THOMISM AND PREDESTINATION

THOMISM AND PREDESTINATION

Principles and Disputations

Edited by Steven A. Long, Roger W. Nutt,
and Thomas Joseph White, OP

SAPIENTIA PRESS
of Ave Maria University

Cover Design: Kachergis Book Design

Cover Image: Titian, *Christ and the Good Thief*

Printed in the United States of America.

Library of Congress Control Number: 2016936550

ISBN: 978-1-932589-79-5

CONTENTS

THOMISM AND
PREDESTINATION

INTRODUCTION

Steven A. Long

The ensuing volume engages a profound and difficult subject that is central to the Catholic theological tradition. Below I introduce the volume's contributions in a substantive essay rather than in a conventional summative description. This leads to unevenness, because in addition to the normal *minima natura* of reference to the works in question, I engage some essays to a greater degree than others. Beyond question, this unevenness is a function of the limitations of the author (and also of the limitations of space, since engaging all pieces at the same length would have yielded a much longer introduction). Essays reveal the predilections and contingent limitations of the essayist, and as the remarks below attempt more than the conventional introduction, these limitations are on full display. In particular, there are places where intonations of long-standing conversations with the authors in question assert themselves—perhaps nowhere more evidently than in the introduction of the essay by my friend (and astute critic) Michael Waldstein (chap. 11, this volume). That introduction (and indeed his essay) continues a longstanding conversation that is and has been fruitful for us both. If it carries the ring of a late-night discussion between the two of us on the lanai, one hopes that may be further inducement to appreciate the book. In any event, one hopes that the words below may be of some service and interest. Whether aided or distracted by this introduction, the reader should

1

turn to the essays themselves, serene in the knowledge that these are of far greater intelligible density than either a conventional introduction, or a full-bodied introductory essay, is able to compass. These essays merit serious attention, and their richness exceeds the capacity of the most robust introduction sufficiently to delve.

～

Three striking facts encouraged us to orchestrate a conference addressing the Thomistic understanding of predestination and the disputations—*ad intra* and *ad extra*—to which it has given rise.

First, the extent and nature of this central doctrinal conversation are to a great degree *terra incognita* among many theologians and philosophers today. There are many reasons for this. Doubtless the work of authors happily defending the normative primacy of an ignorance of seven hundred years of doctrinal development is part of this equation.[1] That such a position is convenient for the slothful, pleasant to the historicist, and obliging toward modernity has not hurt such views.[2] But there is also the pronounced doctrinal and historical complexity of the subject, combined with its central importance in Catholic thought, rendering the subject *forbidding* even for those who have not ruled out the consideration of the tradition.

Distinctively complicating the matter further, for a brief while the subject was thought to have been shown somehow to be one no longer requiring essential and distinct consideration in theological formation. Following upon the distinct claims of Rahner and of de Lubac to have superseded the contexts for consideration of nature and grace derivative of the preceding seven hundred years, it was widely thought that the questions and problems addressed in those years could simply be swept aside as disutile. In addition, speculative works in the Thomistic tradition somehow came to be popularly but misleadingly referred to as "manualism"—as though, for example, the several writings of Garrigou-Lagrange on the mystical life, dogmatic theology, and philosophy; or the moral

---

1. These remarks target no "school" but rather the simple fact that the whole commentatorial period in its contributions to the Church's doctrine and life is something that has for many theologians become either a "known unknown" or even, in some cases an "unknown unknown."

2. These remarks, too, target no properly theological school as such, but rather sloth, historicism, and the tendency toward servile subordination of truth to contingent and controvertible apologetic judgments.

theology of Pinckaers; or the books of Maritain; or the texts of the Salmanticences, John of St. Thomas, Cajetan, and Báñez were not profound and challenging theological and philosophic works. One thinks also of accomplishments such as that of Del Prado (*De gratia et libero arbitrio*), the requisites for the *understanding* of which—quite apart from concurrence or dissent—are simply not enjoyed by those who, bereft either of the speculative penetration of the thought of the *Doctor Communis*, or the historical depth and profundity of de Lubac's contemplation of the Fathers, are armed only with genealogical glosses, aesthetic preferences, and philosophic eclecticism.

These convergent influences—occurring in roughly the same time frame as the analytic and linguistic movements of philosophy in Anglophone thought, and the influence of phenomenological and broadly existential considerations in Europe—for a time effected a virtual amnesia regarding the actual teaching of Aquinas. For St. Thomas's theology is *scientia* and not a mere *resource* for ad hoc historical appropriation as syncretic and apologetic impulses (whether dubious or sound) may command.

The second striking fact is the slowly dawning recognition by theologians that the new theological regimen has not in fact brought forth the expected fruits. Explanations for this are various. But theological antinomianism regarding the tradition, and particularly regarding the moral life, have undeniably become significant problems in the post–Vatican II era. These effects were most certainly not the objectives sought by all critics of commentatorial Thomism—quite the opposite. It might be thought that while one might bring these effects to the doorstep of Rahner (who after the council denied that the Church could define particular moral norms), it would nonetheless be difficult to ascribe these to the *intention* of de Lubac, who always fought against them. Yet these effects have ensued, and the displacement and derogation of commentatorial Thomism—whether in behalf of the supernatural existential or the negation of a proportionate natural end, or of continental or analytic modalities of thought—seems arguably to have powerfully contributed to them.

Because of the strategic importance of the teaching of St. Thomas Aquinas to the magisterium of the Church, which both in the preconciliar and postconciliar epoch has taught that his authority is not simply that of being one among many of the Fathers but rather that of an "authentic teacher,"[3] it is impossible permanently to relativize or derogate his contributions. Yet on many matters, those contributions have, as a matter fact (and one that would be an interesting object of study for the sociology of knowledge), suffered the distortion of a relativization effected by an aversion to the speculative project manifest throughout his work. De Lubac famously lamented the commentatorial Thomists' "disregard for history and their slender critical sense," quoting M.-B. Lavaud that "Exegesis and history concerned them far less than the fundamental nature of things."[4] But it is equally manifest that this observation clearly pertains to Aquinas himself, who was not principally a historical scholar and certainly not what today we would call a "medievalist."

Aquinas was a brilliant theologian and philosopher whose insights can withstand the maximal speculative stress placed upon them, and whose teaching is susceptible of indefinite development and application. It was thus natural that minds sensitive to the need to read texts as the sort of texts they are would emphasize the speculative teleology of Thomas's teaching and seek to extend and apply it. There is a principle here cognate with that of the methodology of the study of sacred Scripture in that a text must be read *as the sort of text it is*. Neither Thomas nor the commentators who sought to further develop and apply his teaching were principally undertaking a project in historical study, but sought to be, as Ramirez famously expressed the matter, a "disciple of faith and a master of natural reason."[5] The structure of the question in the *Summa Theologiae* (*ST*) and the nature of the disputed question indicate an intensive and extensive focus upon truth. It is thus necessary for appreciation of Thomas's teaching to engage it precisely on the speculative level. Today many theologians and philosophers discern the need to

3. Cf. Santiago Ramirez, OP, "The Authority of St. Thomas Aquinas," *The Thomist* 15 (1952): 1–109, and Jorgen Vijgen, "The Contemporary Authority of St. Thomas Aquinas: A Reply to Otto-Herman Pesch," *Divinitas* 49 (2006): 3–26.

4. Cf. Henri de Lubac, *Augustinianism and Modern Theology*, trans. Lancelot Sheppard (New York: Herder, 1968). De Lubac criticizes sixteenth-century Thomists who speak of obediential potency for "their disregard for history and their slender critical sense" and in a note quotes the words of M.-B. Lavaud, OP: "Exegesis and history concerned them far less than the fundamental nature of things" (233).

5. Cf. Jacobus M. Ramirez, "*De Hominis Beatitudine Tractatus Theologicus*," in *Edicion de las Obras Completas*, vol. 3, ed. Victorino Rodriguez, OP (Madrid: Instituto de Filosofia, 1972), 103. "Theologus tamen in hoc medio inveniendo se habere debet ut discipulus fidei et ut magister rationis naturalis."

renew speculative contact with the teaching of Aquinas as a condition for a fruitful understanding of the situation of theology in the twenty-first century.

This leads to the third fact. Predestination, both by reason of its intrinsic importance and because of its centrality for the fortunes of the Thomistic synthesis, is a subject of essential moment both for Catholic theology as such and for Thomistic thought. Given the distinctive work and achievement of the graduate theology program at Ave Maria University, this suggested our unique ability to host a conference uniquely addressing this subject in my adult lifetime.

It soon became clear that some of the most prominent minds engaged on this subject would be able to participate. And so we come to the contributions to the present volume. Foremost among these is chapter 1, by Serge-Tomas Bonino, OP. Father Bonino is the president of the Pontifical Academy of St. Thomas Aquinas, general secretary of the International Theological Commission, former editor of the *Revue Thomiste*, and—like his confrere in this volume, Romanus Cessario, OP—is recipient of the highest theological honor bestowed by the Order of Preachers, that of Master of Theology in the Dominican Order.

Aware at once of the importance of historical context and the priority of the speculative teleology of the text of St. Thomas, he enjoys distinctive awareness of the history, doctrinal complexity, and *status quaestionae* of the questions regarding grace, freedom, predestination, reprobation, and sin. As an author aware of the profound continuity of the Dominican teaching from St. Thomas Aquinas onward, he was from the very first to our minds the optimal keynote speaker.

His essay, "Contemporary Thomism through the Prism of the Theology of Predestination," thus merits prime mention and is situated at the start of the volume, as in a sense all the considerations taken up are situated in relation to it. It is a masterful articulation both of the situation of the Thomistic tradition as such in relation to this question, and a vindication of the synthesis which has animated the teaching of careful students of St. Thomas Aquinas's work for generations. He defends the need for an account that vindicates the universal determining divine causality, the innocence of God, and the primacy of grace, and rejects accounts that deny the need for a prior permissive divine decree as a condition for evil. His rejection of "the absurdity" of "freedom conceived as first cause" is masterful. As Bonino argues, "The reason for the permission of sin (and thus reprobation) is the wisdom of a divine government that conforms to the nature of things as it is thought by divine wisdom. Human nature being fallible in its freedom, God allows it to sometimes fail." Aquinas affirms the divine innocence, the primacy of grace, and the divine universal causality. That God permits defectible free causes freely to defect does not militate against the divine goodness.

In chapter 2, the present author (Steven Long) attempts to address the profound anxiety regarding reprobation that affects the reception and understanding of Thomas's teaching, but turns to this subject only after showing the presence in St. Thomas's texts of what later came to be called the doctrine of physical premotion. The view that because Thomas did not use these precise words he did not hold this teaching exhibits, he says, an "extreme *ipssisima verba*-ism," as Thomas clearly holds that there is a divinely bestowed motion, prior by nature but not by time, which causes the free act of the will in choice, and moves the will to move itself (according to its contingent/free mode) to the perfection of a particular determination. The essay also undertakes critical corrective analysis responding to three major figures—Maritain, Marín-Sola, and Lonergan—whose accounts it designates as unsustainably "revisionist" with respect to the teaching of St. Thomas Aquinas on the subjects of premotion, grace, and predestination. Finally, Long argues that negative reprobation, and the divine permission of evil, must be viewed in light both of God governing things according to their natures—and thus permitting the defectible creature at times to suffer defect—but even more in relation to the rootedness of providence and predestination in the transcendent divine good, mercy, and love. The deontological element, though important, is subordinate, and can never of itself assuage or heal anxieties that only give way in abandonment to the light of divine providence and the omnipotent mercy of God.

In chapter 3, "St. Thomas on the Predestination of Christ," Roger Nutt argues persuasively that "Thomas Aquinas's theology of the predestination of Christ is the locus where he most fully works out and integrates his theology of predestination—theology proper as discourse about God—with the realization of the eternal plan of predestination in the temporal order." As he puts it, "Because Christ's predestination is not ordered (first) to filial adoption by grace, but rather to the diffusion of the divine goodness through the personal union of the two natures in the Word (from which the redemptive effects of eternal predestination are realized in time), Aquinas's complete doctrine of predestination cannot be fully comprehended without reference to the Incarnation and the economy of salvation."

Treating the unfolding of the plan of predestination in time, through the sacraments and human free acts—proceeding always from St. Thomas's analysis and engaging Journet, Cessario, Huetter, Paluch and others—Nutt exhibits the masterful synthesis of Thomas's doctrine as fully articulated in the account of the predestination of Christ.

Thomas Joseph White, OP, in chapter 4 exposits the doctrine of predestination according to the teaching of St. Thomas Aquinas. Emphasizing the transcendence of God in relation to free human acts, he locates the source of sin in the defectibility of the human will and the divine permission of the same as congruent with the divine government of all things respecting their natures. He argues that the classical Catholic doctrine of predestination has become obscured in modern theology owing to a polemical opposition between those who appeal to some version of Calvin's theology and the universalist vision of predestination to which it gives rise as a counterproposal. His argument is that the retrieval of a nuanced understanding of the traditional Thomist position serves to extricate Catholic theology from a set of false alternatives, and allows the right balance of an affirmation of diverse theological principles: the primacy of divine grace in the order of salvation, the transcendent omnipotence of God, the universal offer of salvation, the noncausal permission of evil, and the innocence of God in the face of moral evil." He explains six theses essential to Thomas's teaching:

1. All that is morally good in the human person comes from the creative activity and providential assistance of God.

2. All that the human person does that is morally evil stems from a truly free, morally culpable, and naturally defective initiative of the creature.

3. The mystery of salvation by grace stems primarily from the initiative of God, whose gifts of grace precede all works of cooperation on the part of the free human creature.

4. God offers the possibility of salvation to all human persons. The

mystery of perdition originates from the free defective resistance to or refusal of the mystery of grace.

5. God foreknows all who will be saved from all eternity, and his divine will for their salvation is the effective cause of their predestination to divine glory.

6. God is eternally innocent of moral evil. Reprobation occurs in light of the antecedent permissive decree of God, which is in no way causal of sin.

These propositions are salient, and their intensive contemplation and explication form the heart of the Thomistic tradition regarding predestination.

Michael Dauphinais in chapter 5 explores the ramifications of treating the divine initiative in the theology of Ephesians as an "occasion of joy and thanksgiving rather than of fear and dread, as it has been received at times from the period of the Reformation until the present day." He seeks to understand the Pauline epistle more adequately in order to enter into the Pauline praise of God expressed in the hymn of praise and blessing to God in Ephesians 1:3–6. Appreciating the account of Markus Barth in its rejection of determinism, Dauphinais nonetheless criticizes it for placing the divine and created causality in a competitive relationship which insufficiently regards the transcendence of God. Adverting intensively to Aquinas's commentary on Ephesians, he shows the importance of Thomas's metaphysics of creation for fully appreciating the richness of the teaching of Ephesians 1:3–6.

In chapter 6, Joseph Trabbic undertakes response to the criticism of Father Brian Shanley on the subject of the *praemotio physica*, and particularly to the claim that physical premotion compromises the divine transcendence. In the course of doing so, he explains physical premotion in general, and shows how it is that denial of this doctrine would imply either occasionalism or the rejection of Aquinas's teaching of subordinated secondary causality, neither of which seems to provide a reasonable reading of Aquinas. He engages Shanley's concern over turning into "something created, the very motion by which God moves created agents." This, he notes, "would not be a real objection but only a misunderstanding of the doctrine." He goes on to argue that "Premotionists distinguish between God's action, the motion it produces (i.e., the referent of the term 'physical premotion'), and the action of the created agent. No premotionist says that God's own action, which is identical with God himself, is created. But it is true that the motion produced by God and passively received by the created agent is something created." Further, "premotionists, Shanley believes, tie God to a notion of moving that is essentially mundane, and fail to appreciate how our concepts break down in our attempt to understand *creatio*." But "If he doesn't suppose that he is simply relaying nonsense, then he must believe that he has some understanding of what he's talking about. So, he must also believe that our concepts can apply at least analogically to God's creative action. But if that is how he sees things, then he has not shown us any essential difference between his understanding of how our concepts could apply to the divine *motio* and how premotionists like Garrigou-Lagrange understand them to apply."

Along a path he notes to be similar to those of "Bernard Lonergan, John Farrelly, Francisco Marín-Sola, Jacques Maritain, and William Most," Lawrence Feingold argues in chapter 7 that Thomas's division of grace into operative and cooperative grace is a more fundamental division than that between what came to be called efficacious and sufficient grace. The latter division (efficacious/sufficient) ought, he argues, to be viewed as subordinate to the former (operative/cooperative). "It seems to me that a false dilemma is created when actual grace is divided first into the categories of sufficient and efficacious grace. This is a division with regard to consequence. I see it as introducing a kind of consequentialism into the debate about the nature of actual grace." Arguing that operative grace "incites a desire for salvation," but that cooperative grace continues this motion in us "resistably," he argues that the difference is that of "the initial attraction to salvation" as distinct from "the actual choice of salvific means," and concurs with Marín-Sola and Maritain with respect to the nature and role of the faulty deliberation of the will in cases of resistance to grace.

Feingold argues for an account of contingency and freedom that requires that free acts be unknowable to God by way of divine causality, and knowable to God only through the divine eternal presence, because "the actual movement of free will (with the aid of cooperative grace) *cannot be known with certainty in its causes alone, because the will is a subordinate and contingent cause of its own free act.*" As the author puts it,

"Cooperative grace can be frustrated in the course of deliberation by a final practical judgment contrary to grace's attraction. Nevertheless, it was sufficient to have made possible the completion of the good act." Feingold thus provides a nuanced argument along lines similar to the analyses of Maritain and Marín-Sola.

Thomas Osborne in chapter 8 takes up the profound and delicate issue—which has divided Thomist commentators—over the question of whether, and in what respect, God premotively determines the matter of the sinful act without predetermining to the sin itself. Cajetan—whose position is further articulated by Alvarez and Lemos—held that God does predetermine to the matter of the sinful act without predetermining to the sin itself. Osborne considers the analysis of Cajetan—and the reasoning of Medina, Zumel, and Báñez—before turning to Alvarez and Lemos (great Dominican figures from the *Congregatio de Auxiliis*) as developing and defending the teaching of Cajetan. The difficulty concerns a threefold distinction articulated by Cajetan distinguishing "the act absolutely speaking, the positive entity that places the act in a species, and the privation of rectitude." God causes the act absolutely speaking and does not cause the privation, but what of the positive entity that specifies the sin? Cajetan insists that "sin has a positive malice from its object but a privative malice in its lack of conformity to the law," and the latter privation "is the sin's deformity."

Alvarez, concurring with Báñez but construing the argument as interpreting rather than correcting Cajetan, argues that "relation to a deficient cause is not a positive entity and therefore not caused by God." Osborne notes of Alvarez:

His central point seems to be that the formality of sin is not formally a being, although materially it is one. In other words, the thing that is a sin is a natural being, but it is not a sin insofar as it is a natural being. God causes the sin only insofar as it is a natural being. Although God causes the being that is a sin, he does not cause it as a sin. But the deficient human will causes the sin insofar as it is formally sinful, namely, as related to a deficient cause. The conclusion that God causes sin is invalid because it draws on premises with different appellations of "sin." It is the same logical error as concluding that the sculptor made wood from the premise that the sculptor made a statue, and that the statue is wood. Alvarez identifies the same fallacy and uses almost the same example that Báñez used in his discussion of Biel and Ockham.

Osborne explores the further reasonings of Lemos on the subject and concludes, "The later Thomists were arguably successful in responding to contemporary challenges because they relied not only on Thomas Aquinas's own texts, but also on the conceptual progress made by previous Thomists." The essay is a pellucid explanation of the authentic further speculative development and clarification of the teaching of Thomas by commentatorial minds of great profundity and acuity.

Father Matthew Lamb explains Bernard Lonergan's theoretical exposition of Aquinas's teaching in chapter 9. Identifying the proposition of Lonergan, that, absolutely speaking, causality in itself involves no change in the agent but only in the effect, he concurs with Lonergan that "If then, a *gratia operans* were to produce a contingent effect with irresistible efficacy, it could not be a creature; it would have to be God... Similarly, when God irresistibly produces a contingent effect, he does so, not through a necessitated, but through a contingent cause." Lamb criticizes the recent work by Robert Matava[6] in holding that Lonergan does not "seem to understand application—God's operation in the operations of created agents—in terms of creation," arguing that "Lonergan most certainly does see application as a further differentiation within the context of creation and conservation." He claims that the distinctiveness of Lonergan's position enables him to hold that "Grace as a creature cannot produce any contingent effect with the irresistible efficacy proper only to God," a teaching he considers to have been implicitly rejected by both Báñez and Molina. But grace and physical premotion are created. Thus he holds that even as subordinated causes, they cannot bring about contingent effects efficaciously, which are brought about "through the immediacy of divine causality." One's own action is thus brought about not by one being *moved* by God to move oneself, but solely by having God create one's actions directly, an account that as Matava notes (for he has sympathy with this position about divine creation)[7] has not infrequently been criticized as entailing occasionalism.[8]

---

6. Robert J. Matava, *Divine Causality and Human Free Choice: Domingo Bañez, Physical Premotion, and the Controversy De Auxiliis Revisited*, Brill's Studies in Intellectual History 252 (Leiden: Brill, 2016), 242–321.

7. Cf. Robert J. Matava, "Divine Causality and Human Free Choice: Domingo Báñez and the Controversy de Auxiliis" (PhD Diss., University of St. Andrews, 2010), 256–57.

8. Ibid., 248–51.

With Lonergan, Lamb rejects the insistence of Báñez that the divine motion of which Aquinas speaks—which is not God himself, nor is it the creature's action (which derives from the divinely caused prior motion actuating its potential for agency)—is a created effect. Lonergan's famous comment that "Peter acting" and "Peter not acting" are not really different is said to be simply the assertion that Peter is free to act or not to act (cf. Lamb's footnote 3). As Lamb argues:

Causation is the actuation of the active potency of the cause and the passive potency of the effect. One and the same act actuates both potencies, and this act is the motion produced in the object moved. Causation is therefore inherent not in the cause but in the effect; action and passion are really identical with the motion of the recipient. There is no change in the cause, only in the effect.

Where Báñez raises the issue of how the finite thing that is not in itself a pure agent or cause but in potency to agency achieves the dignity of agency, Lamb with Lonergan focuses upon the intrinsic character of agency as in and of itself not requiring potency. "Thus God creating and redeeming the world involves no change in God, but in the created and redeemed world. And it is also the case with human causation."[9]

---

9. Agency qua agency involves only agency, and so it is wholly accidental to agency that there be motion from potency to act. But the question may remain: does not the creature that is an agent need to be moved from potency to act in order to attain to the dignity of agency? God does not need to be moved from potency to act to be an agent, but is it not essential to the creature that it can only be an agent insofar as moved to agency by a principle that is in act? Lonergan does not seem directly to address the matter in these terms. But if the motion of which St. Thomas speaks in *De malo*, q. 3, art. 2, ad 4 ("Similiter cum aliquid movet se ipsum, non excluditur quin ab alio moveatur a quo habet hoc ipsum quo se ipsum movet." "Likewise when something moves itself this does not exclude that it is moved by another, from which it has even this very thing that it moves itself"), is a *motio realis* of the creature from potency to act, is this not God imparting a real motion to the creature whereby it is moved actually and freely to determine itself? Granted that some "effects" are only said to be so relationally, if we speak of activation of a real power, we speak of a *motio realis* (it being understood that motion is an analogical term referring to the reduction from potency to act). Matava on this point wishes to argue for direct creation and even criticize Lonergan for not doing so (cf. "Divine Causality and Human Free Choice," 261), seemingly contrary to Lamb's reading of Lonergan but placing Matava's substantive position closer to that of Lamb and his reading of Lonergan. With regard to both, those with sympathy for the Thomism of the Dominicans at the *Congregatio* will wonder: does recourse to direct creation avoid occasionalism, follow St. Thomas's mode of analysis, and conform to the metaphysical principle that anything that is moved from potency to act must be *moved* by something in act, *quod movetur ab alio movetur* (such that the motion is finite, granted that the mover is God)? This is a discussion that calls to mind the disputations regarding *created grace*. In any

He argues vigorously alongside Lonergan for a strong theonomic account. For Lonergan, Lamb explains, all that is is intelligible, and all that is good is from God, and evil is a *surd* that "cannot have an antecedent cause or noncause," while evil presupposes the divine permission. This is a remarkable examination and exposition of Lonergan's *sui generis* analysis and theoretical account of Thomas's thought, and it is destined to be read and engaged for many years to come.

In chapter 10, Romanus Cessario, OP, addresses the way in which the Dominican third-order priest Louis-Marie Grignion de Montfort (1673–1716) discussed predestination and the predestined, and his teaching about "how to live the grace of predestination in a way that coheres with the truth about the outpouring of the divine goodness that appears on earth within the 'logic of the Incarnation.'"

Focusing upon the efficacy of divine grace, Cessario quotes de Montfort to the effect that "the Saints tell us that when we have once found Mary, and through Mary, Jesus, and through Jesus, God the Father, we have found all good."[10] As Cessario puts it, "De Montfort knew that only the good draws."

He observes: "One leitmotif of de Montfort's instruction appears in the association that he makes between devotion to Mary and predestination, a claim that the Church has acknowledged as worthy of credence." Of Alan de la Roche, Cessario comments, "Blessed Alan, whom de Montfort venerated, assures his readers that those who cherish a devotion to the 'Hail Mary' display a mark of predestination, whereas those who lack reverence for the *Ave Maria* exhibit a sign of reprobation." He suggests that de Montfort likely discovered the promise of predestination attached to the rosary's "Aves" from Juan de Cartagena, OFM, a former Jesuit who "embodied a fervent opposition to Molinism, as one may surmise when it is discovered that he left the Jesuits after the Society of Jesus had adopted Molinism as their school opinion." Cessario does not hesitate to identify de Montfort as a "popular, anti-Molinist preacher of what I call the grace of predestination."

---

case, the Lonerganian position and Lamb's reading of it (and even Matava's general recourse to creation as the mode of divine causality of free acts) contribute to a mode of analyzing the question that is somewhat different both from Molinism and Congruism on the one hand, and from the Thomism of the Dominicans in the *De auxiliis* controversy on the other.

10. *Le Secret de Marie*, 451, no. 21. A. Somers, trans., *The Secret of Mary* (London: Burns Oates & Washbourne, 1926).

De Montfort's stress on predestination has none of the sad severity of Pascal and the Jansenists, but rather a "confident rejoicing" in the supernatural gifts that God has provided in Jesus and Mary "to an admittedly fallen race." Cessario argues that while de Montfort's teaching is fitted better to the ordinary experience of life than to the salons or classrooms, it never opposes piety to learning but forwards the primacy of living by faith so as to grasp properly the truth of the complicated question of predestination. De Montfort's adroit and profound consideration of Scripture is mentioned here. De Montfort uses the words of Sirach 24:13 (translated by Ronald Knox)—"Et dixit mihi: In Jacob inhabita, et in Israël hæreditare, et in electis meis mitte radices" "And his command to me was that I should find my home in Jacob, throw in my lot with Israel, take root among his chosen race"—in an allegorical interpretation of Mary as Wisdom, developed around the theme of predestination. Cessario cites de Montfort's use of Psalms 87:5 (NAB), "But of Zion it must be said: 'They all were born here.' The Most High confirms this." He points out the importance of de Montfort's teaching that "each of the elect (*homo et homo*) comes to birth in the Blessed Virgin Mary" inasmuch as "She gives birth both to the Head and the members of Christ's Body." To be born of another mother than the one who gives birth to the Head would render the progeny to be monsters. And Mary protects her spiritual children from the malice of sin and the devil.

Most importantly, Cessario points out that for de Montfort, proper knowledge about predestination arises only among the predestined, who accept suffering gladly as a way to participate in Christ. In Mary the Holy Spirit—from whom no divine person proceeds in the Trinity—brings forth predestined offspring, such that Mary may be revered as the spouse of the Holy Spirit. In her assent to the Incarnate Word, the whole grace of the redemption enters the world, and de Montfort teaches the practice of filial tenderness toward Mary and the greatest confidence in her goodness and power to ensure safe arrival in heaven.

Michael Waldstein presents a profound and inherently Thomistic reading of Balthasars's teaching regarding predestination (chap. 11). Beginning with an extended meditation of Johannine texts, he comments:

Many who hear the word "predestination" in a culture deeply formed by Calvin hear primarily the note of limitation. From the mass of those predestined to damnation, some are snatched out to be predestined to live. "I will (θέλω) that where I am those too may be with me." Yet the primary thrust of the prayer is not to highlight the limits of predestination. Granted, Jesus does not state the universality of predestination as a fact. What stands in the center of attention is the expansive movement of the prayer as a whole.

He continues, observing, "In this light one can see why predestination is the very paradise of teleology. It is the one and only way of reaching the end of all human longing, the end that infinitely exceeds all possible human longing: 'What eye has not seen nor ear heard, what has not risen up into the human heart, God has prepared for those who love him (1 Cor 2:9).'" Moving from considerations of Plato and Plotinus, Waldstein then enters into an explanation of St. Thomas's teaching regarding predestination by contrast with that of Karl Barth. He begins by referring to the limited end of created human nature according to St. Thomas, a nature that is nonetheless "theonomic" and an expression of God's wisdom and goodness. "The infinite distance between the natural and the supernatural is the reason why predestination is needed in the first place." As he puts it, "What St. Thomas hears in the word 'predestination' is above all that God sends or shoots us over and across a great distance, *oportet quod ab alio transmittatur*, as an archer shoots an arrow at a target far away." But for Barth, "no such act" is necessary, because he holds that double predestination is God's first act from which everything else derives. "Nature, if it comes into view at all, does so only as an implication of grace."

Balthasar, he argues, seeks to affirm precisely what Barth denies: the consistency of the natural order and of philosophy. Without these, Balthasar insists, the gift of grace is impossible. Balthasar, Waldstein explains, seeks to defend the abstract knowledge of created essences by showing that they are not incompatible with acts and events but rather based upon them: "by adding in concentric circles around this nature the sorts of things in which Barth is particularly interested," Balthasar seeks to arrest his attention with the Catholic tradition. These concentric circles include, Waldstein says, what the word "nature" is first applied to, nature as the essence of a being in the abstract, essence as a principle of movement and activity, defense of this understanding of nature against what he calls Barth's "actualism," and explicit inclusion of the things in which Barth is particularly interested. He continues to note the *concreteness*, according to Balthasar, of the concentric circles around the essence, so as to conclude that Barth's anxieties regarding a "merely" abstract nature is unfounded.

Waldstein, turning to a contemporary author, differs strongly with my (the present author's) work *Natura Pura*, which argues that Balthasar's *intentions* with respect to vindication of nature are hollowed out by his approach, leaving nature as a mere "vacuole" for grace. The "Balthasar criticized by Long is more Barthian than Barth criticized by Balthasar." Focusing upon one quotation from *Natura Pura*, Waldstein argues that the grammar of the English translation led to an incorrect interpretation, but that the German "settles the question definitively."[11] Further, "Long's often repeated objection that Balthasar is opposed to abstraction, that he has a wrongly concrete understanding of nature and so on, seems to arise from the tendency to read Balthasar mainly as speaking about nature in the sense of essence."

Waldstein's most central criticism of *Natura Pura* refers to its reply to Balthasar's claim that "Thomas never entertains, *even hypothetically*, a final goal that could be unmoored from the supernatural vision of God." *Natura Pura* argues that Thomas did expressly entertain a hypothetical natural end unmoored from the supernatural vision of God— the hypothesis of creation *in puris naturalibus*[12]—and that accordingly Balthasar is incorrect. Waldstein argues that a finality is "not truly final"

---

11. On this point regarding the translation of the particular lines, I concur.

12. Steven A. Long, *Natura Pura* (Bronx, NY: Fordham University Press, 2010), 243. "*De malo* q. 5, art. 1, ad 15 teaches that, had man been created *in puris naturalibus* and then died bereft of the beatific vision, this lack of the vision would not be a punishment. For Thomas, a punishment, when it is just, proceeds from fault and is constituted by a deprivation of the natural good of the one punished, contrary to that person's will, and engendering suffering. Clearly, if there were a strong and unconditional natural desire for supernatural beatitude as opposed to a conditional desire to know God under the disproportionate *ratio* of 'Cause of created effects,' then its deprivation would be a punishment, and its deprivation prior to fault would be an unjust punishment. Yet Thomas says it would *not* constitute a punishment. This is not merely because it would not proceed from fault, but because man apart from grace has no unconditional *natural* desire for supernatural beatitude which is not man's natural end, a point made all the stronger in Thomas's words in *De malo* q. 5, art. 3, resp. regarding the *limbo puerorum*: 'Now it pertains to natural knowledge that the soul knows it was created for happiness and that happiness consists in the attainment of the perfect good. But that that perfect good for which man was made is that glory which the saints possess is beyond natural knowledge.' (Pertinet autem ad naturalem cognitionem quod anima sciat se propter beatitudinem creatam, et quod beatitudo consistit in adeptione perfecti boni; sed quod illud bonum perfectum, ad quod homo factus est, sit illa gloria quam sancti possident, est supra cognitionem naturalem.)"

unless it is all-sufficient and ultimate, and so that even *hypothetically* the phrase "a final goal" can have been meant by Aquinas only to refer to the actual ultimate end in the present nonhypothetical order (i.e., supernatural beatitude). Ergo, he concludes, Balthasar is correct.

In *Natura Pura*, I (the present author) take the phrase "natural end" to designate "natural finality"—a finality, *in puris naturalibus* "unmoored from the supernatural vision of God" in the sense of not requiring or constituting in itself an exigency for it, and of limited perfection while participating the eternal law.[13] By contrast, in the proposition in question, by a "hypothetical finality," Waldstein takes Balthasar to refer exclusively to absolutely perfect finality which accordingly refers not to the hypothetical but to the nonhypothetical order (i.e., the concrete providential order in which the supernatural good, owing to revelation, is our ultimate end). If the proposition of Balthasar's in question is read as reducing the hypothesis to the thesis of the concrete order, then Balthasar cannot have intended to deny the hypothesis of creation *in puris naturalibus*. On the other hand, if the hypothesis is truly reducible to the thesis, how is it even conceivable? Such a reading seems to avoid acknowledging a contingent negation of the hypothesis of pure nature by Balthasar only at the cost of making that negation something absolutely necessary and ineluctable.

As Waldstein puts it, "Even if God had not decided to order us to the supernatural end of his own happiness, our natural end could not be final in the unqualified and absolute sense." This reading seems to construe "final goal" to mean "unqualified" and "absolute" rather than simply "final" or "good" or "end" or "that for the sake of which." Balthasar's express rejection even of a *subordinate* finality of pure nature—"Finally there is the other extreme—and extreme it is, as it has hardly any adherents, or even could for that matter—which leaves room for a full-blown (if subordinate) finality of pure nature in the *de facto* world order (as in

13. Because of revelation, the limits of the natural good are better understood. To posit a limit is to have gone beyond the limit. Because the hypothesis of pure nature is the hypothesis on which God could have created us with only natural aids, but without elevating us in grace and for the sake of the supernatural beatific vision, on that hypothesis we would not have the same understanding of the "limit" of natural good. The paradox of our recognizing a good being both the natural end, while needing to be further ordered vis-à-vis the *finis ultimus*, arguably comes about by virtue of God having created man as susceptible of elevation to the order of grace, and having from the beginning elevated man in grace.

Billot)"[14]—raises complications even for this reading (for it makes clear that whether subordinate to supernatural good or not, it is the idea of any normative or fully natural finality that is being rejected). Might one not think that, had man not been raised to the order of grace, the natural end would unqualifiedly have been man's only end without that end thereby being "unqualifiedly absolute?"[15]

Nonetheless, it is manifest that Balthasar's original intentions, stressed by Waldstein, are better served by Waldstein's judgment to the effect both that there *is* a subordinated natural finality and that Balthasar wholly and fully affirms it. There is a strong case to be made that Waldstein demonstrates that reading Balthasar in this way is the most speculatively penetrating and fruitful way in which to interpret Balthasar: because it aligns more perfectly with the teleological dynamism of Balthasar's initial and express intention in the work. Discerning this teleology enables one to complete the work of the master along lines that preserve the good of the whole, whereas, proceeding differently—even if it were to be exegetically warranted (a judgment from which Waldstein dissents)—cannot fulfill the aboriginal intentions of the author.

Waldstein clearly and strongly argues the Thomistic provenance necessary to interpret Balthasar's account as corrective of Barth. "The end we can reach by our own power remains the defining end from which our specific nature derives: we are rational animals, not angels. Knowledge comes to us through the senses. And yet that *defining* end cannot be our *ultimate* end, because we know it is finite and therefore not truly final." Criticizing Gormaz for his insistence that nature cannot "need" supernatural beatitude absolutely, as though it were due, Waldstein discerns

---

14. Balthasar's rejection targets even natural good/end/finality, which is understood as *subordinate* to the supernatural good and so clearly understood *not* to be absolutely perfect. *The Theology of Karl Barth*, trans. Edward T. Oakes, SJ (San Francisco: Ignatius Press, 1992), 289: "Finally there is the other extreme—and extreme it is, as it has hardly any adherents, or even could for that matter—which leaves room for a full-blown (if subordinate) finality of pure nature in the *de facto* world order (as in Billot)." So, it is not merely the issue of subordination to the supernatural good, but the very affirmation of natural finality *tout court* that Balthasar's text negates. It is astonishing to read Balthasar's words that Billot's position could have no adherents, as Billot himself was one of no mean capacity.

15. St. Thomas Aquinas, *Quod.* I, q. 4, a. 3, resp. "But because it was possible for God to have made man in a state of pure nature, it is useful to consider how far natural love could be extended." "Sed quia possibile fuit Deo ut hominem faceret in puris naturalibus, utile est considerare ad quantum se dilectio naturalis extendere posit."

"the poisonous stench of Baius's legalism." To this he opposes the Aristotelian sense of the transcendence of happiness and argues that "Aristotle is dimly aware" of the need to be "shot across" or "sent across" a great distance that "we cannot overcome by our natural power." Here again we face the difficulty of whether the sense of nature can be exclusively that of the concrete order. If not, how may one be justified in saying *not merely* that nature qua nature is susceptible of elevation and superior perfection through divine grace, *but rather* also saying that nature qua nature and of itself implicates and needs the supernatural order? In any case, Waldstein affirms of nature and grace the profound truth that "Both are deeply theonomic." Thus—and Waldstein's words recall to mind Kevin Flannery's masterful essay "Can an Aristotelian Be a Friend of God?"[16]—he comments of Aristotle that "Had he been told of predestination, it would have been good news for him, as it was to the criminal on the Cross."

Howsoever the argument is assessed that apart from beatific vision all finality is only equivocally designated as end,[17] the strong effort to interpret the argument of Balthasar in an axially Thomistic way is clearly a strong and speculatively penetrating mode of assimilating the intention with which Balthasar undertook his work in *The Theology of Karl Barth*. The remarkable emphasis upon a subordinated and theonomic natural principle affirmed by Waldstein provides a rich middle term that both those who follow de Lubac's reading of nature and grace and those who do not will find instructive and challenging. And it offers a fruitful path for the achievement of the initial intentions articulated by Balthasar in *The Theology of Karl Barth*.

Christopher Cullen, SJ, observes in chapter 12 that while St. Ignatius

---

16. Father Kevin Flannery, "Can an Aristotelian Consider Himself a Friend of God?," in *Virtue's End*, ed. Joshua Hochschild, Fulvio De Blasi, and Jeffrey Langan (South Bend, IN: St. Augustine's Press, 2008), 1–13.

17. One might think that a finite end is unequivocally and really an end, but an imperfect end, and that we might not, in a different order of providence, have been as able as we are now to understand either this imperfection of the natural good or to affirm properly the perfection of the divine life—even while the natural good would remain limited and incapable of bringing perfect rest, and even though the inner life of God would remain infinite Trinitarian fecundity. One might also wonder whether the different semantics of Aquinas and Balthasar do not complicate the analysis. If Balthasar by "final" means only ultimate finality, is this how Thomas uses the term when he speaks of the end of man had he been created in *puris naturalibus*? Surmounting all this is Waldstein's unequivocal and profound affirmation that both nature and grace are theonomic principles.

of Loyola (1491–1556) lived in the context of the Renaissance and Reformation, and frequently is understood purely in the light of humanism and Protestantism, "Ignatius also lived in the midst of the second major revival of Thomism." He attempts to show the important ways in which Ignatius's *Spiritual Exercises* can be understood to be in harmony with classical Thomism. As he puts it, "By examining the congruence between classical Thomism and the *Spiritual Exercises*, 'Ignatius the Thomist' can come into focus." Thus, he suggests, the educational program of Ignatius and the early Jesuits will be seen as proceeding from a transcendent humanism significantly indebted to Aquinas.

Because Ignatius was not a professional theologian, his theological beliefs are to be gleaned from his writings and particularly his spiritual writings. Both Hugo Rahner and Avery Dulles, SJ, Cullen notes, pursued such project. Cullen insists that the condition of accurately understanding Ignatius's theology is, first, that one "take care not to associate Ignatius with later theories that became closely identified with Jesuits, such as that of Molinism, which only developed in the generation after Ignatius... or that of probabilism." He notes the evidence presented by Robert Maryks that Ignatius and the early Jesuits were not probabilists but tutiorists closer in moral doctrine to Bonaventure and Aquinas. Second, one needs "to see the unity of humanism itself as a tradition." That is, humanism is not something wholly new that arises with the Renaissance, but rather there is "a humanism not only of the Renaissance but also of the Scholastics." He quotes R. W. Southern's work *Scholastic Humanism and the Unification of Europe* on this point to some advantage, especially regarding the essentially humanistic character of the seven liberal arts in "every cathedral school of the period from the tenth to the twelfth centuries."

Cullen asserts that "the question is not whether Ignatius was a humanist or a Scholastic; in being the latter, he is necessarily also the former." The difference between Scholastic and Renaissance humanism "is to no small extent an argument over which subjects ought to enjoy primacy within the education of the complete human being." Cullen argues that Ignatius's path is different from that of "Renaissance humanists, such as Erasmus, who reject Scholasticism." To the contrary, "Ignatius sought to hold together both the humanism of the Renaissance, which culminates in the art of eloquence, and the humanism of the Scholastics, which culminates in the wisdom of revelation." Ignatius, Cullen believes, "overcomes this dispute by synthesizing the favored subjects of both the medieval and Renaissance humanists in a carefully ordered plan of studies that culminates in the study of divine wisdom." This is made possible by the spirituality of the *Spiritual Exercises.*

Following the life, intellectual formation, and writings of St. Ignatius with care, Cullen brings his examination to the point of addressing the topic "Ignatian Thomism: Reasons for Choosing Aquinas." He observes the judgments of John O'Malley, SJ, from his book *The Early Jesuits*, noting a variety of reasons for the election of Thomas as the theologian of the society. In addition to a variety of less central reasons, however, O'Malley goes further, Cullen notes, and proposes the importance of two doctrinal reasons: (1) the basic compatibility between reason and revelation and (2) the compatibility between nature and grace. According to O'Malley, these tenets comport better with the *Spiritual Exercises* and *Constitutions* than would a more Augustinian perspective. Aquinas's teaching on human nature makes clear the omnipresence and operation of God in all things.

Yet "O'Malley thinks that the early Jesuits departed from Aquinas on certain other points. For example, he thinks they reject Aquinas's view that theology is principally a speculative doctrine." Further, Erasmus grappled with roughly this same problem, and his solution was "to jettison Scholasticism and replace it with the more rhetorical theology of the Fathers." Ignatius, by contrast, acted differently: "Rather than jettison the Scholastic tradition, he placed it at the center of Jesuit education, as evident in his choice of Aquinas as the theologian of the Society."

There ensues Father Cullen's treatment of the many elements of the *Spiritual Exercises* that reflect a Thomistic view, notably the superiority of the contemplative life to the active, which is manifest in the nature of the *Exercises* as "carefully structured meditations meant to encourage a habit of contemplation." The contemplation of the Incarnation whose motive is clearly articulated to be human salvation is a further Thomistic element.

Specifically, the Thomistic account of predestination may be found in the *Exercises*, in particular in Rules 14 and 15 for "Thinking with the Church." Rule 14 states: "It is granted that there is much truth in the statement that no one can be saved without being predestined and without having faith and grace. Nevertheless great caution is necessary in our manner of speaking and teaching about all these matters." Rule 15 famously discourages speaking much about the subject, and when speaking about it encourages that one do so in a manner that will not cause ordinary people to fall into error by abandoning good purposes and actions and growing "listless" so as to "neglect the works which lead to good and to the spiritual advancement of their souls." But Cullen notes that these are simply concerns with the effects of any misappropriation of the doctrine, not regarding its nature, and spring from the fear of quietism.

Cullen explains that the *Exercises* clearly intend the retreatant to meditate predestination, and hold it to be real, but something of which there is an ignorance on the side of the retreatant. Regarding the second week of the *Exercises*, he writes:

In the points for this meditation, Ignatius leads the retreatant to consider the great ordering and drama in which they find themselves. Ignatius also places the emphasis on what God is doing. It is God who has ordered the plan. It is not as if there is no predestination to glory for the elect and nonelection for the reprobate, and God is waiting for the results. It is rather that we, in our limited consciousness, do not know the ending. But the author of this drama has written an ending, for the whole and for each. And the task of the retreatant is to do a series of spiritual exercises—meditations and contemplations, examens of conscience—in order to be found on the side of justice in the end.

There then ensues the heart of Cullen's treatment, wherein he explains St. Thomas's teaching regarding physical premotion, indicating how understanding this teaching is of invaluable aid for the contemplation of the *Spiritual Exercises*: "An understanding of God's help as a physical premotion within human nature is especially valuable when it comes to Ignatius's *Spiritual Exercises*, because the soul can then be seen as a mirror in which God's movements can be discerned." The exercises "require as a precondition that God is moving us from within. Of course, this is true in the order of grace." But, Cullen reasons, "this also seems true in the order of nature, at least with regard to the movements of the soul as operations of natural powers moving from potency to act." Further, "God is at work in the intimacy of the human soul, in the most profound sort of way, insofar as the powers of the soul move from potency to act in their operations." Cullen's acute perception of the reason for the import of the discernment of spirits in the exercises is profound:

If we understand our souls to be autonomous domains, then it seems that the foundation of the *Exercises* is lost. But if our souls are moved from potency to act by God as Pure Act, the spiritual life is a realm of transcendence.

Addressing nature and grace, merit, and choice, Cullen shows the deep affinity of the *Exercises* with the teaching of St. Thomas Aquinas. Of Jesuit education, he rightly states that "Ignatius worked to create a system of schools; these schools became one of the largest purveyors of Aristotelianism and Thomism in the history of Western education." The historical depth and nuance given to his exploration of "Jesuit Aristotelianism" is remarkable and fascinating. Cullen quotes his late Eminence Avery Cardinal Dulles that:

In the sixteenth century theology was in disarray because medieval scholasticism had been devastated by the mockery of humanists and the hostility of Protestant reformers. The Jesuits together with the Dominicans, were the primary architects of a new, updated scholasticism in which discipline and order were restored.

Reading Cullen's essay, one is inspired to consider that this teleological dynamism is still to be found in a world that very much needs it. Ignatius the Thomist is perhaps more needed today than ever before.

In chapter 13, Barry David relates St. Thomas's teaching on predestination in the *Summa Theologiae* to rival accounts, viewing these accounts according to diverse interpretations of the nature and implications of the gratitude that follows upon divine faith. He distinguishes three claims: that the whole human race attains eternal bliss; that a majority of the race, "and possibly the entirety," attains bliss; and that, "as Aquinas insists, only a minority of the race attains bliss."

He notes the distinction according to which predestination to bliss is universal but predestination to temporal election is not. This is a merely relative distinction, however, because in the first treatment all are viewed as ordained to beatitude. David seems to think that universal salvation is the only fully theocentric account:

By contrast, those opposing a teaching of universal bliss interpret the God–man relationship either by a nontheocentric paradigm combining theocentrism and nontheocentrism or by a strictly nontheocentric paradigm. These paradigms maintain either that man cannot attain eternal bliss or that one portion of humanity attains bliss on account of God's primary causality while the other portion does not because it, rather than God, exercises primary causality. Each view contradicts a consistently theocentric account of the nature of and relationship between God and humanity.

But why, if God governs things according to their natures—and if these natures are defectible—would it be "nontheocentric" for God to permit such defectible natures to fall into defect? And the possibility of such defect is only wholly, immutably, and finally overcome after death. God could have created man in the beatific vision, wholly immobilized in perfect good, but this, though possible to the divine power, is unfitting. Why, then, is the permission of defectible creatures to defect—even though it be with regard to their ultimate supernatural good—absolutely contrary to the theocentric providence that governs all things in accord with their natures, even when moving them beyond their natures?

David argues that Thomas's account of reprobation places sin prior to reprobation; that is, "Because sinning causes the sinner to be abandoned by God and 'deserted by grace' *a gratia deseritur*, reprobation does not incite sinning but ordains the sinner to have an 'eternal punishment' *poenae aeternae*, ultimately due to sinning." True enough that reprobation does not *incite* or *cause* sinning, as it does not deprive the creature of its powers. But the *permission* to fall away is a *nonupholding* in grace, an upholding not absolutely due. As Thomas puts it, "it likewise is part of that providence to permit some to fall away from that end; this is called reprobation."[18] What is this "permission"? Further, as Thomas puts it, "so also reprobation includes the will to permit a person to fall into sin, and to impose the punishment of damnation on account of that sin."[19] But what does "permit" mean here? Because, by virtue of the universal causality of God, anything ontologically positive falls within the sphere of the divine effect, for a defectible thing to defect, God must allow it, and such allowance is not like that of one creature to another. Sin is the reason of damnation, but the *permission* of sin is required, which—with respect to final sin—implies reprobation.

As Thomas says in *ST* I, ad 2, q. 23, "guilt proceeds from the free-will of the person who is reprobated and deserted by grace." That is, reproba-

18. *ST* I, q. 23, a. 3, resp.: "ut permittat aliquos ab isto fine deficere. Et hoc dicitur reprobare."

19. *ST* I., q. 23, art. 3, resp. "Sicut enim praedestinatio includit voluntatem conferendi gratiam et gloriam, ita reprobatio includit voluntatem permittendi aliquem cadere in culpam, et inferendi damnationis poenam pro culpa."

tion is *prior* to final defect, and not its effect: "Sed culpa provenit ex libero arbitrio eius qui reprobatur et a gratia deseritur." As Thomas argues in the ad 3 of the same question, while reprobation does not take away from the power of the person, it does imply conditional impossibility: "this must not be understood as implying absolute impossibility: but only conditional impossibility...that the predestined must necessarily be saved; yet a conditional necessity, which does not do away with the liberty of choice."[20] This requires a profound engagement with Thomas's account of the composite and divided senses of "power" and "possibility." However, it manifests that God alone upholds from defect.

David argues that reprobation is "nontheocentric," whereas predestination is "theocentric." In some critical sense this must be true, as the evil of sin is not caused by God, nor is it necessary for God. But for anything to affect a creature, either positive or negative, it must be subject to divine providence, and predestination—as that part of providence that concerns the order to eternal life—is part of providence. In this sense, it would seem to be theocentric, although this is a sense of which man can have no proper knowledge in this life. Thus the line of Augustine quoted by Garrigou-Lagrange in *Predestination*: "Why God draws this one and not that other, seek not to judge, if thou wilt not err."[21] Viewing reprobation as nontheocentric, David argues that "Thomas's subordination of a theocentric to a nontheocentric paradigm has some merit"—owing to the antagonism of sin vis-à-vis virtue. Yet "his teaching on eternal reprobation contradicts the natures of divine goodness and human responsibility."

David sees the profundity of Thomas's doctrine of predestination as "theological before it is anthropological; it concerns the self-sufficient God who, as *ST* I, q. 19, aa. 2–3, shows, creates by suppositional rather than by absolute necessity." Thus, he argues, reprobation is in a sense an *antithesis* of predestination, serving to distinguish the privileged status of God's elect. But as evil accents the good of which it is the contrary deprivation, so the darkness of evil serves to underscore the centrality and irradiance of the divine light. Because everything—including sin—

20. *ST* I, q. 23, art. 3, ad 3: "non est hoc intelligendum secundum impossibilitatem absolutam, sed secundum impossibilitatem conditionatam, sicut supra dictum est quod praedestinatum necesse est salvari, necessitate conditionata, quae non tollit libertatem arbitrii."

21. Réginald Garrigou-Lagrange, *Predestination*, trans. Dom Bede Rose (St. Louis, MO: Herder: 1939), 44, taken from *In Joan.*, tr. 26.

finally glorifies God and serves God's elect (just as the cruelty of the tormentors serves the patience of the saints), it is difficult to understand why reprobation is not also theocentric inasmuch as it is ordained as part of the universal divine providence (in which evil is permitted only because God can bring from it a greater good).

David seeks to articulate the nature of what he refers to as *confessio* or the explicitly Trinitarian relationship of a mortal person with God. He writes that "while the ontology between divine goodness and human responsibility—and, consequently, between goodness and the predestined—is eternal, the ontology between divine goodness and the reprobated and the elect and the reprobated is contingent." Further, he goes on to argue that, because the doctrine of majority salvation "is more capable of inspiring divine gratitude" than the doctrine of universal salvation, it is objectively preferable. Likewise, David argues that Thomas's doctrine of predestination, while it "upholds the importance of practicing gratitude," nonetheless "militates against recognizing the primacy of the divine goodness." For this reason, Barry holds that "group B's teaching"—that of majority salvation—is superior both to group A (universal salvation) and group C (minority salvation). It is, he claims:

better able to subordinate (1) the contingent to the absolute word, (2) temporal to eternal being, and (3) finite responsibility to infinite divine goodness.

It might be wondered whether there is not an anthropomorphism here, in that as infinitely good in himself, and the source of every Good, God is owed complete gratitude by every sentient being. Sin, and its punishment, convict the one whose moral defect God has permitted, and not God for permitting a defectible agent at times to defect. Yet, on the other side, inasmuch as David's analysis proceeds *ex convenientia*, from fittingness, it presents a *sui generis* analysis whose considerations invite meditation and careful assessment. David's claim is not that the extent of predestination *must* be as described, but—if this reader fathoms the argument—that considerations of the fittingness of the divine pedagogy *suggest* that it be as described.

Barry's systematic comparison of differing views of predestination and reprobation cannot help but move the mind back to first principles both in natural knowledge—especially metaphysics—and in regard to revelation and the Church's *de fide* teaching. One might, however, wonder: is it not better and more generous to hope that one may wholly conform to the divine goodness than to hope that a certain *number* may prove to be that of the elect? Without, of course, in any way denying that there *is* such a number known to God alone? If so, is it not the case that the generosity that alone matters is one to which the *extent* of salvation is wholly accidental? For though the beatific good can only be received as a common good participable by many, it is also the same good *irrespective* of whether it is participated by many, and is infinitely transcendent of the universe. Of course, it is congruous with charity to wish for the salvation of all whom we do not know certainly to be damned, but as this is not a revealed object, this would be not theological hope but human hope. Yet if David's argument is correctly viewed as an argument from fittingness, just so far it would seem not to contradict such reflections, although the content of revelation on these points is a further consideration.

In any event, however, these are questions and alternatives that have preoccupied this question for several centuries now. David offers a remarkably forthright and clear argument for a particular view of the extension of salvation.

～

This lengthy introduction would be insufficient did it not express the gratitude of all those who participated in the conference to those who conspicuously contributed to its existence. First, we are grateful for all that Father Thomas Joseph White and the Thomistic Institute of the Dominican House of Studies did to contribute to the success of the conference, from arcane matters to artwork. We are grateful for the generous support of Ambassador Michael Novak, without whose help this conference well might not have occurred. And, in particular, we are thankful to the Honorable Francis Rooney, former US ambassador to the Holy See, for his willingness to introduce Father Bonino, and to meet with and encourage our graduate students, sharing with us his experience and wisdom. Michael Dauphinais, the chair of the theology department at Ave Maria University, was of constant support and brought a refined prudence, fruit of many years serving the university, to the good of this conference, and we are grateful. Michael Sherwin, OP, not only graciously offered a brilliant paper at the conference, but also volunteered to translate the *viva voce* French remarks of Father Bonino into English. While circumstances did not permit him to contribute to this volume, we are grateful to him for all he gave to the conference. Likewise, Barry David, who spoke at the conference and has contributed to this volume and aided in its translation, generously read the English transcript of Father Bonino's remarks, transmitted to all who chose to use the earphones, during his French lecture. Like Father Sherwin, he of course did double duty! The stalwart efforts of Martin Doman, director of operations at Ave Maria University, in providing, testing, and making the wireless headsets workable enabled simultaneous translation to be possible at a moment when for many reasons this had begun to appear doubtful. Our theology department secretary, Susan Nutt, helped orchestrate innumerable details that were necessary to the good of the conference, and without her constant diligence, prudence, and cheerful generosity, it would have been a lesser event. Our master of arts student Melissa Eitenmiller placed the French and matching English of Father Bonino's lecture into pamphlet form for the conference, while our PhD student Jeremy Johnston has provided helpful final editing corrections of the notes for Father Bonino's essay.

Finally, we are grateful—with a *sui generis* gratitude—to President James Towey and to the chairman of the Ave Maria University board Michael Timmis, for their constant stalwart encouragement and support. Their efforts sustain a graduate theology program and theology conferences that seek to enkindle an acquired contemplation of God, of revelation, and of all things in nature and grace as proceeding from and ordained to God. Thank you, one and all.

CONTEMPORARY

THOMISM THROUGH THE PRISM OF THE

THEOLOGY OF PREDESTINATION

Serge-Thomas Bonino, OP

*translated by Stefan Jetchick; translated and
edited by Barry David and Steven A. Long*

Introduction: "Classical Thomism" in Agony?

Predestination of the Saints and Grace was first published in Paris in 1936. In this work, Father Réginald Garrigou-Lagrange, OP, summarizes the numerous studies he had already published on the topic. The *nihil obstat* given by the authorities of the Order of Preachers not only says that the book contains nothing against faith or morals, but also stresses that it is "very suitable to disseminate and defend the doctrine of the Church in this important matter. In addition, it is quite worthy of the doctrinal tradition of the Thomistic school of our Order."[1] In those days, a bril-

---

1. R. Garrigou-Lagrange, *La prédestination des saints et la grâce: Doctrine de saint Thomas comparée aux autres systèmes théologiques* (Paris: Desclée de Brouwer, 1936), 6. "Aptissimum iudicamus ad propagandam et defendendam doctrinam Ecclesiae circa hanc materiam momentosam; insuper plane dignum traditione doctrinali scholae thomisticae et Ordinis nostri."

liant and young thinker of the Dominican province of Toulouse, Father Jean-Hervé Nicolas (1910–2001), arrives at the *Angelicum* in Rome. He had just been ordained a priest in 1935. "You should change your topic!" advised Garrigou-Lagrange when Nicolas told him of his desire to work on predestination.[2] The young Dominican was not discouraged, however, and on July 4, 1938, in the presence of Father Garrigou-Lagrange and the future Cardinal Paul Philippe (1905–84), he argued *summa cum laude* a thesis on "evil and God's universally foreseeing causality."[3] The formidable issues he addressed in this thesis would haunt him unceasingly. Thus it is he who, in 1960, in a substantial article in the *Revue Thomiste*, defends "Classical Thomism"[4] and its doctrine of the antecedent permissive decree, against its radical reassessment, conducted within the Thomist tradition, either by followers of Francisco Marín-Sola, OP (1873–1932), or by Jacques Maritain (1882–1973). Maritain, by advancing the idea of a breakable motion (*motion brisable* in French), thought he could save the absolute innocence of God, and therefore avoid any recourse to the antecedent permissive decree, and subsequently any negative *ante praevisa merita* reprobation.[5] But in 1992, in an article contained in a book tribute

2. Cf. J.-H. Nicolas, "La volonté salvifique de Dieu contrariée par le péché," *Revue Thomiste* 92 (1992): 177–96, here 189.

3. The thesis was published in an article by J.-H. Nicolas, "La grâce et le péché," *Revue Thomiste* 45 (1939): 58–90, 249–70.

4. By "classical Thomism" I mean here, in a neutral way, the authoritative doctrine taught in Dominican "classes" since the *De auxiliis* controversy, without prejudging its fidelity to St. Thomas.

5. Cf. J.-H. Nicolas, "La permission du péché," *Revue Thomiste* 60 (1960): 5–37; 185–206; 509–46. Nicolas mostly discusses, first, F. Muñiz, *Suma teologica de santo Tomás de Aquino*, 4th ed., Biblioteca de Autores Cristianos 29 (Madrid: 2001), 1947; Francisco Muñiz, in *Tratado de Dios uno en esencia/Santo Tomas De Aquino: Traduccion del Raimundo Suarez. Introducciones particulares, anotaciones y apendices por Francisco Muñiz* (Madrid: La Editorial Catolica, 1947), 967–1055, which defends a thesis inspired by F. Marín-Sola. Cf. F. Marín-Sola, "El sistema tomista sobre la mocion divina," *Ciencia Tomista* 32 (1925): 5–54; "Respuesta a algunas objeciones acerca del sistema tomista sobre la mocion divina," *Ciencia Tomista* 33 (1926): 5–74; "Nuevas observaciones acerca del sistema tomista sobre la mocion divina," *Ciencia Tomista* 33 (1926): 321–97; M. D. Torre, *Do Not Resist the Spirit's Call: Francisco Marín-Sola on Sufficient Grace* (Washington, DC: Catholic University Press, 2013). About F. Marín-Sola, cf. M. D. Torre, *God's Permission of Sin: Negative and Conditioned Decree? A Defense of the Doctrine of Francisco Marín-Sola, O.P., Based on the Principles of Thomas Aquinas* (Fribourg: Academic Press Fribourg, 2009). M. D. Torre argues that Maritain's solution is rooted in F. Marín-Sola; cf. his "Francisco Marín Sola OP and the Origin of Jacques Maritain's Doctrine on God's Permission of Evil," *Nova et Vetera* (English ed.) 4 (2006): 55–94. Nichols discusses, second, J. Maritain, "L'existant libre et les libres desseins éternels," in *Court traité de l'existence et de l'existant* (1947), chap. 4; *Oeuvres complètes* 9 (Fribourg:

to Marie-Michel Labourdette, OP, himself a rather "classical" Thomist,[6] Father J.-H. Nicolas solemnly threw in the towel. Without concealing the insoluble problems to which led the abandonment of the antecedent permissive decree, he now ceased trying to defend it.[7]

The itinerary of Father Jean-Hervé Nicolas exemplifies the general trend, apparently irresistible, of contemporary Thomism on issues related to predestination. It's this evolution that I would like to understand and assess. How did we go from a commonly held doctrine, presented by Garrigou-Lagrange in *Predestination of the Saints and Grace*, to the almost general triumph of the Maritain line, with the "classic" line now defended only by a handful of indomitables (gathered in this volume)? The problem seems interesting not only for its doctrinal ramifications, but also because of what it teaches us about the recent history of Thomism, on developments on how to "read" and update St. Thomas.

I proceed in four stages. First, I briefly describe the starting point— that is, the position and assumptions of Father Garrigou-Lagrange— which seems to be opposed by current Thomism. Second, I show how contemporary thinking on predestination among Thomists is linked to recent developments on how to read St. Thomas and how to "be Thomistic." The third part focuses on the crux of the problem: the doctrine of the antecedent permissive decree. I discuss some of the strategies whereby the majority of Thomists now seek to circumvent this thesis, and how a minority is trying instead to justify it. Finally, in the fourth and final part, I conclude by suggesting that the question of predestination is one of the major places in Thomism today where the correct under-

---

Éditions Universitaires, 1990), 87–118. Maritain responds to criticism of J.-H. Nicolas in "Dieu et la permission du mal [1963]," in *Oeuvres complètes 12* (Fribourg: Éditions Universitaires, 1992), 13–123.

6. Cf. M.-M. Labourdette, "Cours de théologie morale, De la grâce," cours polycopié (Toulouse: n.d.), and "Préliminaires. III. La théologie de la grâce," pp. 32–70; idem, "Deux inédits du Père Marie-Michel Labourdette," *Revue Thomiste* 100 (2000): 355–83. (This contains Labourdette's reaction to Maritain's theses.)

7. The "dramatic reversal" by P. J.-H. Nicolas—that is to say, his abandonment of "classical Thomism"—is already attested in 1984 by his annotation of the French translation of the treatise on God of the *Summa Theologiae*, especially in the notes on q. 23. On this matter, see J.-P. Torrell, "Introduction," in Thomas d'Aquin, *Questions disputées sur la vérité: Question V: La providence (De providentia) Question VI: La prédestination (De praedestinatione)* (Paris, J. Vrin, 2011), 352. Cf. Thomas d'Aquin, *Somme théologique*, Tome 1 (Paris: Éditions du Cerf, 1984), 324–35. It is confirmed in his *Synthèse dogmatique*, vol. II, *Complément, De l'Univers à la Trinité* (Fribourg: Éditions Universitaires, 1993), 378–96.

standing of the relationships between faith, theology, and metaphysics is decided.

In principio erat Garrigou-Lagrange

Father Garrigou-Lagrange is a man of synthesis. Insensitive to the charms of "rebellious diversity" that so fascinates postmoderns, he is a contemplative who tries to gather everything into the light of first principles, so as to systematically unify the data. He thus presents a "concordist" theology of predestination. According to his masterpiece, the doctrine of predestination developed itself homogeneously, sometimes by rejecting errors, sometimes by deepening the truth. Moreover, according to him there is a deep underlying continuity of St. Paul, St. Augustine, St. Thomas Aquinas,[8] and finally classical Thomism, which updated the Thomasian doctrine during controversies between various post-Tridentine schools of thought.[9]

The same "concordism" manifests itself in the way Garrigou-Lagrange, in his approach to the theme of predestination, articulates the "three wisdoms": philosophy, theology, and mysticism. For him, the metaphysical doctrine of God's universal causality and the theological doctrine of grace efficacious of itself are mutually corresponding and reinforcing.[10] Moreover, Father Garrigou-Lagrange was himself a disciple of a great theologian who was also a great contemplative, that is, Aquinas,[11] and he wrought the concordism between St. Thomas and St. John of the Cross. It is therefore not surprising that Garrigou-Lagrange also calls for the mystical wisdom that, in the darkness of faith quickened by the gifts of the Spirit, enables the believer to uphold, with supernatural peace, the mystery of predestination because, as he explains, grace makes the believer already participate in the life of God, in whom all are reconciled, in the

---

8. Garrigou-Lagrange also highlights the agreement of St. Thomas with all ancient theologians. Cf., e.g., *La prédestination*, 132: "On these crucial points, almost all former theologians agree, whether Augustinian, Thomist or Scotist; almost all accept the principle of predilection."

9. Ibid., 39. "The answer of St. Paul, St. Augustine, St. Thomas..." Between St. Augustine and Scholasticism, one passes from the implicit to the explicit; cf. 53.

10. The theology of predestination, according to Garrigou-Lagrange, is not limited to the application of a metaphysics to religion, but it is ultimately based on Revelation.

11. Ibid., 44.

eminence of his Deity, all the perfections that seem so hard to reconcile in predestination.[12]

For Garrigou-Lagrange, the problem of predestination, from a Thomistic point of view, is not so much reconciling divine action and human action (because the Thomistic theory of the subordination of two total causes offers an intellectually satisfying solution[13]). No, the problem of predestination is more about reconciling the dogma of universally salvific will with the "principle of predilection" ("No one would be better if he were not loved more"[14]). The latter is the "capstone"[15] of the treatise on predestination: it recapitulates the metaphysical doctrine of the universal causality and the effectiveness of the divine love[16] as well as the revealed doctrine of the absolute primacy of grace.[17]

Predestination and the New Ways to "Read" St. Thomas Aquinas

Since 1936, the way we "read" St. Thomas has undergone profound evolutions that are reflected in the way we understand the teachings of Aquinas on predestination, and the way we try to update them in the context of contemporary theology.[18] Here I discuss four.

12. Ibid., 254. "Grace, by a secret instinct reassures us about our salvation, and about the intimate conciliation in God of infinite justice, infinite mercy and sovereign freedom. Grace, by this secret instinct, reassures us thusly, because it is a real and formal participation of the divine nature, of God's inner life, of the deity itself, in which are identified, without any distinction, all the divine perfections."

13. Ibid., 248. "There is certainly a mystery in reconciling the freedom of our meritorious acts with God's infallibly effective decrees; but still more obscure is the mystery of evil permitted by God." The Thomistic concept of the relationship between divine action and the creature's action, no matter how satisfactory, obviously doesn't remove mystery, especially in its application to the supernatural order.

14. Ibid., 37. "The *first challenge* was always conciliation of predestination with the universal salvific will."

15. Ibid., 93.

16. Ibid., 201. "This principle appears in the philosophical order as an obvious corollary of the principles of causality and the universal causality of God, author of all good" (91).

17. Ibid., 221. "The basis of the predilection principle is not only evident in the natural order, but it is revealed."

18. There is an excellent *status quaestionis*, which leads us from R. Garrigou-Lagrange to H. J. M. J. Goris, in M. Paluch, *La profondeur de l'amour divin: Evolution de la doctrine de la prédestination dans l'œuvre de Thomas d'Aquin*, Bibliothèque Thomiste 55 (Paris: J. Vrin, 2004), chap. 1, "L'interprétation de la doctrine thomasienne sur la prédestination au XXᵉ siècle."

Scriptural Renewal

Contemporary Thomism first noted and benefited from the *scriptural ressourcement* of theology in the twentieth century. It therefore desires to be more attentive to the biblical roots of theology in St. Thomas,[19] noting for example the interest of Aquinas's comments on the Epistles of St. Paul for the question of predestination.[20] But the scriptural renewal has had the effect of freeing predestination theology from the sometimes narrow context in which modern scholastic discussions had locked it up, to place it in a broader perspective—that of a theology of salvation history. If contemporary Thomism has had no difficulty integrating the Trinitarian and Christological dimensions of predestination—St. Thomas already teaches that Christ's predestination is the model and cause of our own[21]—the emphasis on biblical predestination's communal and "economic" character has made it more difficult to see, in texts such as Romans 9–11, the immediate foundation of an individual predestination theology for definitive eschatological salvation.[22] Thus, as writes Torrell, "the application of these general categories of salvation history in the case of individuals could only lead to a series of misunderstandings."[23]

In truth, Father Garrigou-Lagrange, who refers here to the work of Father Marie-Joseph Lagrange, didn't ignore this aspect but felt that the principles implemented in "general predestination" also applied to "individual predestination."[24] The application is without a doubt less im-

---

19. Cf., recently, P. Roszak and J. Vijgen, eds., *Reading Sacred Scripture with Thomas Aquinas: Hermeneutical Tools, Theological Questions and New Perspectives*, Textes et Études du Moyen Age 80 (Turnhout: Brepols, 2015).

20. Cf. Paluch, "*La profondeur de l'amour divin*," 7; M. Levering, "Aquinas on Romans 8: Predestination in Context," in *Reading Romans with St. Thomas Aquinas*, ed. M. Levering and M. Dauphinais (Washington, DC: Catholic University of America Press, 2012), 196–215.

21. Cf. Thomas Aquinas, *ST* III, q. 24, aa. 3–4.

22. For St. Paul, the subject of predestination seems to be especially the union to Christ and to the Church in this life. He also uses the concepts of predestination and reprobation concerning the role of each community in the history of salvation. Thus, when God is said to reject some, it is an "economic reprobation" (Journet), bound to a phase in salvation history.

23. J.-P. Torrell, "Introduction," in Thomas d'Aquin, *Questions disputées sur la vérité*, 35. See also 320.

24. Cf. Garrigou-Lagrange, *La prédestination*, 224. "Saint Paul, speaking of the predestination of Gentiles and the reprobation of Jews, *formulates general principles*, which clearly apply, as noted by Fr. Lagrange (*Comm. sur l'Epître aux Rom.*, c. ix) to individuals, according to the principle that God works in us (in each one of us) the willing and the doing (Phil. ii, 13)." Cf. also ibid., 109–10.

mediate than he thought. Nevertheless, contrary to a number of theologians who inferred too quickly that predestination was a false problem, the "classical" question of individual predestination to eternal life within general predestination in Christ cannot be discounted. We are all predestined to live in Christ in the Church, but we do not all actualize this vocation. To say with J.-H. Nicolas: "Setting these problems in the broader context of redemptive divinisation and incarnation allows us to situate them in their proper place, and also to project upon them the light of the whole Christian mystery, but this doesn't eliminate their specific difficulty or render useless their study."[25]

Patristic Renewal

Contemporary Thomism then benefited from patristic renewal. Here again, it was better shown how St. Thomas thought within the tradition and knew how to integrate the contribution of the Fathers into his theological synthesis. Among others, this can be seen in St. Thomas's interest in the distinction, found in St. John Damascus, between antecedent will and consequent will.[26] Yet many contemporary Thomists, usually eager to emphasize the happy continuity between St. Thomas and the Fathers, paradoxically feel that, in the case of predestination, patristic and especially Augustinian references have been a serious handicap. We are therefore invited to liberate Thomas from Augustine, as today it's widely believed that the theology of the last St. Augustine, that of the anti-Pelagian controversy, is "one of the most devastating misconceptions in the history of Western theology."[27] "Classical Thomism" knew the differences between Thomas and Augustine (and even more between

25. J.-H. Nicolas, *Les profondeurs de la grâce* (Paris: Beauchesne, 1969), 78.

26. Cf. L.-M. Antoniotti, "La volonté divine antécédente et conséquente selon saint Jean Damascène et saint Thomas d'Aquin," *Revue Thomiste* 65 (1965): 52–77; Paluch, *La profondeur de l'amour divin*, chap. 8, "Le changement du schéma interprétatif de la volonté divine."

27. O. H. Pesch, *Thomas d'Aquin, Grandeur et limites de la théologie médiévale: Une introduction*, Cogitatio fidei 177 (Paris: Éditions du Cerf, 1994), 180. To pick just one example, C. Taylor, in his great book *L'âge séculier* (Paris: Seuil, 2011), attributes an extremely negative role to what he calls, not without abusive oversimplification, the "judicial and penal" model of Christianity—"we suffer because we have sinned" (558), initiated by St. Augustine with his doctrine of original sin, *massa damnata*, and redemption through suffering. He believes that, especially in its Calvinistic form, its repulsiveness leads to anti-Christian exclusive humanism. Cf. 1105: "The consequences of the hyper-Augustinian framework thoroughly repelled consciences in previous ages, and helped push people away from faith and toward exclusive humanism, in a gradual way, as the anthropocentric shift grew stronger." Cf. also 145–47.

Thomas and modern Augustinianism), for example, on the place of original sin as the reason for reprobation,[28] but it had also clearly seen the
continuity between the Thomistic doctrine of predestination and what is
the living heart of Augustinianism in what makes it most Christian: the
absolute primacy of grace over works.

Demonization of "Commentators"

The most spectacular change since Garrigou-Lagrange is certainly the
marginalization or even the "demonization" of "commentators,"[29] in this
case Báñez. For Garrigou-Lagrange, commentators had only clarified, according to the homogeneous development model, the unique Thomistic
doctrine by applying Aquinas's principles to new issues that arose in the
post-Tridentine context. If Garrigou-Lagrange thought some commentators had done this more successfully than others (he opposes "strict"
Thomists to "moderate" Thomists, and considers himself a "moderate"),
he did not doubt the substantial loyalty of the school. The current trend,
however, attempts to preserve the modernity of St. Thomas by disconnect-
ing him from a Thomistic school that, it is believed, would have dragged
him down into debates foreign to him (as the De auxiliis quarrel). This
Thomistic school, influenced by the intellectual context of its time, would
have also introduced concepts (such as physical premotion or the antecedent permissive decree) that distort our understanding of St. Thomas.

28. Although St. Thomas sometimes mentions original sin contracted by the sons of
Adam as the objective reason why God does not will eternal salvation for some (cf. Thomas
Aquinas, *Quaestiones disputatae de veritate*, q. 6, a. 2, ad 9), "Thomas linked predestination
much less to the historical situation of Original Sin (as did Augustine) than he did to the
natural, essential condition of the rational creature. Predestination for Aquinas was not so
much rescuing individuals from the *massa damnationis*, as it was a rescue of the rational
creature from his potential defectibility with regard to his supernatural end." M. Harper
McCarthy, *Recent Developments on the Theology of Predestination* (Rome: Pontificia Uni-
versitas Lateranensis–Pontificium Institutum Joannes Paulus II studiorum matrimonii et
familiae, 1995), 61–62.

29. On the current way of assessing commentators, cf. S.-T. Bonino, "Historiographie
de l'école thomiste: Le cas Gilson," in *Saint Thomas au XXᵉ siècle, Actes du Colloque du
Centenaire de la Revue Thomiste* (Paris: Centre National de Livre-Saint Paul, 1994), 299–313;
idem, "La tradition thomiste," in *Thomistes ou de l'actualité de saint Thomas* (Paris: Parole
et Silence, 2003), 241–53.

Thomas versus Thomas

But commentators are not solely responsible because, we are told, the system they've developed, and which we'd now like to leave behind, is not without roots in the Thomasian corpus. Just as two—the predestined and the reprobate—clashed in the womb of Rachel according to Scripture (Gn 25:22–23), there would be in the Thomasian corpus an internal conflict between two understandings of predestination.[30] Such is the thesis defended by Father F. Daguet in his *Theology of the Divine Purpose in St. Thomas*: there would be an explicit line, Augustinian in its tendency, and an implicit line, based on other principles. Father Daguet would have us favor the implicit line today, because it would correspond more to the principles of Christian faith.[31] Thus, as suggested by J.-H. Nicolas in his commentary on question 23, you have to play either the principles or the spirit against the (too Augustinian) letter.[32]

But what are these principles? How should they be determined? The historical-critical method is essential here because it avoids project-

---

30. More broadly, Nicolas admits that "in this area, the relations between grace and freedom in the texts of St. Thomas are not always perfectly consistent, neither with each other nor with other parts of his most proven teachings." "La volonté salvifique," 179. Thus the doctrine of negative reprobation taught in *ST* I, q. 23, a. 5, would contradict God's innocence taught elsewhere. Cf. J.-H. Nicolas, ed., Thomas d'Aquin, *Somme théologique*, tome 1 (Paris: Éditions de Cerf, 1984), 330n7: "We are embarrassed to see, in this *ad* 3, reprobation presented as programmed by God before the creature's initiative to avoid grace. Isn't this finally putting in God the initiative of sin *against the most explicit statements of St. Thomas himself?*... This is one of the moments in the question where Saint Augustine's influence can be felt the most, and not without damage."

31. Cf. F. Daguet, *Théologie du dessein divin chez Thomas d'Aquin, Finis omnium Ecclesia*, Bibliothèque Thomiste 54 (Paris: J. Vrin, 2003), chap. 6, "Le dessein salvifique de Dieu frustré par le péché de l'homme?" According to Daguet, the current magisterium of the Church requires us to go beyond the express line of thought of St. Thomas: "Henceforth, it's the universality of God's purpose and His perseverance in the gift of grace that are clearly stated, and correspondingly the freedom of man to acquiesce or to escape from it" (341). Eager to avoid inclusion of sin in God's original plan, Daguet endorses the Maritainian theses. But he sometimes exaggerates these theses to the point of concealing the dissymmetry, nevertheless claimed by Maritain, between the line of good and that of evil, by submitting both salvation and damnation ultimately to our choice, which is the logic of semi-Pelagianism. "Between the two wills, antecedent and consequent, are held all free acts of the creature and, ultimately, the one whereby it will determine itself to salvation or reprobation" (317); "Man has the first initiative of sin, he also has the last word concerning his salvation" (325).

32. "One could say, against the letter of St. Thomas, but by using his own principles." Nicolas, *Somme théologique*, 1:335n13.

ing onto Aquinas our own desires. Far from being an atemporal system that came down from heaven, St. Thomas's Thomism is a "work-in-progress theology," a doctrine that evolves and whose internal balances are changing, as was shown for predestination by the substantial work of M. Paluch. But the direction of these evolutions helps us better understand the structure of Thomasian teachings and fundamental principles.[33] On the question of predestination, in fact, two significant developments have taken place. First, St. Thomas evolved in the direction of a stricter "Augustinism" starting from the time when, after the *Quaestiones disputatae de veritate*, he learned of the semi-Pelagian controversy and gained insight on the theological and spiritual issues of the *initium fidei*.[34] According to J. Wawrykow, the theology of grace in St. Thomas then moved from a certain priority given to human action (*Scriptum*) to a clear affirmation of Divine action's absolute priority (*Summa Theologiae*).[35] Second, this theological insight went hand in hand with a deepening of the metaphysics of divine causality: St. Thomas, drawing all the consequences of an approach of *esse* as an intensive act, can now emphasize the transcendence of a divine causality that reaches to the ultimate determinations and modalities of its effects.[36] Thus, in the *Scriptum*, the certainty of predestination is still based on eternal foreknowledge of God, and in *Quaestiones disputatae de veritate*, it is based on a statistical model that could be called "the machine gun principle": God, by "spraying" the predestined—that is, by multiplying the graces that objectively solicit his will—eventually will "touch" him. On the contrary, in the later works, predestination's certainty is based on the effectiveness of the causal action of God, a causal

33. At the end of the thirteenth century, the author of *Articuli in quibus frater Thomas melius in Summa quam in Scriptis* had already made a systematic survey of the places where St. Thomas had spoken better in the *Summa* than in the *Scriptum* so as to determine his most authentic thought. Cf. R.-A. Gauthier, "Les 'Articuli in quibus frater Thomas melius in Summa quam in Scriptis,'" *Recherches de Théologie Ancienne et Médiévale* 19 (1952): 271–326, esp. 300–314; idem, "Concordances," *Bulletin Thomiste* 9 (1954–1956): 935–43.

34. Cf. H. Bouillard, *Conversion et grâce chez S. Thomas d'Aquin: Étude historique,* Théologie 1 (Paris: Aubier-Montaigne, 1944).

35. Cf. J. Wawrykow, "Grace," in *The Theology of Thomas Aquinas*, ed. R. van Nieuwenhove and J. P. Wawrykow (Notre Dame, IN: University of Notre Dame Press, 2005), 199–221, esp. 199–202.

36. On this evolution, cf., e.g., B. McGinn, "The Development of the Thought of Thomas Aquinas on the Reconciliation of Divine Providence and Contingent Action," *The Thomist* 39 (1975): 741–52; H. J. M. J. Goris, "Divine Foreknowledge, Providence, Predestination, and Human Freedom," in *Theology of Thomas Aquinas*, 99–122, esp. 112–15.

action that controls the ultimate determinations of created actions. But this "high" model of God's action in creatures inevitably raises the question of the causal relationship between this sovereign causality of God and moral evil that occurs in the free actions of the creature, and may lead to the horror of eternal damnation.

Can We Do without the Antecedent Permissive Decree?

The crux of the contemporary debate on predestination, at least within the Thomistic school, focuses on how to understand the doctrine of reprobation (imposed by the Catholic dogma of hell) in a manner consistent with, on the one hand, the dogma of God's universal salvific will and, on the other hand, God's innocence, a theme that is of decisive importance for the spiritual sensitivity of our time.[37] Yet the classical Thomistic doctrine on the necessity for a permissive decree of God antecedent to each particular sin logically leads to the thesis of a negative reprobation *ante praevisa demerita*: God freely chooses, in his wisdom and goodness, to not prevent such a person from committing a sin that will never be forgiven. This doctrine is a stumbling block (sometimes even, as for Maritain, an object of deep indignation[38]). How, on the one

37. For the "second," see Nicolas, *Synthèse dogmatique*, 2:378n11: "this principle [that God in no way desires the fault of evil] can and must serve as an absolute hermeneutical rule to interpret all texts of St. Thomas concerning the origin of evil that is sin." It is significant that M. Levering (*Predestination: Biblical and Theological Paths* [Oxford: Oxford University Press, 2011]) labels chapter 5, dedicated to the twentieth century, based on its approach to predestination: "The Twentieth Century: God's Absolute Innocence." T. Osborne appears to me overly optimistic when he writes: "I am not here concerned with the objection that the Thomist position entails that God is responsible for evil actions. This objection does not seem particularly difficult for me, and has been overwhelmingly refuted by J. H. Nicolas." "Thomist Premotion and Contemporary Philosophy of Religion," *Nova et Vetera* 4 (2006): 607–32, esp. 614n17.

38. In a somewhat blunt way, D. B. Hart writes: "The immediate and vulgar response of most Christians to this style of theology is to dismiss it as absurd and repulsive. The more considered and sophisticated response, however—by one of those delightful coincidences that are all too rare—is usually the same." "Impassibility and Transcendence: On the Infinite Innocence of God," in *Divine Impassibility and the Mystery of Human Suffering*, ed. J. F. Keating and T. J. White (Grand Rapids, MI: William B. Eerdmans, 2009), 299–323, esp. 307. Labourdette, "Deux inédits du Père Marie-Michel Labourdette," 361, invited Maritain to more respect for his opponents: "I clearly see the darkness and the enormous difficulties of this teaching, and especially the odious presentation that can be made of it (in this regard,

hand, is it compatible with the universal salvific will? If God, even before a person has committed any good or evil, allows this person to fall, freely yet infallibly, in a sin that will never be forgiven, can we still claim that God "sincerely" wants the salvation of this person? How, on the other hand, would God not be an accomplice of sin by allowing this to happen? Under the combined pressure of these two principles—universal salvific will and innocence of God—we are ordered to renounce the antecedent permissive decree.

Yet the doctrine of the antecedent permissive decree is also the result of several inescapable doctrinal constraints. It is, first, a consequence of the doctrine of the *Ipsum Esse subsistens'* sovereign causality vis-à-vis the creatures he creates, maintains, and moves to good.[39] To this divine causality's universality in the metaphysical order corresponds, second, revealed doctrine of the absolute primacy of grace in the order of supernatural salvation, with its spiritual corollary, the fundamental role of humility in the Christian life, which is the real issue of St Augustine's struggle against semi-Pelagianism. "What distinguishes you? What hast thou that thou didst not receive?" (1 Cor 4:7).[40] Finally, third, within the framework of Thomistic theology of divine science, as a science based on causation, the doctrine of the antecedent permissive decree seems to be the only way to account for the way God knows real sins. Opponents of the antecedent permissive decree attack mostly the first point (the way we understand God's action in creatures), but because the three doctrines are bound up as a system, they try to allow the two others without recourse to the first. Mission impossible.

---

may I say that the tone of p. 97 annoys me a bit: those who struggled with these difficulties, and I think it was with 'seriousness,' and without being deprived of the sense of human drama as too many of their scholiasts, are still Bañez, Lemos, John of St. Thomas; I do not think that all of which you remind us so well regarding the coexistence of temporal development with the immutable eternity had escaped them, or that they were fooled by imagination of the 'script' written in advance ...)."

39. In the line of efficient causality, the effective failure of the creature is unthinkable without the cessation of the motion to good by the First Cause. Cf. Labourdette, "Deux inédits du Père Marie-Michel Labourdette," 361. "I still can't see (even though I'd love to! your solution is so liberating!) how we could maintain the *antecedent* character of the divine motion for the conservation of good by denying the anteriority of a permission (permissive decree) in the case of evil."

40. Cf. P.-M. Hombert, *Gloria Gratiae: Se glorifier en Dieu, principe et fin de la théologie augustinienne de la grâce*, Collection des Études augustiniennes: Série Antiquité 148 (Paris: Institut d'Études Augustiniennes, 1996).

"God Determinant or Determined God,
no Middle Ground"?

Father Garrigou-Lagrange's famous dilemma, which expresses the doctrine of God as pure act, is the keystone of classical Thomism. Therefore its opponents seek to destroy this deadlock, this "venerable error,"[41] by proposing alternative models for the relationship between divine causality and the spiritual creature's free action.[42]

A first strategy is to reject outright the doctrine of physical premotion. Hence some think that an interpretation of St. Thomas's metaphysics that emphasizes the primacy of *esse* as the proper effect of God the Creator does not need physical premotion to explain the passage from power to operation.[43] Others are even more radical. The very problem of physical premotion would be the pure product of the ontotheological drift afflicting metaphysics and modern theology, reducing them to a form of sacred rationalism oblivious to the true transcendence of God: "The God of physical premotion is not fully transcendent, but merely supreme; he is not a fully primary cause, but merely a kind of 'infinite' secondary cause,"[44] "the first element of a physical chain of movement."[45] In order to avoid this, Harm Goris notes that, because the action of God in the creature participates in the mystery of God, it is beyond our understanding and must be viewed in the perspective of apophatic theology, dear to the Utrecht Thomistic Institute.[46] The thesis of physical premotion

41. Hart, "Impassibility and Transcendence," 300.

42. Nicolas, "Dieu et la permission du mal," presents, in order to refute them, the "efforts to exclude the antecedent permissive decree": (1) exclusion of predetermination (1.1, divine causality without motion; 1.2, undetermined divine motion); and (2) recourse to conditioned divine predetermination (2.1, divine predetermination with created conditioning positive as well as negative: Marín-Sola, Muñiz; 2.2, divine predetermination with created conditioning in the line of evil only: Maritain).

43. Cf. Nicolas, "La permission du péché," 9–13. Cf., e.g., J. De Finance, *Être et agir dans la philosophie de saint Thomas* (Rome: Librairie Éditrice de l'Université Grégorienne), 224–34. Among more recent advocates of this position, cf. D. Burrell, *Freedom and Creation in Three Traditions* (Notre Dame, IN: University of Notre Dame Press, 1993), 95–139.

44. Hart, "Impassibility and Transcendence," 309, relying on Heidegger's reading of the destiny of Western metaphysics, interprets "modern Thomism" as a perverse form of ontotheology.

45. Goris, "Divine Foreknowledge," 100. Cf. also B. J. Shanley, "Divine Causation and Human Freedom in Aquinas," *American Catholic Philosophical Quarterly* 72 (1998): 99–122.

46. Ibid., 115. "God's incomprehensible act of giving being as such, including his modal qualifications, allows us to say that the Creator sustains the causal action of creatures and

would therefore lower the transcendent actions of God in his creation to a form of predicamental action. Everything happens for these authors as if we had to choose between the *prima via* and the *quarta via*. This debate is reminiscent of that between compatibilists and incompatibilists concerning the theology of providence.

A second strategy to overcome Father Garrigou-Lagrange's dilemma is, while maintaining the need for a divine motion at the root of a created action, to deny that this divine motion is the cause of the very specification of this free act. This would be a motion indefinite "by excess," in the sense that the divine motion that leads the will to good would suffice to virtually actualize the particular determinations chosen only by the will.[47] This is sometimes put forth on the basis of the metaphysics of the real distinction between being and essence, and it is argued that the exercise of the free act (corresponding to *esse*) comes from God, while its specification (corresponding to *essentia*) comes from the creature, provided that this determination by the second cause is purely negative: it is not "more" being, but a limitation.

These attempts to get around the Garrigaldian dilemma face considerable metaphysical difficulties, starting with their consequences on the question of divine science. If the determination of the free act is removed from the predetermining causality of God, how can God still know it? All the Thomasian doctrine on God's omniscience (intrinsically bound up to revealed doctrine on providence's universality) is indeed based on God's universal causality, because God doesn't know created reali-

---

gives being to their effects in accordance with the necessity or contingency of the secondary causes. 'Presence' and 'causation' are said analogously of the Eternal One and of the Creator, and signify modes of presence and of causation that elude our grasp."

47. Cf. Nicolas, "La permission du péché," 13–18. Among more recent advocates of a specific nondetermination of the free act of the creature by God, cf. L. M. Antoniotti, "La présence des actes libres de la créature à l'éternité divine," *Revue Thomiste* 66 (1966): 5–47, esp. 26: "The operative motion that is the source of all the natural order's cooperating motions is a motion undifferentiated by excess… [the person] contracts and particularizes the motion specified by the good in all its magnitude, as a power limits the act it receives. This is why no divine intervention other than the motion to good as good is required in the pure line of natural specification for the person to confer a defined 'thisness' to the singular action he freely elicits"; J.-P. Arfeuil, "Le dessein sauveur de Dieu: La doctrine de la prédestination selon saint Thomas d'Aquin," *Revue Thomiste* 74 (1974): 591–641, esp. 621: "The proper action of the creature, insofar as it brings determinations to the *esse*, is subsequent to the action of God creating the *esse*, but it precedes the production of the *esse* insofar as it's the ultimate perfection that actualises the perfections which are the created causes' proper effects."

ties by leaning over the balcony to find out, but by knowing himself as their cause. Unless we assume God learns something from creatures, we must maintain that God knows directly only what he causes. As for sin, God knows it indirectly by knowing the gap between what should be and what actually is (i.e., private election of moral rectitude), a failure known infallibly by God, not by causing it, but through a permissive decree.

Some then sought to unravel the link between divine science and divine causality, especially by using the theme of the presence of creatures and their free acts in God's eternity, which St. Thomas invokes when dealing with future contingents.[48] But isolating this particular theme from the general doctrine of divine science, and still more claiming it as a substitute, would be to seriously err in method. God's presence to free acts, necessary for the object to have a certain intelligibility, is in no way the *medium* of divine science: it's the effect of divine causality and cannot suffice, independently of it, to account for divine science. "All his creatures, spiritual and corporal, [God] does not know them because they are, but they are, because he knows them."[49]

In his 1992 *retractatio*, J.-H. Nicolas explains that he long maintained the doctrine of the antecedent permissive decree, "not without efforts to rearrange it, to solve the problem of God's foreknowledge of sin," and recognizes frankly that once this doctrine is set aside, "the problem [of divine science of sin] remains."[50] He then suggests that God knows sin by a kind of reverse connaturality: "God knows it [the will] as faltering, at the instant of reason when it conceives sin in its heart, by a kind of reverse connaturality, the loved being perceived as suddenly separating itself and breaking love's bond."[51] Not only is the proposed solution hard

48. Cf. *ST* I, q. 14, a. 13.

49. Augustin, *De Trinitate* XV, XIII, 22. "Universas creaturas, et spirituales et corporales, non quia sunt, ideo novit Deus; sed ideo sunt, quia novit." Quoted by St. Thomas in *De veritate*, q. 2, a. 14; *ST* I, q. 14, a. 8, sed contra. Cf. Labourdette, "Cours de théologie morale," 61. "God does not know created beings because they are present, it's because He knows them *voluntate adjuncta* that they are present; He has of them a causal science. About evil, we say: God doesn't know it because it happened without Him expecting it; He knows it because He permits this evil to influence a positively willed subject."

50. J.-H. Nicolas, "La volonté salvifique," 186.

51. Ibid., 193–96. Cf. idem, *Synthèse dogmatique*, 2:396n53. "How could God know them [the sins] since He in no way wants them? Such a difficult question! If we must, as I'm currently inclined, give up the notion of the antecedent permissive decree, which had been developed to solve this problem, maybe we can think of a kind of knowledge by connaturality."

to understand, but it also inevitably leads to a theology of suffering in God and its inherent difficulties. Suffering, presented as an actively assumed passivity, becomes in a way the *medium* of the knowledge of sin.[52]

The Dissymmetry between the Line of Good and the Line of Evil

Jacques Maritain, meanwhile, intends to rigorously maintain the doctrine of physical premotion, at least in the order of good, that is, in the production of the good act. For in the dissymmetrical order of evil, the doctrine of the antecedent permissive decree seems to him totally incompatible with the doctrine of God's innocence.[53] He then falls back on the concept of a "breakable motion." God moves the creature to good, but the motion can be "broken," made sterile by a "nihilisation" under the creature's full initiative. The coherence of the concept of a "breakable motion" has led to many discussions.[54] Recently again, Father F. Schmitz has argued that a resistible, or in other words "breakable," divine motion (in the composite sense) would be just as self-contradictory as "a square circle."[55] Divine motion is not a vaporous entity, whose form depends on the created will's determinations. "If it is true that St. Thomas conceives divine motion, not as a kind of dynamic quality impressed into the will by God, but as God's immediate action on the will, communicating a certain act to the operative power by mode of influx, in order to lead it to its vital operation, it is metaphysically impossible for divine motion to fail obtaining its effect."[56]

But just as the indeterminate motion had to face the question of divine science of sin, the breakable motion thus breaks up on the theological

---

52. Same logic for Hart, "Impassibility and Transcendence," 314. "Just as the incarnate Logos really suffers torment and death not through a passive modification of his nature, imposed by some exterior force, but by a free act, so God can 'suffer' the perfect knowledge of the free acts of his creatures, not as a passive reaction to some objective force set over against Himself, but as a free, transcendent act of giving being to the world of Christ."

53. Cf. Maritain, "Dieu et la permission du mal," 87–88n9. "It's not the sinner, it's God, who by His sole almighty will, makes evil enter into the divine plan; *voilà*, in the question of evil, the cornerstone of bañezism and neo-bañezism."

54. Cf. Nicolas, "La permission du péché," 193–206; S. Long, "Providence, liberté et loi naturelle," *Revue Thomiste* 102 (2002): 355–405.

55. F. Schmitz, *Causalité divine et péché dans la théologie de saint Thomas d'Aquin: Examen critique du concept de motion "brisable"* (Paris: L'Harmattan, 2016), 171.

56. Ibid., 177.

principle of the primacy of grace in the order of salvation, defined by the Church against semi-Pelagianism. Even if Maritain wishes to contest this consequence,[57] the breakable motion theory inevitably leads to attribute to the creature—to its nonresistance to divine motion—the last word in the matter of our salvation. "To say that non-nihilisation is in no way a created initiative is pushing the paradox to the point of contradiction. For the power to nihilate is obviously the power not to nihilate, such that it's an initiative not to take an initiative, which we could take."[58] That God does not save us without our consent is an essential truth, but we must immediately add, against all semi-Pelagianism, that this consent itself, which is nonresistance to grace, is already the effect of his grace "Hoc ipsum quod aliquis non ponit obstaculum ex gratia procedit."[59]

The Antecedent Permissive Decree as the Default Solution

Thomists who fail to see how we can, without serious inconvenience, dispense with the antecedent permissive decree can't exempt themselves from offering a version that takes into account, where possible, criticism of its adversaries.[60] But the doctrine of permission of sin would probably

57. For Maritain, nonresistance to sufficient grace does not require efficacious grace because it isn't, he says, anything positive. The universal predestination (contained in sufficient grace) becomes special predestination once the will does not nihilate.

58. Nicolas, "La permission du péché," 199. Cf. Labourdette, "Deux inédits du Père Marie-Michel Labourdette," 360. "The 'to not nihilate' implies a prevenient motion. Saint Thomas says that, just as a creature, apart from the creative influx, can only fall back into nothingness, a will created outside this prevenient motion, can only fail, freely of course, but infallibly. God *preserves* in good as He preserves in being; without which he who doesn't nihilate 'discerns himself' [1 Cor 4:7] and would bring to his salvation something that is only his and which doesn't come from God."

59. Cf. Thomas Aquinas, *Lectura in epistolam ad Hebraeos,* c. 12, lect. 3 (#689). "Sed contra. Quia si gratia non datur ex operibus sed tantum ex hoc quod aliquis non ponit obstaculum, ergo habere gratiam dependet ex solo libero arbitrio, et non ex electione Dei, quod est error Pelagii. Respondeo. Dicendum est quod hoc ipsum, quod aliquis non ponit obstaculum, ex gratia procedit."

60. Some authors, using the "classical" idea of a mutual precedence of efficient and material causes in the sinful act (the will's failure precedes, in the order of dispositive causation, the refusal of the motion to good, which is first in the order of effectiveness), propose the idea of a reprobation *simul ac praevisa demerita.* Torrell agrees with this thesis he finds in M. Paluch: "Rigorous concurrency of a twin-faced process: it's *at the same time* that free will deserves reprobation, that God causes the sinner's abandonment." "Introduction," in *Questions disputées sur la vérité,* 353. But if the failure is, in a certain order, the cause of the refusal of the motion to good, it remains to be explained how the failure itself is possible.

not elicit as much perplexity if it didn't also apply to final impenitence, which leads a person to eternal damnation. How can God allow the unfathomable evil of damnation, the apparent failure of his universal salvific will? *Quaestio tremenda*, which touches the very roots of the problem of evil.[61]

We can—and must—reply that the cause of eternal damnation is the stubborn resistance of the sinner to the end, despite the objective moral motions whereby grace unceasingly solicits the rebellious will. But we still have to clarify the relationship between this resistance and God's efficient causality.

The simplest solution (which constitutes by far the most common "theodicy," including from the pulpit) is to say that God is purely and simply powerless against a created freedom that resists all his advances. God in his infinite mercy encircles the will, but he cannot act in it. In this case, damnation depends only on us. It is the consequence of our resistance or nonconsent to grace. Unfortunately, in this model, in which God is denied access to our will and is thus reduced to being a cause among others, it seems that our salvation is also the result of a consent, about which only our freedom has ultimately the decisive initiative!

In reality it's necessary, in Catholic theology, to maintain that this resistance, which is fully ours, would not be possible without some divine permission.[62] Thus Maritain, for whom our resistance is not preceded by

---

Cf. Labourdette, "Cours de théologie morale," 70. "The refusal of grace is always a penalty: penalty of previous sins, but penalty also of the very sin it's about, since in a way this refusal is preceded by my failure. But if there is something which precedes both this refusal and that failure, it's divine permission."

61. In a question where so many existential issues are involved, much prudence, quickened by charity, is required for the theologian. Every believer has his "portable theodicy," i.e., his personal way of reconciling his experience of evil and his faith in God. This "theodicy" is rooted in the history of his life of faith, and it maintains a vital link with his intimate experience of God. Thus any discussion of evil must be done in a context of humble charity, as it is liable to destabilize this vital complex, where lived faith and philosophical or theological representations of God that are more or less adequate intermingle. We will welcome with fear and trembling the warning of C. Journet, *Le mal: Essai théologique* (Saint-Maurice: Saint-Augustin, cop., 1988), 18: "The most orthodox doctrine, if repeated without being immersed back into the flame where it was born, if it is not imbued by some secret power of the Gospel, will betray, it could become poisonous, and how then could we not fear to cause scandal, where we thought we were bringing light?"

62. Cf. Nicolas, "La permission du péché," 544. "[The problem] is born from this indisputable truth, admitted by all, that God could prevent moral evil in general, that He could, in each particular case, preserve from evil the free creature without infringing on its freedom, and nevertheless that He does not. That is the mystery."

any permissive decree, recognizes that God could effectively break this resistance by nonbreakable motions, as he sometimes does especially in the supernatural order.[63] If he doesn't do it, when he could do it, he therefore somehow *permits* this resistance. Why? Because, say the Maritainians, God does not want to force the will: he wants to be chosen, loved with a love of preference. But would an act elicited under the effect of an unbreakable motion be forced or less free? Such a concept would be in complete opposition to the thought of St. Thomas.

Therefore God doesn't allow sin in order to respect a created freedom, in which his action could only do violence, but "because He wanted to create free beings and He wants to govern them in a manner consistent with this nature."[64] The reason for the permission of sin (and thus reprobation) is the wisdom of a divine government that conforms to the nature of things as it is thought by divine wisdom. Human nature being fallible in its freedom, God allows it to sometimes fail.[65]

A reflection on the reason for the permission of sin can only be a posteriori. If we must admit that there are spiritual creatures that perish (if only Satan), and if we maintain that God's causal action can't be limited extrinsically by the creature, then we must also admit that God, in his wisdom, has reasons (reasons of fittingness and not necessary reasons) to permit damnation, and it is legitimate to inquire about them. But we can in no way deduce a priori the permission of sin (and negative repro-

63. Maritain, "Dieu et la permission du mal," 48–49: "It goes without saying that God can give to some persons *unbreakable motions the first time around*. Their freedom will be divinely removed from its natural fallibility, and they will act well without the risk of failing, and will be divinely protected against the possibility of a non-consideration of the rule. But it's also clear that this is not the ordinary case."

64. Nicolas, "La permission du péché," 543.

65. Cf., e.g., Schmitz, *Causalité divine*, 205. "If God does not effectively will the salvation of all spiritual creatures, it may be because He can't will *with a consequent will* such an object; not because of an extrinsic limitation to His causal power by the creature, but because such an object would be incompatible with divine wisdom, given what the defectible creature is, intrinsically." Such a justification of the permission of sin by the general order and the good of the universe, which seems to be the one used systematically by St. Thomas, is hotly contested in the name of Christian "personalism." Can someone's eternal destiny be subordinated, "sacrificed," to the good of a universe this person transcends, by this person's very ordination to God? Isn't the Christian God the one who leaves the ninety-nine sheep to rescue the single lost sheep? We would need here to agree on the content of the "good of the universe." If it's true that the created person is not subject to the good of the physical universe, or even to the good of the political community, this person is no less integrated into a metaphysical and moral order of which it's only a part.

bation) as if it were a means to a good end, as, for example, the manifestation of God's righteousness (even if sin, once committed, becomes an opportunity to manifest this justice).[66]

Theology against Metaphysics?

Peter Abelard said: "I don't want to be a philosopher if this means I must reject St. Paul, I don't want to be Aristotle if this means the door of Christ is closed for me."[67] One of my Toulouse colleagues, an excellent Thomist yet hard-core anti-Báñezian, usually concludes our discussions by declaring that he too will always choose Jesus Christ in a contest between metaphysics and Christ. But is it really necessary to choose between the God of metaphysics and the God of love revealed in Jesus Christ?[68] As M. Paluch says, "the necessity of sacrificing Theology on the altar of Philosophy or Philosophy on the altar of Theology...cannot be easily accepted by any Thomist. Such a situation questions the harmony between reason and faith, a harmony that is far too important for the Thomistic tradition to give up without a struggle."[69]

The debate on predestination invites us to avoid both a unilateral determination of theology by metaphysics (theology is not a sacred metaphysics) as well as a unilateral determination of metaphysics by theology

66. It has sometimes been argued in "classical Thomism" that negative reprobation was a way for God to manifest the gratuitousness of the supernatural and his sovereign freedom, which in choosing some, necessarily rejects others. Nothing in the logic of "classical Thomism" requires nor justifies these positions. Nicolas has recognized that the biblical doctrine of election didn't imply of itself exclusion and disapproval of some. Election means freedom of divine action, not the rejection of some. If there is reprobation, the reason lies elsewhere, even if by accident the reprobation may be the opportunity to manifest the gratuity of the supernatural and God's freedom. "La volonté salvifique," 192.

67. Pierre Abélard, "Confessio fidei ad Heloisam: Abelard's Last Letter to Heloise? A Discussion and Critical Edition of the Latin and Medieval French Versions," ed. Charles S. F. Burnett, Mittellateinisches Jahrbuch 21 (1986): 152–53.

68. The contradiction could also be between the metaphysical God and the ethical God; cf. Paluch, "La profondeur de l'amour divin," 204. "Thomas is thus faced with a choice between the coherence of morality and that of the metaphysical vision of God. This is also the same choice that faced, mutatis mutandis, Molina and Bañez, Marín Sola and Garrigou-Lagrange, Maritain and Nicolas."

69. M. Paluch, "Recovering a Doctrine of Providence," Nova et Vetera (English ed.) 12 (2014): 1159–72, esp. 1168–69. For Maritain, according to Paluch, "philosophy is forced to serve theological purposes" (1167), whereas "the solution presented by Nicolas is metaphysically coherent," but "Theology with its concern for divine innocence and God's universal salvific will is forced to follow a philosophical coherence."

(metaphysics would lose its value as interlocutor for theology). We must rather accept a fruitful tension that compels both the metaphysician and the theologian to deepen their own certainties based on those of their counterparts.

Certainly, it is not in itself (methodologically) sinful to consider "re-thinking" certain aspects of metaphysics (which is a perfectible science) to better uphold the truths of faith.[70] But metaphysics is not malleable at will. As Benedict XVI has repeatedly reminded us along the lines of *Fides et ratio*, faith, in order to avoid falling into fideism, must welcome philosophical reason as an authentic, autonomous partner, with which to confront itself.[71] Metaphysics—especially one that culminates in the rational approach to the Creator God—aids theology (which is sometimes tempted by insufficiently criticized anthropomorphic models) to maintain a keen sense of the transcendence of the *Ipsum Esse subsistens*.

In the question of predestination, absent a positive demonstration of the full conciliation of metaphysical truths and truths of faith, as well as between the truths of faith themselves (e.g., between the sovereign Lordship of God, his love for each person and his permission of a sin that leads to damnation), the Thomist theologian, like every believer, holds in

70. The manner in which St. Thomas has deepened the ontological status of the accident in light of the Eucharistic dogma has here an exemplary value. Concerning predestination, the operation may lead to quite different results. If, for Maritain and the second Nicolas, the innocence of God is the fundamental theological principle that leads them to abandon the theory of the divine science of evil using the antecedent permissive decree (without finding a satisfactory alternative), on the other side, the theological principle of the absolute primacy of grace, required by the condemnations of semi-Pelagianism, calls for and confirms a "high" metaphysical conception of divine causality.

71. Cf. Benedict XVI, *Address to the University of Rome La Sapienza*, January 17, 2008: "I would say that Saint Thomas's idea concerning the relationship between Philosophy and Theology could be expressed using the formula that the Council of Chalcedon adopted for Christology: Philosophy and Theology must be interrelated 'without confusion and without separation.' 'Without confusion' means that each of the two must preserve its own identity. Philosophy must truly remain a quest conducted by reason with freedom and responsibility; it must recognize its limits and likewise its greatness and immensity. Theology must continue to draw upon a treasury of knowledge that it did not invent, that always surpasses it, the depths of which can never be fully fathomed through reflection, and which for that reason constantly gives rise to new thinking. Balancing 'without confusion,' there is always 'without separation': philosophy does not start again from scratch with every thinking subject in total isolation, but takes its place within the great dialogue of historical wisdom, which it continually accepts and develops in a manner both critical and docile. It must not exclude what religions, and the Christian faith in particular, have received and have given to humanity as signposts for the journey."

the dark that this conciliation is possible,[72] and as a theologian establishes that it's not impossible.[73]

Such is, in my opinion (and this will be my conclusion), the genius of Thomism in an area where the theologian knows that his science has reached its limits. He doesn't want to sacrifice any of the problem's data, metaphysical or theological: neither the universal determining causality of pure Act, nor grace's primacy, nor God's innocence and his saving will. The theologian surrenders neither to the absurdity of a contradiction between the Word of God and right reason, nor to the apologetic cop out of a created freedom conceived as first cause. He contents himself (but that's a lot) to lay out the mystery in its rightful place, that is, to turn one's gaze toward the superintelligible essence of a God in whom power, wisdom, and goodness kiss.

72. The main idea of M. Levering in his work *Predestination* is that "the relationship of His [God's] superabundant love for all and His election of some cannot be understood by us" (11) but must be held. "Until the eschaton, these two affirmations cannot be resolved in one" (178).

73. Nicolas, "La permission du péché," 534: "All the theologian can do is show that between this revealed mystery [reprobation] and the other truths of faith concerning the infinite goodness, infinite justice and infinite wisdom of God, we can not discover any opposition." Schmitz, *Causalité divine*, 193n336: "The partial answers provided by the classical Thomists don't allow us to perceive positively the agreement between the infallible efficacy of any divine motion, and the universal salvific will. However, even if we do not judge them fully satisfactory, the arguments they put forward suffice to prove that there is no obvious incompatibility between the two assertions. It's not because the conciliation of these two points isn't clear, that we must reject an otherwise certain metaphysical conclusion, under the pretext of saving a truth of faith. It is better to simply confess our ignorance about the conciliation of these two truths rather than give up one or the other, which would cause us to sink either in heresy or in the absurd."

2

ST. THOMAS AQUINAS,

DIVINE CAUSALITY, AND THE MYSTERY

OF PREDESTINATION

Steven A. Long

Introduction

The question of predestination involves questions of the authoritative
teaching of the Church which inescapably imply questions of scriptural interpretation, of the content of the tradition, and of the teaching of
St. Thomas Aquinas, whose authority is—as Ramirez demonstrates for the
preconciliar period,[1] and as Jörgen Vijgens demonstrates with respect to
the postconciliar magisterium[2]—not merely the authority of one more of
the fathers, but that of an "authoritative teacher." Moreover, as St. Thomas
argues in the *Summa Theologiae* (*ST*) I, q. 1, a. 7, ad 1, because the theologian through *sacra doctrina* does not enjoy a quidditative knowledge of
God, knowledge of the effects of God in nature and in grace must "stand
in" for the lack of this knowledge in the theologian's acquired contempla-

---

1. Santiago Ramirez, OP, "The Authority of St. Thomas Aquinas," *The Thomist* 15 (1952):
1–109.

2. Jorgen Vijgen, "The Contemporary Authority of St. Thomas Aquinas: A Reply to
Otto-Herman Pesch," *Divinitas* 49 (2006): 3–26.

tion of God. Since, among all the effects of God, the effect of *esse* is most universal,[3] Thomas sees that wisdom regarding this effect is essentially necessary for the theologian. Thus, metaphysics as the science of being *qua* being enjoys a privileged instrumentality within *sacra doctrina*.

This essay addresses the metaphysics of predestination and reprobation, acknowledging that while the metaphysical issues are essential and necessary, these subjects are also by their very nature a matter of divine revelation. The aim is partially to address the difficulty that is found by many theologians and philosophers not only with the teaching of St. Thomas that predestination is prior to the prevision of merit,[4] but even more crucially, with his teaching that reprobation is prior to prevision of demerit.[5]

In this essay I proceed in the following way. First, I advert to his account of the relation between free acts of will and the divine causality, referring to God's motion of the human will. This doctrine—which later came to be known as the doctrine of "physical premotion"—articulates a profound analysis regarding how it is that human freedom lies within the transcendent divine providence. *This teaching must be considered because, lacking such an analysis, it would be impossible for the plan of divine predestination to be—as St. Thomas insists that it is—the cause of grace and free actions. This, in turn, would imperil both the universality of divine causality and the primacy of grace in the supernatural life.* By contrast, Thomas's teaching retains human freedom, but not a human freedom that implies what would be an impossible antinomy of "created aseity" as though any creature could possess a liberty of indifference to the divine causality. Second, and more briefly, I point out the implications that flow from the affirmation of the divine simplicity in understanding grace as such. Third, I briefly respond to three of the most important twentieth-century accounts attempting to revise St. Thomas's teaching with respect to grace, efforts principally undertaken for the sake of avoiding Thomas's express teaching regarding predestination and reprobation *ante previsa merita*. The efforts are those of Jacques Maritain, Marín-Sola, OP, and Bernard Lonergan, SJ. Fourth and finally, I suggest a way of understanding Thomas's express teaching regarding reprobation that does

---

3. *ST* I, q. 45, a. 5, resp.   4. *ST* I, q. 23, a. 5, resp.
5. *ST*, I, q. 23. a. 3, ad 1, 3; q. 23, a. 5, ad 3.

not seek to remove the mystery, but rather to clarify how this teaching in no way implies a denial of the divine innocence or goodness.

St. Thomas's Express Teaching Regarding Physical Premotion

As has been noted above, the nature of human freedom in relation to divine causality is a central constituent of this question, since predestination cannot be the cause of grace and of free actions if free actions cannot be caused by God. Some scholars have denied that Thomas ever held a doctrine rightly characterized by the terms "physical premotion." (Here I think, in contemporary terms, of the observations of Brian Shanley, OP, recently approbated in a conspicuous footnote by John Wippel in an article titled "Metaphysical Themes in *De malo* 1."[6]) After all, the phrase "physical premotion" as such was never used by St. Thomas Aquinas. This is often thought to settle the matter. Yet it is proper to distin-

---

6. John Wippel, "Metaphysical Themes in *De malo*, 1," in *Aquinas's Disputed Questions on Evil: A Critical Guide* (Cambridge: Cambridge University Press, 2015), 30n58: "Many Thomists, influenced by the terminology of Dominic Báñez, claim that Thomas therefore holds that God moves free created agents with a 'physical pre-motion.' Not finding this terminology in Thomas's texts, I recommend against using it because it slants Thomas's solution in the direction of a determinism he did not defend. For similar reservations about Báñez's position, see Shanley, *The Thomist Tradition*, 107, n. 56; 204–205. Limitations of space preclude a fuller examination here of Aquinas's effort to reconcile divine concurrence (and foreknowledge) with human freedom." Note that the claim about determinism hangs in empty, speculatively underdetermined, space. Is it truly possible that the view that affirmation of divine causality necessarily requires affirmation of some determinate actual effect is being confused with an undifferentiated yet somehow objectionable "determinism"? What is objectionable? Either we are not told, or Father Shanley implies that premotion is mechanistic, a reduction or denial of the divine transcendence, too categorial. But these are allegations for which the speculative foundation is not to be found. Premotion is not a mechanism; the divine premotion is indeed transcendent of the categories, as all creatures can move only if they first be moved by God. This confusion regarding the reality of the divine motion is remarkable, as is likewise the failure to provide anything remotely akin to a textual support for the claim that Thomas did not defend what the term of art "physical premotion" designates (the terminology having been developed to respond to the claim that Thomas does not teach there to be a real—what is intended by "physical"—motion bestowed by God that is ontologically prior to the self-motion of the rational creature). To the contrary, St. Thomas repeatedly asserts that there is a real motion bestowed by God, prior by nature to the rational creature's free act, which moves the creature from potency to act with respect to its own self-motion. But (as applied to the rational creature's acts of free choice—the present subject) this is simply what "physical premotion" means (God moves every creature according to its nature).

guish the nature of a teaching from pedagogic terminology that may help in explaining it. For example, St. Thomas does not introduce the distinction between essence and existence with the phrase "the real distinction of essence and existence," a phrase which seems *precisely as such* to appear nowhere in his writing. Yet he does hold that essence and existence are real principles, principles of being, and he does hold them to be distinct in all creatures. And so we do not distort his meaning by using the phrase "real distinction of essence and existence," a phrase that is pedagogically helpful. Likewise, the term "physical" in the phrase "physical premotion" means "real"; the "pre" in "premotion" refers to an ontological as distinct from temporal priority (as, e.g., the cause is prior to the effect even when they are simultaneous in time); and "motion" refers to the actualization of potency. It is true that Thomas does not use the term "physical premotion." But in several distinct texts, especially in the middle and later part of his writing, St. Thomas does affirm that there is a *real* motion bestowed by God to every creature, a motion that is *ontologically* prior to any action whatsoever on the part of any creature, including volitional action: *and this is what "physical premotion" means.* Those who reject the doctrine because Thomas does not use this precise formulation are exhibiting what one might call a semantic *ipsissima verba*-ism that obstructs their acknowledgment of Thomas's manifest and express teaching. Such a view should, in fairness, likewise refuse to speak of the real distinction of essence and existence, because—although this is manifestly the teaching of Aquinas—he does not use this precise phrase. If one prefers "real premotion" to "physical premotion," there is no objection, because the teaching referred to is in any case identical (and the sense of "physical" in the expression is "real," "actual," "ontological," etc.).

Before referring to a few of the texts wherein St. Thomas affirms the divine motion of the will as ontologically prior to action and necessary to move the rational creature from potency to act with respect to its own act of free choice, it helps to consider St. Thomas's doctrine that the agent causality of God extends to all being as such, to anything that properly exists in whatsoever manner. For example, *ST* I, q. 22, a. 2, resp., unequivocally refers to divine *agent causality* and states: "But the causality of God, Who is the first agent, extends to all being not only as to constituent principles of species, but also as to the individualizing principles; not only of things incorruptible, but also of things corruptible. Thus all things that exist in whatsoever manner are necessarily directed by God towards some end; as the Apostle says in Romans 13: 'Those things that are of God are well ordered.'"[7]

Yet nonetheless the action of the creature must be its own, *and be brought forth from and by the creature through its own powers.* Thus God cannot simply "create" our actions *apart from us,* but must *move us freely to move ourselves.* Indeed, since according to Aquinas motion is nothing other than the reduction of potency to act (as he states in *ST* I, q. 2, a. 3, resp.: "Movere enim nihil aliud est quam educere aliquid de potentia in actum"), and the rational creature is in potency to self-motion in freedom prior to moving itself, for God to be first cause of these volitional acts is by the nature of the case for God to move the creature to move itself (God is not alone first efficient cause of esse, but first mover). This is precisely what St. Thomas teaches, which involves an account both of the nature of freedom and of the nature of the divine motion. To deny the ontologically prior divine motion whereby God applies every created power to act[8] and moves us to move ourselves will imply either occasionalism (which denies that God brings forth acts through the powers and secondary causality of creatures) or else imply denial of the universality of the divine causality (carrying the hazards not only of semi-Pelagianism or even Manicheism, but also of a deistic rather than theistic doctrine of God). Such alternatives appear neither to be compatible with the teaching of St. Thomas Aquinas nor to properly articulate Catholic doctrine.

In *ST* I-II, q. 9, a. 4, resp., Thomas argues that the will must be moved by God as exterior mover, referring to the first motion of the will. But he argues from a *principle* that applies beyond the first motion of the will and that extends to the application of the natural motion of the will in free choice: "For everything that is at one time in potency and at another in act, needs to be moved by a mover."[9]

---

7. *ST* I, q. 22, a. 2, resp.: "Causalitas autem Dei, qui est primum agens, se extendit usque ad omnia entia, non solum quantum ad principia speciei, sed etiam quantum ad individualia principia, non solum incorruptibilium, sed etiam corruptibilium. Unde necesse est omnia quae habent quocumque modo esse, ordinata esse a Deo in finem, secundum illud apostoli, ad Rom. XIII, *quae a Deo sunt, ordinata sunt.*"

8. Cf. *Summa contra gentiles* III, ch. 67: "Sed omnis applicatio virtutis ad operationem est principaliter et primo a Deo." "But every application of power to operation is principally and first from God."

9. *ST* I-II, q. 9, a. 4, resp.: "Omne enim quod quandoque est agens in actu et quandoque in potentia, indiget moveri ab aliquo movente."

In *ST* I-II, q. 109, a. 1, resp., St. Thomas states: "And thus howsoever perfect a corporeal or spiritual thing is taken to be, it is not able to proceed to its act unless it first be moved by God."[10] Both the rational agent who does not choose and the rational agent who does choose enjoy the natural motion of the will—according to Aquinas bestowed by God—whereby the will is objectively ordered to universal good, and wills happiness. But no agent of whatsoever dignity can even *proceed to its act* unless it first be moved from God. The creature that is in potency with respect to its own free self-motion must be moved from potency to act with respect to this self-motion.

In *De malo*, q. 3, a. 2 ad 4, Thomas clearly articulates the thesis of a real ontologically prior divine motion whereby the rational creature is moved freely to determine itself—that is, physical premotion: "When anything moves itself, this does not exclude its being moved by another, from which it has *even this* [my emphasis] that it moves itself. Thus it is not repugnant to liberty that God is the cause of the free act of the will."[11] According to this express teaching, God is the cause of the self-motion of the will by *moving it* to its own self-motion. This is precisely what is designated by the phrase "physical premotion." Further, we have no more warrant for holding that this motion occurs *only through final causality* than we have for supposing that the proof for God as Prime Mover in *ST* I, q. 2, a. 3, refers solely to God as final cause, as though the first and fifth ways were identical.

As Thomas makes clear in *ST* I, q. 83, a. 1, ad 3, just as one thing can cause another thing without being the first cause of that thing, so the rational creature can cause its own free acts, and move itself, without being the *First* Cause and *First* Mover of its free acts.[12] Thomas also insists

---

10. *ST* I-II, q. 109, a. 1, resp.: "Et ideo quantumcumque natura aliqua corporalis vel spiritualis ponatur perfecta, non potest in suum actum procedere nisi moveatur a Deo."

11. *De malo*, q. 3, art. 2, ad 4: "Similiter cum aliquid movet se ipsum, non excluditur quin ab alio moveatur a quo habet hoc ipsum quo se ipsum movet. Et sic non repugnat libertati quod Deus est causa actus liberi arbitrii."

12. *ST* I, q. 83, a. 1, ad 3: "Dicendum quod liberum arbitrium est causa sui motus; quia homo per liberum arbitrium seipsum movet ad agendum. Non tamen hoc est de necessitate libertatis, quod sit prima causa sui id quod liberum est; sicut nec ad hoc quod aliquid sit causa alterius, requiritur quod sit prima causa eius. Deus igitur est prima causa movens et naturales causas et voluntarias. Et sicut naturalibus causis, movendo eas, non aufert quin actus earum sint naturales; ita movendo causas voluntarias, non aufert quin actiones earum sint voluntariae, sed potius hoc in eis facit; operatur enim in unoquoque secundum eius

in *ST* I-II, q. 9, a. 4, ad 2, that for an act to be violent it must be not only extrinsic but also contrary to the movement of the will, whereas the divine motion bestowed to the will whereby it is moved freely to determine itself *cannot* be against the movement of the will because it is "the will that wills, though moved by another" and the will cannot "will and not will the same thing."[13]

Thomas asserts in *ST* I-II, q. 6, a. 1, ad 3, that "every motion whether of the will or of nature proceeds from God as the first mover."[14] He will also argue in *Summa contra Gentiles* (*ScG* III, ch. 67, that God is "the first and principal cause of the application of every power to act" and that God is not only the prime object of appetite, but also the *prime agent of willing*, and even that "every movement of a will whereby powers are applied to operation is reduced to God as first object of appetite and first agent of willing."[15] This last proposition makes plain that cooperative grace lies

---

proprietatem." "Free will is the cause of its own movement, because by his free will man moves himself to act. But it does not of necessity belong to liberty that what is free should be the first cause of itself, as neither for one thing to be cause of another need it be the first cause. God, therefore, is the first cause, Who moves causes both natural and voluntary. And just as by moving natural causes He does not prevent their acts being natural, so by moving voluntary causes He does not deprive their actions of being voluntary: but rather is He the cause of this very thing in them; for He operates in each thing according to its own nature."

13. *ST* I-II, q. 9, a. 4, ad 2: "Ad secundum dicendum quod hoc non sufficit ad rationem violenti, quod principium sit extra, sed oportet addere quod nil conferat vim patiens. Quod non contingit, dum voluntas ab exteriori movetur, nam ipsa est quae vult, ab alio tamen mota. Esset autem motus iste violentus, si esset contrarius motui voluntatis. Quod in proposito esse non potest, quia sic idem vellet et non vellet." "To the second it should be said that it does not suffice for the nature of violence that the principle be extrinsic, but to this it must be added that it be without the concurrence of the patient. Which does not happen when the will is moved by an exterior [principle], for it is the will that wills, though moved by another. But this movement would be violent, were it to be against the movement of the will. Which in the proposed case is not possible, because thus the will would will and not will the same thing."

14. *ST* I-II, q. 6, a. 1, ad 3: "omnis motus tam voluntatis quam naturae, ab eo procedit sicut a primo movente."

15. *ScG* III, ch. 67: "Quicquid applicat virtutem activam ad agendum, dicitur esse causa illius actionis: artifex enim applicans virtutem rei naturalis ad aliquam actionem, dicitur esse causa illius actionis, sicut coquus decoctionis, quae est per ignem. Sed omnis applicatio virtutis ad operationem est principaliter et primo a Deo. Applicantur enim virtutes operativae ad proprias operationes per aliquem motum vel corporis, vel animae. Primum autem principium utriusque motus est Deus. Est enim primum movens omnino immobile, ut supra ostensum est. Similiter etiam omnis motus voluntatis quo applicantur aliquae virtutes ad operandum, reducitur in Deum sicut in primum appetibile et in primum volentem. Omnis igitur operatio debet attribui Deo sicut primo et principali agenti." "Whatsoever agent applies active power to the doing of something, it is said to be the cause of that action. Thus,

also within the divine motion of the will, which extends the intention of action into actual operation in moving us to move ourselves to act, and even in externally supporting the act.

The self-motion brought about by God is our own act of choice, and both God and the creature are total causes of the effect. The self-motion of the creature brought forth by the divine motion is in its own order both wholly a *cause* and simultaneously an *effect*, such that God brings about the actual determinate perfection of human willing. This dependence upon God as first agent cause of willing is in the natural order prior to, and distinct from, the order of grace.

But how, then, if the free act of the will is an effect lying within divine causal providence, is rational choice free? For St. Thomas, rational choice is free owing to the *nature* of the will as a proximate cause. Thomas teaches in *ST* I, q. 82, a. 2, ad 2, that the will is ordered to *universal good* and *cannot be fully actuated or compelled by any finite object*, inasmuch as knowledge of every finite object is compatible with viewing it as in some way "not good." Further, as he argues in many places, for example, in *De malo*, q. 16, a. 7, ad. 15, *contingency and necessity are discriminated not in relation to the First Cause, but in relation to the proximate cause.* A contingent cause is changeable so as to bring about a great variety of effects, whereas a necessary cause is unchangeable and brings about one effect.[16] By reason of its rational nature, the will is in choice a radically contingent cause insusceptible of complete actuation or compulsion by any finite good, although it does have a necessary and natural motion

---

an artisan who applies the power of a natural thing to some action is said to be the cause of the action; for instance, a cook of the cooking which is done by means of fire. But every application of power to operation is first and principally made by God. For operative powers are applied to their proper operations by some movement of body or of soul. Now, the first principle of both types of movement is God. Indeed, He is the first mover and is altogether incapable of being moved, as we shown above. Similarly, also, every movement of a will whereby powers are applied to operation is reduced to God, as first object of appetite and first agent of willing. Therefore, every operation should be attributed to God, as to a first and principal agent."

16. "Et ideo necessitas et contingentia in rebus distinguuntur non per habitudinem ad voluntatem divinam, quae est causa communis, sed per comparationem ad causas creatas, quas proportionaliter divina voluntas ad effectus ordinavit; ut scilicet necessariorum effectuum sint causae intransmutabiles, contingentium autem transmutabiles." "And therefore necessity and contingency in things are distinguished not in relation to the divine will, which is a universal cause, but in relation to created causes which the divine will has ordered proportionately to the effects, namely in such a way that the causes of necessary effects are unchangeable, and of contingent effects changeable."

toward the good in general. Thus *every choice is by its nature objectively free*—and, furthermore, every volition short of the beatific vision is in its exercise contingent—while nonetheless *every choice* (and every volition) *lies wholly within the divine causality such that the least actuation of the will derives from the divine motion.* God causes necessary things necessarily and contingent things contingently, including the contingent acts of our own free will. Even evil acts are divinely caused in their being, truth, and good, although not in their deprivation of the rule of reason and charity.

The distinction between the composite and divided senses of "power" or "possibility" is important here.[17] For example, I retain the power to stand even while I sit, but it is not possible to actuate both powers at the same time, and so this power is said to be possessed in the "divided" sense because these powers cannot be actuated together even though both are truly possessed. By contrast, in the composite sense of power, one power may be actuated even together with actuation of another power, as the powers to walk and chew gum can be actuated simultaneously. The creature moved to freely move itself is *not* not moved, and so even at the instant that it freely moves, it is said to retain the *power* not to move itself in the *divided sense.* Thus the Blessed Virgin Mary from all eternity was ordained freely to assent to the Incarnation, and retained the power not to do so at the instant she was moved freely to assent, while of course she could not simultaneously freely assent and freely not assent. Thus, in the composite sense, one cannot be moved freely to act, and not act, because this is a contradiction in terms; in the divided sense, however, one retains the *power* to act otherwise, even at the instant when one is moved freely to determine oneself in choice. Freedom is the *mode or nature* of human choice, but human choice is an action, and the human agent must be moved by God from potency to act with respect to its own self-determination in freedom for an act of free choice to occur. This is to say that there are two kinds of created liberty: the kind that exists within providential causality, and the kind that does not exist because *nothing* is absolutely outside of divine providential causality. So much for a brief consideration of the divine motion of the will in free choice.

17. Cf. *ScG* I, ch. 67.

Divine Simplicity

The doctrine of the divine simplicity enters into this consideration. In *ST* I, q. 28, a. 2, ad 1, for example, Thomas argues that

nothing that exists in God can have any relation to that wherein it exists or of whom it is spoken, except the relation of identity; and this by reason of [propter] God's supreme simplicity.[18]

There is and can be *no change*, and *no dependence upon the creature*, in God, inasmuch as God is Pure Act. The immutability of God is not only a metaphysical necessity but it is also revealed, affirmed throughout Sacred Scripture and Sacred Tradition, a de fide teaching of the Church. That it is a de fide teaching is apparent in the conclusion to the creed of the first general council, Nicaea, in 325, the original creed rather than the more familiar Nicene-Constantinopolitan Creed, where, speaking of the Eternal Son, it is affirmed that "However those who say 'there once was when he was not,' and 'before he was born he was not,' and He was made from nothing," or who say that God [the Son of God] may be of another substance or essence or may be subject to change and alteration, the Catholic Church anathematizes."[19]

Metaphysically, the only difference between God causing X, and God not causing X, is not a change *in God*, but rather *the being of the creature*. This is a simple function of the truth that the divine perfection is not limited by any potency whatsoever; it is Pure Act. Whatsoever degree and kind of actuality that God causes will exist. Thus, if we speak of created grace—rather than of the Uncreated Grace Who is God Himself— the bestowal of grace is necessarily always *efficacious* in at least some respect. Thus bestowal of grace requires some determinate effect, because the contrary is tantamount to the suppression of grace as such. There is no way to distinguish a putative "effect" that is absolutely and in every respect *indeterminate*, from *the absolute absence of any effect whatsoever*. To affirm that God bestows grace cannot be equivalent to holding that

18. "Nihil autem quod est in Deo, potest habere habitudinem ad id in quo est, vel de quo dicitur, nisi habitudinem identitatis, propter summam Dei simplicitatem."

19. Peter Hunermann, ed., *Denzinger*, 43rd ed. (San Francisco: Ignatius Press, 2012), 51, no. 126. "Eos autem, qui dicunt "Erat, quando non erat"; "Antequam nasceretur non erat"; "Quod de non exstantibus factus est"; "vel ex aliasubstantia aut essentia dicentes aut convertibilem aut demutabilem Deum [Filium Dei], hos anathematizat catholica Ecclesia."

God does *nothing*. Thus, because the only signification of God giving grace to the creature is a real, determinate, actual effect in the creature, every grace is necessarily efficacious with respect to some determinate actual effect, even while it may signify only a remote capability or "sufficient" grace with respect to *something else* to which it is further related. Another way of saying this is to observe that, absolutely speaking, *nothing* cannot have a real relation to *something*. So, if we say that some grace establishes a capability or a remote order to another good, for this to be true, it must already be something actually determinate that can be related in this way. For example, *attrition* or imperfect sorrow for sin may be further ordered to *perfect contrition*.

As Thomas holds in his treatment in *ST* I, q. 22, a. 1, God as universal cause *cannot* be impeded by any finite cause, because all finite causes can only be, and only operate, within the universal causality of God. *This is the difference between the causality of God, and the causality of any creature.* Thomas teaches in *ST* I, q. 22, a. 2, ad 1, that a particular cause can be impeded, but nothing can impede the universal causality of God. This view is not equivalent to the proposition—as Michael Torre supposes in his book defending Marín-Sola, *Do Not Resist the Spirit's Call*[20]—that the end of an act must in every case be attained if the act is caused by God, because God may permit—or perhaps even ordain—a degree of determinate actuality that falls short of a possible effect to which the actuality in question is still in some way potentially related. Rather, the point is *pre-*

---

20. Michael Torre, *Do Not Resist the Spirit's Call: Francisco Marín-Sola on Sufficient Grace* (Washington, DC: Catholic University of America Press, 2013), 253. His examples—e.g., that wet paper may not burn—truly lack sense in relation to the simple divine will, which cannot be impeded. The problem—never adequately cognized by Marín-Sola, nor by Torre, nor by many others to the present day—is that in relation to the divine simple will, whatever the object of this will is *will infallibly be*. Whether this object could be impeded in itself is irrelevant, because in relation to the simple divine will, it becomes hypothetically necessary. What is possible regarding a motion in itself is not the same as what is possible for it in relation to the simple divine will. The effect simply willed by God—whether a nudge or a complete act—must infallibly be. The object thus simply willed does not cease to be hypothetically necessary because in itself it could be otherwise. Failure to grasp this is to fall short of Thomas's entire teaching on this subject, for it is everywhere implicit. A particular cause may be impeded, but the universal causality of God cannot be impeded—the order of a particular cause may be escaped, but not the order of the universal cause (*ST* I, q. 22, a. 2, ad 1). Further, if we take the proposition that "every end of providence is attained" to refer to the simple divine will, to providence *simpliciter*, then it is Cajetan who is correct, and Ferrariensis whose criticism is problematic (cf. 252–53n106).

cisely that *whatever degree and kind of actuation, whether in the order of nature, or in the order of grace, that God wills cannot fail to be achieved by God,* unless we wish to abandon the doctrine of the divine omnipotence and the primacy of grace.

Of course, in itself, a created motion can be impeded. But, taken in relation to God, if an effect is simply willed by God, then the effect cannot be impeded, *not because of its own nature taken separately,* but because of its relation to the causality of God. Of itself, a peach is corruptible, but should God simply will to sustain the peach indefinitely, it will not corrupt. In *De veritate,* q. 6, a. 3, St. Thomas distinguishes between a thing considered in itself and a thing considered in relation to something else. As he argues in his central answer:

> For, even though free choice can fail with respect to salvation, God prepares so many other helps for one who is predestined that he either does not fall at all or, if he does fall, he rises again. The helps that God gives a man to enable him to gain salvation are exhortations, the support of prayer, the gift of grace, and all similar things. Consequently, if we were to consider salvation only in relation to its proximate cause, free choice, salvation would not be certain but contingent; however, in relation to the first cause, namely, predestination, salvation is certain.[21]

As Thomas famously puts it, speaking of volition in *ST* I-II, q. 10, a. 4, ad 3, "If God moves the will to anything, it is incompatible with this supposition, that the will be not moved thereto."[22] These considerations move Thomas, alongside Augustine, to teach that predestination is the cause of merit, and that while reprobation is not the cause of sin, it is itself prior to the prevision of demerit.

Intra-Thomistic Efforts at Revision

What I have said barely scratches the surface of Thomas's account. But here I turn to three twentieth-century arguments that attempt to revise

---

21. *De veritate,* q. 6, art. 3: "Liberum enim arbitrium deficere potest a salute; tamen in eo quem Deus praedestinat, tot alia adminicula praeparat, quod vel non cadat, vel si cadit, quod resurgat, sicut exhortationes, suffragia orationum, gratiae donum, et omnia huiusmodi, quibus Deus adminiculatur homini ad salutem. Si ergo consideremus salutem respectu causae proximae, scilicet liberi arbitrii, non habet certitudinem, sed contingentiam; respectu autem causae primae, quae est praedestinatio, certitudinem habet."

22. *ST* I-II, q. 10, a. 4, ad 3.

the classical Thomistic account, and make a brief response, before closing with a suggestion concerning our understanding of reprobation. I state the revisionist accounts without varnish, and respond without embellishment.

First is the argument of Maritain. He argues that although God can efficaciously bring about the free act of the creature, God normally first gives an initial grace that may be "negated" or "nihilated" or "fractured" or "broken," and only if that grace is not negated, or nihilated, or fractured, or broken does God move the will infrustrably yet freely. Thus, *if* the creature does not negate or break the initial divine prompting, *then* God will give the positive and infrustrable efficacious grace.[23] But there is a problem: in a real subject, the negation of negation is something positive. If I say of a real person that "he does not *not* have a nose," this is not really different from the affirmation that "he has a nose." It makes no sense to say, if only I do not *not* have nose, then God will *give me a nose*, because in a real subject "not *not* having a nose" is really the same as having a nose. In a real subject, negation of negation is a positive effect. Thus to say that the creature does not negate a grace is simply to say that God has efficaciously bestowed grace. We default to the original position: either God bestows grace, or does not. Maritain's account is justly famous, owing to its simplicity, depth, and a certain grandeur, and it seems superior to me to the account of Marín-Sola, with which it is at times compared, as it does not affirm that one can achieve a greater effect in the supernatural order with a lesser grace, as Marín-Sola seems to do (as shall be taken up below). Yet this account of Maritain's runs aground upon a paralogism. I write this observation as one who for many years held this position, a position whose semantics are very close to those of the classical teaching, but diverges from it unnecessarily in substance.[24]

23. See Jacques Maritain, *Existence and the Existent*, trans. Lewis Galantiere and Gerald B. Phelan (New York: Pantheon Books, 1948), esp. chap. 4, "The Free Existent and the Free Eternal Purposes," 85–122, and more particularly 94, 100n10. See also idem, *St. Thomas and the Problem of Evil* (Milwaukee, WI: Marquette University Press, 1942), 26–30, 33, 34, 36–38.

24. Torre, *Do Not Resist*, 253n108, argues in response to my criticism of Maritain that Maritain modified his account (seemingly implying that the criticism is unfitting). But Maritain did not substantially modify his account in a way that frees his analysis of the present criticism. Negation of negation is, in a real subject, something positive. To say that if the creature does not negate or shatter a grace, that *then* God will give an unshatterable grace, is to confuse a conceptually diverse naming with a real diversity in reference. If I do not *not* have a nose, this is only a conceptually different formulation than is represented by the af-

Second is the argument of Father Marín-Sola, OP, who affirmed that in light matters with little difficulty a creature could, with a divine activation of grace ordained by God for one effect, turn it to another effect. It is this argument that moved Garrigou-Lagrange to criticize him so stridently, because it implies that the free creature can bring about an effect that exceeds the divine causality. But no particular cause can operate outside the universal causality of God. Thus each grace is efficacious for some real effect and is only a potency with respect to any further effect. Nor may a creature by its own finite agency *prolong* a grace efficacious for one effect so as to *extend it to another*, as Marín-Sola clearly suggests may occur over short time periods with only light temptation,[25] just as the

---

firmation that I have a nose, but it is not really different. The negation of negation of grace is not different from the grace itself: grace is either bestowed or is not (unless the proposition is that not God, but God *and* man, cause grace, which is closer to Molina than to Aquinas). If "shattering" is not "negating" but is construed as something positive, we would have an even worse account (because as first and principal cause of the application of every power to act, then God would be moving the agent not merely to the matter of sin, but to the formal sin itself constituted by the putatively positive "shattering," which is both (1) something Maritain would never have argued and (2) something in itself impossible).

25. Torre, *Do Not Resist*, 120n34. This is a little like saying that over short time periods and with only light temptation the creature can bring something from nothing: the creature cannot cause an effect in grace, save through a divine motion ordered to such a determinate effect, and if the aid given is determined to a particular effect, the creature cannot prolong or extend it on its own initiative to some further effect, as though the creature were itself divine. In this matter, Marín-Sola is bewitched by the phenomenology of action to the loss of metaphysical rectitude of judgment. On the other hand, this question ought not be confused with the question—e.g., taken up by the Salmanticences—whether someone in grace can undertake ordinary good acts in small matters and in the absence of temptation, without specially added grace. Torre insists that the Salmanticences (cf. 155) hold the view of Marín-Sola (and himself) that one may perform a further act in the supernatural order without a specifically added grace. Here again, he has oversimplified something rather complex. What the Salmanticences considered were acts that would not be possible for the agent, were the agent not in the state of grace, but for which nonetheless nature *in the state of grace* is a sufficient principle: always presupposing the efficacy of the divine motion in the natural order with respect to God as natural end, as well as the motion of grace to the supernatural end, but given the distinction of these motions. Insofar as such acts may be specified by natural goods and involve no hardship or temptation with respect to the supernatural order, these acts require the further aid of God moving the agent, but do not necessarily require a further specific grace. E.g., the Salmanticences' view would be that a further specific grace is hardly required for a man in the state of grace to perform the good act of eating a pear, while nonetheless of course the help of God moving the agent to this act in the natural order is required. Cf. *Cursus Theologicus, Tomus Nonus* (Paris and Brussels: 1878), disp. 2, no. 49, p. 162. Without necessarily concurring with the general treatment of the Salmanticences regarding the analysis of the relation of nature and grace—toward which I am nonetheless well disposed by reason of its strong insistence on the proportionate natural good—one can see that this is not to say that in the order of grace the least further effect may

activation of my limbs to run is not the activation of my mind to contemplate or of my fists to fight.

Márin-Sola also proposes that grace may be "fallibly efficacious" and compares it to an arrow whose flight may be impeded.[26] But a grace "fallibly efficacious"—like a God "partially omnipotent"—is contrary to the divine simplicity and to the very nature of grace, which is always efficacious with respect to some effect, and, equally, not efficacious with respect to other effects. Without efficacy with respect to any determinate effect whatsoever, the claim that God bestows grace becomes empty. *De veritate*, q. 6, a. 3, has already been cited, but the following observations from the reply to the seventh objection (ad 7) are decisive:

A thing can be said to be possible in two ways. First, we may consider the potency that exists in the thing itself, as when we say that a stone can be moved downwards. Or we may consider the potency that exists in another thing, as when we say that a stone can be moved upwards, not by a potency existing in the stone, but by a potency existing in the one who hurls it.

Consequently, when we say: "That predestined person can possibly die in sin," the statement is true if we consider only the potency that exists in him. But, if we are speaking of this predestined person according to the ordering which he has to another, namely, to God, who is predestining him, that event is incompatible with this ordering, even though it is compatible with the person's own power. Hence, we can use the distinction given above; that is, we can consider the subject with this form or without it.[27]

---

be achieved without further actuation of the creature by God precisely in grace. Every quantum of further operative perfection with respect to the order of grace requires its principle in grace, which must be bestowed by God. Thus the agent is necessarily in need of further aid from God with respect to further perfection in the order of grace, and the agent cannot transubstantiate one grace into another because acts are specified by their objects and ends. Thus the grace of remorse is not simply of itself the grace of contrition, or of approaching the sacrament of penance.

26. Torre, *Do Not Resist*, 27–28.

27. *De veritate*, q. 6, a. 3, ad 7: "Ad septimum dicendum, quod aliquid potest dici posse dupliciter. Uno modo considerando potentiam quae in ipso est, sicut dicitur quod lapis potest moveri deorsum. Alio modo considerando id quod ex parte alterius est, sicut si dicerem, quod lapis potest moveri sursum, non per potentiam quae in ipso sit, sed per potentiam proiicientis.

Cum ergo dicitur: praedestinatus iste potest in peccato mori; si consideretur potentia ipsius, verum est; si autem loquamur de praedestinato secundum ordinem quem habet ad aliud, scilicet ad Deum praedestinantem, sic ordo ille non compatitur secum istum eventum, quamvis compatiatur secum istam potentiam. Et ideo potest distingui secundum distinctionem prius inductam, scilicet cum forma, vel sine forma consideratio subiecti."

Considered in itself, any motion may be impeded, but considered in relation to the simple divine will, whatsoever degree and kind of actuation God wills occurs, in the mode in which God wills it. That is, God brings about necessary things necessarily, and contingent things contingently. There is no change in God that pertains to divine agency, but only the being of the effect, and so to suppress the effect or render it indeterminate is to deny the causality. As Thomas expressly teaches that the universal divine causality cannot be impeded, whatever degree of aid God ordains to bestow is received: neither more nor less.

Marín-Sola also accused the classical Thomistic reading of St. Thomas's teaching undertaken by Báñez, Cajetan, John of St. Thomas, and others, of being closer to that of Calvin or Jansenius than to Aquinas. He confused *efficacious grace*—which can be but with hypothetic necessity is not resisted—with the Jansenist *irresistable grace*, which simply cannot be resisted.[28] This is a remarkable error. Marín-Sola's admirers to this day evince failure to understand why his superiors might have thought that accusing the classical Thomistic tradition of Calvinism or Jansenism indicated a lapse of judgment. I incline to the view that this teaching of Marín-Sola's is contrary to the teaching of Aquinas and doctrinally ill founded.

Marín-Sola held that Thomas's use of the "divided sense" of capacity was rare. But, to the contrary, whenever we retain a power to do differently than we are doing *now*, the sense of such power is the divided sense (because it is not possible to act and not act, to will and not will, simultaneously). Freedom is not the capacity to violate the law of noncontradiction, and as Thomas understands it the divided sense of possibility is not rare at all, least of all with respect to acts of human willing (for inasmuch as God efficaciously ordains the Blessed Virgin Mary freely to assent to the Incarnation, she does not lose the *power* to resist assenting, but she does not *wish* to resist and does not resist). The modality of the action is free (because freedom is denominated by the nature of the proximate cause and not by the relation of this cause to God) and the power for the contrary is not suppressed: the object does not of itself necessitate the will. But, within the efficacious divine motion, the created will is perfected such that the creature does not wish freely to resist and does not freely

28. Torre, *Do Not Resist*, 129.

resist. Because each grace is efficacious for *something* (for otherwise it would be an indeterminate nothing rather than a grace), the distinction between the divided and composite senses is manifestly of frequent application and of central importance in understanding the relation of free will and grace.[29]

The third revisionist account is that of Bernard Lonergan, SJ. Like Maritain, Lonergan is in seraphic discourse with the entirety of the Thomistic tradition. It is arresting to see his responses to John of St. Thomas, Báñez, Del Prado, Garrigou-Lagrange, and others. In his famed *Grace and Freedom: Operative Grace in the Thought of St. Thomas Aquinas*, however, he makes assertions that I do not believe survive a sufficient encounter with St. Thomas's text. The most central of these is the arresting claim that, according to St. Thomas Aquinas, the motion in the creature from

29. Marín-Sola speaks of the antecedent will as needing to be a "real, sincere will of beneplacito." Torre, *Do Not Resist*, 99. Torre ardently and eloquently defends his position, somewhat too clearly, implying that God must "take a look" to determine what God shall do. Cf. 270n18: "There is little, if any, difference between a simple will and a conditioned intent. In both, we want a good and are inclined to obtain it, but only on condition that we discover nothing un-choiceworthy about it." Clearly, however, God does not "discover," and whatever is positive in the creature exists because God has caused it: the divine simplicity, together with its necessary entailment that the divine effect be determinate, continually eludes the analysis of Marín-Sola and Torre. Thomas unequivocally and clearly teaches that the divine antecedent will is called "antecedent" because it is a will of that which is an antecedent to something else (cf. *ST*, I, q. 19, a. 6, ad 1) because there is no before and after in God. Torre also cites A. Michel, OP, in defense of the notion that the antecedent will is a "true" will of beneplacitum in God (326n43). Yet this citation makes clear that Michel considers the antecedent will to be other than a velleity only "in its genre," that is, with respect to that which is an antecedent with respect to something else, and not with respect to the further good, toward which the antecedent *is* an antecedent. No one ever denied, that with respect to the willing of the antecedent that this was a "true" and "genuine" will in God, in the sense that this antecedent good is rooted in the divine causality. But that does not mean that the "antecedent willing of salvation" is the willing of salvation *simpliciter*, or that by itself it is efficacious for this, nor yet again that a "fallible" premotion (which putatively can be or not be in some respect) can in that respect be denominated a "grace." The antecedent will is real in that it brings about effects preparatory to further things, but it is merely a *willingness* and not a *simple willing* of those further things. In all this, Torre represents the thought of Marín-Sola while nonetheless at times acknowledging what is obvious, that the antecedent will is in a sense a will *secundum quid* (269). At least this is true with respect to the further good, with respect to which the antecedent willed by God *is* an antecedent. The teaching of Thomas in the *Summa Theologiae* regarding the antecedent will is largely ignored (for Torre insists that the antecedent will is not a velleity or a willingness, but antecedent will is the will of something that *is* an antecedent, as Thomas unequivocally teaches in *ST* I, q. 19, a. 6, ad 1, and this is the respect in which it is simple will, i.e., merely "in its genre" but not with respect to the further good).

not acting to acting—and hence derivatively, from not willing to will-ing—is not a *motio realis*, not a real motion. I repeat that claim: according to Lonergan, the motion in the creature from not acting to acting, and hence from not willing to willing, is not a *real motion*. The problem about divine causality and freedom would largely vanish if the transition from potentially willing to actually willing were not a real motion requiring a real mover as the condition for our self-motion. As Lonergan puts it in his work *Grace and Freedom*:

To later scholastics this seemed impossible a priori: they held that "Peter not acting" must be really different from "Peter acting." They refused to believe that St. Thomas could disagree with them on this; in fact, St. Thomas dis-agreed. (72n26)

In the same chapter of that work, Lonergan notes that causing is not something real in the agent causing, but exists rather in the effect, or at most in the relation between or nexus of agent and effect. He responds to the proposition that everything must move from potency to act in or-der to cause, by observing that were this true, then there could be no First Cause.[30] Precisely as stated, *this proposition of Lonergan's is true*. With respect to causing *as such*, potency is not essential. Otherwise, it would be impossible for God—who is Pure Act and in whom there is no potency whatsoever—to be the First Cause. Every agency is, as such, *act*. Thus agency as such does not make any reference to transition from potency to act, because it is accidental to agency as such that it be related to potentiality, which is what the texts from St. Thomas that Lonergan adduces suffice to show.

However, although it is accidental to *agency* as such, and to the agent *qua agent*, that it pass from potency to act with respect to acting—be-cause God is the First Cause and there is no potency in him, and because agency is agency and the definition of agency makes no necessary ref-erence to potency—*nonetheless*, it is not accidental to the created being that acts that it is not Pure Act, and so likewise it is not accidental that the finite agent is not identical with its operation, not purely an agent. Consequently, it is not accidental to the finite agent *as* finite agent that *for it to act, it* must pass from potency to act. Even angelic knowers re-

---

30. Cf. Bernard Lonergan, SJ, *Grace and Freedom* (New York: Herder and Herder, 1971), 65–66.

quire divinely infused species to actuate their knowing. Moreover, the human subject is not always an agent in act—it is not always acting— and, in particular, the human agent is not always *choosing*. Granted that there is nothing about acting as such absolutely speaking that requires potency, a finite subject that acts is not its own agency; it is really distinct from its agency. *Thus the finite subject needs to be moved from potency to act in order to attain to the dignity of acting.*

It remains true that to acting or agency *as such*, it is accidental that there be transition from potency to act, just as it is true that to being *as such* potency is accidental. However, it is *not* accidental that potency pertains to finite creatures, because the creature, qua creature, is not Uncreated Pure Act. Thus the created human subject who acts must first acquire *the dignity of being an agent*, which it can only do by passing from potency to act with respect to acting. It is a *tautology* that the agent qua agent is in act—that, as Lonergan puts it, "operation involves no change in the cause as cause"[31]—but this does not mean that everything that is an agent is pure act and thus in no need of being moved from potency to act with respect to its agency *as a condition of acting*.

Lonergan makes the further suggestion that "the Aristotelian premotion as understood by St. Thomas affects indifferently the mover or moved, agent or patient."[32] But this is false with respect to the elevation of a creature to the dignity of agency: for it is the creature that is an agent that must be elevated to agency rather than the creature that is the patient. In Lonergan's analysis, premotion accounts merely for patient or agent being brought into causal *proximity* or perhaps for the being of the patient as created by God.[33] But this account fails to acknowledge that

31. Ibid., 71.
32. Ibid.
33. Ibid., 89. "Because the agent cannot act infinitely, it must have an object upon which or with respect to which it acts. Because the creature cannot create, it cannot provide itself with the objects of its own activity. Because God alone can create, God alone can provide such objects, and this provision is not by chance but in accordance with the divine plan. Therefore God applies all agents to their activity." This expresses a truth but is far from being an adequate account of *applicatio* according to St. Thomas, whose use of the term refers to an ontologically prior causal motion requisite to action, and not merely to the divine provision of a patient to a creature mysteriously self-actuated, as though the creature were its own agency, which is impossible. In the example from *ScG* III, ch. 67, it is true that the fire is already active qua fire, but is not active qua cooking and must be applied further to this act. In this case, it is true that this occurs by way of local motion, and that the food might perhaps be brought to the flame as easily as the flame to the food (although it isn't so

what necessitates divine "premotion" is that the finite subject of agency is not simply of itself in act and so needs to be moved to act. The creature is not its own being, nature, or operation, and thus it is not accidental that it must be moved by God from potency to act with respect to its own agency: for example, in willing, man must be moved by God from potency to act with respect to his own self-determination in freedom.

Lonergan's analysis thus reduces Thomas's teaching to a mere tautology about agency. Of course operation involves no change in the cause as cause, because the agent qua agent is *in act*; but how is it that the creature that is not its own act comes to be in act? This question Lonergan does not ask, because he has not considered that agency qua agency must come to pertain to creatures that are not their own agency. Lonergan denies that "Peter acting" is really different from "Peter not acting." But this is simple error. It is true that causation does not involve any real change in the cause as cause, but that does not mean that no change in the creature as creature is required for the creature to achieve the dignity of agency. Agency does involve and require a real change in the creature in relation to its being a cause, for the created thing is not simply and purely a cause by its very essence or being, it is not identical with its operation but really distinct from it, and must be moved from potency

---

clear this meaning is intended in the passage). But in the case of the natural desire of the will for happiness, this natural motion of the will must be further applied to objects of choice toward which the will is in potency, and toward which it will only be in act, not merely because of physical proximity or the creation of a patient, but because it is moved by God from potency to act with respect to its self-determination in freedom by the divine *applicatio* of the natural motion toward happiness to this contingent act and object of choice. Moreover, the attainment of physical proximity through motion is itself an actuation, albeit clearly of a lower sort. In any case, it is an enormous error to suppose that because it is accidental to agency qua agency that there be motion from potency to act, that therefore any created being can be an agent without being moved from potency to act with respect to agency, precisely because no creature *is* its own being, nature, or operation. Thus, e.g., even the thing that becomes a torch must be lit if it is to be a torch; once lit, it must be applied in actual motion (a motion that, in the case of intellect or will, is clearly not merely a matter of physical proximity or creation of a patient). No creature is its own being, nature, or operation, and so every creature must be elevated to the dignity of agency through divine causality, and if the creature has an active power, this must, to achieve its effect, be applied by God, who is the first and principal cause of the application of every power to act. Some motions may be lower ones involving mere physical proximity. This is absolutely and clearly not the case with intellect and will. One does not will something as an end nor—for a more proper illustration—freely choose it, merely because of its physical proximity or because God has created it. Were this true, one would have consented to dine at many more bad restaurants than perhaps one has chosen to do.

to act with respect to it. It might be thought that Lonergan's claim that "Peter acting" is *not* really different from "Peter not acting" is meant only to distinguish substance from accident. Then the meaning would be: the substance of Peter is not altered by the accident of Peter's acting. However, (1) this is not what the proposition as it stands actually affirms; (2) *if* this is what Lonergan meant, it does not redress the problem, which is that Lonergan does not explain how the thing that is not its own agency is moved to achieve the dignity of agency. While the insistence that operation involves no change in the cause *as* cause is true, it is a tautology that does not address the ontological necessity for created beings to be elevated by the divine motion—moved from potency to act—in order to achieve the dignity of agency.

Lonergan famously comments that for the motion of melting, one need only change the relative positions of the sun and the iceberg.[34] If we presuppose the heat of the sun, this is true, but the heat of the sun presupposes innumerable gaseous explosions and other real motions, without which it would not be an agent of heating—it must be moved from potency to act with respect to that in virtue of which it is an agent of heating. It is remarkable that an abstract proposition about agency as agency could divert a mind of such remarkable penetration from what is absolutely required for created agency as such (and owing to a premise absolutely essential to Aquinas: the real distinction of existence from essence, and the real distinction of act from potency). Moving a thing that is in simple potency with respect to its act into proximity with another (unless that other itself moves it to act), or creating that other in proximity to it, is insufficient to bring forth action. The creature must be moved from potency to act with respect to its own agency, and only if this occurs can it be an agent. With respect to human agency: as only God can move the rational will, imparting to it its natural motion toward happiness, likewise only God can move the rational creature from potency to act with respect to the application of this natural motion in the act of choice. God moves the creature from potency to act with respect to its own self-determination in freedom.

Thus it is the motion from potency to act with respect to acting that requires premotion, and not merely the providential arrangement

---

34. Lonergan, *Grace and Freedom*, 71.

whereby things in act are governed so as to be in proximity to others that they thus may affect. It is this moving of the agent from potency to act with respect to its own agency that is premotion—it is neither God merely placing the agent in proximity to the patient, nor God creating the patient.[35] This is most certainly true of the teaching of Aquinas, who will not admit that anything can so much as proceed to act without first having been moved by God,[36] and clearly this pertains not merely to the natural motion of the will represented in the desire for happiness, but to the *applicatio*[37] of the natural motion in willing this or that contingent object of choice. There are those who do proceed to act, and those who do not, and both desire happiness, but both, for example, do not choose to attend a conference on predestination. Lonergan also considers that

35. One may see how consideration of angelic acts of knowledge might have inclined Lonergan to such an account. He might have thought of the divine infusion of species as merely providing the patient for the angelic cognitive agency. Yet it is clear that for Thomas the very *act* of the angelic cognition is one that occurs because the angelic intellective *power* is actuated by the divinely infused species. I.e., even the angels are not their own operation, and they are *activated* by God, *moved from potency to act*, as the condition for their cognition. In the angelic instance, the divine infusion of species both actuates the angelic intellect and specifies the intellective act (so, in some way, it might in this respect be considered analogically as a "patient" to the angelic intellective agency). But that whereby God actuates the angelic intellect is also that which specifies the resultant act. If one considers only the latter and not the former, it would seem one would have Lonergan's view of premotion and of *applicatio*. But even in the difficult case of the angels this is insufficient, because there is no angelic cognitive agency, save because of the infusion of the species, which *actuates* the angelic intellect, which is not itself in act, save insofar as it is *actuated*, as is the case with every created power. Which is why Thomas clearly teaches that God is the first and principal cause of the application of every power to act (*ScG* III, ch. 67: "Sed omnis applicatio virtutis ad operationem est principaliter et primo a Deo.").

36. *ST* I-II, q. 109, a. 1, resp.: "Et ideo quantumcumque natura aliqua corporalis vel spiritualis ponatur perfecta, non potest in suum actum procedere nisi moveatur a Deo."

37. Of course, at the very lowest level of *applicatio* one may say that whether the meat is moved to the flame, or the flame to the meat, the fire has been "applied" to the meat. But where what is at stake is the application of the natural motion of the will to choice, this requires that the rational creature be moved by God from potency to act with respect to its own self-motion in choice, its own further application of the natural motion of the will to this particular object. This is not a matter of mere proximity—one may be proximate to an object of choice and never choose it—it is a reduction of the will from potency to act with respect to its own self-motion and self-determination. The rational creature is not always actually choosing, and it thus is in potency to its own self-determination and self-motion, and must be moved by God from potency to act with respect to its own self-determination, because (*ST* I-II, q. 9, art. 4): "everything that is at one time in potency and at another in act, needs to be moved by a mover." And (*De malo*, q. 3, a. 2 ad 4): "When anything moves itself, this does not exclude its being moved by another, from which it has even this that it moves itself. Thus it is not repugnant to liberty that God is the cause of the free act of the will."

"If, then, a *gratia operans* were to produce a contingent effect with irresistible efficacy, it could not be a creature; it would have to be God."[38] But this does not consider the distinction mentioned above between a motion taken in itself, and a motion taken precisely in relation to the simple divine will, nor does it distinguish the composite and divided senses of *causa possit deficere* which is required by the principles of St. Thomas.

Predestination and Reprobation

A final word, then, regarding predestination and reprobation. St. Thomas expressly teaches that election and reprobation are *prior to prevision of merit* (merit is an *effect* of predestination), that predestination is gratuitous, and so God is free to grant it to whomever he will, and that predestination is the cause of grace and of free acts, rather than an effect of these.[39] His words about reprobation are clear:

God loves all men and all creatures, inasmuch as He wishes them all some good; but He does not wish every good to them all. So far, therefore, as He does not wish this particular good—namely, eternal life—He is said to hate or reprobate them.[40]

This is simply the implication of the principle of predilection that Thomas affirms in *ST* I, q. 20, a. 3, resp.: "For since God is the cause of the goodness of things, no thing would be better than another, did God not will more good for one than for another." Subjectively, Thomas teaches, God loves everything with the same intensity; but in respect of the good that God wills, he wills more good for some than for others. And so God "wishes all some good," but "So far, therefore, as He does not wish this particular good—namely eternal life—he is said to hate or reprobate them."

These words have elicited many dark broodings and suspicions. The teaching of Thomas regarding divine causality moves critics to assert that the divine permission of evil—which is a "non-upholding in good"[41]—is

38. Lonergan, *Grace and Freedom*, 109.
39. Cf. *ST* I, q. 23, aa. 2–5.
40. *ST* I, q. 23, a. 3, ad 1: "Ad primum ergo dicendum quod Deus omnes homines diligit, et etiam omnes creaturas, inquantum omnibus vult aliquod bonum, non tamen quodcumque bonum vult omnibus. Inquantum igitur quibusdam non vult hoc bonum quod est vita aeterna, dicitur eos habere odio, vel reprobare."
41. *ST* I-II, q. 109, a. 2, ad 2: "Dicendum quod peccare nihil aliud est quam deficere a bono quod convenit alicui secundum suam naturam. Unaquaeque autem res creata, sicut

unjust, unfair, and both inconsistent with the divine innocence and with the antecedent will of God for all men to be saved.

I conclude with three points.

First, the antecedent will that all men be saved is not something antecedent in God, but is rather the willing by God of something that is an antecedent.[42] And the antecedent may be willed without that to which it is an antecedent being willed. Thus something antecedent to salvation and genuinely ordered toward it—real grace—is willed for all men. But owing to created defect, which God permits, the consequent grace of salvation is not bestowed. Objectors believe that the divine innocence is impugned if God wills a grace that is antecedent to salvation, and yet does not will salvation.

Second, we must observe that man's nature is defectible. God could have created us in the beatific vision, but it would be unfitting for man to possess without trial and danger a good infinitely surpassing all real and possible creation. Man naturally is subject to passions; learns experimentally and discursively, over great time; and is subject to many errors. To say that it is unjust for God to permit a *defectible* creature to defect is to postulate that God owes the creature its natural perfection; and to postulate this regarding the last end of supernatural beatific vision is to postulate that God owes the *defectible* creature to be upheld from all defect with respect to the order to supernatural beatitude. But if God permits the defectible creature to suffer defect with respect to the last end, this is reprobation. If any human person should be finally unrepentant, there are only two conceivable options, one of which is contrary to natural and revealed truth. The option that is inconsistent with natural and revealed truth would be a "positive" reprobation in which God somehow positively causes defect, "creates" it like a child lovingly constructing a toy Lego monster. But defect is a deprivation and not an ontologically positive effect. The second option is that God does not uphold the defectible crea-

---

esse non habet nisi ab alio, et in se considerata nihil est, ita indiget conservari in bono suae naturae convenienti ab alio. Potest enim per seipsam deficere a bono, sicut et per seipsam potest deficere in non esse,

42. *ST* I, q. 19, a. 6, ad 1: "Quae quidem distinctio non accipitur ex parte ipsius voluntatis divinae, in qua nihil est prius vel posterius; sed ex parte volitorum." "But this distinction is to be taken not on the part of the divine will itself in which there is nothing before or after, but on the part of the things willed."

ture from all defect even with respect to the last end, and permits the creature to act defectively: negative, not positive, reprobation.[43] But God does not owe the defectible creature to uphold it from all defect, much less from all defect that concerns the supernatural good.[44] Yet all receive more good than is their due, and less punishment, and evil is even more outside the adequate object of the divine omnipotence than is sound to the power of sight. God has infinite power to heal and elevate the human creature even where free defect has been permitted.

Finally, if, and only if, God has power over sin—through the power to redirect, heal, and elevate the human will—can God efficaciously redeem man. The medicine must reach to the root if the root is to be healed. Thus

43. At times the classical application of terminology is confusing, but its principles are clear. God can justly permit (and thus not uphold from) antecedent defect in the defectible creature, or God can uphold from defect, and the latter is a grace. Yet God is not normally said to "withhold" grace except owing to defect, which must first be *permitted* (while the nonupholding in grace mentioned above is not spoken of as a "withholding"). This usage is a function of the *moral* frame of the language; i.e., antecedent defect is antecedent in respect to some motion to the good, and so with respect to that motion to the good God can "withhold" grace as penalty owing to defect. Yet God must first permit the defectible creature to suffer antecedent defect, and this is nonupholding of the free, defectible creature in good: this nonupholding is not spoken of as "withholding" grace because it is not simply "due" as the rectitude with respect to the end is due in relation to that end. The grace of upholding the defectible creature from all antecedent defect is a grace that is not simply due to the defectible creature—it is disproportionate to its nature. While we do not know the extent of permitted final defect, we do know that all human persons receive more aid than is their due, less penalty than is their due, and that "where sin abounded there grace more abounds" (Rom 5:4). The divine antecedent permissive decree with respect to the defectible creature defecting cannot be avoided, as it is as it were a "shadow" that verifies the light, that is, the light of the omnipotent mercy and goodness of God. This is the light of the certain truth that all voluntary perfection is a divine effect, and so the very root of our voluntary life truly can be healed, elevated, and transformed by grace, and that our free acts of will can gently and mellifluously be moved by God to himself as our last end. Both with respect to the human will and with respect to every creature, it is only because the causality of grace extends to it that God can achieve its redemption. The formal motive of our hope is the omnipotent divine mercy, a divine mercy that does not recede from, but brings forth, every created perfection, including the perfection of contingent free acts of the human will.

44. *ST* I, q. 23, a. 5, ad 3: "Neither according to this account is God unjust if He prepares unequal lots for not unequal things. For this would be contrary to the nature of justice if the effect of predestination were given out of a debt and not gratuitously. In those things which are given gratuitously, one can give at will, more or less, provided that no one is deprived his due, without any infringement of justice." "Neque tamen propter hoc est iniquitas apud Deum, si inaequalia non inaequalibus praeparat. Hoc enim esset contra iustitiae rationem, si praedestinationis effectus ex debito redderetur, et non daretur ex gratia. In his enim quae ex gratia dantur, potest aliquis pro libito suo dare cui vult, plus vel minus, dummodo nulli subtrahat debitum, absque praeiudicio iustitiae."

the human will cannot constitute a "no fly zone" for divine causality if God has the power to redeem man: the omnipotent mercy of God is efficacious through the sacrifice of Christ.

While we do not know the radius of the grace of salvation, we have been told in Sacred Scripture that "where sin has abounded there grace yet more abounds" (Rom 5:4). God does not owe it to the defectible creature to preserve it from all defect. But His love and mercy are the irradiant source of every good—including every volitional good—and His grace abounds. The last word is not the limited word of deontological rectitude, which has its true but subordinate place in the divine plan as a divine effect, but rather is the superordinate Eternal Wisdom, Good, and Light. Escaping the morbidity that would dwell only on the fact of man's nakedness before the divine judgment and his lack of any absolute claim in justice to be upheld from final defection (for grace is the *principle* of merit, and as the Council of Trent so wisely taught of God's goodness toward all men, "He wishes the things which are His gifts to be their own merits"[45]), it is crucial to perceive, and to rest in the perception, that God has revealed Himself as Omnipotent Mercy, Whose redemptive Incarnation is infinitely efficacious. It is this that is the very formal motive of hope—and not despair—namely, that God in His efficacious grace truly and infinitely suffices for the salvation of our fallible and defectible freedom. It is this hope that strengthens our abandonment to the Word made flesh Who, by divine decree, is uniquely given to the world through the efficacious grace of the free assent of Our Lady: "Be it done unto me according to Thy word."

45. Henry Denzinger, *Enchiridion Symbolorum: The Sources of Catholic Dogma*, trans. Roy J. Deferrari (Fitzwilliam, NH: Loreto, 1955), 257, no. 810, from chapter 16 of the "Decree on Justification of the Council of Trent."

3

FROM ETERNAL SONSHIP TO

ADOPTIVE FILIATION

St. Thomas on the Predestination of Christ

Roger W. Nutt

Introduction

The positive inclusion and appropriation of Christ's concrete and singular role in the history of salvation has proven itself to be a delicate, if not completely elusive, task in the complex history of the predestinarian debates.[1] It appears that there is an "insuperable tension" between the

---

1. See, e.g., the extremely critical assessment of Augustine's treatment of the Incarnation and mediation of Christ in relation to his doctrine of predestination by Donato Ogliari in "The Role of Christ and of the Church in the Light of Augustine's Theory of Predestination," *Ephemerides theologicae Lovanienses: Commentarii de re theologica et canonica* 79 (2003): 347–64. John Rist's framing of the question is less critical. Rist sees Augustine's doctrine in relation to his critique of the pagan struggle to understand the powers of divination versus that of the foreknowledge of the gods: "Augustine knew that that in his work *On Fate* and *On Divination* Cicero had followed the Sceptics in rejecting divination at the price of abandoning God's foreknowledge (*City of God* 5.1–11). He himself found that too high a price to pay, and his main objection to Cicero—in which he largely follows the Stoics—is that from God's knowledge of the 'fixed order of causes' it does not follow that nothing depends on human choice, for that choice itself is one of the causes God knows (5.9). God knows infallibly the strength and weakness of the human will, so that only in that theologically innocuous sense may actions of the will be said to be 'fixed.'" *Augustine: Ancient Thought Baptized* (Cambridge: Cambridge University Press, 1994), 268.

approaches to predestination that accentuate "God's absolute freedom to choose" and those that underscore "the concrete application in history" of God's "universal love and salvation."[2] Is there any coherent way to traverse this chasm by simultaneously affirming the eternity and priority of predestination as a divine decree *and* the real soteriological significance of the Incarnation and the events of salvation history? Or is it inevitable that one side be conceded so as to salvage the other?

The central claim of this essay is that Thomas Aquinas's theology of the predestination of Christ is the locus where he most fully works out and integrates his theology of predestination—theology proper as discourse about God—with the realization of the eternal plan of predestination in the temporal order. Because Christ's predestination is not ordered (first) to filial adoption by grace, but rather to the diffusion of the divine goodness through the personal union of the two natures in the Word (from which the redemptive effects of eternal predestination are realized in time), Aquinas's complete doctrine of predestination cannot be fully comprehended without reference to the Incarnation and the economy of salvation.[3]

Furthermore, from an existential standpoint, his doctrine of Christ's predestination avoids what Romanus Cessario describes as "a Molinist

---

2. Ogliari, "Role of Christ and of the Church," 355.

3. The well-documented differences between Scotus and Aquinas on the motive of the Incarnation are inextricably linked to the doctrine of predestination. For Aquinas, God's diffusion of goodness is ordered to the redemption of humanity from sin. Scotus, Richard Cross explains, "concludes that Christ would have become incarnate irrespective of the Fall of Adam." This is so because "God predestines Christ's soul to glory," which is prior to anything willed as a result of the Fall. *Duns Scotus* (Oxford: Oxford University Press, 1999), 128. Aquinas affirms the eternity of Christ's predestination but rejects the notion that this eternal decree did not take sin into account. In *ST* III, q. 1, a. 3, ad 4, for example, Aquinas grants the eternal predestination of the Incarnation while also affirming its redemptive character: "Predestination presupposes the foreknowledge of future things; and hence, as God predestines the salvation of anyone to be brought about by the prayers of others, so also He predestined the work of Incarnation to be the remedy of human sin." Further, in *ST* III, q. 24, a. 1, ad 3, on Christ's predestination, Aquinas argues: "If Christ were not to have been incarnate, God would have decreed men's salvation by other means. But since He decreed the Incarnation of Christ, He decreed at the same time that He should be the cause of our salvation." The touchstone of this discussion is ultimately whether Christ is predestined to glory (Scotus) or to the hypostatic union (Aquinas). For a helpful summary of these issues, with an expansive consideration of major thinkers on each side of the problematic, see Trent Pomplun, "The Immaculate World: Predestination and Possibility in Contemporary Scotism," *Modern Theology* 30 (2014): 525–51.

ethos" that is frequently concomitant with theories of predestination, namely, "the typically modern temptation to safeguard the autonomy of human freedom by detaching it from the divine motion that 'moves' all created things that exist."[4] Christ's predestination—the apex of the divine plan of salvation—constitutes a divinely initiated motion in which the created order is gratuitously moved to its supernatural end through the fullness of grace enjoyed by the Incarnate Word. It is not claiming too much to assert that Thomas presents the totality of his doctrine of predestination only within his articulation of the predestination of Christ. The predestination of Christ thus stands as a foundational point of reference for understanding Thomas's integral teaching on the subject, not to mention the manner in which his considerations point a way beyond the tensions between the eternal-theocentric and salvation-historical approaches to the question.[5]

Preambulatory Observations

In his meditative little book on grace, Charles Journet offers a word of warning about the proper mode of discourse when treating predestination. "If we forget," Journet cautions, "that God is a God of love, if we speak [about predestination] without steeping [it] in the atmosphere of divine goodness that knocks at men's hearts, we may well say what would seem theologically—or rather, verbally, literally—exact, but what would in fact be a deformation, misleading and false."[6] Journet's friendly advice corresponds perfectly with Thomas's manner of proceeding when

4. Romanus Cessario, "Premotion, Holiness, and Pope Benedict XII, 1724–30: Some Historical Retrospects on *Veritatis splendor*," in *Theology and Sanctity*, ed. Cajetan Cuddy, OP (Ave Maria, FL: Sapientia Press of Ave Maria University, 2014), 243.

5. Speaking of contingency and causation in relation to the use of 1 Tm 2:4 ("God wills all to be saved") by Albert, Thomas, and Scotus in their commentaries on Lombard's *Sentences*, Franklin T. Harkins notes: "Although much modern scholarship on these high medieval *magistri in sacra pagina* has emphasized the philosophical nature of their work in general and of their *Sentences* commentaries in particular, it has paid noticeably less attention to how their particular philosophical engagement informed their exegeses of Scripture and, conversely, how scriptural and theological questions gave rise to new philosophical insights." See his "Contingency and Causality in Predestination: 1 Tim. 2:4 in the *Sentences* Commentaries of Albert the Great, Thomas Aquinas, and John Duns Scotus," *Archa Verbi* 11 (2014): 35–72, at 35.

6. Charles Journet, *The Meaning of Grace*, trans. A. V. Littledale (Princeton, NJ: Scepter, 1996), 47.

discussing predestination, namely, to remain steeped in the doctrine of the divine goodness.

The divine motion to sanctify the creature cannot be divorced from the salvific work of Christ, which is the centerpiece of the eternal plan of predestination. In a helpful summary statement that accentuates this point well, Daria Spezzano argues:

> The entire graced journey of the human person to beatitude is properly understood as a particular manifestation of God's goodness, willed in the plan of divine wisdom for that individual. Thomas places it within the larger context of the communication of divine goodness, which is the *ratio* of creation and the effect of divine love.[7]

The place of the Incarnation within the plan of the manifestation of the divine goodness may be quite obvious on the surface, but perhaps, too, it is not always appreciated and integrated within treatments of the doctrine of predestination as much as it could be.[8] Authors have tended to reflect on the doctrine of Christ's predestination in two related but distinguishable ways. On the one hand, Christ's predestination is taken to affirm the revelation of Christ's two natures: the divine nature, and the human nature *predestined* in the flesh to descend from David's lineage.[9] This account says little about the relation of the Incarnation to pre-

---

7. Daria Spezzano, *The Glory of God's Grace* (Ave Maria, FL: Sapientia Press of Ave Maria University, 2015), 46.

8. In addition to the biblical texts that commonly ground discourse about predestination, such as the passages in Paul's letter to the Romans that discuss predestination and election in terms of the preordained plan for salvation of the elect (see, e.g., Rom 8:29, and generally Romans, chapter 9) and Paul's teaching in Eph 1:5 that God "has predestined us in love to be his sons through Jesus Christ," there is also a text affirming the predestination *of* Christ in the greeting of the letter to the Romans, where Paul affirms that the Son of God "was descended from David according to the flesh and predestined (Latin text) [or destined] Son of God in power according to the Spirit of holiness" (Eph 1:4). Unlike the word *prooridzo*, which Paul uses in Rom 8:29, 1 Cor 2:7, and Eph 1:5 and 1:11, the Greek word used in Rom 1:4, ὁρισθέντος, does not have the preposition "pre" (pro in Greek) attached to it. The Vulgate renders this word as *praedestinatus*. It seems that Latin authors from Jerome onward did not perceive a substantial distinction between being "destined" or "predestined" by God. For a helpful summary of the biblical doctrine of predestination, see Matthew Levering, *Predestination: Biblical and Theological Paths* (Oxford: Oxford University Press, 2011), 13–35.

9. See, e.g., Peter Lombard, *The Sentences, Book 3: On the Incarnation of the Word*, trans. Giulio Silano (Toronto: PIMS, 2008), 41 [distinction X, chap. 1 (29), 1]. As Lombard explains: "Whether Christ, according to his being a man, is a person or anything. It is also usual for some to ask whether Christ, according to his being a man, is a person, or even is anything." "If it is then asked," Lombard wonders in reference to Paul's affirmation in Rom 1:4 of Christ's predestination, "whether the predestination which the Apostle recalls is of the

destination as such or the realization in time of God's eternal plan for all those predestined in Christ. Augustine,[10] on the other hand, integrates the parameters of Christological orthodoxy with the realization of the divine plan to restore all things under Christ's headship.[11] In this light, the predestination of Christ is the highest instance of predestination[12] (also having significant anti-Pelagian connotations[13]).

Divine Goodness and the Motive of Predestination

Thomas's sympathies in treating the predestination of Christ lie in the direction mapped out by St. Augustine, in which the Christological aspects of Christ's predestination according to his human nature are treated in relation to their soteriological significance.[14] He opens his

---

person or of the nature, it can truly be said that the person of the Son, which existed always, was predestined according to the human form taken, namely that the same person, being man, be the Son of God and the human nature was predestined that it be united personally to the Word of the Father." Ibid., 44 [distinction X, chap. 3 (31)].

10. For a helpful summary of the doctrine of predestination in the patristic period, with developed consideration of Augustine, see Levering, *Predestination*, 36–67.

11. See, e.g., St. Augustine, "On the Predestination of the Saints," in *Four Anti-Pelagian Writings*, Father of the Church 86, trans. John Mourant and William J. Collinge (Washington, DC: Catholic University of America Press, 1992), 254 [31].

12. "These things," Augustine notes, "God beyond all doubt foreknew that he would accomplish. This then is that predestination of the saints, which appeared most clearly in the saint of saints." Ibid., 254. Likewise, invoking Rom 1:4, Augustine reasons that the predestination of the human nature of Christ to union with the Word establishes "an elevation [of human nature] so great, so lofty, and so sublime that our nature could not be raised higher...just as that one man was predestined to be our head, so we, being many, are predestined to be his members." Ibid., 255.

13. "Anyone who can discover in our head," Augustine challenges, "the merits which have preceded his unique generation, let him seek in us his members those merits which preceded our multiple regeneration." Ibid., 255. The incarnation, Augustine cautions, "was not given to Christ as a recompense, but rather given, so that he should be born of the Spirit and the Virgin, apart from all the bond of sin." Ibid.

14. In his *Commentary on the Letter of Saint Paul to the Romans*, 1:4, Thomas affirms the parameters of Christological orthodoxy with the following interpretation: "predestination must be attributed to the very person of Christ. But because the person of Christ subsists in two natures, the human and the divine, something can be said of him with respect to either nature...It is in this way," Thomas continues, "that he is said to be predestined according to his human nature. For although the person of Christ has always been the Son of God, nevertheless it was not always a fact that, while existing in a human nature, he was the Son of God; rather, this was due to an ineffable grace." St. Thomas Aquinas, *Commentary on the Letter of Saint Paul to the Romans* (Lander, WY: Aquinas Institute for the Study of Sacred

treatment of predestination in the *Prima Pars* of the *Summa Theologiae* (*ST*), question 23, by affirming that the rational creature is predestined by God—hardly a significant contribution. What is worthy of note, however, about his affirmation of the rational creature's predestination by God is the *ratio* that he puts forward for the fittingness of this predestination—the very one that Journet urges to be kept in mind. The predestination of the rational creature is fitting because of the twofold end to which the creature is directed by God. On the one hand, providence directs creatures to a proportionate natural end, which, Thomas affirms, "created being can attain according to the power of its nature."[15] On the other hand, there is the end of eternal life "that consists in seeing God, which is above the nature of every creature."[16] This end, Thomas teaches, "exceeds all proportion and faculty of the created nature."[17] Thomas affirms the special grace-filled divine direction of the creature to beatitude by using the passive verb *perducitur* and the participle *transmissa*. The creature is "led" and "carried" or "transmitted" by God to the end of eternal life. What makes this divine direction of the creature fitting is that the *ratio* of the ordering, in Thomas's words, "pre-exists in God...as the *ratio* of the order of all things towards an end."[18] This makes it fitting for God to predestine precisely because, Thomas reasons, "the *ratio* in the mind of the doer of something to be done, is a kind of pre-existence in him of the thing to be done."[19]

Therefore the fittingness of the predestination of the rational creature by God is rooted in the preexistence of the reality of what the creature is predestined to in God himself. The motive by which God moves the

---

Doctrine, 2012), 19 [cap. 1., lect. 3, #51]. The maintenance of the synthesis of the Council of Chalcedon, however, is not where Thomas concludes his treatment of Christ's predestination. In all of his works, including his commentary on Lombard's *Sentences*, he further develops his doctrine of predestination in light of the reality of Christ's. This broader articulation unfolds a *ratio* that Thomas introduces in his general doctrine of predestination and carries through to his discussion of Christ's predestination. This broader *ratio*, which includes the sanctification of the creature in history, is the primary focus throughout the remainder of this essay. See also Steven C. Boguslawski, OP, *Thomas Aquinas on the Jews: Insights into His Commentary on Romans 9–11* (New York: Paulist Press, 2008), esp. 8–11.

15. *ST* I, q. 23, a. 1. Translations from the *Prima Pars*, with an occasional slight modification, are taken from Laurence Shapcote, OP, trans., *Summa theologiae, Prima Pars 1–49*, ed. John Mortensen and Enrique Alarcón (Lander, WY: Aquinas Institute for the Study of Sacred Doctrine, 2012).

16. Ibid.   17. Ibid.
18. Ibid.   19. Ibid.

creature toward the end of beatitude is within God's own eternal being. It is true that human nature has an obediential potency to be elevated in this fashion, but the question that Thomas raises is about God—whether it is fitting for God to predestine. Commenting on this article, Reinhard Hütter explains that Thomas's use of fittingness in this context "rejects these alternatives [whether the fittingness stems from one of either of the rational creature's twofold ends] by referring the matter to the mystery of God's goodness which is identical with God's justice as well as mercy, utterly unfathomable in the glorious simplicity of the divine perfection."[20]

Hütter's insight underscores a foundational element of the entire Christian doctrine of predestination, one that is often obfuscated by the complexity of the issue, namely, that the *ratio* of the movement or transmission of the rational creature to eternal life by God is the divine goodness itself. In a telling passage in the *Summa contra Gentiles*, Aquinas roots the divine motive to create and to assimilate creatures to God solely in the divine goodness: "nothing else moves God to the creation of creatures, save his own goodness, which he willed to communicate to other realities by a manner of assimilating them to himself."[21] This principle is something that he carries forward from his treatise on God to his treatment of the Incarnation and the predestination of Christ.

Thomas draws upon this insight much more so than is generally evident in isolated discussions on predestination and salvation in Christ. In his work on the development of the doctrine of predestination in the thought of Thomas Aquinas, Michal Paluch confirms this point by highlighting a shift in emphasis that can be observed in Thomas's articulation of predestination between the *Prima Pars* and the *Tertia Pars* of the *Summa Theologiae*.[22] Given that several years and several thousand pages of material stand between the composition of *ST* I, q. 23, and *ST* III, q. 24, which considers the predestination of Christ, perhaps readers should not be surprised by some disparity in Thomas's language. Yet in *ST* III, q.

20. Reinhard Hütter, *Dust Bound for Heaven: Explorations in the Theology of Thomas Aquinas* (Grand Rapids, MI: William B. Eerdmans, 2012), 164.

21. *Summa contra Gentiles* II, ch. 46. "Ad productionem creaturarm nihil aliud movet Deum nisi sua bonitas, quam rebus aliis communicare voluit secundum modum assimilationis ad ipsum." My translation.

22. See Michal Paluch, *La profondeur de l'amour divin: Evolution de la doctrine de la prédestination dans l'œuvre de Thomas d'Aquin*, Bibliothèque Thomiste 55 (Paris: J. Vrin, 2004), 245.

24, Thomas refers back to the discussion of predestination that was put forward in *ST* I, q. 23, a. 1 and 2. "As is clear," Thomas teaches, referring to *quae in prima parte dicta sunt*, "predestination, in its proper sense, is a certain Divine preordination from eternity of those things which are to be done in time by the grace of God."[23] This statement is an adequate summary of the formulations in *ST* I, q. 23, but it is not reducible to any of the definitions that Thomas had set forth earlier. For example, the "direction of a rational creature towards the end of life eternal" (*ST* I, q. 23, a. 1) or the "type of the ordering of some person towards eternal salvation, existing in the divine mind" (*ST* I, q. 23, a. 2).[24]

The shift in emphasis to which Paluch draws attention from *ST* I, q. 23, to *ST* III, q. 24, stems from Thomas's coupling of the eternal divine preordination that constitutes predestination in the divine mind with the working-out in time of that preordination in the Incarnation and gift of grace.[25] This coupling is significant for a complete understanding of Thomas's teaching on predestination. As Joseph Wawrykow notes, "There are in fact two aspects of, or 'notes' to, providence. Primarily, providence is the ordering by God of every creature to their ends: it is the plan that God has for their fulfillment. Secondarily, however, providence also involves the implementation of this plan that extends to all creatures. God orders; God implements the ordering, bringing every creature to the end set for it by God."[26] The movement from the treatment of predestination in terms of discourse about God to the implementation of the divine plan in Christ indicates the reason for the shift in Thomas's emphasis: he is speaking of the same divine reality in the *Tertia Pars*, but from the aspect of its implementation.

23. *ST* III, q. 24, a. 1. Translations from the *Tertia Pars*, with occasional slight modification, are taken from Laurence Shapcote, OP, trans., *Summa theologiae, Tertia Pars 1–59*, ed. John Mortensen and Enrique Alarcón (Lander, WY: Aquinas Institute for the Study of Sacred Doctrine, 2012).

24. Following Paluch, *ST* I, q. 23, a. 1, defines predestination as "ratio...transmissionis creaturae rationalis in finem vitae aeternae," whereas *ST* III, q. 24, a. 1, defines it as "quaedam divina praeordinatio ad aeterno de his quae per gratiam Dei sunt fienda in tempore."

25. Thomas does make reference to grace and merit (i.e., to things done in time) in relation to predestination in the *Prima Pars* without developing them in conjunction with the Incarnation. See, e.g., *ST* I, q. 23, a. 5. For a helpful presentation of this point, see Joseph Wawrykow, *God's Grace and Human Action: "Merit" in the Theology of Thomas Aquinas* (Notre Dame, IN: University of Notre Dame Press, 1995), 156–64.

26. Joseph Wawrykow, "Grace," in *The Theology of Thomas Aquinas*, ed. Rik Van Nieuwenhove and Joseph Wawrykow (Notre Dame, IN: University of Notre Dame Press, 2005), 200.

The Diffusive Nature of the Divine Goodness and the Fittingness of the Incarnation

This focus on the temporal implementation of predestination accentuates the importance of the divine goodness in Thomas's account of predestination. This *ratio* creates a bond—solidified on predestination—between questions 1 and 24 of the *Tertia Pars*, and much of the intervening material. Thomas inaugurates both questions by inquiring of the fittingness of something pertaining to Christ, the Incarnation in the case of the former question, and his predestination in the case of the latter.[27]

The *ratio* that Thomas gives for the fittingness of the Incarnation is theocentric in nature, namely, that "the very nature of God is goodness."[28] So Thomas seats the fittingness of the Incarnation in the divine nature.[29] The fittingness of the Incarnation is on account of the divine goodness, Thomas reasons, because "it belongs to the essence of goodness to communicate itself to others."[30] Furthermore, the Incarnation is not simply a common mode of participation between God and creation. Rather, Thomas adds that the Incarnation is the communication "of the highest good...in the highest manner." The Incarnation reaches this zenith, Thomas reasons, "by His so joining created nature to Himself that one Person is made up of these three—the Word, a soul and flesh."[31]

Thomas then develops a threefold *magis conveniens* and *convenientissium* for the Incarnation of the Son rather than the Father or Holy Spir-

---

27. For a helpful discussion of the predestination of Christ in Thomas's work, see Levering, *Predestination*, 82–83.

28. *ST* III, q. 1, a. 1.

29. For a treatment of the ontology of the hypostatic union with reference to its historical implications, see Thomas Joseph White, OP, *The Incarnate Lord: A Thomistic Study in Christology* (Washington, DC: Catholic University of America Press, 2015), 73–125.

30. *ST* III, q. 1, a. 1. For a presentation of Aquinas's appropriation of the work of Dionysius in his treatment of the diffusion of divine goodness, see Fran O'Rourke, *Pseudo-Dionysius and the Metaphysics of Aquinas* (Notre Dame, IN: University of Notre Dame Press, 2005), esp. 225–74. See also Bernhard Blankenhorn, OP, *The Mystery of Union with God: Dionysian Mysticism in Albert the Great and Thomas Aquinas* (Washington, DC: Catholic University of America Press, 2015).

31. Ibid. John of St. Thomas likewise recognizes the God-centered basis for Thomas's discussion of the Incarnation. "Saint Thomas discusses the fittingness of the Incarnation from the side of God," he observes, "which is that he might communicate himself to the creature in the fullest manner." See John of St. Thomas, *Introduction to the Summa Theologiae of Thomas Aquinas*, trans. Ralph McInerny (South Bend, IN: St. Augustine's Press, 2004), 154.

it.[32] He derives the second reason for the special symmetry (*congruentiae*) of the Incarnation of the Son and not the Father or the Holy Spirit, from the end of the hypostatic union, which, interestingly, he states to be "the fulfilling of predestination."[33] How so? The Incarnation of the Son brings the plan of predestination to a more perfect fulfillment than would an Incarnation of the Father or the Holy Spirit, because the divine preordination is ordered to a heavenly inheritance that "is bestowed," Thomas observes, "only on sons."[34] The Incarnation as such is not fitting under the *ratio* of the divine goodness in a generic sense, but is further specified by the ordination to adoptive sonship—to a special conformity of the saints to the reality of the Word's eternal sonship. "That by Him," Thomas argues, "Who is the natural Son, men should share this likeness of sonship by adoption."[35]

In his commentary on Romans, Thomas explicitly links God's eternal plan to communicate the divine goodness with the Son's wish to communicate his sonship to the faithful. "For just as God willed to communicate his natural goodness to others by imparting to them a likeness of his goodness," Thomas notes, "so that he is not only good but the author of good things, so too the Son of God willed to communicate to others conformity to his sonship, so that he would not be the only Son, but also the firstborn among sons."[36]

Furthermore, when considering whether, given the sinful creatures' distance from God, it is fitting for God to adopt, Aquinas yet again appeals to the divine goodness. "God is infinitely good: for which reason He admits His creatures to a participation of good things," and this, for the rational creature, "consists in the enjoyment of God, by which also God Himself is happy and rich in Himself."[37]

---

32. For an exposition of Thomas's purposes in this challenging question, see Joseph Wawrykow, "Hypostatic Union," in *The Theology of Thomas Aquinas*, ed. Rik Van Nieuwenhove and Joseph Wawrykow (Notre Dame, IN: University of Notre Dame Press, 2005), 233–37.

33. *ST* III, q. 3, a. 8.   34. Ibid.

35. Ibid.

36. St. Thomas Aquinas, *Commentary on the Letter of Saint Paul to the Romans* (Lander, WY: Aquinas Institute for the Study of Sacred Doctrine, 2012), 235 [cap. 8, lect. 6, #706]. Translation slightly modified.

37. *ST* III, q. 23, a. 1. In *ST* I-II, q. 110, a. 1, Thomas speaks of grace in terms of both participation and predestination: "the second [meaning of the word grace] is a special love, whereby He draws the rational creature above the condition of its nature to a *participation of the*

It is interesting to look at the question devoted to Christ's predestination under the light of this recurring theme: fittingness, each time Thomas invokes it, is affirmed in relation to the divine goodness. When he offers his tweaked definition of predestination as "a certain Divine preordination from eternity of those things which are to be done in time by the grace of God," he immediately connects this definition with the superlative communication of the divine goodness that is realized in the hypostatic union: "Now, that man is God, and that God is man is something done in time by God through the grace of the union."[38]

Predestination as the Father's Gift to Christ— and to the Faithful through Christ

In the structure of the third part of the *Summa Theologiae*, Thomas locates his treatment of predestination within a twofold order. First, the question on Christ's predestination is included in a group of eleven questions, commencing with question 16, that, in Thomas's words, "consider the consequences of the union."[39] Within this grouping of topics that follow upon the union, Thomas identifies a second subgrouping of questions on Christ's subjection, prayer, priesthood, adoption, and predestination. This group of topics, Thomas explains, pertains to "such things as belong to Christ in relation to the Father." So, Christ's predestination is (1) a consequence of the union and (2) something that belongs to Christ (*secundum quod homo*) in relation to the Father.

Thomas thus views the hypostatic union as the realization of the diffusion of the divine goodness, which in turn corresponds to the fittingness of the predestination of Christ, as it accomplishes and implements in time the divine preordination to sanctify the rational creature in grace toward the end of eternal beatitude.

There is a kind of connecting member that is provided here for the

---

Divine good; and according to this love He is said to love anyone simply, since it is by this love that God simply wishes the eternal good, which is Himself, for the creature. Accordingly when a man is said to have the grace of God, there is signified something bestowed on man by God. Nevertheless the *grace of God sometimes signifies God's eternal love, as we say the grace of predestination*, inasmuch as God gratuitously and not from merits predestines or elects some." Emphasis added.

38. *ST* III, q. 24, a. 1.

39. See the preface to *ST* III, q. 16.

overall plan of the *Summa* and Christ's place therein. "It cannot be said," Thomas argues in defense of the fittingness of the predestination of Christ,

that God has not from eternity pre-ordained to do this in time: since it would follow that something would come anew into the Divine Mind. And we must admit that the union itself of natures in the Person of Christ falls under the eternal predestination of God. For this reason do we say that Christ was pre-destined.[40]

How can this temporal aspect of the eternal plan be reconciled with Thomas's insistence that predestination, properly understood, is a theo-logical reality in the strong sense of the word "theological"—something whose *ratio* is in the goodness of the divine essence and not in the crea-ture? Thomas identifies his treatment of the predestination of Christ as a consequence of the hypostatic union, and further as an instance of Christ's relation (*secundum quod homo*) to the Father and not to the faithful. To what degree does the properly theological nature of predesti-nation allow for Christological and temporal components?

To respond to this difficulty, Thomas argues that "two things may be considered in predestination. One on the part of eternal predestination itself: and in this respect it implies a certain antecedence in regard to that which comes under predestination."[41] This is the properly theological domain of predestination. From another perspective, however, Thomas explains, "predestination may be considered as regards its temporal ef-fect, which is some gratuitous gift of God."[42]

In relation to the order of questions, however, how does the "gift" of predestination pertain to Christ's relation to the Father and not the Fa-ther's or Christ's relation to the predestined? Thomas clarifies this point by excavating the thread between Christological orthodoxy on the one hand, and the eternal plan for the predestination of Christ on the other: from both the eternal and the temporal point of view, "we must say that pre-destination is ascribed to Christ by reason of his human nature alone: for human nature was not always united to the Word; and by grace bestowed on it was it united in Person to the Son of God."[43] The hypostatic union is a singular, gratuitous effect realized in time of the Father's eternal plan.

---

40. *ST* III, q. 24, a. 1.   41. *ST* III, q. 24, a. 2.
42. Ibid.   43. Ibid.

Given the unmerited gratuity of the predestination of Christ's human nature to the grace of personal union with the Word, to what degree can the Incarnation as such be said to contribute anything whatsoever to the realization of the plan of salvation. Thomas readily concedes that "on the part of the act of predestination," on the side of its eternity in God, "Christ's predestination cannot be said to be the exemplar of ours: for in the same way and by the same eternal act God predestined us and Christ."[44]

Christ's predestination, however, as an unmerited gift from the Father, can be considered in relation to those predestined from the perspective of its term or *ad quem* point of reference. "In respect of the good to which we are predestined," Thomas notes that Christ "was predestined to be the natural Son of God, whereas we are predestined to the adoption of sons, which is a participated likeness of natural sonship."[45] In other words, the perfection of filiation communicated to the creature in predestination resides in the natural sonship of the Incarnate Word.[46]

Furthermore, Thomas speaks of the "manner of obtaining this good" to which predestination is ordered, "that is, by grace." So how does God move the rational creature (in time) to the good of participation in eternal life—how is the divine goodness diffused? Christ's predestination to natural sonship—personal union—exemplifies adoptive filiation because "human nature in Him, without any antecedent merits, was united to the Son of God: and of the fullness of His grace we all have received."[47]

So Christ's predestination does relate to the predestination of the saints as possessing the perfection of natural sonship to which they are ordered to participate, and the means to this participation, namely, his own fullness of grace. In his discussion of Christ's grace, Thomas articulates a connection between Christ's own enjoyment of the fullness of grace and the derivation of grace by his members from this fullness. Christ enjoys the fullness of grace first because

44. *ST* III, q. 24, a. 3.

45. Ibid.

46. Thomas underscores the participatory nature of predestination: "Christ is the measure and rule of our life and therefore our predestination, because we are predestined to adoptive sonship, which is a participation and image of natural sonship." *Commentary on the Letter of Saint Paul to the Romans*, 17 [cap. 3, lect. 3, 48].

47. *ST* III, q. 24, a. 3.

the nearer a recipient is to the inflowing cause, the more it receives. And hence the soul of Christ, which is more closely united to God than all other rational creatures, receives the greatest outpouring of His grace. Secondly, in His relation to the effect. For the soul of Christ so received grace, that, in a manner, it is poured out from it upon others. And hence it behooved Him to have the greatest grace; as fire which is the cause of heat in other hot things, is of all things the hottest.[48]

As a result, the human nature of Christ becomes, through its predestination to union with the Word, the created source of the diffusion of the divine goodness in the temporal order.

Affirming that the exemplar realities of predestination reside in Christ's predestination does not clarify the manner, if there be one, of any causation that can be attributed to Christ in history. In fact, as Thomas recognizes in an objection, it seems impossible, given his general teaching on predestination as an eternal reality in God, that Christ's predestination exercises any soteriological influence on the faithful. "For that which is eternal has no cause," Thomas affirms in an objection, "But our predestination is eternal. Therefore Christ's predestination is not the cause of ours."[49]

To address the causal relation of Christ's predestination to that of the saints, Thomas again turns to the distinction between the act and the term of predestination. In so doing, he gives explicit articulation to his affirmation in the *Prima Pars* of the role that secondary causes have within the unfolding of the divine plan. By the eternal act of predestination in God, Christ's predestination cannot be the cause of the saints, Thomas teaches, "because by one and the same act God predestined both Christ and us."[50] This seems to negate any causal agency on the part of Christ in relation to the communication of grace. Yet Thomas further argues that "Christ's predestination is the cause of ours: for God, by predestinating from eternity, so decreed our salvation, that it should be achieved through Jesus Christ."[51] Here Thomas makes explicit how secondary causes are related to the eternal plan of predestination: "eternal predestination covers not only that which is to be accomplished in time, but also the mode and order in which it is to be accomplished in time."[52]

---

48. *ST* III, q. 7, a. 9.   49. *ST* III, q. 24, a. 4, ob. 1.
50. Ibid., corpus.   51. Ibid.
52. Ibid.

These reflections on causality raise the question of a putative equivocation to which Thomas is especially sensitive in his commentary on Lombard's *Sentences*. In what sense can predestination as an eternal decree, Christ's predestination to natural sonship, and the predestination of the saints be treated under any common notion? "In predestination there are two things," Thomas recognizes in his commentary on the *Sentences*, "one eternal, namely the very operation of God, and another that is temporal, namely the effect of predestination."[53]

From the formally theological perspective, no created agency, not even Christ's, causes God's eternal decree. "Therefore our predestination as that to which is eternal in itself, does not have a cause but," Thomas quickly adds, "as to the effect it can have a cause, namely in so far as its effect is produced by means of some created cause."[54]

This establishes a connection between Christ's predestination and that of the saints: "according to this," Thomas affirms without hesitation, "the cause of our predestination is the predestination of Christ. Efficiently in so far as he is the mediator of our salvation; and formally in so far as we are predestined children of God in his image; and finally, in so far as our salvation overflows from his glory."[55]

The believer is furthermore granted a participation in Christ's fullness through the providential establishment of the causal efficacy of the sacraments. "Divine providence" provides for each thing, Aquinas notes, "according to the mode of its condition. Divine wisdom, therefore, fittingly provides man with the means of salvation, in the shape of corporeal and sensible signs that are called sacraments."[56] This does not mean that the sacraments of the Church somehow constitute a parallel plan of salvation other than the one realized in Christ. Rather, Aquinas explains, "Christ's passion is, so to say, applied to man through the sacraments."[57]

Thomas even addresses the vexing question of reprobation in the context of the universality of Christ's headship over all. Christ's headship and predestination, Thomas explains, is related to all in some real way,

---

53. *Scriptum super III Lib. Sententiarum*, ed. R. P. Maria Fabianus Moos, OP (Paris: 1933), dist. X, solutio III, #118 (p. 352). My translation.

54. Ibid., pp. 352–33.

55. Ibid., #117 (p. 353). "And therefore," Thomas concludes, "the predestination of Christ and ours is not of one univocal *ratio*, but according to analogy."

56. *ST* III, q. 61, a. 1.

57. *ST* III, q. 61, a. 1, ad 3.

but limited by the degree of participation that is actuated in each person through the temporal unfolding of the divine plan. Thomas argues:

> Hence we must say that if we take the whole time of the world in general, Christ is the Head of all men, but diversely, for, first and principally, He is the Head of such as are united to Him by glory; secondly, of those who are actually united to Him by charity; thirdly, of those who are actually united to Him by faith; fourthly, of those who are united to Him merely in potentiality, which is not yet reduced to act, yet will be reduced to act according *to Divine predestination*; fifthly, of those who are united to Him in potentiality, which will never be reduced to act; *such are those men existing in the world, who are not predestined, who, however, on their departure from this world, wholly cease to be members of Christ*, as being no longer in potentiality to be united to Christ.[58]

Predestination to participation in Christ's headship is therefore a real potency—not a mere possibility—in all wayfarers. For those who are saved, the predestination of Christ to headship is the actuating principle of this potency to participation by faith and charity. Death definitively impedes this potency for real, saving participation in Christ from being brought to act in the reprobate.

Conclusion

The doctrine of predestination has vexed and troubled not a few of the greatest and subtlest of Christian thinkers, as other essays in this volume highlight. Recurring spiritual problems that have plagued Christianity—from Pelagianism in all its forms, to questions about the relation of divine causality to human freedom and autonomy, to spiritual aberrations like Quietism and Jansenism, to name just a few—are all related in some way to unhelpful articulations of the doctrine of predestination. Romanus Cessario raises the following important question regarding the decline in the practice of the faith that results from problematic accounts of predestination: "Why would someone grow tired of prayer, asceticism, and in some cases aspects of the moral life?" The predestination of Christ points the way to the only lasting solution to this problem. "The answer may lie," Cessario explains, "in the manner in which such persons attempt prayer, asceticism (which may include the discipline of study), and

---

58. *ST* III, q. 8, a. 3. Emphasis added.

a life of virtue. *Those who seek to sustain themselves spiritually by relying on their own energies always grow weary of conversion.*"[59] Thomas's doctrine of the predestination of Christ clarifies just how concretely the divine aid has entered the created order and operates to move creatures, in Christ, to glory.

To return again to the work of Daria Spezzano, it is worth quoting at length a helpful summary that she makes of many of these themes:

> As the creature is conformed to the Word by wisdom in the intellect, so it is also conformed to the Word insofar as it is through the Word that God carries out the divine plan of wisdom for the universe and for each individual creature, manifesting his glory. The predestination of the elect to beatitude, toward which they move by participation in the Word and Love through wisdom-perfected charity, fully reveals the splendor of God's glory—the knowledge and praise of the divine goodness—in the divine plan of providence.[60]

If the rich doctrine of the predestination of Christ does not change the general parameters of Thomas's treatment of predestination, it certainly adds light and clarity to understanding how the eternal reality of predestination unfolds within the temporal order and how the Incarnation realizes the divine plan under the *ratio* of the goodness of God. Thomas accomplishes an elusive theological task with his doctrine of the predestination of Christ, namely, the articulation of a theocentric account of the unfolding of the divine plan that is integrated with the created means by which God graciously moves the predestined toward their supernatural end.[61]

---

59. Cessario, "Premotion, Holiness, and Pope Benedict XIII," 238.

60. Spezzano, *Glory of God's Grace*, 340.

61. It is interesting to note, as a final but underdeveloped observation, how Thomas appropriates the distinction between operative and cooperative grace, which is frequently parsed in discussions of predestination, in his treatment of the efficacy of sacramental penance in relation to the remission of sin: "it belongs to grace to operate (*operari*) in man by justifying him from sin, and to co-operate (*cooperari*) with man that his work may be rightly done. *Consequently the forgiveness of guilt and of the debt of eternal punishment belongs to operating (operantem) grace*, while the remission of the debt of temporal *punishment belongs to co-operating (cooperantem) grace*, in so far as man, by bearing punishment patiently with the help of Divine grace, is released also from the debt of temporal punishment. Consequently just *as the effect of operating grace precedes the effect of co-operating grace, so too, the remission of guilt and of eternal punishment precedes the complete release from temporal punishment*, since both are from grace, but the former, from grace alone, the latter, from grace and free-will." *ST* III, q. 86, a. 4, ad 2. Emphasis added. This concrete example helps to accentuate the manner of the historical unfolding of the plan of predestination in the faithful through the sacraments that derive their efficacy from Christ.

4

CATHOLIC PREDESTINATION

The Omnipotence and Innocence of Divine Love

Thomas Joseph White, OP

Introduction

Augustine gave initial form to the Western Catholic doctrine of pre-destination in his disputes with Pelagianism in the fifth century. His principal concerns were to underscore the primacy of the activity of the grace of God with respect to all human consent and merit in the process of salvation, and to demonstrate the primacy of the divine foreknowl-edge and will with regard to all outcomes that occur in the created order and in human history.[1] God foreknows from all eternity those who will be saved as well as those who will be reprobated.[2] His election of those who are saved is the primary and infallible cause of their salvation, in-dependently of any foreseen merits on the part of the elect.[3] This vertig-inous claim caused the opponents of Augustine to fear that he had com-promised a right understanding of God's goodness and moral innocence. Does God from all eternity simply exclude many from election arbitrari-ly so that they have no genuine possibility of salvation? Are those who

---

1. Augustine, *On Grace and Free Will*, chaps. 15, 20, 24.
2. Augustine, *On the Predestination of the Saints*, chaps. 11, 19.
3. *On Grace and Free Will*, chap. 45; *On the Predestination of the Saints*, chaps. 29, 36.

do evil obliged to do so by the neglectful absence of sufficient assistance offered to them on the part of God? If so, how is God possibly good?[4] Against these concerns, weighty counter-concerns can be leveraged. If God does not foresee all outcomes prior to their unfolding in history, is he really eternal and omniscient? If God cannot from all eternity both know and cause all the good that we do as creatures, can he effectively save the world by his sovereign power, and redeem the world from injustice and evil by his mercy and grace? Consequently, can he really be good in any effective way without being omniscient and eternal in just the way that the Augustinian doctrine of predestination says that God is?

The conundrums of the Augustinian theory gave rise to subsequent disputes over centuries that were resolved insightfully by the Second Council of Orange (529 AD) and the ninth-century councils of Quiesy and Valence.[5] These local councils sought to establish a Catholic doctrinal balance internal to Augustinianism. They clarified a definite twofold claim regarding the mystery of predestination. First, those who attain to salvation do so only because of the primacy of God's grace and assistance given to them from all eternity in order to lead them up the pathway toward salvation. The predestination of the elect depends upon the eternal creative power and goodness of God, who always takes the first initiative. Second, those who are reprobated and suffer eternal damnation do so only because they have culpably rejected the grace of God that was antecedently offered to them. Their reprobation is not caused primarily by God, and in no way impugns the goodness of Christ or his moral innocence. Christ died so that all human beings might be offered the possibility of salvation. All who are saved have God alone to thank for taking the initiative to save them and to sustain them in a state of grace so that they might persevere. All who are damned have themselves alone to blame for

4. For helpful studies of Augustine's critics, see Alexander Y. Hwang, *Intrepid Lover of Perfect Grace: The Life and Thought of Prosper of Aquitaine* (Washington, DC: Catholic University of America Press, 2009), chaps. 3–5; D. Ogliari, *Gratia et Certamen: The Relationship between Grace and Free Will in the Discussion of Augustine with the So-Called Semipelagians* (Leuven: Leuven University Press, 2003).

5. Second Council of Orange, 529 AD, can. 3–25 and conclusion (Denz. 373–97); Synod of Quiercy, 853 AD, chaps. 1–4 (Denz. 621–24); Synod of Valence, 855 AD, can. 1–6 (Denz. 625–33), in *Denzinger: Compendium of Creeds, Definitions, and Declarations on Matters of Faith and Morals*, 43rd ed., ed. Peter Hünermann, Robert Fastiggi, and Anne Englund Nash (San Francisco: Ignatius Press, 2012).

their rejection of grace. In the words of Augustine, God never abandons us unless we first abandon him.[6]

This mature, early medieval formulation of the doctrine of predestination was deeply influential among the Latin doctors of the Scholastic age, even into the Renaissance era. It has its own challenges as a way of thinking, and is difficult to hold with any right degree of balance or subtly. Today, however, it has been largely lost from view owing to the emergence in the modern period of two rival conceptions of the Augustinian patrimony, both of which obscure the traditional doctrine, and which in some ways are mirror images of one another.

The first of these is that of John Calvin, a subtle thinker whose views should not be caricatured. Calvin posited a number of tenets that were to have great influence in modern debates, among his critics as well as defenders. Here we may list briefly a number of his core ideas: the thesis that grace is irresistible and infallibly converts the hearts of those to whom it is given;[7] the thesis that God gives this grace only to a part of the human race (the elect or predested);[8] the thesis that there is no distinction to be made between the divine will and the divine permissions of evil, so that all that happens in salvation history is in some way the transparent expression of divine volition (including the moral evil of human beings that may prepare them for just reprobation on the part of God);[9] the thesis of the radical depravity of the human person, who is incapable of choosing what is morally good from a right motive without a prior initiative of divine grace acting upon the subject;[10] and the thesis that only those are saved who have explicit faith in the Gospel (and not any kind of implicit faith by way of nonspecifically Christian tenets of

6. See the Synod of Valence, can. 2 and 3, Denz. 627–28: "Nor do we believe that the wicked thus perish because they were not able to be good; but because they were unwilling to be good, they have remained in their own vice...we faithfully confess the predestination of the elect to life and the predestination of the impious to death; in the election, however, of those who are to be saved, the mercy of God precedes the merited good. In the condemnation, however, of those who are to be lost, the evil they have deserved precedes the just judgment of God" (translation slightly altered).

7. See John Calvin, *Institutes of the Christian Religion (ICR)* III, chap. 24, where God's election and his grace are depicted as being always intrinsically effective and irresistible.

8. *ICR* III, chap. 21, no. 1.

9. *ICR* III, chap. 23, no. 8. Calvin expressly refuses the distinction between God's will and his permissions.

10. *ICR* II, chaps. 2–3; III, chap. 23, no. 3.

belief), so that only visible members of the Church may be saved.[11] To this we can add the following theses, which may well be in Calvin but are disputed and were promulgated by some of his disciples: the notion that Christ died only for the elect (selective atonement theory),[12] and the notion that God from all eternity wills positively that many be reprobate independently of or prior to their foreseen demerits (so-called double predestination).[13]

In general today, when people speak of predestination, they often presume some part of this configuration of things, one in which (to speak critically) it seems that divine willing must supervene upon free agency in history such that the human being seems inexorably driven by a kind of transcendent necessity toward either the ends of grace and salvation or those of moral evil and damnation assigned from God eternally pre-existent to all that occurs in time, and according to a divine voluntarism whose motives cannot be fathomed or understood. At the logically arguable extreme of this theory, one might stipulate that all that occurs in the domain of moral evil serves just as profitably to give glory to the omnipotence and justice of God as all that occurs in the domain of moral goodness. Hell glorifies God in one way, heaven in another.

Karl Barth offers an interpretation of the Augustinian heritage that is in some ways directly opposed to that of Calvin, one that has echoes in various modern Catholic thinkers. Following a thesis of the twentieth-century French Reformed theologian Peter Maury, Barth inverted central features of the Calvinist paradigm while maintaining others.[14] God is the primary author of salvation by grace alone, and grace that is given to the elect works by way of infallible efficacy. (It is not ultimately

11. *ICR* III, chap. 2, no. 3.

12. Compare *ICR* II, chap. 16, and III, chap. 22, no. 1–6. On diverse interpretations of the theology of atonement and election in the Reformed scholastic tradition, see Richard A. Muller, *Christ and the Decree: Christology and Predestination in Reformed Theology from Calvin to Perkins* (Grand Rapids, MI: Baker Academic, 2008).

13. Consider *ICR* III, chaps. 21–24, and Muller's summary of the subsequent interpretation of Theodore Beza in *Christ and the Decree*, 79–96. It is commonly thought that the Synod of Dordt deemphasized this aspect of Calvin's thought, and those who have maintained it are sometimes deemed "hyper-Calvinist" in the Reformed tradition.

14. See the treatment of election particularly in *Church Dogmatics* II, 2, sections 32–33, and II, 3. In section 33 (154–55), Barth mentions the influence of Pierre Maury's essay "Election et Foi," presented at the Congrès International de Théologie Calviniste in Geneva in 1936. G. W. Bromiley and T. F. Torrance, trans., *Church Dogmatics*, 4 vols. (Edinburgh: T&T Clark, 1936–75). Hereafter cited as *CD*.

resistible.[15]) From all eternity, God has willed that the elect be saved and is able to effectuate his determination of man for salvation through all the mediations of creaturely historical processes.[16] Thus far we are with Calvin. In differentiation from traditional Reformed doctrine, however, Barth holds that Christ is the elect one, who has died for all human beings, such that in him all human beings have been elected to eternal life.[17] Meanwhile, according to Barth, Christ alone has experienced the dereliction of the passion and descent into hell in substitutionary atonement for all of humanity, and so Christ alone is reprobate. He alone was forsaken so that we might be saved.[18] Consequently, God elects all human beings to salvation in Christ, and so we rightfully may dare to hope that all will be saved.[19] God has a kind of kenotic or self-emptying respect for the freedom of his creatures in allowing them to do evil, but God is also able in his transcendent freedom to incorporate all the outcomes of our all too human works of evil into his plan of redemption, not only making himself the subject and victim of this evil in the passion, but also making use of his own human death and resurrection in such a way as to exalt humanity forever into life with God in Christ.[20] Here Augustinianism is placed at the service of an eschatological universalism that seeks to vindicate the goodness and innocence of God in the face of humanity's history of suffering and moral evil.

This second strategy safeguards aspects of the Augustinian theology of predestination. But it does so by making the doctrine an appendage to a Christological universalism. The notion that human free refusal of the mystery of God might really have eternal consequences is disavowed or placed in theoretical suspension. In the wake of Barth, the thesis of

15. *CD* IV, 1, section 58, 86–88: "Is grace as such ever *sufficiens* without being *efficax*? Is it ever effective objectively without being effective subjectively?...Does the fact that man believes he can evade or resist it mean that we can speak of a grace which is not effective?... But the grace of the one God and the one Christ, and therefore the objective grace which never comes to man except from God, must always be understood as the one complete grace, which is subjectively strong and effective in its divine objectivity, the grace which does actually reconcile man with God."

16. *CD* II, 2, section 35, 338–40.

17. *CD* II, 2, section 35, 410–19.

18. *CD* II, 2, section 35, 449–58, 494–97.

19. See the cautious but relatively clear direction of thought articulated in *CD* II, 2, section 35, 417–19.

20. See the particularly interesting discussion of God's use of the figure of Judas in *CD* II, 2, section 35, 502–6.

factical damnation is perceived in much of Christian theology even as a potential threat to the very existence of a coherent Christian theology.[21] Such an idea would eclipse an authentic understanding of the power of God in the service of his triumphant goodness. If all are not saved, then God's transcendent innocence is imperiled, and so is the very truth of Christianity.

We find in the eschatology of Barth an inversion of the problem brought on by Calvin specifically. Neither theology seems to depict adequately a world in which God's sovereign love for the creature is echoed by analogy in the creature's real capacity to love God freely, and so also to refuse grace freely and turn away from the mystery of Christ. For both Calvin and Barth, in contrast to the Council of Trent, Grace is deemed irresistible. With Calvin it is given only to some, while with Barth it is ultimately accorded to all. This leads critics of the Calvinist paradigm to the concern that for Calvinists the souls of the reprobate never truly had the possibility of accepting God's grace. This leads critics of the Barthian paradigm to the concern that for Barthians the elect never really had the possibility of the free, final refusal of God's grace. In either case, the triumph of the divine will seems to require an eventual vanquishing or eclipsing of the human will, no matter how sublimely this resolution is portrayed. The inverted Calvinism of Barth, while reaching a much more benign outcome than that the theology of double predestination, seems to veer toward a form of Gnostic dualism in which our historical decisions in time have no ultimate capacity to effect eternity, as real decisions we make in this life—of love or lovelessness—have no proportionate bearing upon the state we inhabit before God for all eternity.[22]

Hans Urs von Balthasar famously stated that "love alone is worthy of belief."[23] Is this statement true? Adequate depiction of divine love is more a *sine qua non* condition for theology than a sufficient condition

21. See the helpful analysis of Richard Schenk, "The Epoché of Factical Damnation: On the Costs of Bracketing Out the Likelihood of Final Loss," *Logos* 1 (1997): 122–54.

22. I explore this argument at greater length in Thomas Joseph White, *The Incarnate Lord: A Thomistic Study in Christology* (Washington, DC: Catholic University of America Press, 2015), chap. 9.

23. Hans Urs von Balthasar, *Love Alone: The Way of Revelation* (London: Sheed and Ward, 1968). Here, following Barth, Balthasar expresses the idea of universal salvation for all as a hope, rather than a certitude (78–80). Yet he does characterize this hope as one pertaining to the "effective" intervention of God in the lives of all persons, over and above all their finite refusals (79).

as such. After all, divine wisdom is worthy of belief, too, and so is divine truth. We might restate his claim in a more qualified fashion, therefore, by saying that whatever is genuinely worthy of belief must always shine forth with the radiant splendor of divine love. Without love there is no theology. In the medieval Augustinian paradigm of the doctrine of predestination, divine love predominates both in God's actions with regard to the predestined and in a real sense also with regard to the reprobate, both in God's expressions of eternal omnipotence and his expressions of divine innocence. The key to this balance is found in the twin affirmations of the universal offer of the possibility of salvation (which is motivated by God's love for all in Christ), and that of the real possibility of human refusal (which follows from God's perennial loving respect for each spiritual creature in its genuine freedom). God in his omnipotence gives grace to all and leads some inexorably to eternal life. God in his innocence allows human beings to refuse his grace, permitting some to persist in their willful refusal of the mystery of Christ. If we wish to avoid an unhelpful dualism that divorces God's providence from any real relation to history, there has to be a clear intellectual bridge that extends from the world of human choice making to the eternal consequences of human decisions. At the same time, this history has to be interpreted in light of the transcendent omnipotence and innocence of God, so that each of these attributes together shine through in the mystery of human salvation as well as in the mystery of the human refusal of divine grace. In all of this, the mystery of God's eternal love has to be made manifest, or else we have failed to reflect adequately upon the mystery of the Gospel of grace.

Principles

In what follows, I pose six principles that I take to be normative for any sufficiently balanced Catholic account of predestination. In doing so, I have recourse to principles drawn from the thought of Thomas Aquinas as the common doctor of Catholic theology. I am not presuming that only Thomists may advance the six principles in question. In fact, the contrary is the case. What is presumed here is merely that Aquinas and some of his subsequent interpreters in the Thomistic tradition provide us with a refined account of the doctrine predestination, one that rightly underscores both the omnipotence and innocence of God, the primacy of grace and the reality of human freedom, the eternity of divine fore-knowledge and the real distinction between what God wills and what God merely permits or tolerates. The Thomist account is able to hold these features in healthy tension in such a way as to present us with a mystery that is both luminous and obscure, intelligible and numinous. The balance and depth of this account preserve the truths of the New Testament and of the Augustinian heritage of Western theology in consonance with the sound principles of realistic metaphysics and of ordinary human experience.

All that is morally good in the human person comes from the creative activity and providential assistance of God.

The scriptures of the Old and New Testament teach that God is the author of all created being.[24] As understood in the Catholic tradition, this teaching has a clear metaphysical content.[25] God is the author and giver of all that exists, not only in its historical origins (a first beginning of creation in time), but also in its actual existence. This means that all that is exists only insofar as it is actually given being by God. It is also ontologically good by virtue of its existence. Goodness is in some sense coexistent with being.[26]

Human freedom is a reality included among all that exists, itself a property of the voluntary faculty in a human soul. The voluntary faculty is in effect the appetite of human intellect or reason.[27] We may eventually learn to love, desire, and choose freely what we first come to know rationally.[28] Knowledge gives rise to love, and love gives rise to freedom. To choose freely is natural to human beings, because human beings are rational animals. Reason and freedom are embedded ineluctably in the human spiritual soul as constitutive of human identity, specifying ontologically what kind of reality we are. Because we are given being by God in each moment to be this kind of being, so too we are given by God in each moment to be an autonomous self-mover, a rational animal who makes free decisions by knowledge and by love.

24. Gen 1:1; Is 43:1; Ps 115:15; Wis 7:17–22, 11:18; Jn 1:1–3; Col 1:16–17.
25. Consider, e.g., the influential ruminations on creation ex nihilo of Augustine in *Confessions*, XII, esp. chap. 38.
26. Aquinas, *On Truth*, q. 1, a. 1; *Summa Theologiae (ST)* I, q. 5.
27. *ST* I, qq. 82–83.
28. *ST* I, q. 83, a. 3; I-II, q. 13, aa. 1–2.

We can conclude from this first principle two things. First, if we begin from realistic metaphysical premises, there is no rivalry possible between God as the first cause of our existence who gives us *to be*, and human free agents as secondary causes who are truly free in and of themselves.[29] Created causes are causes in and of themselves even as they are causes only ever from and because of God. The condition of the possibility for there to be human free agents is the Creator, who gives them being and sustains them in existence precisely as free rational creatures in each moment. Aquinas distinguishes between created causes that act by necessity and contingent free causes.[30] The former act by the requirements of the internal principle of their natures and have predictable results, as when water "necessarily" dissolves various substances if they are immersed within it. The latter, however, are determined from within by rational deliberation. We cannot tell in advance what a given person will choose, even if we can make predictions that are more or less likely. It is precisely this kind of real, contingent freedom that we experience in everyday life that God sustains in being by virtue of his creative causality.

Second, all that we choose that is authentically morally good is a gift of God. This is the case even in the order of created nature, prescinding from any consideration of the gift of grace and the mystery of salvation.[31] God gives us the kind of existent nature that can make morally praiseworthy actions, and so he is the primary author of all that is morally good in us just insofar as these actions exist.[32] This does not mean that there is no such thing as a genuinely morally praiseworthy or blameworthy act, as we shall come to say shortly. On the contrary, the principle of nonrivalry just established means that human actions can be authentically free and morally good primarily because God causes them to be. This metaphysical principle, when rightly understood, does not undermine human freedom, but establishes it as real. The transcendent exemplar of human spiritual freedom is the divine freedom of God, and it is only because there exists a primary cause of spiritual freedom that our created human freedom can come into existence.[33] What this claim does

---

29. *ST* I, q. 19, aa. 4 and 8; q. 105, a. 4, ad 2.   30. *ST* I, q. 19, a. 8; q. 82, aa. 1–2.
31. *ST* I, q. 47, a. 1.   32. *ST* I, q. 19, aa. 2 and 4; q. 105, a. 5.
33. As Jean-Baptiste Gonet pointed out in his critique of Molinism in the *Clypeus theologiae Thomisticae contra novos eius impugnatores* (Cologne: 1671), p. 1, tr. 3, disp. 6, 1:285b–362a, esp. aa. 5–6, 296b–318a. See the analysis of Ulrich G. Leinsle, *Introduction to Scholastic Theology* (Washington, DC: Catholic University of America Press, 2010).

imply, however, is that all that is genuinely praiseworthy in a human being's moral action is also always more fundamentally an ontological gift from God. We depend always upon God the Creator for all the moral good that exists within us.

For Aquinas, this is the case not only just insofar as such a given good moral action exists, but also insofar as God's help or *auxilium* is required for every free agent who moves himself from potency to act, from the capacity to do something good to the act of doing it.[34] We are self-movers who make voluntary free decisions, and are not compelled to act from any external created cause. But even when we do self-actuate, we are able to do so only because God, who is not an external created cause but the Creator, is more immanent to our own being than we are to ourselves. In being present to our human freedom, God not only sustains it in existence, but also moves us from within to do the good as only a uniquely transcendent cause can. God alone can act "from within the depths of our being" so as to move us ontologically *to act of ourselves* in the radically free, contingent, and spontaneous way what we are naturally capable of doing. This is not a claim that we are determined passively to act owing to divine causality, but it is the inverse claim. Because God is present in the most intimate depths of our being, moving us to do the good in an authentically natural, human way, therefore (and ultimately only because of this divine activity!) can we truly determine ourselves in genuine freedom to do what is good.

All that the human person does that is morally evil stems from a truly free, morally culpable, and naturally defective action of the creature.

The second principle, which is deeply interrelated to the first, has to do with the origins of moral evil. Here we must reclaim a central tenet of Augustinian thought that was formulated in the face of Manichaeism: evil is the privation of the good, and, consequently, evil is also a kind of privation of being. The morally evil act is an act that is deprived of its right rectitude, and therefore of the fullness of being and goodness.[35]

Aquinas understood the subtly and challenge of thinking through this Augustinian theological claim. On the one hand, all that is in the human person must be good insofar as it exists, and has its primary origin in

34. *ST* I-II, q. 109, aa. 1–2; I, q. 105, a. 4, ad 2.
35. Augustine, *Confessions* VII, xii(18)–xiv(20); *ST* I, q. 48.

God. Therefore moral evil must consist in a defect of human choosing that comes from the creature and that is truly morally culpable. On the other hand, an evil action is something real in itself, a metaphysical mode of being that depends upon God the Creator, who sustains the creature in being even as it commits a moral error that is contrary to the divine will.

Here Aquinas offers us a set of distinct but related ideas that are helpful but that also coexist in some degree of conceptual tension. First, it is clear from Aquinas's treatment of the morally free act in *De Malo*, q. 6, that he takes it as given that a morally free agent who does evil has the power to do otherwise and does not act by necessity. Consequently, the morally evil agent cannot be excused on the basis of the claim that God simply did not give him the power, ability, and fundamental inclination to do the good. On the contrary, it is only because he has all of these that his action is truly morally disoriented and blameworthy. Were this not the case, or were God to withhold the assistance sufficient to the creature to do what is right, the creature would not be culpable.

Some have held that the human will is necessarily moved to choose things.... But this opinion is heretical. For it takes away reason for merit and demerit in human acts, as it does not seem meritorious or demeritorious for persons to do necessarily what they could not avoid doing. It is also to be counted among the oddest of philosophical opinions, since it is not only contrary to faith, but also subverts all the principles of moral philosophy. For if nothing is within our power, and we are necessarily moved to will things, deliberation, exhortation, precept, punishment, praise and blame, of which moral philosophy consists, are destroyed.[36]

Second, in the case of an act of moral evil, it is true, Aquinas notes, that God causes the act to be that is morally evil. And yet here Aquinas also sees the significance of Augustine's stance against Manicheanism: insofar as a reality is, it is from God, but insofar as it is evil, it is subject to a privation that does not come from God. If we apply this to the domain of the morally defective action, then we must say that the creature who misuses his freedom is the primary origin of the moral defect in the act. God is not responsible for the defect of the act.[37] Nor does he will it either directly or indirectly.[38]

---

36. Aquinas, *On Evil*, q. 6. Translation by R. Regan, trans., *On Evil* (New York: Oxford University Press, 2003).

37. *ST* I-II, q. 75, a. 1.

38. *ST* I, q. 19, a. 9; I-II, q. 79, a. 1.

Of course this point may seem in strange tension with the first principle mentioned above: that God as the Creator who is within us "moves" us to each good act we do in such a way that we are truly free only in ontological dependence upon the Creator. Even if we presume that that kind of account of divine causality is compatible with genuine human freedom, is it still compatible with divine innocence? Does such an idea not entail that in the case of the morally evil act, God deprives the human soul of some assistance necessary so that it might avoid evil and do the good?

Aquinas notes that it does not. Here we come to the nonparallelism of good and evil actions. In the "ascendant" order of action oriented toward the good, the prior initiative of God is always present, as the transcendent primary origin of all the good we do.[39] In the case of evil actions, however, Aquinas provides a subtle analysis that is of major significance. An evil action exists and depends upon God for its very being.[40] Furthermore, as with the good actions we do, evil actions depend upon the transcendent internal motion of God, who moves the human soul from ontological potentiality to act or from the capacity to do evil to the real engagement in evil. Nevertheless, the act is only evil because of a prior intention on the part of the created agent that is deprived of rational integrity. In his choice making, the human agent fails to refer sufficiently to the rule of truth.[41] Here Aquinas distinguishes a negation in the act from a privation that results. The negation or nonbeing of the morally evil action is found in the "non-reference to the rule" or the absence of regard for the moral truth in the intellect of the agent. The privation is present subsequently to the negation and results from it.

A sin is an inordinate act. Accordingly, so far as it is an act, it can have a direct cause, even as any other act; but, so far as it is inordinate, it has a cause, in the same way as a negation or privation can have a cause. Now two causes may be assigned to a negation: in the first place, absence of the cause of affirmation; i.e. the negation of the cause itself, is the cause of the negation in itself; since the result of removing the cause is the removal of the effect: thus the absence of the sun is the cause of darkness. In the second place, the cause of an affirmation, of which a negation is a sequel, is the accidental cause of the resulting negation: thus fire by causing heat in virtue of its principal tendency,

39. Logically and ontologically prior, not temporally prior.
40. *ST* I-II, q. 79, a. 2.
41. *ST* I-II, q. 75, aa. 1–2; *On Evil*, q. 2, a. 2.

consequently causes a privation of cold. The first of these suffices to cause a simple negation. But, since the inordinateness of sin and of every evil is not a simple negation, but the privation of that which something ought naturally to have, such an inordinateness must needs have an accidental efficient cause. For that which naturally is and ought to be in a thing, is never lacking except on account of some impeding cause. And accordingly we are wont to say that evil, which consists in a certain privation, has a deficient cause, or an accidental efficient cause. Now every accidental cause is reducible to the direct cause. Since then sin, on the part of its inordinateness, has an accidental efficient cause, and on the part of the act, a direct efficient cause, it follows that the inordinateness of sin is a result of the cause of the act. Accordingly then, the will lacking the direction of the rule of reason and of the Divine law, and intent on some mutable good, causes the act of sin directly, and the inordinateness of the act, indirectly, and beside the intention: for the lack of order in the act results from the lack of direction in the will.[42]

Here St. Thomas is saying that a free action that is not grounded in the truth is deprived of right reason, and therefore ontologically disordered by privation. This falling away from the plenitude of being is the evil in us Augustine noted so well. We diminish ourselves by evil and become less than we were intended to be because we do not refer our actions to the moral truth about ourselves, but walk in the darkness of the lie, one that diminishes our very being.

In this account, Aquinas has preserved a sharp sense of the divine innocence while also affirming divine omnipotence. God does give us the positive being to do what we choose to do, so that we can pass from the capacity to act to the activity. But he is innocent of the disorder of our moral actions because these fall away from the truth, not by a deficit on the part of God but from a deficit that arises from within ourselves, a lack of self-reference to the truth.

Why, though, do we fail to refer ourselves to the truth *prior* to the commission of a morally deformed action? Here St. Thomas pushes his analysis back to the first principle and cause of moral evil: the metaphysical "mystery" of the failure of the will to love the authentic good.[43] Following Augustine, St. Thomas notes that the created will is inherently

---

42. *ST* I-II, q. 75, a. 1. Translation by the English Dominican Province, trans., *Summa Theologica* (New York: Benziger Brothers, 1947). See the helpful analysis of this passage by Jean-Hervé Nicolas in *Synthèse Dogmatique: Complément, de l'Univers à la Trinité* (Fribourg: Éditions Universitaires Fribourg and Éditions Beauchesne, 1993), 361–96.

43. *ST* I, q. 63, aa. 1 and 4.

ontologically imperfect, and is created from nothing. Therefore, unlike the divine will that is perfect, the human will can fail to love and do the good.[44] What is mysterious is that the human being can fail to love what is more noble and perfect, preferring instead what is less noble and perfect, in such a way as to diminish its own nobility and happiness. God does give the morally culpable person the sufficient knowledge, capacity, and inclination to love and choose the good, or else the creature would not be culpable for its evil actions.[45] But the human will can, having all these natural capacities, fall away from the good by a kind of moral unraveling or internal spiritual corruption. This leads to a willful negation of the truth, one that occurs despite a genuine alternative possibility for the good. "They refused to love the truth, and so be saved" (2 Thess 2:10). The disorder in the action originates not from a privation of the gift of being on the part of the Creator, but from a culpable defect in the love of the creature. Creaturely evil originates from the mystery of freely accepted disordered human love.

The mystery of salvation by grace stems primarily from the initiative of God, whose gifts of grace precede all works of cooperation on the part of the free human creature.

This third principle can be articulated somewhat succinctly, and yet is the central claim of the Augustinian teaching on grace. I have said above that all that is ontologically good in the human creature originates from God the Creator, even in the order of nature alone, prescinding from the order of grace. How much more is this the case in the domain of the supernatural, where grace is that infused "gift" of divine life, by which human beings are healed of the wounds of sin, and elevated into a participation in the life of God.[46] Based on a careful reading of the New Testament, medieval Augustinian theologians made unarbitrary distinctions regarding the life of grace in us, noting various effects brought about by the initiative of God. Prevenient operative graces are those that precede our conversion and stir up in us an initial interest in and openness to the mystery of Christ.[47] The grace of "justification" occurs through the in-

44. *ST* I, q. 48, a. 2, ad 3; *On Evil*, q. 1, a. 3, and q. 16, a. 3; See Augustine, *City of God* XII, 5–8. See Nicolas, *Synthèse Dogmatique*, 378–86.

45. *On Evil*, q. 3, a. 2.

46. *ST* I-II, q. 110, aa. 1–2.

47. See Augustine, *On Grace and Free Will*, chap. 33[xvii].

fusion of the "theological virtues" of faith, hope, and charity.[48] These infused habits are the root of "cooperative grace," because they enable us to
act in stable ways in conformity with the life of God in us.[49] Such grace
is sanctifying, in turn, because it can grow more intense over time and
is accompanied by infused moral virtues and the gifts of the Holy Spirit
acting in the soul.[50] By virtue of this cooperation, the Holy Spirit can live
or dwell within the soul in an enduring way as a welcomed guest and
active source of spiritual inspiration and direction.[51] The grace of perseverance is that by which the soul perdures in the pathway of penance
and sanctification even unto death.[52] Finally, beatification results from
God's gift of the *lumen gloriae*, the light of glory, by which the human
soul granted to see the eternal essence of God by immediate intellectual
intuition, to behold the mystery of the Holy Trinity "face to face."[53]

The aim of the doctrine of predestination in this domain is to signal
that in all of these graces—prevenient awakening, justification, sanctification, perseverance, glorification—it is always God who takes the primary initiative in the order of the gift. Christ in the Gospel of St. John
teaches that "no one can come to me unless the Father who sent me draws
him" (Jn 6:44). And likewise St. Paul asks, "What do you have that you
have not received?" (1 Cor 4:7). It follows from this way of thinking about
the mystery of salvation that the gifts of grace, including even those of final perseverance and entrance into eternal life, are never given in view of
foreseen merits on the part of the creature, as if the creature were in any
way to earn *by its own natural powers and efforts* either the initial offer of
grace or the gift of justification or the process of sanctification or the gift
of final perseverance or beatification in eternal life. All of this is always
only God's gratuitous gift, even when the soul is also given the grace to
cooperate with the work of God in it. The creature can only cooperate
freely with the gifts of God because God himself gives the creature infused habitual graces that render possible this stable cooperation.

---

48. *ST* I-II, qq. 62–63.
50. *ST* I-II, q. 113, prologue, and q. 114.
52. *ST* I-II, q. 109, a. 10; q. 114, a. 9.

49. *ST* I-II, q. 111, a. 2.
51. *ST* I, q. 43, a. 4, ad 2; a. 5, ad 3.
53. *ST* I-II, q. 114, aa. 2–3.

God offers the possibility of salvation to all human persons. The mystery
of perdition originates from the free defective resistance to or refusal of the
mystery of grace.

The Catholic Church traditionally claims that God offers the possibility of salvation by grace to all.[54] The idea is contained in Scripture,
overtly in the apostolic teaching of 1 Tm 2:4—"[God] wills all men to be
saved and to come to the knowledge of the truth"—and implicitly in the
unambiguous affirmations that Christ offered his life on behalf of all human beings (1 Jn 2:1–2; 1 Pt 3:18; 2 Pt 3:9). Although Augustine did speculate in various texts that God might only offer salvation to some persons
and not to others, medieval Augustinians were more often universalist
in this respect.[55] Aquinas is quite clear in multiple texts that the offer
of salvation is made to all.[56] Likewise in the seventeenth century, the
Church rejected the theory of limited atonement (found in Jansenius's
Augustinus), and in the twentieth century taught in *Gaudium et Spes* that
God offers to all the possibility of being configured in some way to the
Paschal Mystery of Christ, so as to be saved by his unique grace.[57]

At the same time, the Church has underscored just as insistently that
the grace of God can be resisted or refused. This teaching has clear biblical warrant.[58] Even though Augustine does not have any unambiguous
sympathy for the idea, it is found in Prosper of Aquitaine, Leo the Great,
and the subsequent Augustinian tradition.[59] Aquinas speaks clearly of
the capacity of a soul to place an obstacle (*impedimentum*) to the gift of

---

54. See *Catechism of the Catholic Church*, §§74, 618, 851.

55. For what seems to be an affirmation of the restricted offer of salvation, see Augustine's *On the Predestination of the Saints* I, 8; and *Enchridion*, no. 103. On the medieval Augustinian tradition, see Yves Congar, "Ecclesia ab Abel," in *Abhandlungen über theologische
Kirche: Festschrift für Karl Adam*, ed. Marcel Reding (Düsseldorf: Patmos-Verlag, 1952),
79–108; and Bernard Sesboüé, *Hors de l'Eglise pas de salut* (Paris: Desclée de Brouwer, 2004).

56. See, e.g., Aquinas, *In I Tim.* II, lec. 1, and *In Heb.* XII, lec. 3, for unambiguous affirmations that God offers the grace of salvation to all human persons. Aquinas does have a
restricted notion of salvation offered to children who die without baptism before the age of
reason (limbo), a point I will not consider in this context. See on this topic *The Incarnate
Lord*, chap. 9.

57. Pope Innocent X, in his 1653 document *Cum occasione*, denoted as "impious…
dishonoring to divine piety, and heretical" the proposition of the *Augustinus*: "It is
semi-Pelagian to say that Christ died or shed His blood for all men without exception"
(Denz. 2005). See also Vatican II, *Gaudium et Spes*, §22.

58. See, e.g., Is 50:5; Mt 5:22, 7:1–5, 11:20–24, 12:41–42; Acts 7:51.

59. See the analysis of Prosper, Leo, and their subsequent influence in Hwang, *Intrepid
Lover of Perfect Grace*, chap. 6.

grace and of culpable resistance to the inward workings of grace (*resis-tentem gratiae*).[60] The real possibility of refusal of grace was affirmed doctrinally by the Council of Trent, multiple times in relation to Jansenism, and repeatedly in the modern teaching of the Church.[61]

In the Catholic tradition, there are diverse theories about the working of grace in the soul and about the nature of culpable resistance to grace. Thomists sometimes affirm that God gives grace in an intrinsically effective manner, meaning that whatever grace God wishes us to receive will be received effectively.[62] How, then, can anyone ever resist or refuse the workings of grace? The resistance is based on what the free human creature does once he has received the gift of grace. If a person places an obstacle to the work of grace in himself, the organic effect of that grace can be impeded, as the stem of a tree is maimed or destroyed before it can blossom with fruits. Grace can be given, for example, in a way that is sufficient to move a subject to contrition of sins and to active repentance, but this grace (which works in the form of a power and inclination given to the soul by the Holy Spirit) can be freely undermined or refused out of a wrongly ordered love of the kind we have considered above (with regard to morally evil actions).[63] In the confrontation with the gifts and

---

60. See, e.g., *Summa contra Gentiles* III, ch. 160–61; *On Evil*, q. 3, a. 1, ad 8; *In II Sent.*, d. 27, q. 1, a. 4, ad 4; *On Truth*, q. 24, a. 11, ad 6; *In Ioan.* XV, lec. 5, no. 2055.

61. Council of Trent, *Decree on Justification*, ch. 5; and canons 4, 5, 6, and 17 (Denz. 1525, 1554–56, 1567). See also the condemnation of Jansenius's second proposition, that grace is always irresistible (Denz. 2002), repeated in a variety of forms against Pasquier Quesnel (Denz. 2410–45). See also the *Catechism of the Catholic Church*, §§678 and 2002.

62. See, e.g., Norbert del Prado, *De Gratia et Libero Arbitrio*, part II (Fribourg: St. Paul, 1907), 427–67, 521–67; Jean-Hervé Nicolas, *Les Profondeurs de la Grace* (Paris: Beauchesne, 1969), 184–219.

63. Aquinas, *In Ioan.* XV, lec. 5, no. 2055: "The second question is about the truth of the conditional statement, that if Christ had not done among them works which no one else did, the Jews would not have the sin of disbelief. My reply is that if we speak of any of the miracles indiscriminately, the Jews would have been excusable if they had not been done among them by Christ. For no one can come to Christ by faith unless he is drawn: 'No one can come to me unless the Father who sent me draws him' (6:44). So the spouse says in the Song (1:4): 'Draw me after you.' Therefore, if there were no one who had drawn them to the faith, they would have an excuse for their disbelief. Note that Christ drew by words and by signs, both visible and invisible, that is, by inciting and stirring hearts from within: 'The king's heart is a stream of water in the hand of the Lord' (Prv 21:1). And so an inner impulse to act well is the work of God, and those who resist it sin. If not, Stephen would have no reason to say: 'You always resist the Holy Spirit' (Acts 7:51). And Isaiah (50:5) says: 'The Lord has opened my ear,' that is, the ear of my heart, 'and I was not rebellious.' When our Lord said, 'If I had not done among them the works which no one else did,' we have to understand this

illuminations of grace, the soul can choose what is less noble, true, and good, and prefer what is not supernatural to what is, in such a way as to snuff out the work of grace in itself.

If we consider this last idea in relation to the third principle mentioned above, we might have a reasonable objection to make. How is it that when the soul ascends steadily upward toward God by more perfect actions, God always has the ontologically precedent initiative to lead the soul toward himself by grace, while when the soul turns away or back from the offer of grace, it is the soul that has the precedent and not God? Should we not be more consistent and say simply that in some cases God offers to a soul the effective grace of repentance or perseverance, while in other cases he simply does not offer the soul the grace sufficient for its conversion or its perseverance in sanctity?

According to the theory I am presenting, two extremes are to be avoided. One is the notion that God simply does not offer to human beings the grace that is sufficient to make their salvation really possible, and only makes this offer to some. Such a view obscures the revealed goodness of Christ crucified, and the universality of his love. The other extreme would claim that God offers to all equal grace sufficient for their salvation, and then reacts or responds to the good will each person shows in the use of this initial gift of grace. This latter theory, originating from Luis Molina, suggests that the soul can act supernaturally in quasi-independence from the ontologically prior initiative and sustaining gift of God in the order of grace.[64] It seems inevitably to make the soul the primary author of its own salvation.

The middle way is to affirm that God offers grace truly sufficient for salvation to all such that all have the real possibility of attaining to salvation, and that simultaneously God mysteriously shows a just respect for some who refuse the gift of grace while showing a predilection of mercy for others who he converts to himself. God effectively offers grace to

---

as referring not only to visible works but also to the interior impulses and attractions to his teaching. If these had not been done among them, they would not have sin. It is now clear how they could have been excused, that is, if he had not accomplished miraculous works among them." J. Weisheipl and F. Larcher, trans., *Commentary on the Gospel of St. John*, part 2 (Petersham, MA: St. Bede's Press, 2000).

64. Typical Thomist concerns with the Molinist theory are noted by Réginald Garrigou-Lagrange, *Grace* (St. Louis: Herder, 1952), chaps. 7 and 8, which contain a Báñezian assessment of the Molinist and Congruist accounts of efficacious grace.

some human creatures while allowing them subsequently to turn away from him culpably. God tolerates this out of a mysterious respect for the freedom of his creature, one that is just, and even in a certain sense merciful, because God continues to sustain in being those who culpably refuse his mystery. In other cases, God offers grace to creatures and then pursues them by a kind of persistence of divine mercy. In this latter case, God acts to convert a soul to himself ineluctably and infallibly, so that even if the soul sins gravely, it repents after it sins, and learns little by little to cooperate with the grace of Christ in stable and enduring ways. If God truly offers the possibility of salvation to all, why does God allow souls to turn away from himself freely in some cases, while drawing souls to himself effectively in other cases? Here we confront the Augustinian principle of predilection in the order of salvation. All receive grace such that no one can claim to be inculpable if he rejects the grace of God. But some receive a greater grace than others, so that no one can claim to have earned more favor than others as a result of his own natural merits. If we are saved, it is due to the gift of God working in us. If we are lost, it is due to our own fatal initiative of forsaking the offer of God.

It might seem that one should seek to avoid this schema altogether by insisting unequivocally that God simply offers the same degree or intensity of assistance to each one, and that eternal salvation or final perdition stems uniquely from the work that the human free will does under such conditions. Of course this theory has been developed in detail by the Molinists of the seventeenth century, and especially in the mature formulations of Molinist theory by the so-called Congruists, Robert Bellarmine and Francisco Suarez.[65] The problems with this strategy are multiple, but we can name one that pertains directly to our considerations here. Let us say that we admit that some souls are saved while others are not, and that the theory of *apokatastasis panton* is to be refused. In this case, it is clear that *in the end* some souls must receive greater grace than others, because some are beatified while others are not. Let us also admit that God foresees this outcome from all eternity (i.e., God knows the eschatological future and governs the world in this light). But if these presuppositions are taken for granted, and we then suppose that

65. For a helpful and somewhat sympathetic introduction to Molinism, see Alfred Freddoso, "Introduction to the Problem of Free Will and Divine Causality," http://www3 .nd.edu/~afreddos/papers/freedom%20and%20God.pdf.

the difference of final outcome does not come from the distinction of degrees of grace received *internal to the soul* by the transcendent agency of God, then the differences in outcome can only arise from outside circumstances (such as God arranging the temporal order providentially so that soul A will choose Y while soul B will choose Z). This is in effect the Congruist thesis: that God's predilection consists not first and foremost in the distinction of intensive degrees of grace given to the human soul interiorly, but in the diverse forms of providential assistance given to the soul in exterior fashion (through events in the world that dispose the soul to choose the life of grace freely by its own powers). In Molinism or Congruism, therefore, the mystery of predilection is not avoided but simply moved to another site. By the governance of congruent circumstances external to the act of the created will itself, God disposes some to use their freedom better than others. He knows from all eternity that he will give greater help to some than he does to others.

To avoid any notion of predilection on the part of God, then, one would have to affirm a more radical postulate than one provided by Molinism. One could do this by affirming that (1) all souls in the end are in hell, (2) all souls are saved, or (3) that some are saved and others are not, but that God does not govern the world of his creation in view of ends that he foreknows infallibly and effectively intends from all eternity.[66] The first two options are inherently problematic for doctrinal reasons. What about the third option? In this case, God would *estimate* by an imperfect knowledge that some *might* be lost, but would not know the future yet in an infallible fashion, and would be aiding all souls equally in the interim period.

Evidently, this position denies that God knows future singular contingencies, and therefore undermines the claim of classical theism that God has a comprehensive divine omniscience. This viewpoint, however, implicitly stands in contradiction with the very idea that God is the Creator of the world. Why is this the case? For classical theism, God knows all that is because he is the author of all that exists, and indeed he knows all things by virtue of the knowledge he has of own essence. This must be the case, as God creates all that is based on the knowledge he has of

---

66. For a contemporary version of the latter view, see the "open theism" of Johannes Grössl in *Die Freiheit des Menschen als Risiko Gottes* (Münster: Aschendorff, 2015).

himself and from himself, without prior reference to any other preexisting entities. God knows everything that will come to be by virtue of his omniscience as Creator. Evidently, if this is the case, the third option we have just proposed is not realistic. Because God is truly the Creator of all that exists, he must know the future from all eternity, because he creates it from and through the knowledge he has of his very essence. This future includes a diversity of final states of souls, some that are saved and some that are damned. It is not possible, then, on the supposition of the revealed truth about final beatitude and factical damnation, to avoid some version of the Augustinian principle of predilection. God knows from all eternity that there are some who are to be saved and some who are not. If some are lost, this is not because of any neglect on God's part, but because of his desire to respect created human freedom, which has the capacity to refuse the offer of salvation.

God foreknows all who will be saved from all eternity, and his divine will for their salvation is the effective cause of their predestination to divine glory.

The fifth principle is the most characteristic of the Augustinian theory of predestination. God foreknows all who will be saved from all eternity, and his divine will for their salvation is the transcendent primary cause of their salvation.[67] We can positively state this principle by reconsidering the first and third of the principles mentioned above. God is the primary author of all that is good in us, and all that has being within us is a gift of God. God is also the primary initiator of the gifts of grace we receive, from conversion and justification to sanctification, perseverance, and beatification. If we add to this the notion that God is eternal, and that God possesses within himself a plenary knowledge (from all eternity) of all that he creates and sustains in being, then we must conclude that God has eternal knowledge of all the positive gifts of grace that have ever or will ever be conveyed to creatures in the order of time.[68]

Furthermore, God gives these gifts of grace to the creatures that he beatifies antecedently of any foreseen merits on their part.[69] The reason one must hold this is that the creature cannot elevate itself into the realm of supernatural grace by its own natural capacities.[70] Nor can the crea-

---

67. *ST* I, q. 23, aa. 2, 4.
69. *ST* I, q. 23, a. 5.

68. *ST* I, q. 23, a. 6.
70. *ST* I-II, q. 62, aa. 1–3.

ture who is in a state of grace cooperate with that grace without continued supernatural assistance (the *auxilium* that accompanies the infused theological virtues).[71] Nor can the creature who is actively cooperating with God by grace persevere in the life of grace by its natural powers alone, without the special assistance of God.[72] In short, all that the creature receives in the order of cooperative grace (which is considered "meritorious" in a qualified but real sense) is always, already the gift of God. We can only walk up the pathway toward eternal life because God has already taken the prior initiative to lead us there.

Aquinas goes as far as to say that those who are predestined by God from all eternity to eternal life will be saved "infallibly."[73] By this he does not mean "necessarily" or in a "predetermined" way, if those words connote something in the creature that is compelled or necessitated by the transcendent activity of God. Aquinas here returns to the aforementioned distinction between necessary and contingent causes.[74] If the human being only ever attains to any decisions in life by means of an authentically contingent form of self-determination, then this will be the case also for decisions of the human person made under the effects of grace. We should go further and say that the life of grace according to Aquinas makes a person more free and not less so, more apt to choose contingently and deliberately those authentic goods that alone can ennoble the person, and make the heart truly happy. Nevertheless, when the human person does choose in this way by authentic acts of deliberate freedom, it does so as a finite creature dependent in all that it is qua free agent upon the transcendent creative gift of God, and as a creature stimulated in its inmost ontological core by God's wholly interior, nonviolent premotions. The work of God's grace within us, then, does not

---

71. *ST* I-II, q. 109, a. 9; q. 114, a. 8.   72. *ST* I-II, q. 114, a. 9.

73. *ST* I, q. 23, a. 6.

74. *ST* I, q. 23, a. 6. "Predestination most certainly and infallibly takes effect; yet it does not impose any necessity, so that, namely, its effect should take place from necessity. For...predestination is a part of providence. But not all things subject to providence are necessary; some things happening from contingency, according to the nature of the proximate causes, which divine providence has ordained for such effects. Yet the order of providence is infallible...So also the order of predestination is certain; yet free-will is not destroyed; whence the effect of predestination has its contingency. Moreover all that has been said about the divine knowledge and will [*ST* I, q. 14, a. 13; q. 19, a. 4] must also be taken into consideration; since they do not destroy contingency in things, although they themselves are most certain and infallible."

move us by necessity or any form of physical or psychological obligation. It does so rather as only the creative causality of God can, by causing our very freedom to be and to unfold according to its own exigencies, so that when we choose the good entirely freely and spontaneously, we do so in absolute dependence upon the ontologically prior, transcendent initiative of God. Because God gives us to do the good that we do in the order of grace, he also may predestine us from all eternity to such free actions, of which he is the primary author and which are entirely transparent to him in his omniscience as God.

God is eternally innocent of moral evil. Reprobation occurs in light of the antecedent permissive decree of God, which is in no way causal of sin.

The final principle serves to underscore in a most ultimate light the nonreciprocity of good actions as distinct from those that are morally evil. God is the eternal author of all that is good in the human person, including especially his or her free cooperation with grace in view of the participation in eternal life. But God never wills moral evil whether directly or indirectly—that is, as a result of God's providential desire—or as a foreseen and indirectly willed consequence of God's original plan for creation.[75] Moral evil exists only because of a culpable deficit arising in the free creature that misuses its capacities for good in order to turn culpably toward what is morally evil. Furthermore, to think rightly about God's eternal knowledge of human actions of evil, we must restate that God offers the real possibility of salvation by grace to all human persons, in some fashion and in some juncture in their personal histories.

At the same time, however, we must also underscore a significant biblical truth: God has an eternal knowledge as God of all past, present, and future actions of moral evil on the part of creatures.[76] He is not surprised by evil actions nor does he learn from them. Rather, as the author of all that exists, he knows all that is or that has being, through and through, including the voluntary deficits of his creatures whom he sustains in existence and to whom he continues to give being, even when they have misaligned moral intentions or when they sin. There is nothing in creation that God lacks knowledge of, including what from our vantage

---

75. *ST* I, q. 19, a. 9.
76. *ST* I, q. 14, aa. 10, 11, and 13.

point we might call the "future of moral evil" that has not yet come to pass. In truth, it is only if God can know the future of moral evil that he can respond effectively to it as God in his omnipotent goodness and mercy, by way of the mystery of the Incarnation, Passion, and Resurrection of Christ; the universal offer of grace; the mystery of the Church; and the eschatological judgment of the human race. If we remove the attribute of omniscience from our account of God in his knowledge of evil, then we also remove from him omnipotence as the Creator who knows all that is as the sovereign author of all that is. Consequently, if we remove from God his transcendent omnipotence so as to make him nescient of all evil, we also remove from God the power of his infinite goodness, innocence, and mercy to *remake the world in the face of creaturely evil*. In short, we remove from God the possibility of being our Savior. If God is truly our Savior, however, then God is omnipotent and omniscient (as well as good, just, and merciful). Consequently, God has an eternal knowledge of the evil we do, without being in any way the cause of that evil. Aquinas stipulates that God has no "divine idea" of evil, but knows it from all eternity as the privation of the goodness he intends for his creatures.[77] In light of the evil he foresees in creatures, God acts by virtue of his justice and mercy in order to redeem the world, principally through the Incarnation, Passion, and Resurrection of Christ.

If all that we have stated thus far is true, then it follows that God foreknows from all eternity the moral evil that his creatures accomplish. This foreknowledge is not causal, because God does not will that such evil transpires. Instead, Aquinas affirms that the transcendent, eternal foreknowledge of God is "permissive." God wills from all eternity to offer the grace of salvation to his creatures, but he also permits *from all eternity* that some freely turn away from his offer of grace.[78] Here again we meet up with the mystery of God's respect for creaturely freedom. Human freedom is imperfect and is naturally subject to potential failure. God permits some to refuse the good and to choose what is evil. The permission of God in this case is not the origin of the defect of the human action. As Domingo Báñez underscores in his reading of Aquinas on reprobation, the creature that is reprobated by God is reprobated only

---

77. *ST* I, q. 14, a. 10; q. 15.
78. *ST* I, q. 19, a. 12; q. 23, a. 3.

negatively (not positively). God does not positively will the damnation of the creature, but merely wills from all eternity to *allow* the creature to freely refuse the grace of God. The creature is then subsequently punished by God. However, the creature truly had the capacity to choose the good and should have done so. It was not denied assistance from God such that it could not have done otherwise.[79]

Here the nonparallelism between good acts and morally evil acts may seem strained to the point of incredulity. After all, if God is the principal author of all that is good in us in the order of grace, and if we are reprobated owing to the bad choices of our human will, then should we not conclude that God from all eternity desires to offer some the grace of a rightly aligned will that is converted to himself progressively over time, while to others he offers only a symbolic grace that is not truly efficacious? In this case, is God not the principal cause of reprobation as well as predestination? While this viewpoint may seem more metaphysically pure to some, and morally horrific to others, it is essentially inadequate both as an interpretation of Scripture and as a metaphysical reading of reality in its true complexity. What is obscured by this reductionistic explanation is the reality of the human evil act as something that truly violates the will of God for the good of the creature but that is simultaneously sustained in being by God and tolerated by his divine providence. That God should be the principal author of our salvation in the order of grace should cause us no offense, and to say so amounts merely to the realistic admission of our absolute dependence upon God in the order of grace. Likewise, however, any adequate theory of God's divine providence must be able to account for the fact that God allows or permits human beings to resist or refuse his grace, to stray from the moral good, to callously do evil, and that this is not unjust on the part of God, but is in some way an expression of his eternal respect for the creature's freedom.

---

79. Domingo Báñez offers this reading of *ST* I, q. 23, a. 3 (on reprobation), in his *Scholastica Commentaria in Primam Partem Summae Theologiae S. Thomae Aquinatis* (Madrid: FEDA, 1934), particularly commenting on ad 3 (491–97). His understanding of Aquinas on this point is indicative of the subsequent teaching of the Thomist school: "Indeed, as St. Thomas indicates in the third solution to this article, reprobation does not remove anything from the power of willing in the reprobate, nor diminish his freedom, just as we have said that the permission, by which God permits someone to sin, removes nothing from the power and freedom [of that person]. Therefore, he freely sins, he who could have not sinned, had he wished" (491; translation of the author).

Furthermore, God responds rightly to the moral evil of creatures who reject him, his grace, and the moral law by punishing them in proportionate and just ways.

What we know from the New Testament is that God's first response to all who sin is the universal offer of the grace of Christ, which is an offer of divine mercy and saving forgiveness in light of the truth. If this is the case, then we can say that the Thomist theory of God's "antecedent divine permissions" of sin from all eternity, far from being an obstacle to the theology of divine innocence, is in some way required if we are to maintain an adequate conception of God's universal offer of salvation to all human beings in the wake of human evil. Because God is wholly innocent, his response to the reality of human sin is the offer of grace and salvation, but because God is God, he also knows from all eternity all that will come to pass in time, including the reality of his rejection by some. This understanding of the universal outreach of God in his innocence is only truly compatible with the affirmation of his perfect eternal knowledge if we think that God foreknows comprehensively from all eternity the evil of the human race, but that he in no way causes it. This is the balance that the Thomist theory of the "antecedent permissive decree" of evil seeks to attain, and it has nothing in common with a voluntaristic desire on God's part to will evil in view of some kind of aesthetic or psychologically vindictive end.

Furthermore, one must consider God's final response to the *definitive and final* rejection of the grace of Christ. Here we come to the mystery of reprobation. God permits from all eternity that some creatures not only resist grace, but also persevere in their rejection of his grace. He then punishes them in light of their culpable rejection of that mystery.[80] Reprobation is not so much the activity of God in his just revindication as it is the inevitable confrontation after death of the sinful human person with the eternal truth of Christ, which in turn manifests the truth of the moral choice of the creature. When this occurs in the wake of the

---

80. *ST* I, q. 23, a. 3, ad 2: "Reprobation differs in its causality from predestination. This latter is the cause both of what is expected in the future life by the predestined—namely, glory—and of what is received in this life—namely, grace. Reprobation, however, is not the cause of what is in the present—namely, sin; but it is the cause of abandonment by God. It is the cause, however, of what is assigned in the future—namely, eternal punishment. But guilt proceeds from the free-will of the person who is reprobated and deserted by grace. In this way, the word of the prophet is true—namely, 'Destruction is thy own, O Israel.'"

creature's persistence in the rejection of God's grace and offer of mercy, then what results is the state of eternal loss or damnation.[81] The Thomist school has always underscored, as does the Church in her official teaching, that damnation is not caused primarily by God, but originates with the creature's refusal of the mystery of grace. Understood in this way, hell is authored only ever by human beings and angels, and not by God.[82] God does permit a creature to turn away from him freely and to persist in refusing his offer of grace. He even permits this from all eternity. Yet he in no way obliges the creature to fall. In the face of moral evil, God remains forever infinitely innocent, from eternity to eternity. "God is light and in him there is no darkness" (1 Jn 1:5).

Conclusion

How do we conclude this study? The six principles enunciated above might seem to exist in serious tension with one another, and it is easy to imagine how some seem directly opposed to others. To maintain the integrity of the mystery, however, the principles should be considered conceptually irreducible to one another in a way that is noncontradictory. We can think about this further by considering how they are interrelated, in three ways. First by considering the way the principles build upon one another like a conceptual ladder, second by considering the way they are bound together like a ring in which each node has an irreducible place. Here we can consider the irreplaceable role of apophaticism in conceiving of this mystery. Finally, we should return to the question of contemporary theology, the analogy of love, and a consideration of the promise of the traditional Catholic theology of predestination.

---

81. *Catechism of the Catholic Church*, §1037: "God predestines no one to go to hell; for this, a willful turning away from God (a mortal sin) is necessary, and persistence in it until the end. In the Eucharistic liturgy and in the daily prayers of her faithful, the Church implores the mercy of God, who does not want 'any to perish, but all to come to repentance' (2 Pet. 3:9)."

82. *Catechism of the Catholic Church*, §1033: "We cannot be united with God unless we freely choose to love him. But we cannot love God if we sin gravely against him, against our neighbor or against ourselves.... To die in mortal sin without repenting and accepting God's merciful love means remaining separated from him forever by our own free choice. This state of definitive self-exclusion from communion with God and the blessed is called 'hell.'"

A Ladder of Ascent

It should be evident that the six principles enunciated above are arranged in two groups of three. One set of principles pertains to the primacy of God in the order of the communication of the good. God gives being to all that exists naturally. God is the giver of grace such that he is the primary author of salvation. God wills to give grace from all eternity effectively in those who he predestines to eternal life. In stating things in this way, we emphasize the love of God as expressed through divine omnipotence and sovereignty. The other set of principles pertains to the primacy of the creature in the order of moral evil. The creature is the principal origin of the privation of truth and of moral rectitude that occurs in the morally deformed free action. The creature is able by a free defection of the will to turn from the truth and to resist or refuse the gift of grace. The creature who does evil and definitively refuses the mystery of grace is permitted to do so by God from all eternity, but this eternal knowledge of God does not cause or incite the ontological and moral defectiveness that occurs in the free action of the creature. In stating things in this way, we emphasize the goodness of God as expressed in his divine innocence. All that is good in us must be traced ultimately to the initiative of God. All that is morally evil in us must be traced ultimately to the defective action of the creature. In the succinct words of Aquinas, citing the Vulgate version of Hosea, "Your destruction is your own, Oh Israel. Your help is only in me" (Hos 13:9).[83]

We might also think of this structure of thought in ascendant pairs, like the vertical lines on either side of a ladder that is joined horizontally at three successive nodes. The ladder passes from what is more evident *quod a nos* to what is more evident *in se*, from what we know best to what must be most true in the light of God. At the base of the ladder is a statement of fundamental ontological and moral realism. On the one hand, all that exists in us is itself received from God who gives us existence. We owe him everything that we are, including the right choices we make in the responsible and diligent use of our freedom. On the other hand, we are not able to blame others and least of all God for the moral evil that we freely succumb to, whether by weakness or egoism. Our moral irre-

---

83. *ST* I, q. 23, a. 3, ad 2.

sponsibility is our own, not the responsibility of others, and any realistic recognition of our moral state before others and especially before God must take this reality into account.

More mysterious is the pairing at the next level. On the one hand, God offers us the grace that can heal and justify, sanctify, and ultimately save us. And in doing so, God is never our debtor but only ever the free giver who enriches us by his mercy and is able in the process to make us beings of gratitude and thankfulness. On the other hand, we must also say that the soul that is naturally capable of evil is also capable of resistance and refusal of the gift of God's grace. The negative side of the ladder that we found at the base (our capacity to fail freely to confirm to the truth in our moral actions) has a correlate at the middle level: our capacity to turn away freely but unreasonably from the mystery of Christ.

Ultimately these two lower levels of the ladder require that we reflect on their transcendent causal precondition, something that is less evident to us, but more evident in itself, in the very life of God. If all that we receive positively in the order of nature and grace has its transcendent origin in the eternal love of God, then God must will from all eternity (in a way that is not entirely comprehensible to us) that we receive all the gifts that he gives us to possess. As a consequence, we must follow Augustine to the logical term of New Testament principles in saying (however remote this may be from our immediate perception) that God must in some mysterious way predestine the elect to the final grace of eternal life. He does so out of his eternal love and goodness. By his eternal foreknowledge he governs the lives of those who he wishes to bring effectively into the sphere of eternal life by the sheer gratuity of his good will. And yet the other side of the ladder obtains to this node or rung of eternal heights as well. For if the creature is lost only because of its own defection from the offer of grace, then we should also say that God merely permits and does not will the loss of any human person or spiritual creature. On the contrary, God offers the possibility of salvation to all out of love for all. He also allows that some should forsake him, however, not because of the absence of a sufficient gift on the part of God, but because of the loving respect God has for free creatures, whom he permits to refuse his grace freely. Such creatures use their capacity to love badly, so as to turn definitively away from the mystery of Christ. Aquinas follows John Damascene on this point in distinguishing between the antecedent and the consequent will of God.[84] God wills that all men be saved—*antecedently*, says Aquinas—but he wills so with the condition that they freely consent to this mystery by the capacity to love that is naturally placed within them, and so God wills *consequently* that those who freely refuse the mystery be allowed to live in self-alienation from the mystery of God, in this life and in the life of the world to come. Salvation comes by way of grace, but this grace can only be consented to freely in love.

A Circle of Concepts

Another way that we might think of these diverse principles is by comparison with an image of a circle or ring, in which the principles form six nodes that bind the ring together but that also remain distinct. They work together insofar as they each cast a positive kataphatic light on the mystery of God's predestination of the saints. But they remain distinct as irreducibly unique points of intelligibility concerning the mystery, points that exist in apophatic tension with one another.

This emphasis on aphophaticism is significant and can be illustrated in two ways. We can reflect on it in one way by stating in succinct fashion what the six principles enunciated above each exclude. First, if God gives us all the positive being and goodness that is present within us, then no account of creaturely freedom should be given that allows creatures to positively enrich or contribute to the development of the very being of God, as if God were to change or develop ontologically in a divine history with creatures in virtue of the choices that they might make. God is the unilateral giver of being, not the receiver.[85] Second, if the human creature is truly capable of the misuse of human free will, then we must exclude the thesis that God is the first cause of moral evil, either by willing it directly or by failing to come to the aid of a creature with sufficient recourse of assistance. Third, if God is the author of all the grace that we receive and we can in no way merit grace by our natural efforts, then all we receive in the order of grace is first and foremost an unmerited gift of God. We cannot earn or gain anything from God by our own natural capacities. Fourth, if God truly offers grace to all human beings but also allows human beings to resist and eventually at times to refuse

---

84. *ST* I, q. 19, a. 6, ad 1.

85. See the arguments to this effect in Thomas Joseph White, "Divine Simplicity and the Holy Trinity," *International Journal of Systematic Theology* 18, no. 1 (2016): 66–93.

his grace definitively, then God is not the author or cause of the human abandonment of God. Fifth, if God is the first principle of all grace we receive from all eternity and predestines us to himself by election, then all who are saved have no one to praise for the gift of grace other than God, who has chosen them in Jesus Christ. As regards our predestination, all is grace! But, lastly, if there are those who refuse the offer of grace from God and persist in this refusal, it is because of the creature's decision that God respects and permits from all eternity, and is in no way a sign that impugns the infinite innocence and goodness of God.

A more ultimate and significant form of apophaticism is epistemic in nature and signals the limited comprehension that we can have of the mystery of predestination. This is the problem of the co-simultaneous intelligibility of the diverse principles enunciated above. One may wish to argue that they are all true, and that although they exist in some conceptual tension with one another, they are not mutually contradictory. But *how* is it that they are all true in God and in his eternal knowledge and will? How is it, for example, that God offers grace to some that leads them inexorably upward into the light of beatitude while offering grace truly sufficient for salvation to others that he permits them to refuse? How does he know of both the predestined and the reprobate from all eternity? How does he sustain in being creatures that do moral evil and that even choose to sin against his initiatives of grace? These are all deeply meaningful questions, but they are also ones that we cannot answer adequately owing to the insufficiency of our human comprehension. We can affirm that all these things are true, and that God is merciful and just to both the elect and to those who reject his grace. We can affirm that all we have that is good in us is from God, and that all that we do that is seriously morally wrong originates with ourselves. How are both these sets of affirmations true simultaneously? The "how" of the divine mysteries is often hidden from us, as in the case of how the Son of God subsists personally in both his divine and human natures (the hypostatic union), or the case of how God in his omnipotence changes bread and wine into the body and blood of Christ (transubstantiation). We can affirm that a given mystery is real and note its diverse luminous intelligible aspects without understanding comprehensively how such a mystery functions from God's perspective, or what its inner shape is as perceived from within the sphere of divine wisdom. Here as elsewhere in theology, we confront a shadowland of light and darkness, one that reveals to us indirectly but really the wisdom and goodness, justice and mercy of God, but one that also leaves the mystery concealed from our complete understanding. What we should say, however, is that the ring that binds these mysteries is one of divine love. God in his love respects the creature's capacity to refuse him in its created freedom, and God in his love moves his creature sweetly and respectfully from within to consent to his mystery of grace. In all things the love of God is glorified, and in all things the capacity in the human person to accept or to forsake divine love freely is respected as a mystery present at the heart of the creature's spiritual life.

Return to the Catholic Heritage: The Analogy of Love

I argued at the beginning of this essay that the classical doctrine of predestination in the Catholic tradition has been largely eclipsed in modernity by the tendency to treat the doctrine as gravitating toward one of two extremes, either one represented by the Calvinist emphasis on the exclusionary offer of salvation or one represented by the Barthian theory of universalism. Both of these interpretations seem to reduce the mystery of predestination uniquely to a question of the realization of the divine will, without sufficient attention given to the mystery of human consent to or refusal of grace. The analogy between divine and human freedom is reduced univocally to the plane of concordance and rivalry, one in which the divine will is seen to triumph ultimately by sublimating all human willing to itself.

Behind this tendency in modern theology is an eclipse of metaphysical analogy in general, and the analogy of divine and human love in particular. This analogy is preserved when one acknowledges adequately the metaphysical and theological mystery of the transcendence of the divine will to the human will. The divine will is the creative cause of human willing, but in such a way that genuine creaturely freedom is preserved, and not illusory. This causality is unlike any merely intracreaturely causality because it gives being to the interior freedom of the creature as free, and sustains its development in authentic freedom. The created agent, meanwhile, is not only genuinely free to do what is in some way good, but can also refuse goodness (at least in certain respects), and even the goodness of God as a chosen final end. It does so even while being sustained in being by the primary cause. Only when theology has truly embraced the mystery of the analogy of divine and human love can it acknowledge the capacity of God to redeem human freedom intrinsically from within without violence done to the creature, while also acknowledging God's respect for the creature's refusal of the love of God, without any prejudice to the prerogatives of divine sovereignty.

The Catholic Augustinian and Thomistic principles outlined above do permit such an acknowledgment of the shape of the mystery. They do so without falling into the inverse error of Pelagianism, according to which human persons would be able to take the first initiatives to save themselves by advancing in the natural order of virtue and merit so as to accede to the world of grace. If salvation occurs by grace alone, but if human beings are also capable of freely refusing this grace, then the Catholic Church is right to underscore a nonparallelism in her perennial doctrine. All that is given to us in the order of grace to lead us toward salvation occurs by virtue of the unmerited first gift of God, who first loved us from all eternity and who predestines the saints to eternal life. All that occurs to undermine the work of grace in us stems originally from the human heart that defects from the stimulus of grace, its infused capacities and inclinations. What you have in the order of salvation, oh Israel, you have from God, who has always loved you. What you lose to your own perdition you lose because of your own decisions, which God allows you to make out of his love and respect for your freedom. But here is our great hope: that God's love is greater than our hearts, and that he will continue to give us the grace to repent, pray, and persevere so long as we do not reject his assistance. This mystery is not exclusive, because God offers the possibility of salvation to all human beings. Consequently, we can preach the Gospel with confidence in the abiding universal assistance of the Holy Spirit, who wills that all human beings accept the Gospel. And, simultaneously, our confident prayer on behalf of the Church should be: "May you bring to completion the good work you have begun in us, Oh Lord." This is the hopeful realism and perennial consolation of a Catholic doctrine of predestination.

5

PREDESTINATION AS THE

COMMUNICATION OF DIVINE GOODNESS

IN AQUINAS'S *COMMENTARY*

ON EPHESIANS

Michael Dauphinais

Balanced theological treatments of the mystery of divine predestination necessarily engage central scriptural references as well as metaphysical accounts of God's relationship to temporal creation. In contemporary treatments of this mystery, there is an understandable shift in emphasis toward the human experience of predestination. Yet it would be a mistake to emphasize the experiential dimension to the exclusion of an adequate metaphysical account of predestination, which alone can help ground our understanding of Christian life. Aquinas offers a balanced approach that treats predestination in its scriptural and metaphysical context while also attending to the Christian experience of salvation. In the theological ordering of wisdom, Aquinas considers first God as the fullness of existence itself (*ipsum esse subsistens*), who creates and redeems the human race out of his own perfection. The foundational distinction between the Creator and the creature thus orients the mystery of predestination. By situating the redemption within God's creative agency, Aquinas emphasizes the giftedness of the redemption of the human race by which we are made to share in the divine nature as adopted sons. When we investigate how Aquinas treats predestination in its scriptural context, we see explicitly how the metaphysical consideration of the priority of divine love in human redemption leads the believer to a response of thanksgiving and praise. Thus the metaphysical perspective allows the divine mystery to become existentially meaningful in Christian life. The context of the scriptural commentary offers Aquinas the opportunity to develop a broad purview of the theology of predestination. As his treatment in his *Commentary on Ephesians* shows, according to Aquinas, "God's predestining will has no other ratio than the communicating of the divine goodness to his sons."[1]

A Contemporary Exegetical Argument against Predestination in Ephesians

In his 1974 *Anchor Bible Commentary on Ephesians*, Markus Barth provides a theologically rich reading of Ephesians.[2] Against much of the academic and Protestant exegesis of his day, he defends the Pauline authorship of Ephesians on the basis of Paul's broad covenantal theology of salvation against "an existentialist theology of individual justification and sanctification."[3] A standard reading of his day was that Paul was focused on individual justification, and because Ephesians does not speak of individual justification by faith, then Paul must not have written Ephesians. Yet Markus Barth sees the strong covenantal and unitive language in Ephesians with respect to Jews and Gentiles as a more mature formulation of themes and questions that dominate Romans and Galatians, among other Pauline writings. Stepping away from the individualistic paradigm and into a covenantal and communal paradigm assisted Markus Barth in seeing Pauline themes in Ephesians, even if they were here expressed in a different manner.

1. *Commentary on Ephesians*, ch. 1, lect. 1, 51 (with modification to the published translation): "Unde patet etiam, quod divinae voluntatis praedestinantis non est alia ratio, quam divina bonitas filiis communicanda." Unless otherwise noted, all translations are taken from Aquinas's *Commentary on Saint Paul's Epistle to the Ephesians*, trans. Matthew L. Lamb (Albany, NY: Magi Books, 1966).

2. Markus Barth, *Ephesians: Introduction, Translation, and Commentary on Chapters 1–3*, Anchor Bible Series (New York: Doubleday, 1974).

3. Ibid., 48.

Barth's covenantal and communal approach is relevant to his interpretation of the question of predestination in Ephesians. For here again, the theological presuppositions one brings to the exegesis shape the exegesis itself. Ephesians 1:3–14 is a beautiful hymn of praise and blessing to God the Father for the tremendous blessing he has bestowed on the faithful in Christ. Paul writes in Ephesians 1:3–6, "Blessed be the God and Father of our Lord Jesus Christ, who has blessed us in Christ with every spiritual blessing in the heavenly places, even as he chose us in him before the foundation of the world, that we should be holy and blameless before him. He destined us in love to be his sons through Jesus Christ, according to the purpose of his will, to the praise of his glorious grace which he freely bestowed on us in the Beloved."[4] That doxology includes—and even highlights prominently—God's having chosen us and having destined us. Seemingly, Paul does not hide God's initiative. The divine initiative is instead the occasion of joy and thanksgiving rather than of fear and dread, as it has been received at times from the period of the Reformation until the present day. How then do we understand this hymn of praise more adequately in order to enter into that Pauline praise of God?

Markus Barth argues that we must be careful to separate the theology of Ephesians from later theories of predestination in order to safeguard that doxology. He explicitly states that "Ephesians cannot be considered the charter of the eternal predestination of one part of mankind for bliss, the other for hell." He ultimately lists seven reasons for this argument: first, Paul's words are "adoring rather than calculating or speculative"; second, there is no impersonal or "anonymous predestining force," but the disclosure of a loving, personal relationship of God as a Father; third, the language is borrowed from election in the Old Testament and does not bring in "earlier or contemporary philosophical discussions"; fourth, the eternal election is not to remain hidden, but God "has made known to us in all wisdom and insight the mystery of his will" (Eph 1:9); fifth,

---

4. Eph 1:3–6 (RSVCE). "Exelexato hemas en auto pro kataboles kosmou" "he chose us in him before the foundation of the world" (1:4; cf. Acts 1:2, 15:7; 1 Cor 1:27, 1:28; Jas 2:5). "Proorisas hemas eis huiothesian dia Iesou Christou" "having predestined us for divine adoption as sons through Jesus Christ" (1:5; cf. Acts 4:28; Rom 8:29, 8:30; 1 Cor 2:7; Eph 1:11). In order to consider Aquinas's commentary in its historical context as well as an interlocutor in the present theological search for wisdom, this article refers both to the Vulgate text of Scripture as commented on by Aquinas and occasionally to the same texts in the Greek and in the Revised Standard Version Catholic Edition.

election is neither of the past nor of "a timeless divine will," and instead God elects in the past, present, and future; sixth, election communicates the forgiveness of sins and thus "is a stronghold in times of temptations and trials"; and seventh, and most important for Markus Barth, election is always in Christ: "the formula 'in Christ' denotes the concentration, summation, revelation, and execution of God's own decision in one person, that is, the Messiah upon whom the Jews had set their hope (1:12)."[5] In each of his seven arguments, Barth employs certain dichotomies: adoring versus speculative, personal versus anonymous, biblical versus philosophical, being made known versus hidden, in time versus timeless, earthly encouragement versus earthly security, and a new community centered on the Messiah versus individualistic salvation. Markus Barth then concludes by distinguishing "decisively between the election of God as praised in Ephesians and a fatalistic belief in an absolute decree." In doing so, Barth associates predestination with fatalism. He further develops this contrast by contrasting fixed plans of God with God's invitation to a relationship:

If the person of Jesus Christ is the prime object and subject, the revealed secret and instrument of God's election, and if he represents all those elected, then all notions of a fixed will, testament, plan, and program of God are not only inadequate but contrary to the sense of Eph 1....Much more it is that person-to-person relationship of love which exists in the relation between God and his Son and is revealed only by the events that manifest this relationship. Thus election has nothing to do with a prescription or schedule. God's election is not an *absolute* decree, but is relative to the Son, his mission, death, and resurrection.

Summing up his argument, he contrasts the living and personal nature of God to the fatalism associated with schemes and plans: "Eph 1 bears testimony to the living God, the Father, the Son, and the Spirit. Everything said is personal, intimate, and functional. An invitation to fatalism under the scheme of double predestination or another deterministic plan cannot be found here."[6]

Much can be agreed with here in terms of Barth's rejection of fatalism and determinism. These philosophical positions exclude human free will and thus the dignity of the rational creature. Nonetheless, Barth's dichot-

---

5. Barth, *Ephesians*, 105–8.
6. Ibid., 109.

omy of fixed versus personal, and determined versus relational, depicts a metaphysics of creation in which the Creator and the creature exist in a competitive relationship.[7] I suggest that Aquinas offers a richer way around these dichotomies in his *Commentary on Ephesians* and thus presents an account of predestination that excludes fatalism. In this biblical setting, Aquinas develops the notion of predestination within the context of the witness of Scripture and his theological understanding of creation and redemption as the communication of divine goodness. Aquinas eschews a fatalistic or deterministic understanding of predestination while maintaining an exegesis of the mystery of redemption characterized by God's eternal love and mercy revealed in Jesus Christ, a mystery that includes what Aquinas will term the "blessing of predestination."

Predestination and the Interpretive Structure of Aquinas's *Commentary on Ephesians*

In order to address Aquinas's presentation of the theme of predestination, it is appropriate to consider how he situates the relevant verses within the themes of the entire letter. Let us begin by observing both the prologue verse Aquinas selected and his organization of the letter, or division of the text offered.[8] To introduce the letter, Aquinas selects Psalm 75:3: "I have strengthened its pillars."[9] It was common for the medieval exegete to identify a unifying theme to the scriptural book under consideration and to present this unifying theme by selecting a verse from another part of Scripture. By selecting "I have strengthened its pillars," Aquinas indicates that the central theme of his *Commentary on Ephesians* will be St. Paul's intention to strengthen the faith of the Christians in Ephesus.[10] Although

---

7. Cf. Robert Sokolowski, *The God of Faith and Reason: Foundations of Christian Theology* (Washington, DC: Catholic University of America Press, 1995). For a more popular exposition, see Robert Barron, *Thomas Aquinas: Spiritual Master* (New York: Crossroad, 1996).

8. As John Boyle has argued, the division of the text is a key interpretive technique in medieval scholastic exegesis. "The Theological Character of the Scholastic 'Division of the Text' with Particular Reference to the Commentaries of Saint Thomas Aquinas," in *With Reverence for the Word: Medieval Scriptural Exegesis in Judaism, Christianity and Islam* (Oxford: Oxford University Press, 2003), 276–83.

9. Vulgate Ps 74:4, "liquefacta est terra et omnes qui habitant in ea, ego confirmavi columnas eius"; RSVCE Ps 75:3, "When the earth totters, and all its inhabitants, it is I who keep steady its pillars."

10. In Aquinas's prologue to his *Commentary on Romans*, he offers a division of the text

Paul did not found the church in Ephesus, he "is justly praised for having strengthened them in [the faith]." Aquinas clarifies as follows: "The Apostle's intention is to strengthen them in good habits, and spur them on to greater perfection. The method of presentation can be seen in the division of the letter."[11] Aquinas then divides the letter into four main sections:

1. The greeting, "in which he shows his affection for them" (1:1–2)

2. The narrative, "in which he strengthens them in good habits" (1:3–3:21)

3. The exhortation, "in which he urges them on to greater perfection [especially unity]" (4:1–6:9)

4. The conclusion, "in which he fortifies them for the spiritual combat" (6:10–24)

The verses on which this essay focuses fall at the beginning of the narrative section "in which [Paul] strengthens them in good habits." Aquinas further subdivides this narrative section into three main sections corresponding to chapters 1, 2, and 3.

First, by giving as a reason Christ, from whom they have received so many gifts (Ch. 1).

Secondly, by reason of they themselves who have been transformed from a former evil condition to their present good one (Ch. 2).

Thirdly, because of the Apostle himself, whose ministry and solicitude has confirmed them in their good state (Ch. 3).

Examining these three reasons together depicts a collective moment of deeper recognition of a good already conferred on the Ephesians by God. The good has been given in Christ, received by them, through the ministry of the Apostle. Aquinas sees in Paul's reiteration of this divine sharing of the good the mode by which Paul strengthens the pillars, or the faith, of the Christians. Chapter 1 concerns Christ "from whom they have received so many gifts." Aquinas thus identifies Christ as the primary means by which Paul "strengthens them in good."[12] Before any men-

---

for the entire Pauline corpus. He writes: "All of the letters are about the grace of Christ. Nine letters consider the grace of Christ as it exists in the mystical body itself." In this context, Aquinas identifies a complementary central theme of Ephesians, namely, "the foundation (*institutio*) of the Church's unity" as an effect of the grace of Christ.

11. *Commentary on Ephesians*, ch. 1, lect. 1, 43.

12. *Commentary on Ephesians*, ch. 1, lect. 1, 44.

tion is made of predestination in Ephesians 1:15, Aquinas has already set the stage for his interpretation of predestination as the sharing of God's own goodness with his human creatures through Christ and his Church.

After dividing the first three chapters, Aquinas further subdivides chapter 1 into three sections, each of which expound different modes of God's blessings (*beneficia*). The first section in verses 3–7 speaks of blessings as given generally to Christians. Aquinas then identifies six blessings offered to the human race generally (*generaliter humano generi*):

First, that of praising (*benedictionis*) [God] in the certainty of future beatitude (1:3).

Secondly, that of being chosen (*electionis*) in the foreordained separation from those headed toward destruction (1:4).

Thirdly, that of predestination (*predestinationis*) in the foreordained community of the good, namely, of the adopted sons (1:5).

Fourthly, that of becoming pleasing (*gratificationis*) [to God] through the gift of grace (1:6b).

Fifthly, that of being redeemed (*redemptionis*), liberated from the punishment of diabolical slavery (1:7a).

Sixthly, that of being pardoned (*remissionis*) by having sin blotted out (1:7b).[13]

This sixfold structure of blessings reveals the manifest goodness of God, who shares his goodness with creatures through the mystery of redemption. Aquinas sees the key to these verses in their doxological character as expressions of praise and thanksgiving to God for specific blessings received from God. Furthermore, those blessings are meant to strengthen the faithful per the overall theme of the letter. Aquinas follows his division of the text by exhorting his reader to the praise of God by stating that Paul "says God should be blessed or praised by you, me, and others with our hearts, tongues, and actions."[14] Blessing God for his blessings becomes the form of Paul's strengthening of the community of the Church. Aquinas connects this theme of blessing directly with that of the virtue of hope, "God has blessed us with hope (*in spe*) in the present, while in the future he will bless us with the reality (*in re*)."[15] God has actively established a relationship that invites a response from the Ephesians. He is resolutely a personal agent capable of a relationship with the

13. *Commentary on Ephesians*, ch. 1, lect. 1, 45.
14. *Commentary on Ephesians*, ch. 1, lect. 1, 45.
15. *Commentary on Ephesians*, ch. 1, lect. 1, 45.

community of the Church, a relationship that begins now, but is a fore-taste of the future.

Election and Predestination as Blessings

Aquinas employs the overall theme of blessing to consider the themes of election and predestination. Aquinas elicits four aspects of the blessing of election: election is free, eternal, fruitful, and gratuitous. It is free because God chose us; it is eternal because it was before the foundation of the world; it is fruitful because we should be holy; and it is gratuitous because election is accomplished not by our merits, but by God's charity.[16] Aquinas emphasizes that this election is a free gift, "not through our merits but from the grace of Christ." Furthermore, Aquinas draws an implication of any election or choosing, namely, that it is a separation, in this case from "those headed to destruction."[17] This is the only occasion in the entire commentary in which Aquinas refers to the separation of those called to eternal life from those headed to destruction.[18] Aquinas displays no interest in the idea of trying to draw a line between the elect and the damned in his biblical commentary. On the contrary, with respect to the theme of election, Aquinas emphasizes the divine initiative in bringing about redemption to strengthen and encourage the faithful. Following Paul in saying that this election remains "before the foundation of the world," Aquinas highlights this aspect by drawing in two other Scriptural passages as comparisons and illustrations: John 15:16, "You have not chosen me; but I have chosen you," and Romans 9:11, "For when the children were not yet born, nor had done any good or evil, that the purpose of God according to election, might stand." Aquinas further points out that Paul's communication of this blessing of election is not meant to be informative, but transformative: "He chose us, I say, not because we were holy—we had not yet come into existence—but that we should be holy in virtues and unspotted by vices."[19] The call to holiness follows upon a ref-

16. *Commentary on Ephesians*, ch. 1, lect. 1, 46.

17. *Commentary on Ephesians*, ch. 1, lect. 1, 46: *praeordinata separatione a massa perditionis*.

18. Aquinas uses the term *separatio* in commenting on Eph 2:1, but there it is only in the context of our separation from God due to sin, not the separation of those chosen from those unchosen. *Commentary on Ephesians*, ch. 2, lect. 1. "Sin is termed a death because by it man is separated from God who is life: I am the way, and the truth, and the life (Jn 14:6)."

19. *Commentary on Ephesians*, ch. 1, lect. 1, 46.

erence to the divine initiative. By emphasizing the call to holiness, Aquinas helps the attentive reader of Scripture avoid a common misunderstanding that places divine election in competition with human action. The eternal character of election calls for a human response and thus does not exclude, but rather presupposes, human freedom. Election serves as an occasion for blessing, as a call for gratitude, and as the exhortation to live up to our calling.

Following the verse structure of Ephesians, Aquinas moves from the theme of election to predestination. Aquinas sees the blessing of predestination announced in Ephesians 1:5–6a, "Having predestinated us unto the adoption of children through Jesus Christ unto himself, according to the purpose of his will, unto the praise of the glory of his grace."[20] He speaks of this blessing as belonging to the "foreordained community of those who are good."[21] The reference to preordination is not associated, as it was for Markus Barth, with any kind of fatalism, but as an announcement of the good news of blessing. Furthermore, Aquinas makes no correlative reference to a preordained community of destruction in his commentary. All of humanity may be under the curse of sin and death, but Aquinas only speaks of the preordination, election, or predestination as associated with redemption.

Within the overall distinction of six blessings in Ephesians 1:3–7, Aquinas further outlines six characteristics of the blessing of predestination. He does so by explicating the specific language used by Paul in Ephesians 1:5. Briefly stated, the six characteristics of predestination are as follows: first, "he destined" means it is an eternal act; second, "us" shows that it has a temporal object; third, "to be his sons through Jesus Christ" shows that it offers a present privilege; fourth, "unto himself" indicates the result is future; fifth, "according to the purpose of his will" shows that it is gratuitous; sixth, "unto the praise of the glory of his grace" shows its due effect. The first four blessings refer to the relationship between time and eternity: it is an eternal act with a temporal object offering a present privilege, the result of which is the

---

20. *Commentary on Ephesians*, ch. 1, lect. 1, 42. Eph 1:5–6a reads "he destined us in love to be his sons through Jesus Christ, according to the purpose of his will, to the praise of his glorious grace" in the RSVCE. Note that the Greek (*proorisas*) and Latin (*praedestinavit*) words include the prefix *pro-* or *prae-*.

21. *Commentary on Ephesians*, ch. 1, lect. 1, 46: "scilicet praedestinationis, in praeordinata associatione cum bonis."

future. The last two blessings also address similar issues of origin and end: the origin of predestination in God and its *telos* in our praise of God.

The Blessing of Divine Filiation and Asymmetry

Aquinas summarizes these six characteristics under the theme that we might become children of God by grace alone (*sola gratia*). Aquinas develops the first three characteristics in particular by saying that God "has forechosen us by grace alone," that we might become children of God. In order to discuss adoptive filiation, Aquinas observes a fundamental principle of causality, "It must be through contact with fire that something starts to burn since nothing obtains a share in some realty except through whatever is that reality by its very nature." He then applies this principle to divine filiation: "Hence the adoption of sons has to occur through the natural son.... Jesus Christ... [is] the mediator who draws all to himself."[22] Aquinas amplifies this causal relation between the natural son and the adopted sons by quoting Galatians 4:4–5: "God sent his Son, made of a woman, made under the law, that he might redeem them who were under the law, that we might receive the adoption of sons." As Aquinas further unpacks the theme of divine filiation, he distinguishes the two ways in which the predestined share a likeness to the Son of God.[23] The first is imperfect, *per gratiam*; the second perfect, *in gloria*. The divine adoption due to grace remains imperfect for two reasons: its reformation only concerns the soul, and the soul retains some imperfection.[24] The divine adoption in glory, however, is perfect and complete: both the body and the soul will be perfected. Aquinas brings in two other Pauline verses to show this glory of the body and the soul: "He will transform our lowly body to be like his glorious body" (Phil 3:21), and "when the perfect comes, the imperfect shall pass away" (1 Cor 13:10). Divine adoption is a sharing in the glory of the eternally begotten Son.

Here we see a central theme that we may learn from Aquinas's *Commentary on Ephesians* about the mystery of predestination. He does not

---

22. *Commentary on Ephesians*, ch. 1, lect. 1, 47: *mediator alliciens.*

23. *Commentary on Ephesians*, ch. 1, lect. 1, 47: "duplex est similitudo praedestinatorum ad filium Dei."

24. Aquinas refers to Eph 4:23–24: "Be renewed in the spirit of your mind, and put on the new man, who according to God is created in justice and holiness of truth."

speak of predestination in terms of an antagonism with human freedom or a deterministic plan. Predestination is the good news of our adoption as children of God by grace alone. Aquinas speaks of divine predestination in its aspect of divine adoption and vice versa. The two implicate one another. Predestination has no intelligibility as an abstract concept; instead, predestination gains intelligibility from its content, namely, the eternal loving act of God in sharing the perfection of his natural son with rational creatures by adopting them as his children. So, too, divine adoption implies a characteristic of predestination. Even in the temporal sphere of humans adopting other humans, adoption expresses a prior decision by the one adopting: the orphan cannot adopt itself or make itself get adopted. The case of divine adoption reveals the same priority of decision, but even more fundamentally because it crosses over between the eternal and the temporal. In order for us to become adopted children of God, human beings must have come into contact in their temporal framework with the Incarnate Son of God. Aquinas indicates that were Christ simply another adopted son, he would be inadequate to bring about our adoption. So, from both the eternal and temporal perspectives on adoption, the act of adoption necessarily originates in the one adopting.

This pattern needs to be observed in all such terms associated with this hymn in Ephesians: adoption, election, predestination, and having been chosen before the foundation of the world. All indicate an asymmetrical relationship between the one adopting, electing, destining, and choosing and the ones being adoption, being elected, being destined, and being chosen. Aquinas employs the principle of causality in divine filiation to show that the natural Son must be prior to the adopted sons. Moreover, the principle of causality implies that the cause and effect must be in contact with each other for the change to occur; thus the natural Son must be in contact with the adopted sons. This asymmetry between God and us is the basis of the good news communicated by Paul. God's actions and decisions to save us constitute the blessings announced in the beginning of Ephesians.

Predestination as Pure Love

Aquinas emphasizes this blessed asymmetry in his comments on the remaining blessings he associates with predestination. Here Aquinas adds an important reality to a full understanding of predestination: divine love. Divine love, according to Aquinas, recommends the blessing of predestination to us. Aquinas thus eschews any fatalistic or deterministic accounts of predestination. Instead it is love calling to love. Here is how he develops his exegesis of these passages. As Ephesians 1:5 says, "according to the purpose of his will," Aquinas comments, "divine predestination is neither necessitated on God's part nor due to those who are predestined." Aquinas does not develop this negative statement into a defense of God's arbitrary freedom, but rather of God's love. He says that divine predestination "springs forth from pure love (*ex amore puro*)."[25] According to its *ratio*, "predestination presupposes election, and election love." In converse order, the *ratio* of love begets election, and election predestination; thus love begets predestination. When Aquinas speaks here of "this immense blessing," he identifies its efficient cause as "the simple will of God" and its final cause as "that we may praise and know the goodness of God." Aquinas does not highlight knowledge of God's power, but rather knowledge of God's goodness as our *telos* or final end. God is a personal agent, an agent acting from love and for love.

Predestination, Creation, and the Communication of Goodness

Subsequent to the consideration of divine love, Aquinas employs the theme of divine goodness as the lens through which to consider the blessing of predestination. To begin, Aquinas makes the observation that "God's will in no way has a cause but is the first cause of everything else." He then continues, however, that God's will can be seen to have a motive in two ways, on the part of the one willing and on the part of what is willed. For the former, God's own goodness is the object of the divine will; for the latter, a created existent (*aliquid esse creatum*) may serve as a motive. These created existents, however, are not the cause of God's will; "rather it is a cause of it happening the way it did."[26] Causation among created

---

25. *Commentary on Ephesians*, ch. 1, lect. 1, 48. "In quo, quarto, commendatur beneficium, quia ex amore puro proveniens, quia praedestinatio secundum rationem praesupponit electionem et electio dilectionem."

26. From the footnotes to the *Commentary on Ephesians* as provided by the translator, Father Matthew Lamb, "Peter's actions are not the cause of God's willing him glory but they are a cause of his attaining glory. They are a cause only because God has willed them to be such; as St. Thomas expresses it: 'There can be no merit on the part of man before God except on the presupposition that God has ordained it' (*S.T.* I-II, 114, 1c). No one insists more

existing things refers to other created existents. Aquinas distinguishes between the Creator and creation, or, in the language he employs here, between causation that lies "within the domain of creatures" and that which lies "within the domain of the Creator."[27] Once the horizon is established as the causality proper to the Creator, then Aquinas must conclude that the causality associated with predestination also be part of the divine creative act. Thus, he writes, "neither can predestination find any reason on the part of the creature but only on the part of God."[28] In order to draw this conclusion, Aquinas considers predestination with the overall *ratio* of God's actions as a creator. If the effect of predestination is a sharing in the divine goodness, then its cause must lie in the divine goodness. The exclusion of human action as a cause of predestination excludes the notion that the rational creature has the ability to create itself or to redeem itself.

The exclusion of human action as a cause of predestination, nonetheless, allows the participation of the rational creature in the cooperation with the gift of grace.[29] Aquinas identifies two effects of predestination: grace and glory. With the realm of what is willed by God, namely, creation, "grace can be identified as a reason for the effects which are oriented towards glory." Aquinas uses the example that Peter receives glory because he fought well with the help of grace. Although grace may be seen as a reason for glory, no such reason may be identified for predestination to grace. Peter was offered grace simply by the sheer gift of God. Aquinas condemns the alternative as "the heretical teachings of the Pelagians who held that the source of good works exists within ourselves."[30] Aquinas then offers the following conclusion, "the reason for predestination is the will of God alone."[31] The context here is the offer of grace, which

---

strongly than Aquinas on the sinner's absolute dependence on God to justify him (*ibid.*, 113); but he equally insists that God's justifying word effects what it says. God's love—unlike created love—presupposes no goodness but rather creates that goodness (*ibid.*, 110, 1c)."

27. On the distinction between God as Creator and all of creation, see Robert Sokolowski, "The Christian Distinction," in *The God of Faith and Reason: Foundations of Christian Theology* (Washington, DC: Catholic University of America Press, 1995).

28. *Commentary on Ephesians*, ch. 1, lect. 1, 49.

29. Aquinas explains that, although there is no cause of the divine will, God does will one thing to an effect of another. Cf. *ST* I, q. 19, a. 5; q. 23, a. 5. When viewed in particular, one effect of predestination may thus be the reason for, or cause of, another. Our free meritorious actions are the effect of grace and yet the cause of glory.

30. *Commentary on Ephesians*, ch. 1, lect. 1, 50.

31. *Commentary on Ephesians* footnote 17. "In the present context 'ratio' is sometimes

must be unmerited, and then the subsequent gift of glory, in which merit
and human action may play a cooperative role.

Aquinas then develops his exegetical treatment of predestination within the idea of the communication of divine goodness. He directly parallels predestination and creation, saying that the reason for both is the will
of God alone. To assign activities to the will of God alone does not merely
exclude other agents, but more precisely identifies the *ratio* of God's agency: "God creates everything and wills it because of his own goodness."[32]
Aquinas then explains that this does not mean that God is acting to attain goodness, but rather to "communicate goodness to others." Aquinas
presents this same theme of the communication of goodness as the fundamental *ratio* of the Incarnation in the *Summa Theologiae*, namely, that
it belongs to the nature of goodness to communicate itself and thus to
the highest goodness to communicate itself in the highest manner.[33] In
the exegetical context of Ephesians, Aquinas follows the lead of the text,
which continues, "unto the praise of the glory of his grace" (Eph 1:6a). The
communication of divine goodness to the rational creatures allows the
rational creature to know the divine goodness. Aquinas observes that this
is not merely the case with respect to predestination, but with all divine
action in relation to rational creatures: "everything that God performs in
reference to rational creatures is for his own praise and glory."[34] As is his
exegetical custom, Aquinas draws in another biblical verse to explicate
the same theme, in this case Isaiah 43:7, "And everyone that calleth upon
my name, I have created him for my glory." Creation is for the glory of
God.[35] To summarize, Aquinas develops the idea of predestination by be-

---

translated as 'motive.' When St. Thomas asserts that 'the reason for predestination is the
will of God alone' he is speaking in terms of the divine causality in itself ('ex parte volentis').
When seen in the perspective of man ('ex parte voliti') grace, as St. Thomas mentioned several lines above, is the reason of predestination."

32. *Commentary on Ephesians*, ch. 1, lect. 1, 50.

33. *ST* III, q. 1, a. 1. "I answer that, To each things, that is befitting which belongs to it by
reason of its very nature; thus, to reason befits man, since this belongs to him because he is
of a rational nature. But the very nature of God is goodness, as is clear from Dionysius (*Div.
Nom.* i). Hence, what belongs to the essence of goodness befits God. But it belongs to the essence of goodness to communicate itself to others, as is plain from Dionysius (*Div. Nom.* iv).
Hence it belongs to the essence of the highest good to communicate itself in the highest manner to the creature, and this is brought about chiefly by 'His so joining created nature to Himself that one Person is made up of these three—the Word, a soul and flesh,' as Augustine says
(*De Trin.* xiii). Hence it is manifest that it was fitting that God should become incarnate."

34. *Commentary on Ephesians*, ch. 1, lect. 1, 50.

35. Aquinas quotes here Is 43:7: "All, who I call by my name, I have created for my glory"

ginning with divine adoption, then divine love, then the divine goodness, then the communication of divine goodness in creation and predestination and its result in divine glory.

As a further way of showing that predestination must be considered from God's perspective and not that of human beings, Aquinas contrasts glory and justice. He notes that Paul exhorts us to the praise of God's glory, not of his justice. Justice would imply a debt, as if God predestined us to be children of God in response to something he owed us. Aquinas instead emphasizes the gratuity of God's gift, "for man to be predestined to eternal life is not due to him—as was said, it is a grace given in perfect freedom."[36] The fact that it is unearned and unmerited is an occasion for Aquinas to remark on its grandeur, because "God gives [grace] without any preceding merits when men are unworthy of it."[37] He cross-references here Romans 5:8: "God commandeth his charity towards us; because, when as yet we were sinners according to the time, Christ died for us." At no point in Aquinas's treatment of predestination stemming from glory as opposed to justice does Aquinas exclude the necessary role of human action and freedom in the execution of predestination; instead, justice is excluded owing to human sinfulness and the biblical notion that God loved us first (cf. 1 Jn 4:10).

Aquinas concludes his primary treatment of predestination by emphasizing the twin themes of God's will alone as the cause of predestination and the desire to communicate God's goodness as the *ratio* of God's will. He first writes, "By now it must be clear how divine predestination neither has nor can have any cause but the will of God alone." He immediately concludes in a striking manner, "This, in turn, reveals how the motive for God's predestining will is nothing other than the communicating of the divine goodness to his sons."[38] Aquinas here employs a se-

---

"omnem, qui invocat nomen meum, in gloriam meam creavi eum"; the RSVCE reads, "every one who is called by my name, who I created for my glory, whom I formed and made." See the *Catechism of the Catholic Church*, §293: "St. Bonaventure explains that God created all things 'not to increase his glory, but to show it forth and to communicate it,'" quoting St. Bonaventure, *In II Sent.* I, d. 2, q. 2, a. 1.

36. *Commentary on Ephesians*, ch. 1, lect. 1, 50.

37. *Commentary on Ephesians*, ch. 1, lect. 1, 51.

38. *Commentary on Ephesians*, ch. 1, lect. 1, 51 (with slight modification to the published translation): "Patet ergo quod praedestinationis divinae nulla alia causa est, nec esse potest, quam simplex Dei voluntas. Unde patet etiam, quod divinae voluntatis praedestinantis non est alia ratio, quam divina bonitas filiis communicanda."

quence of ideas to show God's fundamental plan. Because the simple will of God can have no other cause than God's own goodness, predestination thus has no other cause than the communication of that goodness. This summary highlights two key themes noted above. First, the communication of God's goodness takes the shape of divine filiation. The eternal, natural Son of God communicates adoptive filiation to human creatures similar to the way that it is only through contact with fire that something starts to burn. Second, the communication of God's goodness perfects the rational creature, who is elevated to know God's goodness via grace and ultimately in glory.

Predestination and Human Perfection

Aquinas repeats this teleological approach to predestination in his exegesis toward the end of this great hymn in Ephesians. Ephesians 1:11–12 reads, "In him according to the purpose of him who accomplishes all things according to the counsel of his will, we who first hoped in Christ have been destined and appointed to live for the praise of his glory."[39] Aquinas divides this into three themes: first, the gratuity of the call or vocation; second, the freedom of God's predestination; and, third, the end of both vocation and predestination in praise.

In the first theme, the gratuity of the call, Aquinas refers to the previous verse, Ephesians 1:10, to show that the unification, or restoration, of all things in Christ is an unearned grace. He explains, in causal terms, "grace has superabounded in us and everything has been re-established in Christ...not by our own merits but by a divine choice."[40]

In the second theme, the freedom of divine predestination, Aquinas contrasts our merits and God's initiative. He writes, "the reason for this predestination is not our merits but the will of God alone." In this context, Aquinas emphasizes that the will of God may not be set in opposition to reason. He notes that Paul does not say, "according to his will," but "according to the counsel of his will." Aquinas explains that the addition of "counsel" excludes the understanding that God's judgments are

---

39. Eph 1:11–12. The translation in Aquinas's *Commentary* reads, "In whom we also are called by lot, being predestinated according to the purpose of him who worketh all things according to the counsel of his will; That we may be unto the praise of his glory; we who before hoped in Christ." The Greek word for "predestinated" or "have been destined" is *pro-oristhentes*, the same root as in Eph 1:5.

40. *Commentary on Ephesians*, ch. 1, lect. 4, 60.

irrational.[41] Rather, God's will arises from reason in terms of a "certain and deliberate will."[42] Aquinas's main focus is to consider the causality of predestination on the part of God, not with respect to how it interacts with human causality.

In the third theme, the goal of vocation and predestination as the praise of God, Aquinas connects predestination to the perfection of the rational creation. As Aquinas did each time in the earlier contexts, following the pattern of Paul himself, he connects predestination to the praise and glory of God. He writes, "Through us, who believe in Christ, the glory of God is praised."[43] Predestination thus is not set in opposition to human freedom, but rather is shown to be the fulfillment of human agency and freedom insofar as we reach our perfection, or *telos*, in the knowing and loving of God.

Predestination as Knowing the Love of Christ

The themes of predestination and God's eternal purpose recur in Ephesians 3:19. In the context of his exegesis of this chapter, Aquinas explicates predestination as the revelation of divine love. Aquinas does not present predestination as a hidden mystery, as though the separation of the saved and unsaved is a subject for inquiry. Rather, in his comments on this chapter, Aquinas makes clear that the mystery that is revealed is the mystery of salvation via the Incarnation of the Son of God. It is this mystery of salvation that necessitates the priority and initiative of God's saving action as described by the themes of vocation, election, and predestination.

As Aquinas outlined in his introductory division of the text, the third chapter develops the unique role that the Apostle Paul has played in the communication of God's goodness. Specifically, Paul focused on the manner by which his "ministry and solicitude has confirmed them in their good state."[44] As highlighted in the prologue, Paul's role is to strength-

---

41. Cf. Pope Benedict XVI, "Faith, Reason and the University: Memories and Reflections," September 12, 2006, often referred to as "The Regensburg Lecture," on *Logos* and the divine nature.

42. *Commentary on Ephesians*, ch. 1, lect. 4, 63.

43. *Commentary on Ephesians*, ch. 1, lect. 4, 63 (minor variation to the translation).

44. *Commentary on Ephesians*, ch. 1, lect. 1, 44.

en the faith of the Ephesians. Developing this theme, Aquinas presents Paul's faith as the exemplar cause of their faith when he comments on Paul's words in Ephesians 3:3, "how the mystery was made known to me by revelation, as I have written briefly."[45] He writes that one who knows something best ought to be able to communicate it clearly. In this case, the ability write about the mystery of salvation "briefly" demonstrates that Paul "enjoys a perfect knowledge of the mysteries of faith."[46] Paul's knowledge is certain, full, and eminent. What, then, is this knowledge?

Aquinas explicates the knowledge of revelation by making reference to the vocation of the apostle "to preach among the Gentiles the unsearchable riches of Christ" (Eph 3:8b). Aquinas uses this occasion to distinguish what is unsearchable from what is searchable, what is unknowable from what is knowable, in the rational creature's knowledge of God. He clarifies that Paul's mission is "to reveal and clarify the great and hidden secrets of God." What are these great secrets? Aquinas identifies these great and hidden secrets as "the greatness of Christ and the salvation of those who believe which he accomplished. The entire Gospel concerns these two."[47] The hidden secret thus is not predestination abstracted from the whole, but nothing other than the Gospel in its entirety.

To expound upon this Gospel revelation, Aquinas highlights the themes of goodness, mercy, and love. Developing Paul's language of "riches," Aquinas identifies the specific grace given to Paul, one of proclaiming "the good."[48] Furthermore, the "riches" remain unsearchable because "they are as great as his mercy which can be neither understood nor analyzed."[49] Yet his mercy is neither a pure negation nor a sheer unknowing, as these riches flow from the positive perfection of love. Aquinas emphasizes the wonder that our redemption was accomplished "from an immense love."[50] The greatness of the mystery of redemption reveals its goodness, its mercy, and its love.

---

45. Eph 3:3.

46. *Commentary on Ephesians*, ch. 3, lect. 1, 121.

47. *Commentary on Ephesians*, ch. 3, lect. 2, 127.

48. *Commentary on Ephesians*, ch. 3, lect. 2, 127: "haec gratia data est mihi ut annuntiem bonum.".

49. *Commentary on Ephesians*, ch. 3, lect. 2, 127: "divitiae istae vere investigabiles sunt, quia tanta est misericordia eius, quod intelligi vel investigari non possit."

50. *Commentary on Ephesians*, ch. 3, lect. 2, 127: "quam mirabilis et ex quanta dilectione sit facta adimpletio arcanae redemptionis."

Aquinas continues his exegesis of Ephesians 3 to argue that this mystery exceeds the ability of human knowing owing to the excellence of this knowledge. As is consistent with his understanding of God as the first cause of all created effects, Aquinas clarifies here that "creatures, in whom a trace of their Creator is visible, do not provide us with a perfect understanding of Him."[51] Developing the correlation between modes of causality and modes of intelligibility, Aquinas distinguishes between two modes of God's creative acts: "Now God is the efficient cause of everything; he makes some things whose intelligibility is open [to investigation], namely, those created through the mediation of second causes. Other effects, however, which he immediately produces by himself are hidden in him."[52] As Aquinas articulates near the beginning of his *Summa Theologiae*, we do not know how God is, but rather how he is not.[53]

God's manner, or how, of causing our creation and our redemption simply exceed our comprehension. Although salvation makes use of instrumental causes, these created effects lack proper secondary causality, because salvation in no way belongs to created effects in and of themselves, as created to bring about eternal redemption. Only insofar as created effects are conjoined to divine agency may they instrumentally bring about salvation. As discussed in the above treatment of the opening hymn of Ephesians, Aquinas consistently emphasizes the asymmetrical character of God's actions. In the context of Ephesians 3, he explains that the reasons for God's actions are known to him alone because he alone is the cause of our redemption: "Since God accomplished by himself the mystery of human redemption, this mystery is hidden in him alone. Thus he states that it is hidden from eternity in God, known to him only. Yet, to seek out the secrets of the First Cause is the greatest [wisdom]."[54] Hidden here are not secret decrees of God about who is or who is not saved, but rather the greatness of Christ and his redemption, the very mysteries that have been revealed and communicated through

51. *Commentary on Ephesians*, ch. 3, lect. 2, 127.

52. *Commentary on Ephesians*, ch. 3, lect. 2, 128.

53. *ST* I, q. 2, prologue. "Sed quia de Deo scire non possumus quid sit, sed quid non sit, non possumus considerare de Deo quomodo sit, sed potius quomodo non sit."

54. *Commentary on Ephesians*, ch. 3, lect. 2, 129. Eph 3:8–9: "To me, though I am the very least of all the saints, this grace was given, to preach to the Gentiles the unsearchable riches of Christ, and to make all men see what is the plan of the mystery hidden in God who created all things."

the apostles to the rest of the faithful. Thus Aquinas can declare seeking out this divine mystery to be the greatest wisdom.

Aquinas avoids a sheer apophaticism that would present the mystery of salvation as a simple unknowing. Instead, Aquinas investigates this wisdom that has been unveiled. First, he considers Paul's statement "that through the Church the manifold wisdom of God may be made known" (Eph 3:10). Aquinas differentiates aspects of this wisdom, showing that its fullness and multiplicity comes from Christ. By doing so, Aquinas consistently roots the mystery in its Christological dimension. Aquinas then sees the phrase "the eternal purpose which he has realized in Christ Jesus" (Eph 3:11) as referring to eternal predestination in one of two ways: either, first, to eternal predestination itself, because it is according to wisdom and the Son is himself the wisdom of the Father; or, second, to the fulfillment of eternal predestination, "which God the Father brings to completion through the Son."[55] Aquinas does not present this option as though the interpreter has to choose, as both the act and the fulfillment refer to the same reality under different considerations. This is shown when Aquinas considers Paul's next phrase, "Christ Jesus our Lord, in whom we have boldness and confidence of access through our faith in him" (Eph 3:12). In both ways, the effect of the making known of God's predestination is to grant us "boldness and confidence." Aquinas describes this through the lens of the virtue of hope: both "to the hope of attaining to our reward" and "to the power of attaining to our reward."[56] Predestination implies hope, because the offer of redemption depends upon God and not us. In his *Summa Theologiae*, Aquinas identifies the object of hope as an arduous good, namely, the divine goodness itself, only attainable by God's free communication of his own goodness to his human creatures.[57] Aquinas summarizes this section on the "manifold wisdom of God" by saying that "God's many-faceted wisdom is revealed in the differentiation and pre-determining of the ages, which gives us assurance and access to the Father by faith in him."[58] The revelation has a straightforward effect in

---

55. *Commentary on Ephesians*, ch. 3, lect. 3, 130.

56. *Commentary on Ephesians*, ch. 3, lect. 3, 131.

57. *ST* II-II, q. 17, a. 6: "hope makes us adhere to God, as the source whence we derive perfect goodness, i.e., insofar as, by hope, we trust to the Divine assistance for obtaining happiness."

58. *Commentary on Ephesians*, ch. 3, lect. 3, 131. Cf. ch. 3, lect. 3, 133: "there exist certain

the believers. By means of the unveiling of God's mystery of redemption, which includes predestination, Paul strengthens and confirms the faith of the church in Ephesus and thus in all the faithful.

Aquinas moves from the virtue of hope to the virtues of faith and charity when he comments on Ephesians 3:19, "to know the love of Christ which surpasses knowledge, that you may be filled with the fullness of God." Aquinas explains that "the knowledge of God is necessary for us both in the future life and in the present" and then continues by clarifying that "our faith consists in the divinity and humanity of Christ."[59] Aquinas considers separately the knowledge of the divinity of Christ and that of the knowledge of the humanity of Christ, and shows how each distinctly are necessary. Knowledge of Christ's divinity reveals our call to eternal life. Knowledge of his humanity, however, especially reveals God's love for us. Aquinas writes, "since further knowledge is also necessary—a knowledge of the mysteries of the humanity—he goes on to know also the charity of Christ. For whatever occurred in the mystery of human redemption and Christ's incarnation was the work of love."[60] As was seen above, it is God's love that transcends our knowledge, not his arbitrary will and power. Aquinas connects God's love to the concrete manifestation of that love in the person of Jesus Christ: "It follows that to know Christ's love is to know all the mysteries of Christ's Incarnation and our Redemption."[61] Moreover, these mysteries come from God's immense charity, "a charity exceeding every created intelligence and the [combined] knowledge of all of them because it cannot be grasped in thought."[62] The mystery of predestination exceeds our understanding because it is the mystery of God's charity.

Aquinas reiterates the mystery of God's charity by considering a complementary interpretation of "what is the breadth and length and height and depth" (Eph 3:18) as referring to the Cross of Christ. Here again he

---

intelligible patterns [operative in] the mysteries of grace which transcend the whole of creation" "quod sunt quaedam rationes mysteriorum gratiae totam creaturam excedentes."

59. *Commentary on Ephesians*, ch. 3, lect. 5, 141–42. Note that Aquinas here speaks of faith as the substantive presence of the future life in us. Cf. Pope Benedict XVI, *Spe Salvi*, no. 7.

60. *Commentary on Ephesians*, ch. 3, lect. 5, 144: "Ubi sciendum est quod quidquid est in mysterio redemptionis humanae et incarnationis Christi, totum est opus charitatis."

61. *Commentary on Ephesians*, ch. 3, lect. 5, 144.

62. *Commentary on Ephesians*, ch. 3, lect. 5, 144: "quae ex immensa charitate Dei processerunt, quae quidem charitas excedit omnem intellectum creatum et omnium scientiam, cum sit incomprehensibilis cogitate."

refers to the exalted and mysterious character of the divine love as exceeding our knowledge. As the depth of the Cross refers to its physically being rooted in the ground beneath visible sight, so also "the depth of the divine love which sustains us is not visible insofar as the *ratio* of predestination, as was said above, is beyond our intelligence."[63] Aquinas parallels the hidden *ratio* of predestination with the profundity of the divine love. Aquinas emphasizes the incomprehensibility of Christ's love according to human understanding, "For no one could know how much Christ has loved us." Nonetheless, Aquinas does not therefore lead to a conflict between knowledge versus love in a kind of agnosticism. Instead, he explicitly affirms that charity with knowledge exceeds charity without knowledge: "I hold that such charity [with knowledge of Christ] surpasses a love which is without knowledge."[64] Aquinas finally characterizes this great love, this great communication of divine goodness, as a sharing in the divine nature: "For the human mind and will could never imagine, understand or ask that God become man, and that man become God and a sharer in the divine nature. But he has done this in us by his power, and it was accomplished in the Incarnation of his Son. 'That through this you may be made partakers of the divine nature' (2 Pet. 1:4)."[65] When God communicates his goodness as an act of love, he elevates human nature to participate in the divine nature. This loving elevation of human nature necessarily rests on the divine initiative.

Conclusion: Predestination within the Mystery of the Incarnation

Aquinas, in his theological exegesis of Ephesians, consistently presents predestination within the context of God's initiative in our redemption

63. *Commentary on Ephesians*, ch. 3, lect. 5, 146. "Ibi etiam est profundum in ligno quod latet sub terra et sustinet crucem, et tamen non videtur, quia profundum amoris divini sustinet nos, nec tamen videtur; quia ratio praedestinationis ut dictum est excedit intellectum nostrum."

64. *Commentary on Ephesians*, ch. 3, lect. 5, 146. Aquinas asks in this regard, "Is it not correct that a charity with knowledge is more eminent than a charity without knowledge? It seems that it is not, for then a wicked theologian would have a charity of greater dignity than a holy old woman. I reply that what is discussed here is a knowledge which exerts its influence [on one's life and conduct]. For the force of the knowledge stimulates one to love more since the more God is known, so much the more is he loved....A charity coupled with the above mentioned knowledge of Christ surpasses the love of such people."

65. *Commentary on Ephesians*, ch. 3, lect. 5, 147.

and the communication of his goodness by his loving adoption of us his children. This aspect of the communication of divine goodness offers a broader way of considering divine predestination than was presented in the contemporary biblical exegesis outlined by Markus Barth. Barth viewed that a theological understanding of God's eternal predestining will was at odds with the "personal, intimate, and functional" character of God's actions as presented in Ephesians 1. Barth viewed predestination as a kind of fatalism that deprived both God and human beings of a free and loving role to play in the drama of salvation. He employed language such as "an anonymous predestining force," "calculating or speculative," "a timeless divine will," "a fatalistic belief in a divine decree," and "a fixed will, testament, plan, and program of God."[66] Aquinas employs a different perspective on the question of predestination that allows him to proclaim the blessing of predestination in a way that elevates both divine and human freedom. In particular, he employs the metaphysics of creation as the framework for what we might call the metaphysics of the new creation. Human beings exist as a result of the free and loving act of God sharing his goodness via his creation; so do human beings have the opportunity to live eternally with God owing to his sharing his goodness through his free and loving act of re-re-creation. This divine communication not only brings human beings into existence, but also allows us to know and to love, and thus to respond to God's offer of love. The eternal character of God's purpose and plan does not limit human freedom, but rather encourages us in hope by the revelation of God's unsearchable love in Christ. Finally, the metaphysics of creation means that to ascribe to God's plan an eternal character does not contrast it to human time and human freedom. Instead, God's wisdom and love in creation and redemption constitute and embrace each moment of created time, space, and motion.

In his exhaustive treatment of predestination in Aquinas, the Dominican, Michal Paluch, emphasized the way in which Aquinas integrates the realities of time and eternity and of the Incarnation and predestination in his *Commentary on Ephesians*. Because it addresses directly some of the dichotomies posed by Barth, his comments are worth quoting at length. Paluch summarizes the interplay of the Incarnation and predestination as follows:

---

66. See original references from the introduction.

We see therefore that the Christological dimension highlights the deep link of the doctrine of predestination to the history of salvation. Indeed, it is the *Commentary on the Epistle to the Ephesians* that shows us the illuminating considerations about the link between temporality and the incarnation....In Thomas, there are truths that are not attainable except by their realization in history. The incarnation and predestination, both gifts of grace realized in history, belong, without any doubt, to this order. But there is a difference between them. While the incarnation is already carried out, the predestination that leads us to adoptive filiation, and so to the completion of the purpose of the incarnation, is still in the process of its realization. This situation limits our ability to approach this mystery. Our position in relation to the mystery of predestination is, *mutatis mutandis*, similar to that of the angels with respect to the mystery of the incarnation *ante factum*....In the words of Thomas, we can conclude that we have predestination *in generali*, but we cannot know *in speciali*. It has been made known to us the general plan to make us adoptive sons, but until this plan is in fact accomplished, we will not be able to touch it. In the same way that the realization of the incarnation in the historical person of Jesus Christ was inevitably surprising for the pure spirits who had known *ante factum in generali*, so also will the realization of predestination exceed our imaginations and our speculations.[67]

Predestination is located within the mystery of the Incarnation. Nonetheless, predestination retains its own proper intelligibility, as the adoption of sons must somehow be different from the filiation of the natural son even in history.

67. Michal Paluch, OP, *La Profonduer de l'Amor Divin: Evolution de la doctrine de la predestination dans l'oeuvre de saint Thomas d'Aquin* (Paris: Libraire Philosophique J. Vrin, 2004), 269–70. "Nous voyons donc que la dimension christologique fait ressortir le lien profound de la doctrine sur la predestination avec l'histoire du salut. En effet, c'est le Commentaire de l'Epitre aux Ephesiens qui nous propose des considerations lumineuses sur le lein entre la temporalite et l'incarnation....Chez Thomas, il y a donc des verites qui ne sont saisissables que par leur relatisation dans l'historie. L'incarnation et la predestination, dons de la grace realizes dans l'histoire, appartiennent, sans aucon doute, a cet ordre. Mais il y a une difference entre ells. Alors que l'incarnation s'est deja realisee, la predestination quis nous mene vers la filiation adoptive, donc vers l'achevement du but de l'incarnation, est encore en train de se realizer. Cette situation limite notre possibilite de nous approcher de ce mystere. Notre situation a l'egard du mystere de la predestination est, mutatis mutandis, semblable a cella des anges a l'egard due mystere de l'incarnation ante factum....Pour reprendre l'expression de Thomas, nous pouvons conclure que nous connaissons la predestination in generali, mais nouse ne pouvons pas la connaitre in speciali. Nous avons ete informes sur le dessein general de faire de nouse des fils adoptifs, mais tant que ce dessein ne sera pas reellement accomplice, nous ne serons pas capable de l'embrasser. De meme que la realization de l'incaration dans la personne historique de Jesus Christ a du etre suprenante pour les esprits purs qui l'avaient pourtant connue ante factum in generali, de meme la realization de la predestination depassera nos imaginations et nos speculations."

Aquinas began his commentary with the selection of Psalm 75:3, "I have strengthened its pillars," and saw in those words Paul's overarching aim of strengthening the faithful in Ephesus. The retrieval of Aquinas's exegesis of Ephesians presents the mystery of predestination in its biblical, doctrinal, and metaphysical context as part of the whole mystery of divine creation and redemption. Within this retrieval, Paul's words of predestination may hopefully recover in the ears of the faithful the sound of good news: "He destined us through love to be his sons through Jesus Christ, according to the purpose of his will, to the praise of his glorious grace which he freely bestowed on us in the Beloved" (Eph 1:3–6).

6

PRAEMOTIO PHYSICA AND
DIVINE TRANSCENDENCE

Joseph G. Trabbic

Praemotio physica is among the most controverted doctrines of the Thomistic tradition. There are two general questions that have given the debate its shape over the centuries. First, granted that later authors invented the term *praemotio physica*, can the doctrine be found materially in the writings of the St. Thomas Aquinas? Second, is the doctrine a sound one? Brian Shanley, a distinguished interpreter of Aquinas and the Thomistic tradition, answers both questions in the negative. According to Shanley, the partisans of *praemotio physica*—namely, Domingo Báñez and his disciples—go beyond Aquinas and treat of matters that the Angelic Doctor wisely preferred to leave in the realm of mystery. In advocating premotionism, Báñezians have got themselves into a dangerous spot, thinks Shanley, for their doctrine compromises divine transcendence,[1] human freedom,[2] and the reality of secondary causation,[3] and it further runs the risk of making God the direct cause of evil.[4]

1. Brian Shanley, "Divine Causation and Human Freedom in Aquinas," *American Catholic Philosophical Quarterly* 72 (1998): 101, 111, 116, 120, 121; idem, *The Thomist Tradition* (Dordrecht: Kluwer, 2002), 204.

2. Shanley, "Divine Causation and Human Freedom in Aquinas," 101, 110, 111, 116, 120, 121; *Thomist Tradition*, 107n56.

3. "Divine Causation and Human Freedom in Aquinas," 110–11.

4. Ibid., 116n46.

I believe that Shanley is wrong about all of this, but it is not my intention in this essay to reply to every one of the objections that he raises. The debate has already bequeathed to us plenty of literature on the interpretive issue and on the problems having to do with human freedom, the reality of secondary causation, and God's relationship to evil. I want to focus mostly on Shanley's claim that premotionism compromises God's transcendence, which seems to me to be a fairly nonstandard objection as well as an interesting one.

In the first part of this essay, I give a sketch of what I take to be the essentials of premotionism. Although Shanley singles out Báñez as the author of this doctrine, he does not cite any of his writings. He only cites the expositions of premotionism by Réginald Garrigou-Lagrange and T. C. O'Brien. Accordingly, I also draw upon them and authors who agree with them for my account of premotionism so that I can assume that Shanley and I have roughly the same thing in view. In this part of the essay, I won't completely avoid dealing with some of the various difficulties in the doctrine that incite objections to it—because taking up some of them will, I think, help to make the doctrine more intelligible—but I'm going to keep what I do on that front brief. In the second part of this essay, I argue that premotionism, far from compromising divine transcendence, absolutely requires it. In the final part, I try to respond to Shanley's claims to the contrary.

What *Praemotio Physica* Is

Let's begin with a concise statement of the doctrine of *praemotio physica* and then proceed to an analysis of each of the doctrine's principal parts. Premotionism is the view that God efficiently and predeterminately moves all created agents—that is, all agents other than God himself—to act, every time that they act and in the precise way that they act, by a transient, created motion. This sums up exactly Garrigou-Lagrange's and O'Brien's understanding of premotionism.

Now to what the doctrine holds about the ontological situation of created agents. As O'Brien notes, premotionists maintain that "no created agent is identical with the exercise of its own activity."[5] In other words, unlike God, created agents are not pure act, *actus purus*, but a mixture or

---

5. *New Catholic Encyclopedia*, vol. 11, s.v., "Premotion, Physical."

composite of act and potency. You might say that God is a "pure agent," whereas creatures are "impure agents." Consequently, in the view of pre-motionists, the actions of created agents are never brought about by those agents all by themselves. These acts require the causal involvement of a pure agent, or *the* pure agent, namely, God. Why? Well, a pure agent is an agent that is—if I may be permitted a Heideggerian expression—"always already" (*immer schon*) acting; it's just always in act. That's just what it means to be a pure agent. Created agents, however, because of the impurity of their agency, are not like that; they're not always already acting. Their individual actions are always a movement from being in potency to act to actually acting.[6] But nothing that is in potency to act can give itself that action toward which it is in potency. It cannot do this because *potency* to act is *not* act, just as, for instance, *being able* to mix a martini is not *actually* mixing a martini. The potency must be actualized, then, by something that is already in act that bestows upon the agent the motion whereby it is actualized. This something that is already in act may be another "part" of the created agents (say, their soul or nervous system). But that other part of the created agents cannot be the *ultimate* cause of the subsequent action. Why not? Because, if we're talking about created agents, then *any* action they do will, as we have seen, be a movement from potency to act. Therefore to appeal to any action of created agents as the cause of any of their other actions—while it may, and probably will, be informative about what's happening—will always leave me with the question about the cause of the cause I've identified, and my account will remain explanatorily incomplete. Evidently, the same will be true if I appeal to one created agent as the cause of the actions of another created agent. So long as I remain in the world of created agents—the *ordo creationis*—the best that I can hope for is a kind of endless Derridean deferral, that is, a *regressus in infinitum*.

The cure for the endless Derridean deferral is God, the pure agent. The ultimate cause of any action of created agents is always a pure agent.

---

6. The sort of action I have in mind here is what Aquinas, taking his cue from Aristotle, calls *actus secundus* "second act," or *operatio* "operation," and distinguishes from *actus primus*. Briefly, something's *actus primus* is its very existing, whereas its *actus secundus* is any individual action it carries out. My simple being alive, or living (which is the way living things exist), is thus my *actus primus*, whereas my particular deed of writing, smoking, or drinking is an *actus secundus*. On this distinction in Aquinas, see, e.g., *Super I Sententiarum*, d. 33, q. 1, a. 1, ad 1 (Lethiellieux, I: 766).

If created agents act, but not entirely of themselves, and none of their other actions nor any other created agent can be the ultimate cause of the actions of created agents, the ultimate cause must be a pure agent, for once I posit the pure agent as the cause, I have come to the end of explanation.[7] It is the nature of a pure agent—of God—always to be in act, so I don't have to hunt down a cause of the pure agent's action outside the pure agent itself.[8]

God is therefore the ultimate cause of all the actions of created agents. Said otherwise, God is the *primary* cause of all the actions of created agents. The created agents themselves are the *secondary* and, as it were, instrumental causes of their actions. They are instrumental causes inasmuch as God acts through them to bring about their actions. As premotionists put it, using Aquinas's own language, God "applies" (*applicat*) created agents to their actions.[9]

The motion by which God applies created agents to their actions is the motion to which premotionists refer with the term "premotion." The prefix "pre-" in "premotion" is meant to signal the priority of this motion, but the priority is not temporal. As R. P. Phillips points out, the priority is, rather, logical and causal.[10] The motion originating in God has a priority over the action of the created agent because the former is what *brings about* the latter, not because the former occurs *before* the latter. It probably goes without saying that created agents *passively* receive the motion imparted by God. If this is the very motion that actualizes them when they act, then it could be no other way.

The divine motion, it should further be observed, is a *tertium quid* vis-à-vis God and the created agent. It is neither identical with God nor

7. In my whole argument up to this point, I have done little more than paraphrase Aquinas's arguments for God's existence *ex motu*, of which the best known is in the *Summa Theologiae* I, q. 2, a. 3 (Leonine, IV: 31).

8. This doesn't mean that the pure agent's actions are *self*-caused. That would imply that something got its act going in the first place—even if that something is within the pure agent itself—and that means that its act is the *terminus* of a movement from potency. But that would put us right back in the situation of the acting created agent. If you get what it means for God to be a pure agent, then you will also get why James Mill's question (as reported by his son John Stuart Mill) "Who made God?" is otiose. See John Stuart Mill, *The Collected Works of John Stuart Mill*, vol. 1, *Autobiography and Literary Essays*, ed. J. M. Robson (Toronto: University of Toronto Press, 1981), 44.

9. *Summa Theologiae* I, q. 105, a. 5, ad 3 (Leonine, V: 476).

10. R. P. Phillips, *Modern Thomistic Philosophy*, vol. II (London: Burns, Oates & Washbourne, 1939), 344.

with the action of the created agent it actualizes. Garrigou-Lagrange thus tells us that we must not "confuse the divine motion that is passively received in the [created agent] with the active divine motion that is God himself, or with the operation produced by the [created agent]."[11] Phillips explains this by way of analogy with the heating of water by fire: "there is an active heat in the fire corresponding to the active motion of God; a heat received in the water, and so passively received, which corresponds to physical premotion; and the subsequent action of the hot water on bodies which are in contact with it, corresponding to the action of creatures following on the divine premotion."[12] According to O'Brien, the divine premotion is, more precisely, nothing but "the creature's passage to action."[13]

Phillips's designation of premotion as "physical" raises the question about the meaning of this particular qualifier. Garrigou-Lagrange tells us that "premotion is called physical not out of opposition to the metaphysical or spiritual, but out of opposition to *moral* motion, which draws the will by way of an objective attraction, proposing a good to it."[14] "Physical," in this context, is not intended as a synonym for "material," but as implying a motion other than that exerted by attraction. What we are talking about is an efficiently caused motion as distinct from the moral motion proper to a final cause. God is the efficient cause in question. Norberto del Prado, however, alerts us to the fact that "all physical premotion presupposes moral motion"; that is, all physical premotion also presupposes the motion that derives from a final cause.[15] This is so because what efficient causes do is actualize potencies. Potencies must be directed toward some definite actuality because not to be actualized in any definite way is not to be actualized at all. But to be directed toward

---

11. Réginald Garrigou-Lagrange, *La prédestination des saints et la grâce: Doctrine de saint Thomas comparée aux autres systèmes théologiques* (Paris: Desclée de Brouwer, 1936), 285; B. Rose, trans., *Predestination* (St. Louis: Herder, 1939), 259. Henceforth the page numbers of the English translation appear in parentheses after the page numbers of the French text.

12. Phillips, *Modern Thomistic Philosophy*, 345.

13. "Premotion, Physical." Cf. Garrigou-Lagrange, who describes the same thing thus: "*the passive motion*, by which the creature, that only has the power to act, is passively moved by God to become actually acting." *La prédestination*, 284 (258). The emphasis is his.

14. Garrigou-Lagrange, *La prédestination*, 290 (263). The emphasis is his.

15. Norberto del Prado, *De gratia et libero arbitrio*, vol. 2 (Fribourg: Consociationis Sancti Pauli, 1907), 146.

something, to have a *telos*, is precisely what it is to have a final cause. So, we can conclude that whenever we have an efficient cause, we will always have a final cause. While efficient causation may be in the foreground for premotionists, they assume that final causation also has a necessary role in physical premotion.

You will probably have noticed that in his clarification of the term "physical" in physical promotion, Garrigou-Lagrange relates this specifically to the efficient causation behind the movement of the will.[16] His statement may be somewhat misleading in that regard, for insofar as the term "physical" is meant to tell us that the motion in physical premotion is efficiently caused, this applies to *every* created agent that is actualized by the divine motion, not just to created agents with wills. Nevertheless, this mention of the latter kinds of agents brings into the picture one of the points of greatest controversy in the debate over *praemotio physica*, namely, whether it manages to preserve the freedom of action of created agents with free wills. I'm going to come back to these agents in a moment.

In my summary of premotionism at the beginning of this section, I stated that physical premotion is a transient motion. As O'Brien explains, physical premotion does not bestow upon the created agent something permanent, to wit, "the autonomous power to move itself to act."[17] According to O'Brien, that sort of power could not be conferred on any creature, for that would be to "transform [the creature] into the primary source of existence and act, to make it God."[18] If O'Brien is right about this consequence, then, we are evidently contemplating the absurd. Nothing can be radically autonomous *if it is caused*, because in that case the thing would be in some manner dependent and not autonomous; yet here it is being suggested that God could *cause* a radically autonomous being. Given that this is impossible, we see that it must be admitted that physical premotion is a transient motion.

---

16. In this respect, David Oderberg's more general explanation of the meaning of "physical" in physical premotion seems better than Garrigou-Lagrange's. Thus Oderberg: "It is a physical premotion—not in the sense that it is empirically measurable or subject to the laws of physics, but in contradistinction to merely moral or attractive premotion, whereby God inclines a secondary cause to move by virtue of proposing some end or object to be grasped by the patient as desirable." "Divine Premotion," *International Journal for Philosophy of Religion* 794(3): 209.

17. "Premotion, Physical."

18. Ibid.

I also stated in my summary above that physical premotion is something created.[19] Why this should be so is plain to see. Every Thomist holds that whatever really exists in distinction from God must be created by God, because Aquinas teaches that whatever exists and is not God is created by him.[20] Physical premotion is something distinct from God. The conclusion that physical premotion must be something created, then, is obvious. But while this motion is created, it does not "create" in the strict Thomistic sense of the term; that is, it does not bring anything into being *ex nihilo*.[21] It actualizes a created agent that already exists.

The last two points of the doctrine of *praemotio physica* that I must talk about are best discussed together. The first one is that God's causation in physical premotion is predetermining. David Oderberg says that physical premotion is "predetermining in the sense that the secondary cause infallibly does what God moves it to do."[22] Accordingly, if God moves a fire to heat water, the fire will heat the water without fail; and if he moves me to put $500 on Seabiscuit, I shall put $500 on Seabiscuit without fail. The action that God causes will unfailingly occur and will do so as the specific action that he has caused. In other words, physical premotion is not an indeterminate movement that created agents render determinate by what they, in fact, do. It is not an amorphous energy that it is up to me to channel in particular ways, as, say, "the Force" is in *Star Wars*. How could physical premotion function like this if it is, as I have already said, *passively* received by me?[23] Phillips indicates another problem with supposing that created agents determine the action that is the *telos* of physical premotion: "Such a determination," he states, "since by hypothesis it comes not from God but from the created will, would involve a passivity in Pure Act, inasmuch as God would not be the author but the observer of this determination, and so would be passive with regard to it."[24] Although Phillips is speaking here of created agents with

---

19. Cf. Garrigou-Lagrange, *La prédestination*, 278 (251–52).
20. *Summa Theologiae* I, q. 44, a. 1 (Leonine, IV: 455).
21. Garrigou-Lagrange, *La prédestination*, 282–83 (256–57).
22. Oderberg, "Divine Premotion," 209.
23. Cf. Garrigou-Lagrange, *La prédestination*, 308 (280). Note the mistake in the English translation. In Rose's rendering, we read: "We must take this to mean." Garrigou-Lagrange writes instead: *Il ne faut pas entendre*.
24. Phillips, *Modern Thomistic Philosophy*, 2:345. Cf. Garrigou-Lagrange, *La prédestination*, 275 (249).

wills, the same consideration would be pertinent, *mutatis mutandis*, to created agents without wills.

God predetermines not only the specific action of the created agent through physical premotion, but also its general modality—whether it is necessary, contingent, and/or free. The previous point and this last point are perhaps the aspects of premotionism that most people find problematic. Premotionists hold that God predetermines that this particular action will occur *and* that it will occur necessarily, contingently and/or as freely willed. For many people, talk of a predetermined contingent and/or freely willed action is oxymoronic. There is no question that this can be a hard nut to crack. I'm not going to pretend to crack it here, but I shall still say a few words about how premotionists address this problem, and I shall do this merely with the aim of making the doctrine intelligible.

Aquinas distinguishes between understanding a proposition *in sensu diviso* ("in a divided sense") and understanding it *in sensu composito* ("in a composed sense").[25] Suppose I tell you that Socrates can stand while he is sitting. If by this I mean that Socrates, while he is in fact sitting has at that same time the *power* to stand up in the next moment, then you would probably judge the original proposition I uttered to be true. My proposition, interpreted in this way, is intended *in sensu diviso*. But if by my proposition I mean that Socrates can actually be standing and sitting at the same time, then you would rightly judge my proposition to be false. Interpreted in this way, my proposition is intended *in sensu composito*.

Premotionists turn to this distinction to explain how God can predetermine an action and the action retain its contingency and/or freedom.[26] To go back to an example I used above, if by physical premotion

---

25. *De veritate*, q. 2, a. 13, ad 5 (Leonine, XXII: 90).

26. See Phillips, *Modern Thomistic Philosophy*, 2:349–50. A. J. Freddoso, "Introduction to the Problem of Free Will and Divine Causality," III, A-D (unpublished notes for a 2013 workshop at Mount Saint Mary's College). I don't think Freddoso uses these terms, but the distinction is implied. Freddoso isn't defending premotionism but rather explaining it. He is personally more inclined toward the "Jesuit" position. But he quite interestingly observes that "the strength of that inclination has decreased markedly over time as I have pondered the ramifications of the doctrine of God's transcendence." I don't know whether this means that he's moving in a Báñezian direction. A. C. Pegis's discussion of Molina's response to Báñez's use of the *sensu diviso/sensu composito* distinction is worth reading. See his "Molina and Human Liberty," in *Jesuit Thinkers of the Renaissance* (Milwaukee, WI: Marquette University Press, 1939), 92*ff.*

God moves my will to put \$500 on Seabiscuit, then I shall put \$500 on Seabiscuit without fail. The proposition "I shall put \$500 on Seabiscuit without fail," taken *in sensu diviso*, doesn't entail that I don't retain the *power*—even as I am placing the bet—the next moment to ask for my money back. In other words, I still have the ability to act otherwise, so I am free and the action I do is contingent.[27] The same proposition, taken *in sensu composito*, would exclude my freedom to act otherwise. But this latter sort of freedom should not be defended by anyone, because what it amounts to is a freedom to overturn the principle of noncontradiction, which is not a real freedom at all but a mere fiction.

David Oderberg[28] and Petr Dvořák[29] both believe that the premotionist understanding of freedom can be called "compatibilist." Alfred Freddoso, however, believes that there is a sense in which it can be called "libertarian."[30] I have my doubts about the suitability of either label. Perhaps the safest way to proceed is simply to describe the premotionist account of freedom without labeling it.

The Requirement of Divine Transcendence

I have already had a lot to say about God and his "place" in the doctrine of *praemotio physica* in the previous section. In the present section, I argue that premotionism, as I have explained it, requires a God who is both cosmologically and epistemically transcendent.[31] Put in other terms, the God of premotionism is no item in the world nor identical with the world, and he exceeds every concept I can form of him.

27. Opponents of premotionism might object that this notion of freedom is not yet robust enough for them. There might be more to say about the freedom that premotionism allows that would show it to be stronger than I have presented it here. But that would be a project for another time.

28. Oderberg, "Divine Premotion," 216–18.

29. Petr Dvořák, "The Concurrentism of Thomas Aquinas: Divine Causation and Human Freedom," *Philosophia* 41 (2013): 631.

30. Freddoso, "Introduction," III, C.

31. Here I'm borrowing the language Merold Westphal uses in *Transcendence and Self-Transcendence: On God and the Human Soul* (Bloomington: Indiana University Press, 2004). Westphal also talks about God's "ethical transcendence" and his "religious transcendence." I think a case could likewise be made for the ethical transcendence (in Westphal's sense) of the premotionist God, but I'm not going to pursue that here. I wonder about the logical necessity of Westphal's fourth category: religious transcendence. But I have not come to any definitive conclusions about it.

To begin, I want to back up a little bit to repeat a point I made earlier, that is, that physical premotion *moves* created agents to act; it does not *create* their actions. More needs to be said about this, and I shall let it be said by Garrigou-Lagrange:

although the divine motion, of which we speak, is not creation in the proper sense, it [i.e., the divine motion] can only come from the creative cause (*cause créatrice*), which is the only thing that can produce the whole being of a given effect and all its modes, whether the effect be necessary or free. On this subject, St. Thomas, commenting on Aristotle's *Perihermenias*, 1, 14, says: "The divine will is to be understood as existing outside the order of beings, like a cause that profoundly pervades all being (*totum ens*) and all its differentiae."[32]

Only the "creative cause"—only God the Creator—says Garrigou-Lagrange, can be the source of physical premotion because he alone "is capable of producing the whole being of a given effect and all its modes." Besides quoting what Aquinas states in his commentary on the *De Interpretatione* about God necessarily transcending the order of beings "like a cause that profoundly pervades all being and all its differentiae," Garrigou-Lagrange does not elaborate on his claim that physical premotion must proceed from God the Creator. Looking at Garrigou-Lagrange's other texts, however, we can piece together what he is getting at here.

As I mentioned previously, to "create," as this action is understood by Thomists, is to bring into being *ex nihilo*. It is to give something its being absolutely rather than merely to modify its being in some way. Thus God brings me, Seabiscuit, and my $500 into being not by modifying some preexisting bits of reality but by immediately instantiating the whole of what we are. In another text, Garrigou-Lagrange argues that only God has the power to create in this strict sense because God is "Being itself" (*l'Être même*).[33] He points to *Summa Theologiae* I, q. 45, a. 5, as making the case for this. I shall just convey to you the gist of Aquinas's reasoning there, which is more suggested than explicitly stated. It runs like this: (1) No created being, *A*—which as such merely *participates* in being— can bring another being, *B*, into being absolutely because *A* depends for

---

32. Garrigou-Lagrange, *La prédestination*, 283 (257).

33. Réginald Garrigou-Lagrange, *Dieu, son existence et sa nature: Solution thomiste des antinomies agnostiques*, 11th ed. (Paris: Beauchesne, 1950), 467; B. Rose, trans. *God: His Existence and His Nature: A Thomistic Solution of Certain Agnostic Antinomies*, vol. 2 (New York: Herder, 1936), 138. Henceforth page numbers of the English translation appear in parentheses after the page numbers of the French text.

its being on another. (2) Aquinas's claim could be summarized and re-phrased as: "No existentially *dependent* being can create." (3) The only "being" that could create would be an existentially *independent* being. (4) The only being fitting *that* description would have to be Being itself (*ipsum esse*) or, more precisely, subsistent Being itself (*ipsum esse subsistens*). (5) And this is God. Creating, then, is only possible for God in-sofar as he is *ipsum esse subsistens*. And this is what we have just seen Garrigou-Lagrange assert, too.

Now to how Garrigou-Lagrange understands the transcendence of God as *ipsum esse subsistens*. In his view, *ipsum esse subsistens* is not just one divine name among others. He regards it as the "formal constituent" (*constitutif formel*) of the divine nature.[34] What this means, for him, is that it is "that which we conceive in God as the basic principle that dis-tinguishes him from all creatures and from which we deduce his attri-butes."[35] As we saw a moment ago, no created being can be *ipsum esse subsistens*, for all created beings only *participate* in being. God as *ipsum esse subsistens*, therefore, must transcend the world. And if I understand the world as the totality of created beings, then God still must transcend the world: the totality of created beings merely amounts to a *totality* that *participates* in being. To borrow an example that Frederick Copleston uses against Bertrand Russell: no matter how many chocolates you add together, all you can get is a bunch of chocolates, and never anything that isn't chocolates.[36] Or, to use a favorite example of Garrigou-Lagrange's: "10,000 idiots do not make a single intelligent man."[37]

So, we can attribute cosmological transcendence to God as *ipsum esse subsistens*. But what of epistemic transcendence? Following Aqui-nas, Garrigou-Lagrange holds that the means of our knowledge—that by which I know whatever I naturally know—is what is proportionate to our created intellect.[38] Only creatures, of course, are proportionate to an intellect like ours. Hence it is through creatures that I know whatev-

---

34. Garrigou-Lagrange, *Dieu*, 356–64 (2:16–32).

35. Ibid., 358 (2:19).

36. Bertrand Russell, "The Existence of God," in *The Collected Papers of Bertrand Rus-sell*, vol. 11, *Last Philosophical Testament, 1947–1968*, ed. J. G. Slater and P. Köllner (London: Routledge, 1997), 529.

37. Garrigou-Lagrange, *Dieu*, 262 (1:285): "dix mille idiots ne font pas un homme intel-ligent."

38. Ibid., 713–14 (2:398).

er I know. Given that creatures are radically different from God inasmuch as they only *participate* in being and are not *ipsum esse subsistens*, the knowledge that I can have of God through them doesn't permit me to form any adequate concept of God. This does not mean that my concepts afford me no purchase, as it were, on the divine. But it does mean that they can only be related to God *analogically,* if they can be related to him at all. What Garrigou-Lagrange wants to say is that I can indeed have knowledge of God, but that this knowledge is always in some respect defective or imperfect. So, in the language I have been using, we can also attribute epistemic transcendence to God as *ipsum esse subsistens.*

My purpose in this part of my essay, is to argue that that premotionism, as explained in the previous section, requires a God who is both cosmologically and epistemically transcendent. I have been following the reasoning of Garrigou-Lagrange to make my case. He claims that only God the Creator can be the source of physical premotion. From what we have seen, I think we are now in a position to explain this claim. We know that, for Garrigou-Lagrange, God the Creator must be *ipsum esse subsistens.* But now we need to add that, following Aquinas, he holds that to regard God as *ipsum esse subsistens* is to regard him as *actus purus.*[39] The reason for this is that *esse* as such is an act; it is, as Aquinas understands it, *actualitas omnium actuum*—"the actuality of all acts."[40] This identity of *esse* with act is a commonplace of Thomism. Physical premotion absolutely depends on a God who is *actus purus,* which means, then, that only God the Creator, as Garrigou insists, can be the source of physical premotion. But there is more: if God as *actus purus* is identical with God as *ipsum esse subsistens* and if the latter gives us a God who is cosmologically and epistemically transcendent, then we can conclude that physical premotion requires a God of just such transcendence.

Objections and Replies

Having offered a sketch of the doctrine of *praemotio physica* and argued for the transcendence of the God invoked by the doctrine, I now

---

39. Ibid., 352, 358 (2:11, 19). Cf. *Compendium Theologiae* I, ch. 11 (Leonine, XLII: 86).
40. *De Potentia*, q. 7, a. 2, ad 9 (Marietti, 1953: 192).

turn to Shanley's contention that *praemotio physica* compromises divine transcendence. *Prima facie*, it may appear that this part of my essay has been rendered superfluous by the previous part. Perhaps it has. Whatever the case may be, I now consider and respond to Shanley's contention. I'm going to do this by summarizing his objections and replying to them.

According to Shanley's first objection—in the order that I am presenting them—premotionism compromises God's cosmological transcendence (he doesn't use the language of "cosmological transcendence," but it does express what he means) because it turns into something created, the very motion by which God moves created agents.[41]

I'm not sure what Shanley intends to say in this first objection. If he is saying that premotionism regards as a created being the action *in God* that is the source of the premotion, that would not be a real objection but only a misunderstanding of the doctrine. As I explained earlier, premotionists distinguish between God's action, the motion it produces (i.e., the referent of the term "physical premotion"), and the action of the created agent. No premotionist says that God's own action, which is identical with God himself, is created. But it is true that the motion produced by God and passively received by the created agent is something created. If it is this latter fact that Shanley is pointing to as compromising God's cosmological transcendence, however, then I must confess that I'm at a loss to see how it should. Why should God's acting through a created medium compromise his transcendence of the world? Unless you are an occasionalist, there should be no problem with supposing that God can act through secondary, created causes. But Shanley is no occasionalist, which only makes it harder to understand what he is objecting to here.

As with the first objection, it seems to me there are two different ways you could interpret Shanley's second objection. Both interpretations construe the objection as holding that premotionism compromises God's epistemic transcendence. On the first interpretation, Shanley wants to claim that the divine *motio* can be reduced to the divine *creatio* such that when God "moves" created agents, he is really creating them *ex nihilo*. And the way that "the creative *causa essendi* originates beings," says Shanley, "transcends any mode of mundane moving and so lies beyond

---

41. Shanley, "Divine Causation and Human Freedom in Aquinas," 116; idem, *Thomist Tradition*, 204.

our conceptual ken."[42] But premotionists, Shanley believes, tie God to a notion of moving that is essentially mundane, and fail to appreciate how our concepts break down in our attempt to understand *creatio*.

Now, I don't take Shanley literally when he says that *creatio* "lies beyond our conceptual ken"; that is, I don't take him to mean that I can have no understanding whatsoever of this divine action. The reason I don't read Shanley this way is that he himself says a great deal about what divine creation means. If he doesn't suppose that he is simply relaying nonsense, then he must believe that he has some understanding of what he's talking about. So, he must also believe that our concepts can apply at least analogically to God's creative action. But if that is how he sees things, then he has not shown us any essential difference between his understanding of how our concepts could apply to the divine *motio* and how premotionists like Garrigou-Lagrange understand them to apply.

On the second interpretation of Shanley's second objection, he does not reduce the divine *motio* to the divine *creatio*, but he nevertheless thinks that premotionists fail to appreciate just how different it is from "mundane moving" and how terribly difficult it is for us to understand.[43]

As I hope I was able to make clear in the previous section, premotionists like Garrigou-Lagrange are more than able to recognize that God as *actus purus* radically transcends our concepts, and that these concepts can only apply to him analogically at best.

Conclusion

In this essay I was not able to descend into all the detail that I would have liked to show you—if you needed showing at all—how the Thomistic doctrine of *praemotio physica* doesn't compromise divine transcendence but, on the contrary, requires it. I hope, nevertheless, that I was able to give you some idea about how this can be argued. I also hope that I was able to give you some idea of how Shanley's objections to the contrary can be answered.

42. Shanley, "Divine Causation and Human Freedom in Aquinas," 121.
43. Ibid., 100, 103, 121; Shanley, *Thomist Tradition*, 204.

—————— 7 ——————

GOD'S MOVEMENT OF
THE SOUL THROUGH OPERATIVE
AND COOPERATIVE GRACE

Lawrence Feingold

As a student in Rome in the mid-1990s, my interest in the question of predestination arose following a comment from a professor who said that intractable problems come about when a problem is not rightly posed. He suggested that with regard to the *de auxiliis* controversy, the issue had been posed as a false dilemma. I later discovered that several twentieth-century theologians—including Bernard Lonergan,[1] John Farrelly,[2] Francisco Marín-Sola,[3] Jacques Maritain,[4] and William Most[5]— had developed this thesis.

1. Bernard Lonergan, SJ, *Grace and Freedom: Operative Grace in the Thought of St. Thomas Aquinas. Collected Works of Bernard Lonergan*, vol. 1 (Toronto: University of Toronto Press, 2000), esp. 112–16, 147–48.

2. M. John Farrelly, OSB, *Predestination, Grace, and Free Will* (Westminster, MA: Newman Press, 1964).

3. Michael Torre, *Do Not Resist the Spirit's Call: Francisco Marín-Sola on Sufficient Grace* (Washington, DC: Catholic University of America Press, 2013), 128–30.

4. Jacques Maritain, *God and the Permission of Evil*, trans. Joseph W. Evans (Milwaukee: Bruce Publishing, 1966), 13–18.

5. William Most, *Grace, Predestination, and the Salvific Will of God: New Answers to Old Questions* (Front Royal, VA: Christendom Press, 1997).

What is the mistaken way of posing this problem about grace? I think there are actually several answers to this question,[6] but I am going to emphasize just one of them here. It seems to me that a false dilemma is created when actual grace is divided first into the categories of sufficient and efficacious grace. This is a division with regard to consequence. I see it as introducing a kind of consequentialism into the debate about the nature of actual grace.

A better division of actual grace is given by St. Augustine and clarified by St. Thomas. They first divide actual grace into operative and cooperative. This is a division of two functions of grace rather than two consequences: to begin supernatural action, and to carry it forward into the free and meritorious act.

Distinction between Operative and Cooperative Grace

When St. Thomas treats grace in the *Prima Secundae* of the *Summa Theologiae* (*ST*), he dedicates q. 111 to the division of grace. The first article distinguishes grace that sanctifies the recipient from charisms given to a certain individual in order that he might sanctify others. The second article distinguishes operative and cooperative grace. St. Thomas mentions that this distinction can be applied both to sanctifying and actual grace. Here I look at it as a distinction of actual grace.

From the time of the *De auxiliis* controversy, however, actual graces have generally been divided into two other categories, sufficient and efficacious. This distinction led to the two radically different schools of

6. The horns of this dilemma are well expressed by Marín-Sola: "Thomists have repeated at every turn, and with reason, that there is no middle ground between the *scientia media* and physical and determined premotion to every act, and that, if one rejects one of these, one is bound to end up with the other." "The Thomist System Regarding the Divine Motion," in Torre, *Do Not Resist the Spirit's Call*, 11. See also Réginald Garrigou-Lagrange, *Predestination: The Meaning of Predestination in Scripture and the Church* (Rockford, IL: Tan Books, 1998), 136: "The essence of Molinism consists in a definition of created liberty which includes the denial of the intrinsic efficacy of the divine decrees and of grace, obliging one to admit the theory of the *scientia media*." The problem with this way of posing the problem is that there are good reasons for rejecting both horns of the dilemma. Another way in which I think that the problem was incorrectly posed was that it was assumed that there was no intermediate position between the Molinist and the Báñezian that would preserve an infallible divine providential plan. This is discussed below.

Molinists and Báñezians, who understood this distinction of efficacious and sufficient in two opposing ways. Báñezians see efficacious grace as intrinsically different from merely sufficient grace, whereas Molinists see the difference not in the grace itself, but in the cooperation or noncooperation of the will.[7] It is interesting that St. Thomas does not mention the distinction between sufficient and efficacious *at all* in this question in which the proper division of grace is explained.[8] My thesis is that it makes an important difference whether one starts with the categories of sufficient and efficacious grace, or operative and cooperative, as St. Thomas does. We can then proceed to ask how they are efficacious or fallible, and for what acts.

So let us follow St. Thomas in dividing actual grace into an operative and a cooperative function. To understand this distinction, we have to consider that actual grace is a supernatural movement in which God transmits an impulse to our spiritual faculties of intellect and will, moving us to act for our supernatural end. Because actual grace initiates a human act directed to salvation, it should be analyzed as a kind of movement or change. If we take the deficient analogy of local movement, as in a billiard ball, we find three key elements to consider: an input of force at the point of departure, the passage from the point of departure to the destination, and the arrival at the destination. According to this analogy, operative grace would correspond to the input of force at the point of departure, and cooperative grace would correspond to the passage, which is a self-movement of the will aided by grace, which culminates in the meritorious act that corresponds to the point of arrival. Operative grace efficaciously incites a desire for salvation, and thus it is the starting point or initial impetus. Once desire is incited, we can now freely deliberate

7. See the explanation of the two rival positions by Garrigou-Lagrange, *Predestination*, 234: "For the Thomists, there are two kinds of actual interior graces; one kind is intrinsically efficacious of itself; for it causes us to perform the good act; the other is inefficacious but truly sufficient; for it gives us either the proximate or remote power to perform the good act. For the Molinists, actual sufficient grace is itself either extrinsically efficacious, by reason of our consent that is foreseen by God by means of the *scientia media*, or else it is inefficacious and merely sufficient." See also Domingo Báñez, "Apología en defensa de la doctrina antigua y católica de los maestros dominicanos de la provincia de España contra las afirmaciones contenidas en la 'Concordia' del padre Luis de Molina," in *Domingo Báñez y las controversias sobre la gracia: Textos y documentos*, ed. Vincente Beltrán de Heredia (Madrid: Consejo Superior de Investigaciones Científicas, Instituto "Francisco Suárez," 1968), 128.

8. See Most, *Grace, Predestination, and the Salvific Will of God*, 181.

about and consent to concrete actions that are directed to it or not. When we begin to deliberate, operative grace continues as cooperative grace, moving us to that same end, but now resistibly.

Each subject receives the impulse of the mover according to its own nature. Thus a billiard ball receives movement differently than a cube would, and both receive it differently than a self-moving subject. Because here we are analyzing the movement of a *self-moving* power, we have to distinguish between how we are moved by God without yet moving ourselves (the initial impulse), and how we move ourselves under the impulse of grace in the passage to the completed free salvific action. This distinction corresponds, in fact, to the one given above. The point of departure will be the reception of a movement in which we are moved by God's grace, but not yet self-moving, and the passage to the completed free act aiming at a supernatural end will be a movement in which we are both moved by God and moving ourselves. The intellect, for example, can be moved without moving itself when it receives some infused knowledge. It can then move itself to reason on the basis of the infused knowledge received. Likewise, the will can be moved without moving itself when it is attracted to a new end to which it had not previously been attracted. That attraction can then cause it to move itself to choose means ordered to that newly desired end.[9] This is how St. Thomas defines operative and cooperative grace:

The operation of an effect is not attributed to the thing moved but to the mover. Hence in that effect in which our mind is moved and does not move [itself], but in which God is the sole mover, the operation is attributed to God, and it is with reference to this that we speak of *operating grace*. But in that effect in which our mind both moves [itself] and is moved, the operation is not only attributed to God, but also to the soul; and it is with reference to this that we speak of *co-operating grace*.[10]

To give examples of the respective effects of operative and cooperating grace, St. Thomas writes:

9. See *ST* I-II, q. 9, a. 3: "It is evident that the intellect, through its knowledge of the principle, reduces itself from potentiality to act, as to its knowledge of the conclusions; and thus it moves itself. And, in like manner, the will, through its volition of the end, moves itself to will the means." This explanation of the will's self-movement applies to the supernatural level as well as to the natural. The difference is that in the supernatural order, the end that motivates the choice of means is a supernatural one made known by faith.

10. *ST* I-II, q. 111, a. 2.

Now there is a double act in us. First, there is the interior act of the will, and with regard to this act the will is a thing moved, and God is the mover; and especially when the will, which hitherto willed evil, begins to will good. And hence, inasmuch as God moves the human mind to this act, we speak of operating grace. But there is another, exterior act; and since it is commanded by the will, as was shown above [*ST* I-II, q. 17, a. 9] the operation of this act is attributed to the will. And because God assists us in this act, both by strengthening our will interiorly so as to attain to the act, and by granting outwardly the capability of operating, it is with respect to this that we speak of co-operating grace.[11]

On the basis of an operative grace by which we are attracted to the supernatural good, we can then deliberate about how to attain that good and make a salutary choice. The good deliberation and choice involve self-movement made possible by the operative grace already received, which now *cooperates* with the good movement of the will to consent, choose, and execute actions ordered to salvation.[12] It seems that operative and cooperative grace should generally be thought of as one divine impulse that has different functions by which its initial power is extended and made fruitful over time. St. Thomas says: "Operating and cooperating grace are the same grace; but are distinguished by their different effects."[13]

We can compare operative and cooperative grace to the seed in the parable of the sower in Matthew 13:3–23. The seed is one, but at first it is sown on the soil without any participation from the soil. It then continues to germinate and grow, but only with the participation of the disposition of the soil. In a similar way, the impulse of actual grace is one, but it accomplishes two different kinds of effects, one immediate and the other mediated by the will's own cooperation. Operative grace does not presuppose any prior movement of the will and gives it a new attraction for

---

11. *ST* I-II, q. 111, a. 2.

12. It seems that cooperative grace is not limited to the execution of the exterior act, but would extend to interior acts that are the fruits of the will's self-movement under the influence of grace, such as the interior acts of consent and choice. See Lonergan's analysis in *Grace and Freedom*, 140. "We are led to consider as alone probable the third of the hypotheses listed above: the internal act of will is with respect to the end; the external act is not merely the bodily execution but also the act of the will commanding this execution."

13. *ST* I-II, q. 111, a. 2, ad 4. See Lonergan, *Grace and Freedom*, 130. "Such a definition implies that one and the same grace produces some effects by itself and others in conjunction with free will."

a salvific end (and thus it is also called *prevenient*). Cooperative grace refers to the *subsequent action of that same grace*, which *supports* the movement of the soul to the supernatural good in its free actions of consent and choice, and which presupposes the good and salutary desire of the will that was first brought about by operative grace. Thus it is also called aiding (*adiuvans*) or subsequent grace.[14]

St. Thomas takes this distinction from St. Augustine in his work *Grace and Free Will*, which St. Thomas quotes in this article.[15] St. Augustine, in discussing Philippians 1:6, writes:

For He who first works in us the power to will is the same who cooperates in bringing this work to perfection in those who will it. Accordingly, the Apostle says: "I am convinced of this, that he who has begun a good work in you will bring it to perfection until the day of Christ Jesus" (Phil 1:6). *God, then, works in us, without our cooperation, the power to will, but once we begin to will, and do so in a way that brings us to act, then it is that He cooperates with us.* But if He does not work in us the power to will or does not cooperate in our act of willing, we are powerless to perform good works of a salutary nature.[16]

Because operative grace is the work of God prior to the will's self-movement, it is efficacious of itself. But the whole purpose of operative grace is to enable the will, on the basis of what has been received, to move the intellect to deliberate about how to accomplish concrete steps to the supernatural end, and then for the will *to consent freely* to those steps. This deliberation and consent are accomplished through the aid of cooperative grace, which is the same grace that was originally operative and

14. The Council of Trent, sess. 6, Decree on Justification, ch. 5, refers to operative grace as *excitans* (stimulating or quickening) and *vocans* (calling), whereas it calls cooperative grace *adiuvans* (aiding or helping). Operative grace *touches* the heart and attracts or *calls* one to conversion, whereas cooperative grace *aids* our free consent on the supernatural level.

15. Lonergan argues that St. Thomas's understanding of this distinction is not exactly the same as that of St. Augustine. *Grace and Freedom*, 131–32, 205. St. Augustine, contrary to St. Thomas, conceives of these graces as chronologically distinct acts, for he implies that operative grace changes the will to give it good desires at the beginning of the spiritual life, and cooperative grace perfects it to realize subsequent meritorious works in the maturity of the spiritual life. St. Thomas generalizes their functions, so that operative grace stands at the head of all salvific acts throughout the spiritual life, and cooperative grace is present in all free consent and choice of salvific means, whether at the beginning or summit of the spiritual life.

16. *Grace and Free Will* 17.33, in *St. Augustine: The Teacher, The Free Choice of the Will, Grace and Free Will*, trans. Robert Russell (Washington, DC: Catholic University of America Press, 1968), 288–89. Emphasis added.

is now cooperating with the will's self-movement. Thus the action of operative grace is perfected by cooperative grace. Cooperative grace, by its very nature, is correlative to the will's free supernatural self-movement, which is made possible and aided by grace. God begins by working in the will without the will's cooperation, attracting it to himself, precisely so that he can gain the free cooperation of the will in the process of salvation. The expression "cooperating grace" in the texts of St. Augustine and St. Thomas cited above refers grammatically to the action of God as cooperating with the soul insofar as it has become a self-mover in the supernatural order. Thus we can say both that the soul cooperates with grace, and that grace cooperates with the soul's continued self-movement that grace has initiated.

Thus the action of illumination and attraction aroused by operative grace is attributed to God alone, whereas the free action accomplished through cooperative grace—involving deliberation and consent to some concrete means ordered to the supernatural end—is attributed both to God's grace and to the person willing. Thus we cannot say that Paul illuminated himself or attracted his own will to the supernatural end. It is God who acted through operative grace. We can say, however, that Paul chose to make acts of faith, hope, charity, and to receive baptism, for in those acts his own will was acting as a self-mover under the powerful influence of the grace received, which continued to attract and motivate Paul's will throughout the process.

The end to which operative grace attracts the will may simply be the supernatural end in general—heaven—or it may also be some more particular supernatural good that was not previously desired.[17] Because deliberation and choice concern proximate means to achieve those ends, it follows that cooperative grace is immediately ordered to more particular and proximate ends than operative grace.

---

17. See *ST* I-II, q. 9, a. 6, ad 3. "God moves man's will, as the Universal Mover, to the universal object of the will, which is good. And without this universal motion, man cannot will anything. But man determines himself by his reason to will this or that, which is true or apparent good. Nevertheless, sometimes God moves some specially to the willing of something determinate, which is good; as in the case of those whom He moves by grace, as we shall state later on."

Operative and Cooperative Grace in Scripture

The roles of operative and cooperative grace are manifested in Scripture in numerous places, such as Revelation 3:20: "Behold, I stand at the door and knock; if any one hears my voice and opens the door, I will come in to him and eat with him, and he with me." The action of grace knocking on the door signifies operative grace. But the purpose of the knocking is precisely that one open the door to Christ. This cannot happen without operative grace becoming cooperative, leading the will to initiate deliberation and then to consent to concrete steps of conversion.

Another example is John 6:44: "No one can come to me unless the Father who sent me draws him." God's action of "drawing" or *attracting* the soul toward Christ is the work of operative grace. The purpose of the attraction is that the soul freely *comes* and is converted through cooperation with grace, however. Operative grace begins the process referred to by the prophet Isaiah when he says, "They have sought me that before asked not for me, they have found me that sought me not. I said: Behold me, behold me, to a nation that did not call upon my name" (Is 65:1). That we actually call on God's name, however, is the work of the will cooperating with grace.

Whenever a sinner is suddenly attracted to repentance and a change of life, there is an operative grace that has attracted the mind and the will of the sinner toward God. Examples would be Christ's appearance to Saul on the way to Damascus, the calling of Matthew, or the desire aroused in the heart of Zacchaeus to see Christ as he passed through Jericho. Cooperative grace then continues to be at work in the repentant sinner as he deliberates about changing his life and makes a salutary choice on the basis of the good desire awakened by operative grace. In the case of Zacchaeus, this would be his resolve to give half his goods to the poor and restore fourfold anything unlawfully taken (see Lk 19:8).

Another key text is the parable of the sower in Matthew 13:3–23. The priority of the action of God through operative grace is illustrated by the action of the sower in sowing the same seed in all kinds of soil. The necessity of human cooperation and the real possibility of noncooperation with (or resistance to) the supernatural knowledge and desire we receive from operative grace is illustrated by the different kinds of growth in the different soils. Complete lack of cooperation is indicated in the case of the seed sown on the road, where it remains entirely without fruit. In the rocky or weed-filled soil, some cooperation follows, but not such as to ensure final perseverance. Different grades of cooperation are seen to be possible with the yield of thirty-, sixty-, or hundredfold.

The obstinate lack of cooperation with the movement initiated through operative grace is referred to in Scripture as the "hardening of the heart" or the "stiffening of the neck." A classic text is Psalm 95:8: "Harden not your hearts, as at Meribah, as on the day at Massah in the wilderness." God frequently complains that the Israelites "did not listen or incline their ear, but stiffened their neck, that they might not hear and receive instruction" (Jer 17:23).

The distinction of operative and cooperative grace helps us to understand at what point grace is resistible, which is precisely where the will begins to move itself under the attraction of the prevenient grace. Only when the will is self-moving can it resist or not resist, for only then it can choose, or fail to choose, means ordered to the supernatural end to which operative grace has attracted it.[18]

Efficacy of Operative and Cooperative Grace

Let us now look at the efficacy of operative and cooperative graces and see how they correspond to the traditional distinction between sufficient and efficacious grace and the positions disputed in the *De auxiliis* controversy. We can say first that operative grace infallibly achieves a certain effect: illuminating the intellect and exciting the will. This action does not fail in achieving this effect because here our spiritual faculties are moved and not yet self-moving. Therefore in the reception of an operative grace, the will cannot pose an obstacle to God's movement through deviating from the original impulse by a defective self-movement. That can only happen in what follows on the original reception. Operative

---

18. See Marín-Sola, "A Reply to Some Objections Concerning the Thomist System Regarding the Divine Motion," in Torre, *Do Not Resist the Spirit's Call*, 79. "In this *beginning* [operating grace], by being from God alone, there can be no impediment, just as Adam could not place an impediment that God instill in him the breath of life. In the *continuation* of this life [cooperating grace], there can be an impediment, just as Adam could commit suicide after being created." See also ibid., p. 21.

grace is therefore efficacious for achieving its immediate end, which is to infuse supernatural knowledge and excite the will to be immediately attracted to salvation (or to some more particular salvific end).

In terms of St. Thomas's analysis of the various stages of the complete moral act, the effect of an operative grace is to realize an act of simple volition of the supernatural end. Because simple volition of an end stands at the start of the complete moral act, it can be seen that operative grace works the beginning of each and any salvific act, for without simple volition of salvation, one could not even begin to deliberate about choosing any means of salvation, such as prayer or the sacraments. Operative grace does that which man simply cannot do by way of the will's self-movement. Failure to realize this is the essence of Pelagianism and semi-Pelagianism.

Having been brought by God's operative grace to desire salvation, the will can then direct the intellect to deliberate about means, both remote and proximate, to realize its desire. This begins the process of the formation of an intention for a remote means to be achieved through available proximate means, which are compared with one another. If judged suitable, such means are consented to and one means is chosen, which leads the intellect to order and the will to command the execution in the exterior or completed act, which may be going to confession, baptism, or prayer. In all these integral parts of the complete moral act, the will is able to be a self-mover precisely because of being moved by God to desire our supernatural end. The desire for the salvific end therefore continues to be active in *motivating* a supernatural self-movement of the will.[19] In the passage from simple volition of a supernatural end to actual choice of some concrete means ordered to that end, grace has become cooperative.

St. Thomas traces the playing-out of operative and cooperative grace in an article on contrition, in which he outlines the steps by which the act of contrition is generated:

We may speak of penance, with regard to the acts whereby in penance we co-operate with God operating, the first principle of which acts is the opera-

___

19. The part worked by operative grace remains the primary impulse throughout the integral good action. We can apply the words of Jesus in Jn 15:5 "For apart from me you can do nothing (salvific)." For this reason the analogy used by Molina in his *Concordia*, q. 14, a. 13, disp. 26, of two men pulling a boat, is insufficient. Such an analogy fails to recognize that that impulse given by operative grace works as a principal cause rather than a partial cause.

tion of God in turning the heart, according to Lamentations 5:21: "Convert us, O Lord, to Thee, and we shall be converted."[20]

Supernatural repentance issues forth from operative grace, which leads us, through the continued action of grace, now cooperative, to elicit acts of faith, servile fear, hope, charity, and filial fear.

Resistance

Let us examine, on the contrary, the case in which the will fails to follow the impulse of grace. As we have seen, Scripture shows that actual graces can be resisted, and often are resisted, whether at the beginning or further along in the spiritual life. St. Thomas likewise teaches that actual grace can be resisted.[21] The Council of Trent also teaches this in its Decree on Justification: "Man himself is not entirely inactive while receiving that inspiration, since he can reject it; and yet, without God's grace, he cannot by his own free will move toward justice in God's sight."[22] It was one of the errors of Jansenism, condemned by Innocent X, to teach that "in the state of fallen nature interior grace is never resisted."[23] The greatest problem in the system of Báñez and his followers is the thesis that every salvific action requires an intrinsically efficacious grace,[24] which would seem to be irresistible.

---

20. *ST* III, q. 85, a. 5.

21. See *Summa contra Gentiles* (ScG) III, ch. 159. "Although one may neither merit in advance nor call forth divine grace by a movement of his free choice, he is able to prevent himself from receiving this grace....And since this ability to impede or not to impede the reception of divine grace is within the scope of free choice, not undeservedly is responsibility for the fault imputed to him who offers an impediment to the reception of grace. In fact, as far as He is concerned, God is ready to give grace to all; 'indeed He wills all men to be saved, and to come to the knowledge of the truth,' as is said in 1 Timothy (2:4). But those alone are deprived of grace who offer an obstacle within themselves to grace; just as, while the sun is shining on the world, the man who keeps his eyes closed is held responsible for his fault, if as a result some evil follows, even though he could not see unless he were provided in advance with light from the sun."

22. Council of Trent, Decree on Justification, ch. 5, DS 1525.

23. DS 2002.

24. See the qualification given by Marín-Sola, "The Thomist System Regarding the Divine Motion," in Torre, *Do Not Resist the Spirit's Call*, 27. "The common idea of all Thomists that infallibly efficacious grace is needed for *every* supernatural *act* is inexact. It is required for every *perfect* act, which is what the Thomists call *opus salutis aeternae*, but it is not for easy or imperfect acts....This is a doctrine which is common enough in Thomism... even though these same Thomists appear later to forget it, in other parts of their work." Marín-Sola's thesis is that in his general providence, God gives graces that are resistible or

But how could God's movement fail to obtain its effect? Some would say that this is simply contradictory.[25] How could there be a divine movement that does not actually move the creature? Either God moves the soul or he does not, in which case there is no movement by God at all, and so there is no divine movement that fails to have an effect. I agree. Operative grace does not fail to operate, whenever God chooses to give it. It will always incite a desire for salvation. But we can fail to cooperate with this desire that operative grace infallibly places in us by failing to choose appropriate means ordered toward realization of the supernatural end.

It is easy to resolve this objection by distinguishing two different effects of the same impulse of grace: the initial attraction to salvation and the actual choice of salvific means. Operative grace never fails in realizing its direct effect of moving the soul, which does not yet move itself, to be attracted to the supernatural good. We have seen, however, that the initial movement effected by operative grace is meant to initiate a process of self-movement of the will and intellect that culminates in the realization of a complete good moral act in which there is free consent and choice of means ordered to salvation. This opens up the possibility that the initial operative grace achieves its first effect and still fails to achieve, under the form of cooperative grace, the further effect to which it is ordered.

We can make an analogy here with nature. It frequently happens that a higher cause does not fail in achieving its direct effect, but its ultimate or further effect is frustrated through the failure of a secondary contingent cause acting as an instrument of the higher cause. If a sculptor, such as Michelangelo, seeks to execute a magnificent plan through a broken chisel or faulty piece of marble, the realization of the sculpture will be thwarted through the failure of the instrument or material.

St. Thomas explains contingency in creation precisely in these terms.

---

fallible with regard to the free consent of the will. Only in his special providence does he give graces that are irresistible or infallibly efficacious.

25. See Steve Long, "Providence, Freedom, and Natural Law," *Nova et Vetera* 4/3 (Summer 2006): 588–89. "We may perhaps adjust the saying of Einstein, who commented that 'God does not play dice with the universe,' to note that God does not play dice with the will, moving it in a way that may or may not freely achieve any effect.... It makes no sense to say that the same causal influx that yields being may just as well yield non-being, as though the First Cause were playing darts whilst smoking hashish."

God wills contingent effects to come about for the good of the universe, and thus he assigns to them contingent causes, which can rightly operate or fail.[26] The human will's *self-movement* is such a contingent cause. In operative grace, God moves the will with a movement that of itself is necessary and infallible in achieving its direct effect (illumination of the intellect and simple volition of a salvific end). This effect in turn makes possible a self-movement of the will, which, as an instrument of and co-operator with God's grace, can either rightly operate under the impetus of the initial attraction to salvation by choosing apt means, or in a defective manner shrink from actually choosing means rightly ordered to the supernatural end. A classic example of such a deviation is given by St. Augustine in his *Confessions*. God inspired a desire for chastity in him, but he did not choose to adopt the means, praying: "Give me chastity and self-restraint, but not just yet."[27]

Francisco Marín-Sola[28] and Jacques Maritain[29] have given a good analysis of the faulty deliberation, in which one neglects to consider the right means to that salvific good and ultimately chooses something incompatible with it. As a result of the defective deliberation and its untimely close, the will consents to means incompatible with the supernatural end, and the impulse created in the soul by the operative grace

---

26. See *ST* I, q. 19, a. 8. "Since then the divine will is perfectly efficacious, it follows not only that things are done, which God wills to be done, but also that they are done in the way that He wills. Now God wills some things to be done necessarily, some contingently, to the right ordering of things, for the building up of the universe. Therefore to some effects He has attached necessary causes, that cannot fail; but to others defectible and contingent causes, from which arise contingent effects. Hence it is not because the proximate causes are contingent that the effects willed by God happen contingently, but because God has prepared contingent causes for them, it being His will that they should happen contingently." See also *ST* I-II, q. 10, a. 4. "As Dionysius says (*Div. Nom.* 4) 'it belongs to Divine providence, not to destroy but to preserve the nature of things.' Wherefore it moves all things in accordance with their conditions; so that from necessary causes through the Divine motion, effects follow of necessity; but from contingent causes, effects follow contingently. Since, therefore, the will is an active principle, not determinate to one thing, but having an indifferent relation to many things, God so moves it, that He does not determine it of necessity to one thing, but its movement remains contingent and not necessary, except in those things to which it is moved naturally." See also *ST* I, q. 83, a. 1, ad 3; St. Thomas, *Expositio libri Peryermenias* I, 14: 78–79.

27. St. Augustine, *Confessions* 8.7.17, trans. V. J. Bourke (Washington, DC: Catholic University of America Press, 1953), 213.

28. Torre, *Do Not Resist the Spirit's Call*, 181–87.

29. Maritain, *God and the Permission of Evil*, 44–51.

cannot continue its proper course. This hindrance is the work of the soul alone, caused by a disordered attachment of the will. This is easy to see in the example of St. Augustine mentioned above.

The attachment of the will does not have to cause the hindrance, however, for the deliberation can continue with a consideration of the attraction of the salvific good and an appropriate means to realize it. The will's self-movement during the deliberative process that culminates with consent is thus a contingent cause that can fail to achieve its proper operation. Because the will is a contingent cause, it can cease to cooperate with the initial grace, and the latter's power to cause continued movement under the form of cooperative grace will thus be terminated.

In summary, operative grace is always efficacious for its immediate and direct effect in simple willing or intention, but not always for the succeeding movements of the will, which are aided through cooperative grace to bring the moral act to completion. Operative grace cannot accomplish that without becoming cooperative with the human will, which, through God's aid, can effectively move itself toward that happy conclusion.

Thus we can say that operative grace is always *efficacious* for its direct and immediate effect, and it is *sufficient* to continue the movement (now under the name of cooperative grace) for the realization of the further effect of the free meritorious election.[30] Cooperative grace can be frustrated in the course of deliberation by a final practical judgment contrary to grace's attraction. Nevertheless, it is sufficient to make possible the completion of the good act. The lack is to be ascribed entirely to the poor deliberation that fails to consider what ought to regulate the will's choice.

God's Foreknowledge through Presence to His Eternity

One of the most important objections against the position that I am defending is that it would render problematic God's foreknowledge of our response to cooperative grace. The Báñezian school understands this

30. See Marín-Sola, "A Reply to Some Objections," in Torre, *Do Not Resist the Spirit's Call*, 60, where he stresses the axiom of the Thomistic commentators that there is no sufficient grace that is not also efficacious for something prior. "It is a fundamental Thomistic principle that *all* grace that is *sufficient* for a greater thing is and must be *efficacious* for a lesser thing."

foreknowledge precisely through God's eternal decree to sometimes mercifully grant intrinsically efficacious grace and sometimes to permit such grace to be withheld.[31] The Molinist school answers this question in an opposing way by positing middle knowledge while denying the necessity of intrinsically efficacious grace. God foreknows our consent through knowing all future conditionals. But both positions seem incompatible with St. Thomas's explanation of God's foreknowledge of free actions.

Whenever St. Thomas poses the question about God's knowledge of free human actions in the future, he has a consistent position in various articles throughout his career. He addressed it first in his commentary on the *Sentences*, bk. 1, d. 38, q. 1, a. 5, and in his maturity in *ST* I, q. 14, a. 13.[32] Each time he maintains two points. First, for something to be known with certainty, it must be determined, either in its causes or in its present existence. Future free acts are not determined in their cause, so they cannot be known with certainty in that way, even by God. Second, those free acts are determined in themselves when they are actually chosen in time. This time may be future to us, but to God's eternity all times are present. God thus knows free human acts not through causes, but through their being eternally present to himself in their actuality.

This seems to rule out both of the classic positions of Molina and Báñez. Middle knowledge is excluded because a future conditional is *never* determined in itself, and thus it seems that on the part of the object there is nothing to be known with certainty. This forms the proper basis for the classical Thomist objection to middle knowledge.

The position of Báñez also seems to be excluded, however, because St. Thomas never says that God has knowledge of future free acts through knowing his own infallible predetermining decrees. Quite the contrary! The medium of God's knowledge is always said to be the eternal present,

---

31. See Báñez's commentary on *ST* I, q. 14, a. 13, in *Scholastica Commentaria in Primam Partem Summae Theologicae S. Thomae Aquinatis* (Madrid: Editorial F.E.D.A., 1934), 353. "The created will infallibly will fail with regard to any matter of virtue, unless it is efficaciously determined by the divine will to act well. Thus, from the very fact that God knows that His will does not determine the created will to act well in a given matter, such as that of temperance, He knows evidently that the created will will sin and fall short in the matter of that virtue. Thus, God knows other future contingents in their causes as determined by the first cause, but future culpable evil He knows in its cause insofar as it is not determined by the first cause to act well" (my translation).

32. Between these he treated the question in *De veritate*, q. 2, a. 12; *Quaestiones de quolibet* XI, q. 3, a. 1; *ScG* I, ch. 66–67; *Compendium theologiae*, ch. 133; *De rationibus fidei*, ch. 10.

because free acts are not predetermined in their causes. In *I Sent.*, d. 38, q. 1, a. 5, for example, St. Thomas writes: "It cannot be both that God knows that this man will run, and he fail to run. And this is from the certainty of His knowledge and not on account of His causality."[33]

Some have objected that this is true of created causes, but not of God's own causality.[34] In other words, St. Thomas is saying that God cannot know free future human acts through knowing them in their created causes, but he still could know them in his own eternal decrees to give efficacious grace or permit it to be withheld. This does not seem to be correct, however, and St. Thomas seems to directly state the opposite, for he always explains God's knowledge of future free acts exclusively through their being eternally present to him through his knowledge of vision, and never through knowing his own eternal decrees to grant grace.

Furthermore, in moving the will through actual grace, God realizes a movement of the intellect and will, consisting in illumination and attraction, respectively, which is something created in the soul, actuating an obediential potency of the creature.[35] Hence Thomists speak of created rather than uncreated grace, even though that terminology is not entirely satisfactory. That supernatural illumination and attraction then permit the will to become a self-mover on the supernatural order. In that subsequent graced self-movement, God is moving the will (as first mover) through the intermediary of (1) the effect of his grace and (2) the supernaturally attracted will that moves itself through the power of the grace received.[36] The operative grace was not a contingent cause, because the will that received it was moved and *not yet self-moving*. Thus it infal-

33. My translation. "Non enim potest esse quod Deus sciat simul hunc cursurum, et iste deficiat a cursu; et hoc est propter certitudinem scientiae et non propter causalitatem ejus."

34. See Thomas Osborne Jr., "Thomist Premotion and Contemporary Philosophy of Religion," *Nova et Vetera* 4/3 (Summer 2006): 624–31.

35. Farrelly, *Predestination, Grace, and Free Will*, 163–66.

36. See Osborne, "Thomist Premotion," 627. "This point does not entail that there is an intermediate real being that does the work in moving the will. Indeed, if there were such a being, then it could not predetermine the will so that the agent acts freely. Only the first cause can do so." I agree entirely with Osborne's second statement, but not with the first. In operative grace, I grant that there is no "intermediate real being that does the work in moving the will." In cooperative grace, however, the very attraction received through operative grace, which attraction is not God but a created reality, is moving the will to move itself to choose fitting means to realize the object of its attraction. This attraction thus could be spoken of as an "intermediate real being" that is moving the soul to move itself. It can be said to be intermediate because it is a fruit of God's action, and it is the motive cause of the will's self-movement.

libly achieves the illumination and attraction that are its immediate effects. The will, however, in its cooperation with the attraction given it, is a contingent and free self-moving cause that can fail to move itself in the order of grace by resisting the attraction during the deliberative process, as explained above. Thus the actual movement of free will (with the aid of cooperative grace) *cannot be known with certainty in its causes alone,* because the will is a *subordinate and contingent cause of its own free act.*

St. Thomas explains that God wills certain effects to happen contingently or freely, and God realizes this by supplying them with contingent proximate causes. The will's own self-movement, even when empowered by the reception of grace, is the contingent proximate cause in the accomplishment of the free human act. The operative grace given (which necessarily achieves its first effect) neither takes away the freedom of the ensuing act of free choice nor enables the free choice to be foreknown simply through the fact that such operative grace is given.

To hold that God sufficiently knows the free response to grace simply by knowing his own eternal decrees to grant grace would in effect be to reduce the two categories of operative and cooperative grace to one sole category; all grace would be operative and no grace would empower the will to be a true but defectible self-mover in the supernatural order. For if God is moving the will as a moved mover (through cooperative grace), then insofar as it is a free self-mover, it can of itself defect or not defect, and thus its action cannot be known simply by perfectly knowing its causes. Included here among the causes is God's eternal decree to grant operative grace, and the operative grace itself with its infallible effect in the receiver.

In summary, if God knows our future free acts not only through their eternal presence to him, but also through graces he gives us that would supposedly infallibly achieve their effect, then he would be knowing future contingents in such created causes, which St. Thomas says would annihilate true human freedom and merit.[37] Lonergan makes this charge: "If, then, a *gratia operans* were to produce a contingent effect with irresistible efficacy, it could not be a creature; it would have to be God."[38]

---

37. Lonergan makes this charge: "If, then, a gratia operans were to produce a contingent effect with irresistible efficacy, it could not be a creature; it would have to be God." *Grace and Freedom,* 110.

38. Ibid. See also p. 148: "St. Thomas affirmed divine transcendence: with equal infal-

It follows that God's knowledge of free acts in the future in no way depends on either of the problematic assertions of both the Molinist and Báñezian schools. If we hold, then, that grace is ordinarily resistible with respect to human free action, then this in no way puts one in conflict with St. Thomas's account of God's knowledge of our free acts, nor does it require one to adhere to middle knowledge.

St. Thomas's texts on God's foreknowedge of future free acts point to a third way of understanding God's providential plan. He knows such acts through understanding them neither in their causes nor through middle knowledge, but through their being present to him in his eternity, which embraces all of time as its first cause.

Three Models of God's Providence

The three different ways to understand God's foreknowledge suggest three different models for understanding God's providential plan. The simplest way to understand it would be according to the Báñezian explanation: God predetermines human acts by moving them through intrinsically efficacious movements. In that case, however, the problem is to see how such acts would be truly free. For St. Thomas explains that God wills some events to occur contingently or freely, and God does this by supplying them with *contingent proximate causes*. If God moves the human will by a proximate cause consisting of intrinsically efficacious movements of created grace (physical premotion), however, it is impossible to see how such created causes could be classified as contingent. And if the proximate cause is not contingent, then the act would not be contingent.[39]

A second way for God to execute an infallible providential plan while conserving true creaturely contingency or freedom would be by the Molinist explanation of perfect foreknowledge of what free creatures would in fact freely choose if God were to place them in such and such conditions. This is called God's "middle knowledge" because it is posited as an

---

libility, efficacy, irresistibility, God knows, wills, effects both the ncessary and the contingent....Now, such a transcendence the Bannezian more than admits in God; he transfers it to the *praedeterminatio physica*, a creature, in the hope of saving the freedom of the will; and by that very transference he reveals the thoroughness of his transposition of Thomist thought, which explicitly affirmed the exclusiveness of this divine attribute."

39. See *ST* I, q. 19, a. 8; *ST* I-II, q. 10, a. 4.

intermediate kind of divine knowledge between his knowledge of actual events in history and his knowledge of all possible created events. God knows which graces will be freely resisted and which will not. Thus he supplies a series of internal and external graces for each free creature. Through this kind of conditional foreknowledge, he knows that these graces will produce an effect of salvation that he wills in some free creatures, and also fail to produce it in other free creatures, which he wills to permit. He also foreknows that of the many graces that he gives to each person, some will be resisted and others will be accepted. The problem here is that middle knowledge seems impossible because the object of such knowledge lacks all intrinsic determination.

A third way, excluding middle knowledge, is that God grants operative and cooperative graces according to an eternal plan that takes into account all the possible responses of human freedom, along with the actual responses that he knows in his eternal present. All Thomists hold that God knows all possibilities through knowledge of simple understanding, and that he knows all actualities through his knowledge of vision. These two categories are sufficient, it seems, for God to exercise perfect providence. With these two kinds of knowledge, God is capable of drawing greater good out of all creaturely resistance to grace, adding grace upon grace.

St. Thomas explains how God's providential plan, or predestination, can be infallible with this kind of knowledge. He points out that even if some graces are foreseen to be resisted, other supplementary graces are added that are foreseen to attain their end through the will's free self-movement:

Furthermore, it is clear that the certainty of providence is safeguarded by the wisdom of the divine dispensation, without prejudice to the contingency of things. Even the providence exercised by man can enable him so to bolster up a cause which can fail to produce an effect that, in some cases, the effect will inevitably follow. We find that a physician acts thus in exercising his healing art, as also does the vine-dresser who employs the proper remedy against barrenness in his vines. Much more, then, does the wisdom of the divine economy bring it about that, although contingent causes left to themselves can fail to produce an effect, the effect will inevitably follow when certain supplementary measures are employed; nor does this do away with the contingency of the effect. Evidently, therefore, contingency in things does not exclude the certainty of divine providence.[40]

40. *Compendium Theologiae*, ch. 140, in *Aquinas's Shorter Summa*, trans. Cyril Vollert (Manchester, NH: Sophia Institute Press, 2002), 158.

Thus, even though we remain free to resist God's grace, God still has a providential plan that takes into account our free resistance and eventual cooperation.

Problem of Moving from Potency into Act
without Divine Predetermination

According to the position I am defending, the will moves itself from desiring the supernatural good in general to choosing a particular means to realize it, through the continuing power of the initial grace that continues to be fruitful. The question can be posed: Does the will need a new and distinct intrinsically efficacious grace to make a good choice of means? The Báñezian position is affirmative, and I am arguing for the negative.

Various authors, such as Farrelly,[41] have pointed out that the causality by which God moves the will to be attracted by a universal end—such as happiness in the natural order and supernatural beatitude—is the ordinary way in which he moves the human will to choose particular goods to realize his providential plan. God also gives inspirations that attract the will to desire more particular salvific ends (such as a particular vocation or course of action).[42] Here too, however, the will needs to move itself to choose proximate means to realize these salvific ends.

The key point is that the self-movement of the will, like that of the intellect, is an immanent action that presupposes a faculty that has already been perfected with an initial act that makes possible the self-movement to its subsequent acts.[43] In the case of the intellect, apprehension of first principles eminently contains the conclusions that are grasped through the intellect's self-movement of reasoning. In the case of the will, the desire for the end makes possible the self-movement to consent and the choice of means, because the attraction of the end causes the desirability of apt means.

The will can move itself freely to choose particular goods because it is sufficiently activated by being first moved by God to desire the universal good on the natural or supernatural level. The universal good has all particular goods in potency within it, and reason is sufficient to deter-

41. See Farrelly, *Predestination, Grace, and Free Will*, 192–96.
42. See *ST* I-II, q. 9, a. 6, ad 3.
43. See *ST* I-II, q. 9, a. 3. The acts are referred to as *actus perfecti*; see *ST* I, q. 59, a. 1, ad 3.

mine the ordering of particular goods to the universal good. Thus the actual willing of the universal good plus the deliberation of reason are sufficient in themselves to move the will from potency to act with regard to particular goods. God is still the first mover of this self-determination by which the will chooses particular means. He is not the first mover of this self-determination in the sense of predetermining the will, however. Rather, by moving the will to desire the universal good, he moves the will in such a way that he does not predetermine the particular free choice.

It should be noticed that in this explanation we are not attributing the determination of the choice of means to the will alone as if it were no longer acting under the influence of the impulse of God given through operative grace, being the sole cause of its own determination. It would be a grave mistake to hold, as it seems Molina did, that the righteous human act has two *partial causes*: God giving the attraction to the universal end through operative grace, and man giving the determination to some means through his own self-determination. Molina regrettably used a faulty analogy here, speaking of God and the human will as two partial causes, like two men pulling a boat.[44] Molina's analogy fails to do justice to the primacy of God's action in moving human history through his providential plan. What the analogy fails to see is that God's movement of the will to move itself to achieve the universal supernatural good continues as first or principal cause to be active throughout all the subsequent stages of the moral act, so long as the will does not deviate from its order to the honest or supernatural good. Only at the moment of the deviation can we say that God's grace ceases to be the first mover of the determination of the act. Thus we should say that the human act is caused by a principal cause (God's action in attracting the will to the end) and an instrumental cause (the will's self-movement), both of which are responsible for the entire effect in two different orders, while clarifying that the will is an instrumental cause in a different way from irrational instruments, precisely because it is a free instrumental cause of free acts.

Also, the explanation that I am advocating does not imply that grace is intrinsically undetermined or versatile, which is an objection that Báñez and his school leveled against Molina.[45] God's movement must be

---

44. Luis de Molina, *Concordia*, q. 14, a. 13, disp. 26 (Olyssipone, 1588), p. 174. English translation in Garrigou-Lagrange, *Predestination*, 245.

45. See Báñez, "Apología en defensa de la doctrina antigua," 127–28.

to something determinate in itself. How can there be a true movement that is not determined to some particular destination?

Our analysis of operative and cooperative grace provides an answer. Operative grace is clearly quite determinate in itself in that it excites an actual attraction to some supernatural good, conceived by the intellect as a universal. This attraction may be quite broad—simply salvation in general—or it may also be directed to a more particular salvific good, such as a vocational choice or a particular mission.[46] The attraction to an end does not "predetermine" the particular means to be chosen, but orients the will to choose those means that are judged apt to achieve the end. This initiates a free and fallible self-motion in which deviation may occur, but its goal is given by operative grace.[47]

In other words, operative grace immediately realizes a determinate effect, which is the illumination and attraction received by the intellect and will. This determinate effect makes possible other effects in the supernatural order, such as intention, choice, consent, and execution of particular means. These effects are contained in the illumination and attraction, as particulars are contained in a universal.

Principle of Predilection Objection

Another important objection both to the Molinist position and the one that I am advocating is that it seems that of two men given exactly equal graces, the one who cooperates with that grace makes himself better than another man who does not cooperate, such that one becomes better than another through his own effort and not through a greater gift of divine grace. Luis de Molina writes:

It may happen that two persons receive in an equal degree the interior grace of vocation; one of them of his own free will is converted, and the other remains an infidel. It may even happen that one who receives a far greater prevenient grace when called, of his own free will is not converted, and another, who receives a far less grace, is converted.[48]

---

46. See *ST* I-II, q. 9, a. 6, ad 3.

47. See Alfred Freddoso, "Introduction," in J. Luis de Molina, *On Divine Foreknowledge: Part IV of the Concordia* (Ithaca, NY: Cornell University Press, 1988), 64–65.

48. *Concordia*, disp. 12, pp. 52–53. See the argument of Báñez against this text of Molina in Beltrán de Heredia, *Domingo Báñez*, 125–29.

Garrigou-Lagrange thinks that this answer of Molina contradicts what he calls the principle of predilection, according to which nothing would be better than another if God did not simply will it to be better. The same charge was directed against the quite different position of Marín-Sola.[49] St. Thomas writes: "Since God's love is the cause of goodness in things, no one thing would be better than another, if God did not will greater good for one than for another."[50] From this Garrigou-Lagrange infers:

This principle of predilection, as we shall see, presupposes that the divine decrees concerning our future salutary acts are intrinsically and infallibly efficacious. Otherwise the case might arise in which of two persons who are loved and helped to the same extent by God and who are placed in the same circumstances, one would correspond with the grace received and the other would not. Thus without having been loved and helped more by God, one would prove to be better than the other.... This is what, in opposition to St. Thomas, Molina maintained.[51]

To this objection I would reply that God's gift of grace is always the first cause of every supernaturally good act. Thus nothing can be supernaturally good without God first giving the grace for that act. The creature can never make itself better than God's gift to it. But the creature can make itself worse than God's gift to it. Because the creature is created from nothing, it has the power to cause nothingness by itself. We do this by resisting grace. The creature cannot cause supernatural being in himself independently of God's action. He can, however, block the effect of those graces by not responding to their impulse. Thus if two people receive the same grace, one can freely make himself *worse* than the other by resisting that grace.[52] Ultimately this objection would implicitly presuppose, with Calvinism and Jansenism, that grace can never be resisted.

Another objection is similar. Protestants accuse the Catholic position

49. This objection against his position is given in Marín-Sola, "A Reply to Some Objections," in Torre, *Do Not Resist the Spirit's Call*, 109.

50. *ST* I, q. 20, a. 3.

51. Garrigou-Lagrange, *Predestination*, 36.

52. See the response given to this objection by Marín-Sola, "A Reply to Some Objections," in Torre, *Do Not Resist the Spirit's Call*, 109–22, esp. 112–13. "In effect, it is one thing to *require* ('indiget') a *greater* grace to have a *greater* effort, and this is what Saint Thomas affirms, and it is a very distinct thing that *one is not able*, with a *greater* grace, to have a *lesser* effort, which is what our objector appears to want to conclude. Just as it is one thing to *require* much health in order to work much, which is true, and another very distinct thing that *one cannot*, with much health, work less or not at all, which is false."

(and particularly the Molinist position) of giving rise to boasting, for our cooperation would seem to be something that we could boast about. If we have done better than the next person on account of our free cooperation, then it would seem that we could boast.

First, every good that we do is principally from God, who gives us the capacity to cooperate with him. Luke 17:10 suggests what our attitude should be when we cooperate with grace: we are simply useless servants who have done what we were given to do. Second, any explanation that emphasizes our ability to resist cooperative grace leads not to boasting but to humility. St. Thomas teaches that we should practice fraternal humility by regarding God's gifts in one's neighbor, and one's own failure to correspond to God's gifts in oneself.[53] There can be no boasting because we should think that if others received the same graces that we have, they would probably have corresponded better. Likewise, we should always think that we did not correspond to God's gifts as we should have, but have been at least somewhat negligent, which is all the more distressing in proportion to the abundance and value of the gifts received. This is the attitude of St. Francis Assisi, St. Teresa of Avila, and all the saints. This response would seem impossible in the Calvinist or Báñezian system, in which everything depends exclusively on God's gift of efficacious and irresistible grace. For if grace is intrinsically irresistible, how could one ever justly accuse oneself of negligence in corresponding to God's gifts?

St. Robert Bellarmine expresses this well by saying that if one denies that grace can be resisted, then "no one...could properly accuse themselves of not cooperating with the grace of God as much as they could and should have....However, certainly all the saints frequently accuse themselves of negligence and sloth, and they confess with sighs that they have not cooperated with grace as they should."[54]

Advantages of Using Operative/Cooperative as a Primary Division of Actual Grace

The multiplicity of names for operative and cooperative grace (prevenient and subsequent; *excitans* and *adiuvans*) comes from the great im-

53. *ST* II-II, q. 161, a. 3.
54. St. Robert Bellarmine, *De gratia et libero arbitrio*, bk. 1, ch. 11, in *Opera omnia* (Naples: 1872), 4:290.

portance of this distinction, which is crucial in understanding the priority of God's grace and the necessity of human cooperation. The priority of God's action is shown by the fact that operative grace must come first, presupposing nothing in the will. The necessity of human cooperation is shown by the fact that operative grace, which begins the movement of the will, is meant to pass on into cooperative grace, which aids the will to continue to freely choose salutary acts.

The division of operative and cooperative grace helps to see where grace is infallibly efficacious—whenever it is operative in moving the will without the will yet moving itself—and where it is sufficient in its cooperation with the will (now cooperative grace) but capable of being resisted, and having its impetus terminated by the will failing to choose means rightly ordered to the supernatural end. It also shows how the normal division between sufficient and efficacious can be a misleading division, because one and the same operative grace is efficacious for one thing (exciting the will to simple desire) and sufficient for another (moving the will to move itself to make a free or meritorious act).

This division is also useful in showing the unity of God's action. It would be a mistake to think of operative and cooperative graces as essentially distinct. For one and the same movement of grace begins as operative and then continues to have further effects by becoming cooperative with the will, which can begin to move itself in the supernatural order on the basis of the prevenient grace to consent, choose, and execute. This distinction, by highlighting the essential priority of operative grace in the beginning of every supernatural human act, is also helpful for seeing the nature of the semi-Pelagian error and defending against it.

Most importantly, this distinction brings out clearly the interaction of actual grace and the self-movement of the human will, avoiding the key error that separates the two into competing categories. This distinction highlights the fact that all the free self-movement of the will is carried forward to a supernatural good in virtue of the initial operative grace received. Thus there is no part of the salvific act in which the will is the first mover.

The categories of operative and cooperative grace also make it easier to understand how God moves us according to his providential plan using instrumental causality. As First Mover, God uses created causes, whether natural or supernatural, to move other things. God as principal cause makes use of operative grace as an instrument to illuminate the intellect and attract the will to a supernatural end, which attraction then moves the will to cause the intellect to deliberate regarding suitable means, and the final practical judgment of the intellect causes the will to consent and choose. As a result, the completed salvific act is to be attributed to God as first cause, and to the will as a secondary self-moving cause.[55]

This distinction enables us to understand why intercession for others is not always efficacious. Clearly Mary intercedes for every person, for we are all her children. Still more, Christ on Calvary interceded for all men, and that intercession truly wins graces for all. St. Thomas explains that intercession sometimes fails to win salvation because of an obstacle—hardness of heart—in the person for whom we pray.[56] The obstacle does not block the reception of operative graces, but lies precisely in the will's resistance that renders grace unfruitful and chokes off the opportunity for cooperative grace to continue the action.

Finally, this distinction correlates well with the distinction between God's antecedent and consequent will. That God has a true antecedent universal salvific will has been emphasized in recent centuries against Jansenism. This will implies a potentially salvific effect in the creature, which is the granting of operative graces to all (as the sower in the parable sows on all kinds of soil). God's antecedent will can fail to have its effect, however, for the recipient of operative grace can bring it about (through bad deliberation) that cooperative grace is not given or is rendered unfruitful and cut off.

55. It seems that both Molina and Báñez fall short of understanding the instrumental causality of the will in the free supernatural act. A deficiency of Molinism is that it uses the category of partial causes rather than that of instrumental causality. Báñez, on the contrary, seems to think that this relation of instrumental causality can exist only if God directly predetermines the specification of the free human act. See Lonergan, *Grace and Freedom*, 147–48: "There is a material resemblance between the Molinist *gratia excitans* and the Thomist *gratia operans*, but the resemblance is only material, for the Molinist lacks the speculative acumen to make his grace leave the will instrumentally subordinate to divine activity. But the Bannezian has exactly the same speculative blind spot: because he cannot grasp that the will is truly an instrument by the mere fact that God causes the will of the end, he goes on to assert that God also brings in a *praemotio* to predetermine the choice of means."

56. *ST* II-II, q. 83, a. 7, ad 2: "For it sometimes happens that we pray for another with piety and perseverance, and ask for things relating to his salvation, and yet it is not granted on account of some obstacle on the part of the person we are praying for."

8

HOW SIN ESCAPES PREMOTION

*The Development of Thomas Aquinas's
Thought by Spanish Thomists*

Thomas M. Osborne Jr.

The debate over the predetermination of sin played a persistent role during the *De auxiliis* controversy even if it was not a central issue. In his *Concordia*, the Jesuit Louis de Molina (1536–1600) had argued that God's causal role in sin consists only in his indifferent concursus, and that God does not cause sin even its material aspect.[1] He appeals to the Council of Trent's definition in Session VI, canon 6, which defined against some Protestants that "if anyone says that it is not in human power to adopt

1. Ludovicus Molina, *Liberi arbitrii cum gratiae donis, divina praescientia, providentia, praedestinatione, et reprobatione concordia*, ed. Iohannes Rabeneck (Ona: Collegium Maximum Societatis Jesu; Madrid: Societatis Editorialis "Sapientia," 1953), q. 14, art. 13, disp. 27, pp. 71–173; q. 14, art. 13, disp. 53, memb. 2, pp. 367–84; q. 19, art. 6, disp. 3, pp. 425–30. For some wider issues and context, see R. J. Matava, *Divine Causality and Human Free Choice: Domingo Báñez, Physical Premotion and the Controversy de Auxiliis Revisited*, Brill's Studies in Intellectual History 252 (Leiden: Brill, 2016); Matthias Kaufmann and Alexander Aichele, eds., *A Companion to Luis de Molina*, Brill's Companions to the Christian Tradition 50 (Leiden: Brill, 2014). For a brief discussion of the theological issues in context, see Alister McGrath, *Iustitia Dei: A History of the Christian Doctrine of Justification*, 2nd ed. (Cambridge: Cambridge University Press, 1998), 280–82. The best historical account is still Jacques-Hyacinthe Serry, *Historia congregationum de auxiliis divinae gratiae sub sub pontificibus Clemente VIII. et Paulo V* (Antwerp: 1709).

evil ways, but that God operates in evil acts just as in good, not only per-missively, but even properly and per se, so that the betrayal of Judas is no less his own work that the calling of Paul: let him be anathema."[2] Thom-ists of course both accepted Trent's definition and rejected the common Protestant view that God causes sin.[3] But the Dominicans also rejected Molina's position that God causes a sin's being only by his indifferent concursus. The two most significant Dominican participants in the con-troversy—Diego Alvarez (ca. 1550–1635) and Thomas de Lemos (ca. 1550–1629)—discussed the issue at length.[4]

In 1596, the Dominicans sent Alvarez to Rome in order to report on the controversies over Molinism in Spain. Lemos joined him later and played a far greater role in the ensuing public disputations (1602–6) of the *Congregationes de auxiliis*. Molina's view on the causation of sin was only briefly mentioned in the *Apologia* that Domingo Báñez (1528–1604) and other Dominican theologians wrote for Alvarez's use in Rome. These Dominican authors stated, "For we reckon that statement certain which asserts that God by his previous efficacious assistance concurs with the will of man in the material aspect of sin in the nature (*ratio*) of be-ing."[5] They cited several passages from Augustine and Thomas in favor of this position, along with sacred Scripture and other authorities such as Cajetan. But the *Apologia* did not note that Molina had hit upon an

2. "Si quis dixerit, non esse in potestate hominis vias suas malas facere, sed mala opera ita ut bona Deum operari, non permissive solu, sed etiam proprie et per se, adeo ut sit pro-prium eius opus non minus proditio Iudae quam vocatio Pauli: a.s." Concilium Tridenti-num, Sessio 6, can. 6, in Norman Tanner, ed., *Decrees of the Ecumenical Councils*, 2 vols. (London: Sheed and Ward; Washington, DC; Georgetown University Press, 1990), 2:679. Molina, *Concordia*, q. 14, art. 13, disp. 27, p. 171.

3. For representative passages, see John Calvin, *Institutio Christianae Religionis*, lib. 1.18; lib. 2.4, 5th ed. (Geneva: 1539), pp. 71–76, 101–4. For other texts and authors, see esp. Lemos, *Panoplia Gratiae*, lib. 1, tract. 2, cap. 2, vol. 1, pp. 54–56.

4. Biographical entries on both figures can be found in J. Quetif and J. Echard, *Scrip-tores Ordinis Praedicatorum*, vol. 2 (Paris: Simart/Ballard, 1721), 481–82, 461–64; A. Touron, *Histoire des hommes illustres de l'order de saint Dominique*, vol. 5 (Paris: Babuty/Quillau, 1748), 103–6; Juan Belda Plans, *La Escuela de Salamanca y la renovación de la theología en el siglo XVI* (Madrid: Bibliotecta de Auctores Cristianos, 2000), 870–71. Their involvement in the *De auxiliis* congregation is discussed at length in Touron, *Histoire des hommes illustres*, 106–17.

5. "Nos enim certam reputamus sententiam illam quae asserit Deum suo auxilio efficaci praevio concurrere cum hominis voluntate ad materiale peccati in ratione entis." *Apologia*, p. 3, q. 4, n. 9, in Vincente Beltran de Heredia, *Domingo Bañez y Las Controversias Sobra la Gracia: Textos y Documentos* (Salamanca: Consejo Superior de Investigaciones Científicas, Instituto Francisco Suárez, 1968), 295.

interesting point of disagreement between Thomists. The disagreement between Thomism and Molinism is over whether God causes sin only by his general concursus, which according to Molinists is indifferent to good and bad actions. The disagreement among the Thomists at the time was over the narrower point of whether the material aspect of sin is subject to premotion. Although the Dominican *Apologia* enlisted Thomas and other authorities in favor of this proposition, other Thomists emphatically denied it.

The precise disagreement was over how to hold both that God is the cause of the act of sin and God is not the cause of sin or its deformity. The Mercedarian Francisco Zumel (1540/41–1607), for example, an important ally of Báñez against Molina, directly criticized the view that God predetermines or premoves the material aspect of sin. In the last public dispute of the *Congregationes* (February 22, 1606), Lemos noted that the Jesuits had quoted Zumel in favor of their objection that "if God predetermines to the material aspect of sin, or to the act which is in the sin insofar as it is an entity and an act, he also predetermines to the sin itself."[6] Moreover, Bartholomew Medina (1528–80), Báñez's close Dominican contemporary, had directly attacked the much earlier Thomas de Vio Cajetan (1437–1534) for implying that God is responsible for sin. The source of disagreement among Thomists is over how to hold both that God is the cause of the sin's act and that God is not the cause of sin or its deformity.

I argue that Diego Alvarez and Thomas de Lemos through their participation in the *De auxiliis* controversy developed and defended Cajetan's view of the causation of sin in such a way that they were able to defend the predetermination of the material aspect of sin while at the same time assimilating important aspects from his critics. It is important to recognize that Lemos and his associates hold both that the premotion of sin's material aspect is not necessarily connected with the Catholic faith and that it is knowable by natural reason.[7] Even though they argued that

---

6. "Si Deus praedeterminaret ad materiale peccati, sive ad actionem quae est in peccato, quatenus entitas et actio est, etiam praedeterminaret ad peccatum ipsum." Thomas de Lemos, *Acta omnia congregationum ac disputationum* (Louvain: 1702), col. 1320. Touron, *Histoire des hommes illustres*, 122, repeats the opinion that although Innocent X declared that this book was printed without permission, the lack of permission indicates nothing about the truth of the book's contents.

7. Serry, *De auxiliis*, lib. 5, sect. 3, cap. 9, cols. 765–69; Lemos, *Acta* (February 22, 1606), col. 1357.

other Molinist theses should be condemned as heretical, they held that this rejection of the Dominican thesis concerning sin is simply wrong but not heretical. First, I consider Cajetan's position. Second, I consider the reception of this position by Medina, Zumel, and Báñez. Third, I show that Alvarez and Lemos make distinctions that allow them to incorporate the insights of both Cajetan and his critics.

Cajetan discusses God's causation of sin in the relevant article of the *Summa Theologiae*, namely, *ST* I-II, q. 79, a. 2: "Whether the act of sin is from God?"[8] This approach to the question depends on his understanding of the specific difference between good and evil acts in the same commentary on *ST* I-II, q. 18, a. 6, and on the definition of sin in *ST* I-II, q. 71, a. 6. In general, Cajetan argues that God causes the act's positive being, which includes its specific difference.

In his commentary on *ST* I-II, q. 18, a. 6, Cajetan notes that there is a twofold evil in morals.[9] There is a privative aspect, which is an aversion from the good, and a positive being, which is formally contrary to a good act. This second aspect is a conversion toward an intended good. This intended good object specifies the act. Consequently, an evil act is specifically distinct from a good one because of its intended bad object. Although evil truly and properly speaking is the privation of a due good, in another sense evil describes a genus of acts, along with the specific differences and species that it contains. Although Thomas does not in this article state that the genus and specific difference in morals is positive, Cajetan notes that he does clearly argue for this thesis both in the *Prima Pars* of the *Summa Theologiae* and at greater length in the *Summa contra Gentiles* III, ch. 9.[10]

According to Cajetan, God is the cause of the positive entity that specifies the act, whereas God is in no way a cause of the privation that follows upon it. In his commentary on *ST* I-II, q. 71, a. 6, he argues against John Duns Scotus's (ca. 1266–1308) thesis that the nature of sin consists

8. "Utrum Deus sit causa peccati?" All citations of Thomas are from the Leonine unless otherwise indicated. Cajetan's commentary is printed in the Leonine alongside the *Summa Theologiae*. For a consideration of Cajetan's position in light of its sources and its reception by later Thomists, see James R. Maloney, *The Formal Constituent of a Sin of Commission* (Somerset, OH: Rosary Press, 1947), and to a lesser extent Matava, *Divine Causality and Human Free Choice*, 91–93.

9. Cajetan, *In I-II*, q. 18, art. 6, n. 2 (Leonine, vol. 6, p. 132).

10. *ST* I, q. 48, a. 1, ad 2; *ScG* III, ch. 9. See also *De Malo*, q. 1, art. 1, ad 4; *ST* I-II, q. 79, a. 1, ad 1.

mostly in a privative disorder rather than a positive one.[11] According to Cajetan, Scotus fails to distinguish between the genus of evil simply speaking, and the genus of evil actions. A sin's privative disorder places it only in the genus of evil strictly speaking. This evil follows on the agent's intention, but it is not specified by it because no agent intends the evil as such. A sin's species is taken from the sinner's intention, which is positive even though it is necessarily connected with a disorder. He compares an act of intemperance to an act of cooling. The privation of heat follows on that which is cold because it is something cold. The act of cooling is specified by coldness. Similarly, an act is intemperate because of its intemperate object, such as eating during a fast day. The privation of temperance follows on the intemperate object, which is something positive.

Cajetan applies these distinctions to the discussion of whether God causes a sin. In *ST* I-II, q. 79, a. 2, Thomas argues that God is the cause of the sin's being and act, but not of its defect. According to Thomas, the defect cannot be attributed to God any more than a limp can be attributed to the agent's moving power. The deficient effect is traced not to the act's universal cause but to a deficient proximate cause. In this case, the limp might be reduced to a deficient shin, and the sin is reduced to the deficient human will. God is the cause of the act that is a sin, but he is not a cause of the sin. In his commentary, Cajetan notes that John Capreolus has responded clearly and profusely to the medieval objections against Thomas's position.[12] But Cajetan thinks that a clear and complete explanation should focus on the way in which the act's positive being is both related to the deformity of sin and to its effective cause.

Cajetan makes a threefold distinction between the act absolutely speaking, the positive entity that places the act in a species, and the privation of rectitude.[13] It is indisputable that God causes the act absolutely speaking and that God does not cause the privation. The question is whether God causes the positive entity that specifies the sin. He notes that a sin has a positive malice from its object but a privative malice in its lack of conformity to the law. This latter privation is the sin's defor-

---

11. Cajetan, *In I-II*, q. 71, art. 6, nn. 5–7 (Leonine, vol. 7, p. 10).

12. Cajetan, *In I-II*, q. 79, art. 2, n. 1 (Leonine, vol. 7, p. 77), refers to John Capreolus, *Defensiones*, d. 37, d. 37, q. 1, art. 3, ad argumenta Aureoli et Durandi (vol. 4, 428–32, 434).

13. Cajetan, *In I-II*, q. 79, art. 2, nn. 2–9 (Leonine, vol. 7, p. 78–79). For the threefold distinction, see also Cajetan, *In I-II*, q. 72, art. 1, n. 3 (Leonine, vol. 7, p. 13).

mity. Because only a deficient agent can cause a deformity, and God is in no way deficient, it follows that God cannot cause this deformity. Such an effect can only come from a deficient agent, such as the human will. Nevertheless, the act of sin is from God insofar as the act has perfection even from a human agent. Consequently, God causes the act insofar as it is specified by its object, even though he does not cause the consequent privation. Therefore Cajetan is able to hold that God causes everything positive in a sin's act, including its species, even though God in no way causes the act's malice.

In his much later biblical commentaries, Cajetan argues that God can encourage and otherwise lead humans to sin. For instance, he interprets in this way Jesus's command to Judas in John 13:27, "What you do, do quickly."[14] Moreover, in his commentary on 2 *Regum* (Sam 2), he states that God wills sin insofar as it is a punishment of other sins.[15] According to many later Thomists, the view that God is a moral cause of sin is incompatible with Scripture and with Trent, at least if held with respect to intrinsically evil acts.[16] Later Thomists can be at least cautious concerning his view about willing sin as a punishment.[17] Although Cajetan's biblical commentaries are relevant to the debate over God's causation of sin, they play only a peripheral role in the controversy over whether God predetermines the material aspect of sin. The focus in this narrower discussion is over the *Summa* commentary's thesis that God causes a sin's species and specific difference.

Medina and Zumel directly criticize Cajetan's account. Medina's discussion lies squarely in the contexts of late Scholastic theology and the rejection of Protestant beliefs, whereas Zumel is particularly concerned with the later controversy over the predetermination of sin. In his com-

---

14. Cajetan, *Ientacula Novi Testamenti*, q. 6, ientaculum 6, q. 2 (Cologne, 1526), 71v–72r.

15. Cajetan, *In omnes authenticos veteris testamenti historiale libros comentarii* (Rome, 1533), fols. 148v, 156v.

16. See Melchor Cano, *De locis theologicis*, lib. 2, cap. 4, ad 7–8 (Salamanca, 1563), pp. 15–19; Báñez, *In I-II*, q. 79, art. 4 (vol. 2, pp. 225–27); Zumel, *In I-II*, q. 709, art. 3, dub. 1, p. 494. Lemos provides a more cautious reading of Cajetan in his *Panoplia Gratiae* 2, tract. 1, cap. 27, n. 369, p. 58. Gonet rejects the view that God is a moral cause but does not attribute it to Cajetan in his *Clypeus Theologiae Thomisticae*, vol. 3, tract. 5, disp. 6, art. 3, n. 49 (Venice, 1772, p. 263).

17. For contrary views, see Zumel, *In I-II*, q. 79, art. 2, disp. 3, pp. 490–91; Lemos, *Panoplia Gratiae*, lib. 2, tract. 1, cap. 38, esp. nn. 455, 457, pp. 74–76, esp. 75. Báñez defends Cajetan in his *In I-II*, q. 79, art. 4, dub. 3 (Leonine, vol. 2, pp. 246–51).

mentary on *ST* I-II, q. 79, a. 2, Medina's recitation of the various positions indicates the polemical context.[18] After rejecting the opinions of
the Protestants Martin Luther (1483–1546), John Calvin (1509–64), and
Philip Melanchthon (1497–1560) that God is the cause of sin, Medina
states, "it is most difficult to explain how the sin's act is from God, and
not the sin."[19] He gives opinions taken from Catholic theologians, namely, Peter Lombard (ca. 1096–1160), Durandus of Saint-Pourçain (ca. 1270–
1334), Gregory of Rimini (ca. 1300–1358), William of Ockham (ca. 1285–
1347), Gabriel Biel (d. 1495), John Duns Scotus, Thomas de Vio Cajetan,
Melchor Cano (1509–1560), and Dominic de Soto (1495–1560). Only the
last three had lived during the Reformation, and Cajetan had written his
commentary before it began.

It is significant that Medina considers and rejects the positions that
were developed by Dominic Soto and Melchor Cano, who were his close
predecessors. Dominic Soto had argued that God is a natural, not moral, cause of sin.[20] According to Medina, it would be even worse to be a
natural cause than a moral one, because a natural cause of sin seems to
be bad in its nature. Although Cano had perhaps even more clearly used
this distinction between the natural and moral cause, Medina attributes
to Cano the position that the specific difference and formal nature of a
sin is a being of reason and therefore not something that is real.[21] In his
criticism of Cano, Medina refers to his own commentary on *ST* I-II, q. 71,
a. 6, where Medina had rejected this account of the specification of sin
by a being of reason in favor of Cajetan's position that sin is specified

---

18. Bartholomew Medina, *In I-II*, q. 79, art. 1, in *Scholastica Commentaria in D. Thomae
Aquinatis Doct. Angelici Primam Secundae* (Cologne, 1618), cols. 1002–88.

19. "Explicare quomodo actio peccati sit a Deo, et non peccatum, est dificillissimum."
Medina, *In I-II*, q. 81, art. 1, col. 1082.

20. Medina, *In I-II*, q. 79, art. 1, col. 1085. See Dominic Soto, *De natura et gratia*, lib. 1,
cap. 19 (Florence, 1549; reprint, Ridgewood, NJ: Gregg, 1965), fols. 71v–72r.

21. Medina, *In I-II*, q. 79, art. 1, col. 1085. See Melchor Cano, *De locis theologicis*, lib. 2,
cap. 4, ad 7–8, pp. 15–19; Cano, *Relectio de sacramentis*, p. 4 (Salamanca, 1550), fols. 45r–46v.
I cannot find an exact source for Cano, but the description of the position and the attribution to Cano can be found in Báñez, *In I-II*, q. 71, art. 6, n. 11, vol. 2, p. 64; Gabriel Vazquez,
In I-II, q. 79, art. 2, disp. 129, nn. 22–26, in *Commentariorum ac disputationum in primam
secundae S. Thomae*, 2nd ed. (Madrid, 1613), pp. 772–73. Zumel, *In I-II*, q. 71, art. 6, disp. 8,
p. 164, mentions the position as one that Cano taught. Vazquez was a Jesuit who indicated
that he first publicly defended Soto and Cano on this issue in 1582. Medina's source could be
the unpublished lectures listed in Quetif and Echard, *Scriptores*, vol. 2, p. 256. Báñez claims
that Cano attributed this opinion to his teacher Vitoria, but that he could not find it in his
writings. Báñez was a student of Cano, who was a student of Vitoria.

by a positive entity.[22] Medina states that because sin involves not just a privation but also a positive being, its difference cannot be only a being of reason.[23]

In the commentary on *ST* I-II, q. 79, a. 2, Medina rejects Cajetan's position that God causes this positive entity that specifies the sin because it would make God responsible for sin.[24] According to Medina, this statement that God causes the positive entity would imply that God is the cause of moral evil, and further that he moves men to sin. Moreover, it would follow that sin would conform to God's will. It seems ultimately to lead to the position that he attributes to Gabriel Biel, namely, that God is not the author of sin because God is not bound by the law in the way that humans are.[25] In general, Medina thinks that his Thomistic predecessors hold positions that err by somehow implying that God is responsible for sin.

Báñez and Zumel were the most prominent among the first theologians who responded to Molina. Although Zumel in his *Quaestiones variae* only briefly rejects the premotion of the material aspect of sin, he develops his arguments at great length in his commentaries on the *Summa Theologiae*. Unlike Medina, Zumel argues that Cajetan's understanding of the positive aspect of sin is both un-Thomistic and untrue.[26] According to Zumel, the sin's material aspect is intrinsically connected to moral evil, which is simply a privation. For this reason, Thomas in his discussion of sin mentions only that it lacks due measure. But Zumel is not far from Medina's position when he states that "the position of Cajetan, which concedes that God is the cause of a sin, with respect to its formal nature (*ratio*), which constitutes its species and essence, is absolutely to be rejected, insofar as it concedes God to be the cause of sin, insofar as it is a moral evil, although afterwards he denies that he is the cause of sin from the part of aversion."[27] Although Zumel zeal-

---

22. Medina, *In I-II*, q. 71, art. 6, cols. 949–50.

23. Medina, *In I-II*, q. 71, art. 6, cols. 948–49.

24. Medina, *In I-II*, q. 79, art. 2, cols. 1084–85.

25. For this aspect of Biel's position, see Gabriel Biel, *Collectorium circa quattuor libros sententiarum*, 2, d. 37, q. un., art. 3, dub. 1, ed. Udo Hofman and Wlifrid Werbeck, 4 vols. (Tübingen: Mohr, 1973–1992), 2:643.

26. Gregory of Valentia, a Jesuit participant in the *De auxiliis* disputations, also argues that Cajetan misinterprets Thomas on this issue in his *In I-II*, disp. 2, q. 13, punct. 3, in *Commentariorum Theologicorum*, vol. 3 (Lyons: Cardon, 1609), cols. 247–53. Valentia's own interpretation is criticized especially in Alvarez, *In I-II*, q. 71, art. 6, disp. 28, n. 18, p. 373.

27. "Sententia Caietani, quae concedit Deum esse causam peccati, quantum ad ratio-

ously defended the premotion of good acts, his rejection of Cajetan's understanding of sin's causation moves him to reject the position that God premoves and predetermines even the material aspect of sin.[28] Zumel added a lengthy section to his commentary's discussion of providence in order to attack this view of premotion.[29] He thinks his rejection of such premotion follows from the statements of the Council of Trent and the Council of Orange that God does not cause sin in the way that he causes good acts.[30] Zumel and Medina are not unique in this opposition to Cajetan on this issue. Gabriel Vazquez (1549–1604), a Jesuit theologian who belonged to this generation, stated at his time that Cajetan's opinion "is rejected with merit by everyone."[31]

In his published commentary on the *Prima Pars*, Báñez briefly treats the causation of sin.[32] He mentions only Cano by name, although he describes one position that seems to incorporate elements from Cajetan and Soto as well.[33] Báñez notes that human free choice causes both the privation and aversion of a sin, although God causes only the conversion. Even the positive conversion and object of the act has a positive deformity. God causes the conversion but not the positive deformity. Up to this point, his discussion reflects themes that were developed by Cajetan. Báñez continues by reciting a point that has been attributed to Soto, namely, that God is only the natural cause of an act that is morally bad and not its moral cause. Báñez concludes, "And this mode of speaking suffices for the present place."[34]

---

nem formalem, quae consitutit eius speciem et essentiam, absolute reiicienda est, quatenus concedit Deum esse causam peccati, in quantum est malum morale, licet postea neget esse causam peccati ex parte aversionis." Zumel, *In I-II*, q. 79, art. 2, disp. 2, in Francisco Zumel (Çumel), *In Primam Secundae Sancti Thomae Commentarium* (Salamanca, 1594), 1:476.

28. Zumel, *Disputationes Variae*, vol. 3, disp. 5, sect. 1, appendix, in Francisco Zumel (Çumel), *Variarum Disputationum R. Patris Magistri Francisci Çumel*, 3 vols. (Lyons, 1609), 209–10.

29. Zumel, *In I*, q. 22, art. 4, disp. un., appendix, in Francisco Zumel (Çumel), *Commentaria in Primam Partem S. Thomae, tomus primus* (Salamanca, 1509), 609–11, 612–17.

30. Zumel, *In I*, q. 22, art. 4, appendix, p. 612.

31. "Merito ab omnibus reiicitur." Vazquez, *In I-II*, q. 79, art. 2, disp. 129, n. 15, in Gabriel Vazquez, *Commentariorum ac Dispoutationum in Primam Secundae S. Thomae* (Alcala, 1614), 770.

32. Báñez, *In I*, q. 49, art. 2, in *Scholastica Commentaria in Primam Partem Angelici Doctoris S. Thomae*, 2 vols. (Douai: Borremans, 1614), 1:453–54.

33. Alvarez, *In I-II*, q. 71, art. 6, disp. 128, n. 13 (incorrectly numbered, but between pp. 372 and 373), is cautious about Báñez's description of various positions.

34. "Et hic modus dicendi prop praesenti loco sufficiant." Báñez, *In I*, q. 49, art. 2, p. 454.

In the *Apologia*, Báñez and the other authors state that the conclusion that God predetermines the material aspect of sin is entailed by the thesis that God is the cause of every positive being. They argue:

God is the first cause of whatever positive created entity; for if God is a being essentially (*per essentiam*) he must be the cause of whatever being through participation. But the material aspect of sin in the genus of being precisely considered is a certain positive entity existing outside of its causes. Therefore God is the first cause of that in the nature (*ratio*) of being: therefore God by his previous efficacious help causes with the will that entity of sin as it is a being.[35]

At least verbally in its use of "positive entity," this argument resembles Cajetan's commentary on the *Summa* rather than that of Medina. Cajetan is cited in support of their view, but there is no reference to Soto or Cano. Consequently, the *Apologia* represents to some extent a shift toward Cajetan's opinion, or at least a distance from positions that were recently taught by Spanish Dominicans.

In his commentary on *ST* I-II, q. 71, a. 6, Báñez is similar to Medina in that he defends Cajetan's understanding of sin as something positive against various other views, such as Cano's reported view that sin formally consists in a being of reason. Báñez mentions it not as Cano's own view but the view that Cano attributed to Vitoria.[36] According to Báñez, the act's formality and specific difference can only be understood with reference to the rule of eternal law and natural reason.[37] This relation is real and presupposes that the act has a real formality that is its basis (*fundamentum*).

In his commentary on *ST* I-II, q. 79, a. 4, Báñez also defends in part

35. "Deus est prima causa cujuscumque entitatis positivae creatae; nam cum Deus sit ens per essentiam, debet esse causa cujuscumque entis per participationem. Sed materiale peccati in genere entis praecise consideratum est quaedam entitas positivae extra suas causas existens. Ergo Deus est prima causa illius in ratione entis: ergo Deus auxilio efficaci praevio causat cum voluntate illam entitatem entitatem peccati ut ens est." *Apologia*, p. 3, cap. 4, n. 9, p. 295. In addition to the *Summa Theologiae*, see Thomas, *II Sent.*, d. 37, q. 2, art. 2, sol. (vol. 2, 952); De Malo, q. 3, art. 2, resp. Alvarez gives a similar argument as a reformulation of the *Sentences* commentary's argument in his *De auxiliis divinae gratiae*, lib. 3, disp. 24, n. 19, pp. 201–2.

36. Báñez, *In I-II*, q. 71, art. 6, dub. 1, in Domingo Báñez, *Comentarios Inéditos a la Prima Secundae de Santo Tomás*, ed. Vicente Beltrán de Heredia, vol. 2 (Salamanca: Consejo Superior de Investigaciones Científicas, Patronato "Raimundo Lulio," Instituto Francisco Suarez, 1944), 61–74. For a discussion, see Matava, *Divine Causality and Human Free Choice*, 90–95.

37. Báñez, *In I-II*, q. 71, art. 6, dub. 1, n. 13, p. 65.

Cajetan's understanding of how God causes sin.[38] This text may reflect continuing revisions in light of the debate with Molinists.[39] In dubium 1 of this commentary, Báñez combines two positions that Medina rejects, namely, Cajetan's position that God causes the natural being of sin and the position that God is a natural and not a moral cause of sin.[40] He rejects Cajetan's position that God is the cause of the moral malice and the privation of rectitude.

Báñez does not simply accept or reject Cajetan's thesis that God causes the sin's contrariety, but he distinguishes between a sin's natural and moral contrariety. When there is a positive contrary, the presence of one contrary entails the absence of another. For instance, cold is contrary to heat, and consequently the heating of water entails the privation of cold, and the cooling of water entails the privation of heat. This distinction between the natural and the moral contrariety of a sin is not the same as the distinction between a sin's natural and moral species. For instance, theft and receiving just payment might both fall under the same natural species of taking metal. Báñez is not concerned with this natural species, but with the way in which the theft involves both a natural and a moral contrariety. The act by its nature will have certain features that make it incompatible with justice. But it is not sinful unless an agent with the requisite knowledge freely choses it. Báñez writes:

For, although these acts of justice and injustice have a moral quality to them and are freely exercised by man, nevertheless, free choice (*liberum arbitrium*) supplies that specification which is from the act's object, is natural to it, and is owing to the nature of the thing. Accordingly, the contrariety that is found in them is natural, because it arises from contrary objects. But that some act be a sin does not pertain to it except by relation to free choice, which was obliged not to perform an act of that species.[41]

---

38. Báñez, *In I-II*, q. 79, art. 4, dub. 1–2, pp. 203–45.

39. Vicente Beltrán de Heredia, "Introducción," in Báñez, *Comentarios Inéditos a la Prima Secundae de Santo Tomás*, 2:10–18. See Matava, *Divine Causality and Human Free Choice*, 96n166.

40. Báñez, *In I-II*, q. 79, art. 4, dub. 1, nn. 19–22, pp. 209–12. The position is unattributed in this text, but see note 21 above.

41. "Nam, quamvis ipsi actus justitiae et injustitiae sint morales et libere exerceantur ab homine, tamen specificationem quae est ex objecto suo est eis naturalis et ex natura rei, liberum arbitrium illam tribuit; sic etiam contrarietas quae in illis invenitur naturalis est, quia consurgit ex objectis contrariis. Quod autem alter actus sit peccatum, non convenit ei nisi respectu liber arbitrii, quod tenebatur non operari actum illius speciei." Báñez, *In I-II*, q. 79, art. 4, dub. 1, n. 24, p. 213.

For instance, it might be naturally contrary to justice for me to take fifty dollars from this man who does not owe me money. But it is morally contrary to justice only insofar as I knowingly take money that does not belong to me.

By distinguishing between the two kinds of contrariety, Báñez explains how it is true both that God does not cause sin, and also that he is the total cause of every natural being that is in the act of a sin, including that which specifies it morally. Báñez connects the two kinds of contrariety with the earlier view that God is a natural and not a moral cause of sin by distinguishing between the natural aspect of a sin's specification and its deficiency with respect to the rule. Báñez writes, "God is the efficient real and physical cause of all the natural aspect which is in the act of sin, and even is the cause of the real contrariety with respect to the natural aspect which is found in the act of sin and in the act of virtue, but he is not the cause with respect to every specific moral aspect."[42] The created agent in freely choosing sin is the moral cause of the act because of the deficiency in relation to the rule. The agent is bound to follow the rule. God only causes the natural effect, which is the positive being of the act, and his action is not bound by such a rule.[43]

We have seen that Báñez uses the distinction between natural and moral contrariety in order to accept a modified version of Cajetan's thesis that God causes the sin's contrariety while at the same time rejecting the otherwise plausible implication that God is a cause of moral evil. These two contrarieties seem to be connected to previous Thomistic distinctions between moral and natural effects, and between moral and natural causes. Báñez does not entirely deny that God can be a moral cause of evil, however.[44] In dubium 2 of the same commentary, for instance, he states that God can morally cause only those acts that are evil merely on account of their circumstances or ends. But he thinks that Cajetan's position on the moral causation of intrinsically evil acts contradicts the Council of Trent. According to Báñez, the Scriptural texts that Cajetan adduces can all be interpreted differently.

---

42. "Deus est causa efficiens realis et physica totius naturalitatis quae est in actu peccati et etiam est causa contrarietatis realis quantum ad naturalitatem quae invenitur in actu peccati et in actu virtutis, non autem est causa contrarietatis quantum ad omnem moralitatem specificam." Báñez, *In I-II*, q. 79, art. 4, n. 22, p. 211. See also n. 23, pp. 212–13.

43. This statement partly resembles Biel's position that God does not cause evil because he is not obligated by law in the way that humans are. See the text cited in note 24 above.

44. Báñez, *In I-II*, q. 79, art. 4, dub. 2, nn. 46–47, pp. 225–29.

Although Báñez argues that God cannot predetermine the will to any sin with respect to its formal aspect, he holds that God does premove and predetermine sinful acts with respect to their material aspects, including both those that are evil by their circumstance and end as well as intrinsically evil acts. In his last conclusion, he states, "God by his intrinsically efficacious and predeterminative assistance (*auxilium*) of the will premoves it to the substance and entity of an act intrinsically evil from its object, before the will determines itself to it."[45] In this unpublished commentary, Báñez's conclusion directly contradicts that of Zumel, and it seems to be derived ultimately from those aspects of Cajetan's theory that Zumel rejects.

Báñez's commentary may represent a shift among Dominican Thomists toward accepting Cajetan's theory of the causation of sin's contrariety to virtue by limiting such causation to a merely natural contrariety. The debate over the Thomistic understanding of God's causation of sin preceded the *de auxiliis* controversy, and was ultimately rooted in Cajetan's attacks on earlier theologians and schools. Spanish Thomists such as Medina and Zumel not only had philosophical reservations about Cajetan's account, but they also worried that it was inconsistent with the more recent decrees of the Council of Trent. Báñez was among the first to rehabilitate and defend a modified version of Cajetan's view.

Although Alvarez does not mention Báñez's position as developed in the unpublished commentary, his account closely resembles it in his defense of Cajetan's understanding of God's causation of sin and his use of it to account for the thesis that God premoves and predetermines the material aspect of sin. Nevertheless, he also uses the distinction between natural and moral contrariety to preserve Medina's thesis that the act of sin insofar as it is caused by God has a nature that is distinct from that of the sin. He discusses such a predetermination of the act of sin briefly in his *De auxiliis divinae gratiae*, and at greater length in his commentary on *ST* I-II, q. 70, a. 2.

In his *De auxiliis*, Alvarez distinguishes between several positions on the premotion of sin.[46] He states that the premotion of the being in an act

---

45. "Deus auxilio physico intrinseco efficaci et praedeterminativo voluntatis praemovet illam ad substantiam et entitatem actus ex objecto et intrinsece mali, prius natura quam voluntas se determinet ad illam." Báñez, *In I-II*, q. 79, art. 4, dub. 2, n. 48, p. 229.

46. Diego Alvarez, *De auxiliis*, lib. 3, disp. 24, nn. 1–10, in *De auxiliis divinae gratiae et human arbitrii viribus et libertate libri duodecim* (Rome, 1610), pp. 193–97.

of sin is held not only by Augustine and Thomas, but also by Thomists such as Capreolus, Cano, Medina, Báñez, and Cajetan. He distinguishes between some recent theologians who believe that God premoves and predetermines the will to good acts but not to the material aspect of sin and those who hold that God causes sin only with a general indifferent concursus. Molina and allied Jesuits hold the second position. The first position probably belongs to Zumel.

Alvarez tries to show that the disagreement between theologians such as Zumel and Alvarez's own Dominican colleagues is merely verbal. He distinguishes between two senses of "as material" *pro materiali*.[47] In the first sense, it indicates a relation to the formal aspect of sin. In this first sense, Zumel rightly argued that God does not predetermine or premove the material aspect of a sin. In the second sense, "as material" indicates the act's entity insofar as this entity is an act and separable from the act's malice. It is only in this second sense that God can be said to premove and predetermine sin "as material." Consequently, on Alvarez's reading, Thomists such as Zumel who deny the premotion of sin's material aspect are denying something different from those who defend such premotion. The first deny that God premoves a "material aspect" that is understood as related to the formal, whereas the second assert that God premoves a "material aspect" that is understood as only the sin's natural being.

In his commentary on the *Prima Secundae*, Alvarez develops Cajetan's view that sin is specified by a positive entity, and he makes a further distinction that indicates how God can cause this positive entity without causing malice.[48] First, in his defense of Cajetan's view, he argues that sin cannot formally consist in a relation, whether it be a categorical relation or a relation of reason. According to Alvarez, it is Cano who seems to have held that a being of reason constitutes sin's malice and perhaps that it consists in a relation of reason. Alvarez notes that a relation cannot be contrary. Consequently, it is the sin itself that is contrary to the object of the virtue. Therefore the sin's contrary positive being cannot be a categorical relation or a relation of reason. Alvarez notes, however, that "it can be explained to consist through a transcendental relation of disagreement."[49]

47. Alvarez, *De auxiliis*, lib. 3, disp. 24, n. 23, p. 203.

48. Alvarez, *In I-II*, q. 71, art. 6, disp. 128, nn. 21–22, p. 374. He briefly addresses God's causation of sin in p. 375n25.

49. "Per relationem transcendentalem discovenientiae possit explicari." Alvarez, *In I-II*,

But a transcendental relation is something that belongs to a category other than relation.[50] For example, "head" signifies a transcendental relation, because although the head is related to the rest of the body by a categorical relation, the head itself is not such a relation. Real relations or relations of reason follow from such transcendental relations.

Alvarez uses a distinction from Capreolus in order to show that Cajetan's view is not vulnerable to Medina's objections. Capreolus makes a distinction that Medina accepts, namely, between the defect or privation that follows from an act's essence considered in itself and the defect or privation that involves a relation to a deficient agent who is held by law to act differently.[51] The loss of bodily integrity through rape or seduction and the privation of coolness in the presence of heat are both examples of the first privation. In these examples, the agent that causes the act's essence also causes the resulting deformity. The rapist causes the privation of integrity, and the heat causes the privation of coolness. But the privation in a moral act is not always an effect of the natural effect's cause. For instance, someone might through invincible ignorance or the losses of reason cause another's death and yet not be the cause of the act of murder. Similarly, Jacob approached Leah thinking that she was Rachel. Consequently, Capreolus argues that God causes only the act in its natural species and not the act in its moral species.[52] Although Alvarez thinks that Cajetan's position better explains the causation of sin, he does not reject Capreolus's approach, which is based on Thomas's statement that "the deformity of a sin does not follow the species of an act insofar as it is in the genus of nature; yet thus it is caused by God; but it follows the species of an insofar as it is moral, as it is caused by free choice."[53]

---

q. 71, art. 6, disp. 128, nn. 21–22, p. 374. This passage resembles Báñez, *In I-II*, q. 71, art. 6, dub. 1, n. 13, p. 65.

50. John of St. Thomas, *Cursus Philosophicus, Log.*, q. 17, art. 1 (in Reiser ed., vol. 1, 577a–579a). There is a somewhat misleading account in A. Krempel, *La doctrine de la relation chez saint Thomas: Exposé historique et systématique* (Paris: Vrin, 1952), 645–70.

51. Capreolus, *Defensiones*, lib. 2, d. 37, q. 1, art. 3, ad primum (vol. 4, pp. 428–29).

52. For the distinction in Thomas, see Steven J. Jensen, *Good and Evil Actions: A Journey through Saint Thomas Aquinas* (Washington, DC: Catholic University of America Press, 2010), 40–41; Thomas M. Osborne Jr., "The Goodness and Evil of Objects and Ends," in M. V. Dougherty, *Aquinas's Disputed Questions on Evil: A Critical Guide* (Cambridge: Cambridge University Press), 126–45, at 132–33.

53. "Deformitas peccati non consequitur speciem actus secundum quod est in genere nature: sic autem a Deo causatur; sed consequitur speciem actus secundum quod est moralis, prout causatur ex libero arbitrio." Thomas, *De Malo*, q. 3, art. 2, ad 2. Cited by Capreolus,

The related distinction between the two contrarieties plays a central role in Alvarez's adoption of Cajetan's view. According to Alvarez, the positive entity in a sin that is contrary to virtue can be considered in two ways, namely, as naturally contrary to virtue and as morally contrary to virtue. Alvarez writes, "God is the cause of the conversion to the object contrary to virtue by a natural contrariety, not however as it is contrary to it by a moral contrariety, and in this sense Cajetan is to be explained when he says that the conversion to the object contrary to virtue is from God."[54] This distinction between the kinds of contrariety is the same as that made in Báñez's unpublished commentary. But whereas Báñez seems to think that he is modifying Cajetan's position, Alvarez sees it as a way to interpret Cajetan.

Alvarez's arguments for the use of this contrariety are based not on Cajetan's texts but on reasoning about the truth of the matter.[55] Alvarez argues that God cannot cause the conversion to the object insofar as it involves a moral contrariety because moral evil is caused by such moral contrariety. Consequently, both the conversion to the object as involving moral contrariety and the moral evil constituted by it are intrinsically ordered to the deficient will as their cause and not to God. Alvarez's reasoning is not much different from that of Medina. Their varying responses to Cajetan might be explained by their different readings of him. Medina rejects Cajetan because he understands Cajetan to hold that God causes a positive entity that is the specific difference that places an act in its moral genus. Alvarez defends Cajetan because he thinks that Cajetan holds that God causes the positive entity that places the act in the natural genus, and that the sin's disorder follows from this genus. If Alvarez agreed with Medina and Báñez on Cajetan's position, he would reject precisely that part of it rejected by Báñez.

Once this distinction between the two kinds of contrariety is made, Alvarez responds at length to Medina's criticism of Cajetan on the causation of sin by showing that Medina's objections concerning God's

---

Defensiones, lib. 2, d. 37, q. 1, art. 3, ad primum Aureoli et ad secundum Durandi (vol. 4, pp. 429, 434).

54. "Deus est causa conversionis ad obiectum contrarium virtuti, contrarietate naturali, non autem, ut contrariatur illi contrarietate morali, et in hoc sensu explicandus est Caietanus quando ait, conversionem ad obiectum contrarium virtuti esse a Deo." Alvarez, *In I-II*, q. 79, art. 2, disp. 168, nn. 13–14, p. 502.

55. Alvarez, *In I-II*, q. 79, art. 2, disp. 168, n. 14, p. 502.

responsibility for evil and his causation of sin are valid only if Cajetan is discussing God as the cause of a moral contrariety.[56] He agrees with Medina that if God were to cause the moral contrariety, then God would be the cause of sin and move agents to sinful acts. Alvarez uses Capreolus's discussion of Jacob and Leah to illustrate the difference between the two kinds of contrariety. Simply speaking, approaching Leah would be a sinful act for Jacob. But on account of Jacob's ignorance, the act is contrary to virtue only naturally and not morally.

This natural contrariety is not what places the act in its natural species as opposed to its moral species. Alvarez is using Capreolus's example in a context that includes the distinction between not only the act's natural and moral species, but also between the act's natural contrariety and its moral contrariety to virtue. The two distinctions are related but not the same. Jacob's act in its natural species is a reproductive act. In itself, the reproductive act might be an act of adultery, fornication, or rendering the marriage debt. The natural species is not on its own contrary to virtue. Nevertheless, the reproductive act, because of its natural species, cannot be knowingly performed by Jacob on Leah without belonging to a sinful moral species. This act's natural species entails a natural contrariety to virtue because it is performed by Jacob with Leah. Only Jacob's ignorance prevents the act from falling under the species of adultery.

Alvarez's distinction between the natural and moral characteristics of the act helps him to address the way in which God causes an act's species. If Cajetan is right that sin is more formally a positive entity than a privation, then it seems to follow that God causes sin or that there is a being that is not caused by God. Alvarez presents a standard objection to Cajetan that clearly shows the difficulty:

Moral evil in its formal aspect, either indicates a real entity, or not. If the first is admitted, therefore God is the cause of moral evil in its formal aspect, and consequently of sin, or now there is admitted some positive being in sin which is not from God, which is against the second dictum [of Cajetan]. If the second is admitted, therefore the species of moral evil or of sin is not something positive: but privative, which is against Cajetan.[57]

56. Alvarez, *In I-II*, q. 79, art. 2, disp. 168, n. 16, pp. 502–3.
57. "Malum morale pro formali, vel importat entitatem realem, vel non. Si detur primum: ergo Deus est causa mali moralis pro formali, et consequenter peccati, vel iam detur in peccato aliqua entitas positiva, quae non sit a Deo; quod est contra secundum dictum. Si detur

Alvarez responds to this objection by stating that relation to a deficient cause is not a positive entity and therefore not caused by God.[58] His central point seems to be that the formality of sin is not formally a being, although materially it is one. In other words, the thing that is a sin is a natural being, but it is not a sin insofar as it is a natural being. God causes the sin only insofar as it is a natural being. Although God causes the being that is a sin, he does not cause it as a sin. But the deficient human will causes the sin insofar as it is formally sinful, namely, as related to a deficient cause. The conclusion that God causes sin is invalid because it draws on premises with different appellations of "sin." It is the same logical error as concluding that the sculptor made wood from the premise that the sculptor made a statue, and that the statue is wood.[59] Alvarez identifies the same fallacy and uses almost the same example that Báñez used in his discussion of Biel and Ockham.

Thomas de Lemos more or less follows Alvarez's distinctions in order to reconcile different Thomists. In his account of the last public disputation of the *Congregationes de auxiliis*, for instance, he notes, "without doubt Zumel only says that with respect to the material aspect of sin, as namely it connotes an order to the formal, men are not moved by God."[60] He notes that Zumel never explicitly rejected the thesis that the Dominicans were defending, namely, that God premoves or predetermines acts insofar as they do not connote any sort of deformity. In this text he refers to Zumel's longer treatment in the commentary on the *Summa Theologiae*.[61] Lemos develops his own views in his magisterial *Panoplia gratiae*, which was published posthumously only in 1674. In this work he also expresses the opinion that Zumel should be understood as referring only to the material aspect of sin insofar as it involves and connotes an order to the sin's deformity, although he refers only to Zumel's brief discussion in the *Disputationes variae*.[62]

---

secundum: ergo species mali moralis seu peccati non est aliquid positivum, sed privativum, quod est contra Caietanum." Alvarez, *In I-II*, q. 79, art. 2, disp. 168, n. 15, p. 502.

58. Alvarez, *In I-II*, q. 79, art. 2, disp. 168, n. 17, p. 503. Almost the same discussion can be found in Báñez, *In I-II*, q. 79, art. 4, n. 23, p. 212.

59. See the attribution of a similar point to Ockham and Biel by Báñez, *In I-II*, q. 79, art. 4, n. 17, p. 208.

60. "Nempe Zumel, tantum dicit: quod ad materiale peccati, ut videlicet connotat ordinem ad formale, non moventur homines a Deo." Lemos, *Acta*, col. 1358.

61. Lemos, *Acta*, col. 1320.

62. Lemos, *Panoplia Gratiae*, lib. 2, tract. 1, cap. 26, n. 366, p. 57.

Lemos considers the causation of sin in the context of both providence and premotion. We noted the separation between the two discussions in Zumel, but it is particularly reflected in the work of Molina and Lessius, whom Lemos criticizes at length. With respect to the causation of sin, he more or less follows Alvarez's account, but he develops his views at greater length and more explicitly ties the different kinds of contrariety to the distinction between the act's natural and moral species.[63] In this way, Lemos more clearly aligns his view with that of earlier Thomists such as Capreolus. In his discussion of sin's premotion, for example, he first mentions that God is in no way a moral cause of sin. He then invokes the distinction between the genus of nature and the genus of morals. He explains that when someone without reason kills or fornicates, he commits only the act in its natural species and not as it is a sin. Similarly, even when an agent in his right mind sins, God causes only the act in its natural species. Lemos concludes that God does not predetermine sin because he is a cause of a sin's natural species and not its moral species. The moral species is permitted but not caused by God.

Lemos more clearly applies this distinction to the arguments against Cajetan. Lemos interprets Cajetan as holding that God causes the positive entity that specifies the act in its natural species but not that which constitutes it in its moral species.[64] For instance, Lemos like Alvarez responds to the common objection that would make God the cause of sin because of the way in which sin is understood as involving a positive entity. Lemos's presentation of the argument can be formulated as follows:[65]

Major premise: The formal and specific character of a bad moral act is something real and positive.

Minor premise: But God is the cause of all positive entities.

Conclusion: Therefore God is the cause of cause of the formal aspect of a moral sin.

Lemos distinguishes between different meanings of the major and minor premises in such a way that the conclusion does not validly fol-

---

63. Lemos, *Panoplia Gratiae*, lib. 3, tract. 4, cap. 26, n. 296, p. 272.

64. Lemos, *Panoplia Gratiae*, lib. 3, tract. 4, cap. 27, nn. 310–11, p. 275.

65. "Formale et specificum actus mali moralis, seu peccati moralis ut est formale illius, est aliquid reale et positivum, sed totius realitatis positivae Deus est causa, ergo formalis peccati moralis, seu mali moralis ut formale illius est, Deus est causa." Lemos, *Panoplia Gratiae*, lib. 3, tract. 4, cap. 27, n. 313, p. 275.

low.[66] First, the major premise could either refer to the formal and specific character insofar as it is formally morally evil, or insofar as it is something that the deformity necessarily follows. Considered as formally morally evil, it is false that the formal and specific character is a positive entity. Considered as that which the deformity and privation of law and reason follows, however, the formal and specific character is a positive entity. Similarly, the major premise could either refer to God as only about positive entities as entities, or it could be about the entities insofar as a deformity and privation of reason follows them. God is a cause of the first but not of the second. Consequently, the argument establishes only that God is the cause of the sin's positive entity, and not that he is a cause of the formal sin insofar as it is a sin formally.

Lemos's reply to this argument appears to be a clearer development of Alvarez's position that the formality of a sin is materially but not formally a being, which is rooted in Báñez's distinction between the act's natural and moral contrariety to virtue. Insofar as the sin is an act, it has a natural being that makes it sinful if it is chosen by a created will. This natural being is not the same as the act's natural species. For example, the sin of adultery belongs to the natural species of reproduction, but as a natural being, this reproductive act has features that make it sinful if it proceeds from free choice. The sin's positive entity is such that privation and defect necessarily follow such choice, as proceeding from a defective agent. The distinction is between considering the formality of sin as chosen by the sinner (formally) and considering it apart from the choice (materially).

One of Lemos's original contributions to the discussion is in his application of this theory to the different parts of the human act. In his discussion of God's providence, he devotes a chapter to the role of premotion in the causation of willing the end, deliberating, and choosing.[67] In the following chapter he shows how premotion works differently with respect to the material aspect of sin.[68] After discussing texts from the Fathers (especially Augustine) and Anselm that support his account, Lemos reproduces a text from Thomas's commentary on chapter 9 of St. Paul's *Epistle to the Romans*, in which Thomas explicitly follows Augustine in holding that God in some way moves the sinner to sin.[69] Like Thomas,

66. Lemos, *Panoplia Gratiae*, lib. 3, tract. 4, cap. 27, n. 313, pp. 275–76.
67. Lemos, *Panoplia Gratiae*, lib. 2, tract. 1, cap. 9, pp. 14–18.
68. Lemos, *Panoplia Gratiae*, lib. 2, tract. 1, cap. 10, pp. 18–23.
69. Thomas Aquinas, *Super epistolam ad Romanos lectura*, cap. 9, lect. 3, n. 781, in *Super*

Lemos wishes to hold both that God in some way moves the sinner's will toward what is sinful and also that God does not cause the sin.

Lemos describes four steps of the sin in order to explain how God premoves its material aspect.[70] First, God in his judgment permits the sin. Second, he inclines the will to the good in general. Third, although God applies the intellect and will to their acts concerning the relevant matter of deliberation and choice, he merely permits the error. Fourth, the disordered agent places an impediment to God's sufficient premotion in such a way that God does not provide further efficacious help to judge or choose correctly. The first three steps indicate how God is causally responsible for the sin's natural being. The third and fourth steps explain how the agent is responsible for the sin. In the third step, it is the agent as a deficient cause who makes an error in his deliberation and choice. In the fourth step, it is the agent who resists God's help. Lemos's account shows for Thomists that the agent is primarily responsible for resisting God's help and the corresponding deficiency.

In this text, Lemos notes that this discussion is explained by Cano's distinction of how God is the natural cause of a sin's natural being but in no way the moral cause of what gives the act its moral species. Lemos states that Cano rightly explains this position by saying that "God is the natural cause of every motion and action according as they pertain to the being of nature; but he is not the moral cause of them according as namely they enter the genus of morals."[71] Following Alvarez, Lemos combines Cano's use of the distinction between natural and moral causality with the interpretation of Cajetan as stating that God is a cause of the sin's positive entity that has a natural contrariety to virtue. We have seen that Báñez's unpublished work also embraces this approach. Lemos embellishes but does not substantially alter the framework that Alvarez and Báñez had established. In his use of the distinction between the sin's natural and moral species, Lemos might even be seen as drawing closer to the tradition represented by Capreolus.

---

episotlas S. Pauli lectura, 8th ed., 2 vols., ed. Raphael Cai (Turin: Marietti, 1953), 1:141–42. Lemos, Panoplia Gratiae, lib. 2, tract. 1, cap. 31, n. 405, p. 66. He had already mentioned this text in cap. 10, nn. 125, 128, pp. 20–21.

70. Lemos, Panoplia Gratiae, lib. 2, tract. 1, cap. 31, n. 405, pp. 66–67.

71. "Dicens, quod Deus est causa naturalis omnium motuum et actionum secundum quod pertinent ad esse naturae; non autem est causa moralis eorum secundum videlicet quod ipsae genus moris ingrediuntur." Lemos, Panoplia Gratiae, lib. 2, tract. 1, cap. 31, n. 406, p. 67.

On this particular issue of the premotion of the material aspect of sin, Alvarez and to some extent Báñez clarified and developed Cajetan's understanding of God's causation of sin by making two key distinctions. First, Báñez and perhaps more clearly Alvarez distinguished between the positive entity, which is a natural being that specifies the act, and the moral defect, which specifies the act as a belonging to a moral species. Báñez thinks that by doing so he is changing Cajetan's position so as to remove its implication that God causes moral evil. In contrast, Alvarez and Lemos use this distinction to interpret Cajetan as holding that the positive entity is sin naturally but not morally contrary to virtue.

Second, Alvarez especially distinguished between the two different senses of the "material aspect of sin." Consequently, he could both assent to Zumel's claim that God does not cause a material aspect that is intrinsically ordered to the formal aspect, and that God does premove and predetermine a material aspect that is a positive entity. As a result of making these two distinctions, Alvarez and Lemos were consequently able to respond to a standard objection against Cajetan's view, namely, that if God causes the positive entity of sin, then God causes sin. Although much of the debate is formulated in a context that predates the *de auxiliis* dispute, the motivation for the development by these later authors came from those who objected against the Dominicans that if God premoves and predetermines the material aspect of sin, then God premoves and predetermines sin.

This Thomistic development illustrates how philosophical clarity concerning the same issue can develop in response to problems that have distinct historical contexts. Cajetan was at least in part responding to the Scotistic claim that sin is essentially a privation. Cano and Soto were replying to the teaching of some Protestants that God causes sin in the way that he causes good acts. Báñez, Alvarez, and Lemos were at least partially concerned with Molina's thesis that God does not premove the material aspect of sin. The later Thomists were arguably successful in responding to contemporary challenges because they relied not only on Thomas Aquinas's own texts, but also on the conceptual progress made by previous Thomists.[72]

72. Special thanks to Steven Jensen, Ross McCullough, and R. J. Matava.

9

THE MYSTERY OF

DIVINE PREDESTINATION

Its Intelligibility According to Lonergan

Matthew Lamb

Introduction

In his masterful presentation of contemporary Thomism and predestination, Father Serge-Thomas Bonino concludes by stating that Aquinas and his genuine followers acknowledge the divine mystery of God's predestination:

He doesn't want to sacrifice any of the problem's data, metaphysical or theological: neither the universal determining causality of pure act, nor grace's primacy, nor God's innocence and his saving will. The theologian surrenders neither to the absurdity of a contradiction between the Word of God and right reason, nor to the apologetic cop out of a created freedom conceived as first cause. He contents himself (but that's a lot) to lay out the mystery in its rightful place, that is, to turn one's gaze toward the superintelligible essence of a God in whom power, wisdom, and goodness kiss.

Lawrence Feingold has presented some aspects of Father Bernard Lonergan's retrieval of Aquinas's theory of operative and cooperative grace. He correctly shows that this approach provides insights into why relating divine causality and human freedom was not a problem for Aquinas, as it became later in the *de auxiliis* controversies.

My essay emphasizes the unique achievement of Lonergan's analysis of operative and cooperative grace, and how he also understood the further problems facing the later theologians, such as Báñez and Molina. Lonergan offered additional solutions to these problems based upon his theoretical analysis of Aquinas.[1]

Theoretical Framework

Other theologians might have used the terms "operative" and "cooperative" grace, but none set them in the theoretical framework of the development of Aquinas with the precision of Lonergan. Similar to others, Lonergan shows how Aquinas developed the theoretical context of habitual grace as *operans* and *cooperans*. Yet he also indicates the specific developments in Aquinas (1) on the virtues as perfecting man, (2) on their necessity in the light of Pelagianism and twelfth-century Augustinianism, and (3) finally on the need for prevenient action of grace on free will for justification.[2]

A breakthrough in Aquinas's theory of operation occurred in the *Summa Theologiae*. There he was the first to show that both habitual grace and actual grace are both operative and cooperative. Lonergan affirms with Aquinas that any change brought about by the exercise of the will is a change in the effect, not in the cause as such. Peter as *posse agere* and *actu agere* is the same Peter; the change is in the effect that Peter's act brings about.

From Aristotle and Aquinas, Lonergan realized that causation is a relation of dependence in an effect on its cause. Causation is the actuation of the active potency of the cause and the passive potency of the effect. One and the same act actuates both potencies, and this act is the motion produced in the object moved. Causation is therefore inherent not in the cause but in the effect; action and passion are really identical with the motion of the recipient. There is no change in the cause, only in the ef-

---

1. This leads Lonergan to agree with Réginald Garrigou-Lagrange's criticism of Molina; cf. Bernard Lonergan, *Grace and Freedom: Operative Grace in the Thought of St. Thomas Aquinas*, ed. F. E. Crowe and R. M. Doran (Toronto: University of Toronto Press, 2000), 111.
   2. Ibid., 44–65, 193–251.

fect. Thus God creating and redeeming the world involves no change in God, but in the created and redeemed world. And it is also the case with human causation. Lonergan is illustrating the will as an active potency within the order of execution in the will: Peter is free to act or not to act.

Father H. D. Gardeil, OP, further clarifies this point by contrasting the freedom of the human will in the order of specification and in the order of exercise.[3] He illustrates the difference as follows: If I want to go to a town and there are two different roads to it, I can specify which one I will take; but if there is only one road, I still have the freedom of exercise. "Consequently my will remains free to decide to go or not to go. And this power to will or not to will is called freedom of exercise." He goes on to remark that even when the agent does not have freedom of specification, the agent is still free to act or not to act.

So Peter decides to drive or walk to the town. He actuates the active potency of his will and the passive potency of the car or his legs to walk. One and the same act actuates both potencies, and this action is the motion produced in the object moved, for example, the car or his legs (the effect). That the cause as cause (Peter) is not changed is clear in the fact that on the way he can change his mind and not go; he remains free to act or not to act.

A fundamental issue confronting both the Patristic and Scholastic theologians was the revelation that the Triune God freely creates and redeems the world. There was no necessity for such divine causality. Indeed, Aquinas often applied his notion of "contingent necessity" to all causation in time. Lonergan provides the theoretical and historical developments in Aquinas's use of Aristotelian premotion by incorporating it into a higher synthesis of terrestrial contingency and Divine Providence foreseeing, planning, and bringing about every event:

The Thomist higher synthesis was to place God above and beyond the created orders of necessity and contingence: because God is universal cause, his providence must be certain; but because he is a transcendent cause, there can be no incompatibility between terrestrial contingence and the causal certitude of providence.[4]

---

3. Ibid., 66–73, 252–69. Lonergan mentions that, for Aquinas, "Peter not acting" and "Peter acting" are not really different (73n26). He is illustrating active potency within the order of execution in the will: Peter is free to act or not to act. See H. D. Gardeil, OP, *Introduction to the Philosophy of St. Thomas Aquinas*, vol. 3, *Psychology* (Eugene, OR: Wipf & Stock, 2009), 214–15.

4. Ibid., 81–82.

Universal Instrumentality

This higher synthesis enabled Aquinas to elaborate the universal in-strumentality in all the created hierarchy of causes as they are present in God's eternal wisdom and love. All created events past, present, and future are present in God's eternal presencing:

Since therefore God is eternal, His knowledge must have the mode of eterni-ty, which is to be totally simultaneous without succession. Hence although any time is successive, nonetheless His eternity is present to all times by one and the same and indivisible eternal *now* (*nunc stans*). Similarly, He knows all temporal things, no matter how successive they are, as present to Himself, nor is any of them future with respect to Himself...Hence Boethius remarks that [God's knowledge] is better called providence than pre-knowledge: be-cause it is not as if it were of the future. Rather He knows all things by one glance as present, as it were reflected in His eternity. It can, however, be called pre-knowledge inasmuch as He knows what is future for us, but it is not future for Him.[5]

The eternal Triune God creates the totality of all things, and so the di-vine act of creating embraces all created things and events. Yet this does not impose any necessity on the things or events because the eternal God is not "before" time in any temporal sense of the word. God knows what is going to happen, and which choices every human being is going to make, next year, next century, and so on. While these events are future to us, they are all present to God in his eternal *esse-intelligere-amare*. As Lonergan writes:

If the future is known with certainty, then necessarily it must come to be; and what necessarily must come to be is not contingent but necessary. But St. Thomas denies that God knows events as future. He is not in time but an eternal "now" to which everything is present. Hence when you say, "If God knows this, this must be," the "this" of the apodosis must be taken in the same sense as the "this" of the prodosis. But the "this" of the prodosis is present, therefore, the "this" of the apodosis is present; it follows that "this must be" is not absolute but hypothetical necessity, as [Aquinas often states] "it is neces-sary that Socrates runs, if he runs."[6]

---

5. Thomas Aquinas, *In I Sent.*, d. 38, q. 1, a. 5c; my translation. On God's knowledge of singulars, cf. *Summa Theologiae* (*ST*) I, q. 14, a. 11.

6. Lonergan, *Grace and Freedom*, 107; *In I Sent.*, d. 38, q. 1, a. 5, ad 4m.

Thus the entire universe, embracing all things including all extensions and durations, is under the egis of contingency and hypothetical necessity. Lonergan sees how Aquinas links creation and conservation with application. It is clear that Lonergan never replaces creation and conservation with application. Rather, he shows that

once St. Thomas had grasped a theory of providence compatible with Aristotelian terrestrial contingence, he began at once to argue that the creature's causation was caused not merely because of creation and of conservation but also because of application, instrumentality, cosmic hierarchy, and universal finality.[7]

Divine transcendence is proper only to God and not to any creature, including *gratia operans*. As Lonergan writes, "*If then, a gratia operans were to produce a contingent effect with irresistible efficacy, it could not be a creature; it would have to be God....* Similarly, when God irresistibly produces a contingent effect, he does so, not through a necessitated, but through a contingent cause."[8]

It is amazing that a recent study by Robert J. Matava on *Divine Causality and Human Free Choice* has a chapter on Lonergan's views and yet completely ignores Lonergan's analysis of universal instrumentality. This is especially puzzling because Matava mistakenly claims that Lonergan holds that the created antecedents efficaciously cause the free acts in some similarity to Báñez's physical premotion.[9] On the contrary, Lonergan emphasizes that no creature or combination of creatures, no cosmic sets of hierarchal causes, can substitute for God's efficient infallible immediate causality.[10] Matava thinks that Lonergan does not "seem to understand application—God's operation in the operations of created agents—in terms of creation."[11] Lonergan most certainly does see application as a further differentiation within the context of creation and conservation. It could be argued that Lonergan's position on the immediacy of divine causality would enhance Matava's efforts in that regard.[12]

---

7. Lonergan, *Grace and Freedom*, 89.
8. Ibid., 110–11; my emphasis. See also *ST* I, q. 19, a. 8.
9. Robert J. Matava, *Divine Causality and Human Free Choice: Domingo Báñez, Physical Premotion and the Controversy De Auxiliis Revisited*, Brill's Studies in Intellectual History 252 (Leiden: Brill, 2016), 222–41.
10. Lonergan, *Grace and Freedom*, 66–118, 252–383.
11. Ibid., 236.
12. Matava, *Divine Causality and Human Free Choice*, 242–321.

Divine Causality

Grace as a creature cannot produce any contingent effect with the irresistible efficacy proper only to God. This is precisely the genius of Aquinas's understanding of divine causality. Lonergan was able to pinpoint why for Aquinas there was no problem reconciling God's causality and human freedom. Neither Báñez nor Molina understood the immediacy of divine causality as Aquinas had. Physical premotion is created; it is not God. Therefore efficacious and sufficient grace is not adequate in grasping Aquinas's position. On the one hand, Báñez does not have God cause the sinner's sinning, but sufficient grace makes it impossible for the sinner to do what is right. Merely sufficient grace is not sufficient! On the other hand, Molina's *scientia media* sets up a hypothetical order where God knows *futurabilia* of either graced or sinful acts. In such a hypothetical order, God is not God, as Lonergan puts it, referring to Garrigou-Lagrange. God appears to be determined by a creature.[13]

St. Thomas avoids both these errors by two fundamental theoretical steps. First, for him, the "ratio" of God's providence governs all things, even the least, immediately.[14] Particular things and events are to be understood within the whole providential order of God. The second theoretical step is that, having worked out the providential order, from his *Summa contra Gentiles* (*ScG*) onward, Thomas developed the theorem that God applies all agents to their activity. This theorem is the analogy of operation:

As Newton affirmed a "law" of gravitation, as Einstein affirmed a "theory" of relativity, so too St. Thomas affirmed the analogy of operation, namely, that the causation of the created cause is itself caused; that it is a procession which is made to proceed; that it is an operation in which another operates. The fundamental point in the theory of operation is that operation involves no change in the cause as cause.[15]

In terms of divine causality, therefore, Aquinas gives us three sets: "Thus he distinguishes between what God wills to happen, what he wills not to happen, and what he permits to happen."[16]

---

13. Lonergan, *Grace and Freedom*, 111, 273–348.
14. *ST* I, q. 103, a. 6. The ratio of providence governs all things immediately. The execution of this providence can be mediated by the hierarchical order of all things in the universe.
15. Lonergan, *Grace and Freedom*, 90; see also note 3 above.
16. Lonergan, *Grace and Freedom*, 111–12.

For Aquinas and the Patristic traditions, it is clear that revelation has provided a far more perfect knowledge of God than any philosophy could attain. Eternity is not simply an abstraction; eternity is the Triune God. Moreover, eternity is not opposed to time; eternity creates and redeems time. As God is simple, infinite understanding and loving, so God is eternal. There is no extension or duration in God. This divine eternity, as divine infinity and simplicity, cannot be imagined, nor can it be understood and conceived, except by God. We can, however, affirm that God is eternal and understand analogically that affirmation. There are major breakthroughs in the philosophical and theological grasp of this analogical understanding of the affirmation that God is eternal. Those breakthroughs occurred in the works of Augustine, Boethius, and Thomas Aquinas.

As mentioned under universal instrumentality, Aquinas insists that what God wills to happen, or not to happen, or permits does not hinder the free wills of intellectual creatures. For there is no past or future in God's eternal presencing *now* (*nunc stans*) that embraces all things and events, including all free acts by intelligent creatures.[17]

Predestination

Because divine providence means that God directs all created things toward their end, when it comes to human beings providentially directed to the absolutely supernatural end of the beatific vision, this providential ordering is predestination. "Thus it is clear that predestination, as regards its object, is a part of providence."[18] Lonergan clarifies why Aquinas insists that predestination belongs to God alone, and is not something in the predestined. "Praedestinatio non est aliquid in praedestinatis, sed in praedestinante tantum."[19] The implementation of providential predestination is divine governance, and God governs each and every particular event as within the whole of creation and redemption.

---

17. Thomas Aquinas, *Super I Sententiarum*, d. 40, q. 3, a. 1. This line of argument runs throughout Aquinas's writings, e.g., *ST* I, q. 14, a. 13; *Expositio super Librum de Causis* 11, 30. Cf. Brian Shanley, "Eternal Knowledge of the Temporal in Aquinas," *American Catholic Philosophical Quarterly* 71 (1977): 1–28.

18. *ST* I, q. 23, a. 1.

19. *ST* I, q. 23, a. 2. "Predestination is not something in the predestined, but only in the one predestining."

The analogy based on Aquinas's theory of operation leads Lonergan to remark that contingent truths predicated of a divine person do not add anything to the divine person but a "relation of reason," for the three divine persons are pure act. But the truth does involve a "created ad extra term" in order for the truth to exist:

why does this *adaequatio,* which relates and equates divine knowledge not to the event *in causis* but to the event *in se ipso,* eliminate the problem of necessity from divine foreknowledge? Because once the event is, it can no longer be necessitated; any necessity then is necessarily hypothetical necessity: and that is compatible with contingence. *Omne enim quod est dum est necesse est esse.*[20]

Lonergan analyzes the contingent predication also in his Christology.[21] The "ad extra terms" are antecedently in the divine free choice (e.g., this concrete universe with its manifold natures, the humanity of Christ, operative and cooperative habitual and actual graces, natural and supernatural acts of intelligent creatures, beatific glory, reprobation of the damned). Because there is no "before" or "after" in the Divine Nature and Divine Persons—all created things and events being present as present in the Triune God's infinite *esse-intelligere-amare*—all of the created ad extra terms are in no way rigorous determinants of the divine free choice. God alone has this property of transcendence:

It is only in the logico-metaphysical simultaneity of the atemporal present that God's knowledge is infallible, his will irresistible, his action efficacious. He exercises control through created antecedents—true enough; but that is not the infallible, the irresistible, the efficacious, which has its ground not in the creature but in the uncreated, which has its moment not in time but in the cooperation of eternal uncreated action with created and temporal action. Again, the antecedents per se always per se incline to the right and good. But the consequent act may be good or it may be sinful: if it is good, all the credit is God's, and the creature is only his instrument; but if it is evil, then inasmuch as it is sin as such, it is a surd (preceded, indeed, by a divine permission which is infallible without being a cause or non-cause), and so in the causal order a first for which the sinner alone is responsible.[22]

20. Lonergan, *Grace and Freedom,* 326. Lonergan calls attention to this repeated affirmation by Aquinas from his *Commentary on the Sentences,* through the *Summa contra Gentiles* to the *Summa Theologiae.*

21. Lonergan, *The Ontological and Psychological Constitution of Christ* (Toronto: University of Toronto Press, 2002), 94–99; idem, *The Incarnate Word* (Toronto: University of Toronto Press, 2016), 441–47, 455–57, 737–39, 753–57.

22. Lonergan, *Grace and Freedom,* 117–18. Lonergan also refers to Thomas Aquinas, *De*

While predestination bestows on the elect both their merits and the consequent reward, the reprobate have their sins from themselves alone, and so sin is a cause of punishment in a way that merit is not a cause of glory.[23] Neither Báñez nor Molina were able to account for these reflections by Aquinas on contingency and sin. Sin is a surd as an irrational, objective falsity, and so cannot have an antecedent cause or noncause. Sin as moral evil (*malum culpae*) means that the sinner attempts to withdraw himself from the divine order; he does so by forcibly removing a good from the divine order or *telos* in which it is truly a good. So this withdrawal, as seeking a good against the divine order in which it is a good, does rightly bring punishment on the reprobate.[24]

Yet while neither Báñezians nor Monlinists grasped the full implications of Aquinas's position, they were struggling with a very real problem about the divine permissive will. The problem was how to account for the intelligibility of the mystery of predestination by reconciling divine causality and the divine permissive will. It was God's permissive will, permitting sins while not in any way causing them, that was a key factor in the long-running *de auxiliis* controversy. After some ten years of debates between Dominicans and Jesuits, Pope Clement VIII set up the *Congregatio de auxiliis* in 1598. During his reign and that of two successors, there were some eighty-five conference debates in the presence of the popes over twenty years. With no resolution, a papal decree told both sides to await a final decision of the Holy See, which never came.[25]

The intelligibility of the mystery of predestination is clear in relation to God's eternal presence embracing all temporal contingent events. There is no future or past in God; all of the created universe, including all intelligent creatures and their acts, is present in God's knowing-willing. The ad extra terms (e.g., operative habitual and actual graces, natural operative habitual and actual motions) are creatures and so are contin-

---

veritate, q. 22, 8; and *ST* I-II, q. 79, a. 1, ad 1, where Aquinas corrects Augustine on the hardening of Pharaoh's heart.

23. Lonergan refers to Thomas Aquinas, *In Rom.*, c. 9, lect. 2, 763–64; *ST* I, q. 23, a. 3c and ad 2; *ScG* III, ch. 163.

24. Lonergan, *Grace and Freedom*, 113–18.

25. Cf. Matthew Levering, *Predestination: Biblical and Theological Paths* (Oxford: Oxford University Press, 2011), 98–274. Levering mentions Matava's dissertation. As I argued above, Matava does not adequately understand Lonergan's theory of universal instrumentality with its divine eternal presencing of all concrete extensions and durations.

gently hypothetically necessary. Only God can cause a contingent event with irresistible efficacy. Divine premotion is the created ad extra term affirming the truth that one who dies in the state of grace is predestined. The predestined's death is a hypothetical necessity: if...then. So God freely moves the human will by his operative and cooperative graces as created ad extra terms, resulting from the immediacy of the divine *esse-intelligere-amare* willing this concrete universe.[26]

Thus it is clear that what God from all eternity wills to happen (predestination) or not happen (reprobation as punishment for those dying in mortal sin) embraces the totality of creation/redemption. Divine causality has created ad extra terms (beatific vision and hell as punishment), manifesting their hypothetical necessary contingency. But what about God's universal permissive will? The moral evil of sin (*malum culpae*) is caused only by the sinner, and God permits but in no way enters into the objective falsity of sin. There is no intelligibility of sin as sin that takes a created good and removes it from the divine order in which it is a good.

To seek the "why" and "how" of the divine universal permissive will is to enter the realm of the divine ideas. That is, to ask why out of all possible worlds God chose this one in which intelligent creatures would sin. Now only God comprehends all his divine ideas and possibles. No finite intellect, even of the blessed, can comprehend all possibles. Not even the human intellect of Christ could do so.[27] God's universal permissive will therefore depends upon the divine ideas present in God's own infinite *esse-intelligere-amare*. As Lonergan writes, "The mysteries of faith are mysteries only to us because of their excess of intelligibility; but the *mysterium iniquitatis* is mysterious in itself and objectively, because of a defect of intelligibility." As Aquinas writes, God "in no way wills the evil of sin, which is the privation of right order toward the divine good." God only permits the sin that is caused by the sinner, who alone is responsible for this privation.[28]

In *ST* I, q. 19, a. 9, ad 3, Aquinas sums up his position:

The statements that evil exists, and that evil exists not, are opposed as contradictories; yet the statements that anyone wills evil to exist and that he wills it not to be, are not so opposed; since either is affirmative. God therefore neither

26. See the section "Divine Causality" and notes 7 and 8 above.
27. *ST* III, q. 10, a. 1; I, qq. 15 and 16.
28. Lonergan, *Grace and Freedom*, 115; *ST* I, q. 19, a. 9c.

wills evil to be done, nor wills it not to be done, but wills to permit evil to be done; and this is a good.

In permitting moral evils in a universe God wills into existence, he is able to bring good out of evil. Similar to the *Felix culpa* of the Paschal Vigil, Aquinas reiterates how the whole provides the order to the divine good.

God and nature and any other agent make what is best in the whole, but not what is best in every single part, except in order to the whole. And the whole itself, which is the universe of creatures, is all the better and more perfect if some things in it can fail in goodness, and do sometimes fail, God not preventing this...as Augustine says (*Enchiridion* 11) "God is so powerful that He can even make good out of evil." Hence many good things would be taken away if God permitted no evil to exist; for fire would not be generated if air was not corrupted, nor would the life of a lion be preserved unless the ass were killed. Neither would avenging justice nor the patience of a sufferer be praised if there were no injustice.[29]

Only God's infinite intelligence, wisdom, and love comprehend why he chose this concrete universe. Through revelation, the faithful know that by his redemption Christ, as truly the Son of God and of Mary, brings life out of death, grace out of sin, good out of evil.

Conclusion

By faith, we know that God brings good out of evil. This knowing is in the truth of judgment (*an sit*). Comprehension is understanding as the first act of the mind (*quid vel quare sit*). Knowing is of what is actual. We cannot know the divine ideas or possible universes as they are known and comprehended only by an infinite divine mind. All sins and moral evils, no matter how multiple and widespread they are, can trump God's infinite wisdom and goodness. Although modern theologians seek to make sin intelligible by ascribing some divine causality, whether by modifying either merely sufficient grace or a divine knowledge of *futurabilia*, Lonergan follows Aquinas in distinguishing clearly divine causality from divine permissive will. Intelligent creatures' free wills by sinning can never be first causes. When they sin, they seek to remove

29. *ST* I, q. 48, a. 2, ad 3.

goods from the divine teleological order in which they are good. Thus sinners do not cause something to exist, but rather remove something from the order in which it exists as good. Privation is neither causation nor predestination. Divine causality always produces ad extra terms, whether natural or supernatural. Divine permission, however, has no such ad extra terms. God permits moral evils and sins. Sinners futilely seek to disrupt the divinely ordered universe in its processional return to its Creator and Redeemer.

10

AVE MARIA!

The Grace of Predestination

Romanus Cessario, OP

Et dixit mihi: In Jacob inhabita,
et in Israël hæreditare,
et in electis meis mitte radices.

—*Sirach 24:13*

Background

Overview of the Doctrine

Throughout his published works, the Dominican third-order priest Louis-Marie Grignion de Montfort (1673–1716) explicitly discusses, as one may expect from his historical context, predestination and the predestined.[1] All in all, the references to *prédestination* and *prédestiné* occur in about forty-five places. By way of contrast, *réprouvé* appears only about half as many times. One might argue, however, that everything de Montfort taught or wrote or preached sets forth authentic Catholic

---

1. For information about de Montfort and the Dominicans, see Louis Le Crom, SMM, *Saint Louis-Marie Grignion de Montfort* (Étampes: Clovis, 2003), 332.

doctrine on predestination.[2] Why? De Montfort locates his teachings on predestination within the rich and complex structure of sacramental mediation that characterizes Catholic life. During a period of enormous conceptual confusion, this zealous priest, who did not hesitate to avail himself of the available secondary literature, taught incessantly how to live the grace of predestination in a way that coheres with the truth about the outpouring of the divine goodness that appears on earth within the "logic of the Incarnation."[3]

At the pinnacle of the Church's sacramental mediation, which includes both persons and things, stands the Blessed Virgin Mary. According to de Montfort's teaching, Our Lady does not obscure, as some critics have suggested, the person of Jesus Christ or the indispensable place that baptism holds in the sacramental practice of the Catholic Church. On the contrary, his *Ad Jesum per Mariam*, as Pope John Paul II has reminded us in *Redemptoris Mater*, centers on "consecration to Christ through the hands of Mary, as an effective means for Christians to live faithfully their baptismal commitments."[4] To dispel misconceptions about this "consecration" requires careful theological analysis. In a word, no created mediation, including that of the Blessed Virgin Mary, stands as an obstacle between the devout soul and God.[5] On the contrary, each mediation affords an immediate contact with the good God.[6] De Montfort, although he is realistic about the destructive character of sin, does not envisage the members of the human race as sinners trapped in the hands of an angry God. Instead, he comforts his followers with assurances such as this one: "The Saints tell us that when we have once found Mary, and

2. De Montfort's views on predestination follow the pattern that Aquinas sets down in his *Summa Theologiae* (*ST*). As Father Gilby has remarked about *ST* I, q. 23: "The present purpose is to map the causality engaged in predestination as a part of Providence, to serve as a preparation for the study of the theology of justification and Christ's saving work." See vol. 5 (1a. 19–26) of the Blackfriars edition of the *Summa Theologiae*, *God's Will and Providence*, trans. Thomas Gilby, OP (London: 1967), 107na.

3. See Pope John Paul II, *Fides et Ratio*, no. 94.

4. Pope John Paul II, *Redemptoris Mater*, no. 48.

5. See Louis-Marie Grignion de Montfort, *Le Secret de Marie* in *Œuvres Complètes de saint Louis-Marie Grignion de Montfort* (Paris: Éditions du Seuil, 1966), 451, no. 21. All citations from the works of de Montfort come from this French edition with its paragraph number and page reference. Translations are mine except where indicated.

6. The early Jean-Luc Marion discusses the theme of immediate mediation in *The Idol and Distance: Five Studies*, trans. T. A. Carlson (New York: Fordham University Press, 2001), 162–80.

through Mary, Jesus, and through Jesus, God the Father, we have found all good."[7] De Montfort knew that only the good draws.

As a convenient way to promote consecration through Mary among Catholics, de Montfort resorts to images such as the relationships between sun and light or heat and fire. He searches for metaphors to emphasize the "intimate union" that exists between Mary and her Divine Son and into which the Christian people are drawn.[8] These images obviously proved attractive to the ordinary people who were the beneficiaries of de Montfort's ministry. His facility for using imaginative language endeared de Montfort to his audiences. How else may one explain something that one of his French biographers, a certain Father Pauvert, observed in 1875? "Historians," he calculated, "have written more about this humble country missionary, who rarely preached in cathedrals, than about the great orators or kings of the past."[9]

One leitmotif of de Montfort's instruction appears in the association that he makes between devotion to Mary and predestination, a claim that the Church has acknowledged as worthy of credence.[10] In a text from his *True Devotion*, for example, de Montfort cites the fifteenth-century Dominican blessed, Alan de la Roche (ca. 1428–75), a Breton who promoted the rosary prayer in the form that we know it today.[11] Blessed Alan,

7. *Le Secret de Marie*, 451, no. 21. Translation by A. Somers in *The Secret of Mary* (London: Burns Oates & Washbourne, 1926).

8. For an important text that describes this immediacy, see *Traité de la Vraie Dévotion*, 525, no. 63. For further discussion, see Romanus Cessario, OP, *The Seven Last Words of Jesus* (Paris: Magnificat, 2009), chap. 5.

9. M. l'Abbé Pauvert, *Vie du vénérable Louis-Marie Grignion de Montfort, missionaire apostolique, fondateur des prêtres missionnaires de la compagnie de Marie et de la congrégation des Filles de la Sagesse* (Paris: H. Oudin, 1875), xx. "Signe de contradiction après sa mort comme pendant sa vie, il excita chez ses partisans le besoin de tracer son histoire pour répondre aux calomnies, en sorte que cet humble missionnaire de campagne, qui prêcha si rarement dans les cathédrales, a trouvé plus d'historiens que nos grands orateurs; que dis-je, plus d'historiens que nos rois." Today the interested reader may choose from more than one hundred biographies of Louis de Montfort.

10. See Pius XII, *Mediator Dei* (November 29, 1947), no. 176: "devotion to the Virgin Mother of God, a sign of 'predestination' according to the opinion of holy men."

11. De Montfort, *Traité de la Vraie Dévotion*, 655, 656, no. 250. See also 509, 618, 619, nos. 40 and 200. De Montfort aims to show that the claim about Mary and predestination enjoys the support of solid theological opinion that reaches back to the Church Fathers. See also the seventeenth-century author Johannes Andreas Coppenstein, OP, *Beati F. Alani redivivi rupensis tractatus mirabilis: De ortu atque progressu psalterii Christi et Mariae eiusque confraternitatis* (Venetiis: Apud Paulum Baleonium, 1665). For a modern edition of Blessed Alan's *Il Psalterio di Gesú e di Maria*, see the Italian translation of the work under the direction of Roberto Paola (Conegliano, Italy: Editrice Ancilla, 2006).

whom de Montfort venerated, assures his readers that those who cherish a devotion to the "Hail Mary" display a mark of predestination, whereas those who lack reverence for the *Ave Maria* exhibit a sign of reprobation.[12] This promise of predestination that is attached to the rosary's "Aves" originated, it is held, with St. Dominic, who learned of it from the Virgin Mary herself. De Montfort notes that, in the fifteenth century, Blessed Alan promoted this tradition that associates the rosary prayer with the founder of the Dominicans.[13]

For his part, de Montfort probably discovered the aforementioned reference in a book by a seventeenth-century author, Juan de Cartagena, OFM (1563–1618), whose homilies, the *Homiliae Catholicae*, were available readily in printed editions. Cartagena was a former Jesuit turned Franciscan who wrote on Mariology. What is more important, Cartagena embodied a fervent opposition to Molinism, as one may surmise when it is discovered that he left the Jesuits after the Society of Jesus had adopted Molinism as their school opinion.[14] To sum up, de Montfort emerges as a popular, anti-Molinist preacher of what I call the grace of predestination. As his writings witness, this French priest exhibits an *instinctus*, or a touch for ushering souls into the hands of the Blessed Virgin Mary.

The Historical Setting

In 1713, a few years before de Montfort died, Pope Clement XI (d. 1721) promulgated the controversial but effective bull *Unigenitus*. This document opened the final phase of the Jansenist controversy in France.[15]

12. See Alan, *Il Psalterio*, chap. 11, pp. 152–53. An example of de Montfort's veneration for the author appears in 1706, when Father de Montfort asked to say Mass at the altar in the Dominican convent in Dinant dedicated to Blessed Alan. See J.-C. Laurenceau, "Rosary," in *Jesus Living in Mary: Handbook of the Spirituality of St. Louis Marie de Montfort*, ed. P. Gaffney (Bay Shore, NY: Montfort, 1994), 1056.

13. For an up-to-date report on St. Dominic and the Rosary prayer, see Guy-Thomas Bedouelle, *Dominique ou la Grâce de la Parole*, 2nd ed., ed. P.-B. Hodel (Paris: Éditions du Cerf, 2015), 320–26.

14. For further information, see Sabino A. Vengco, *Juan de Cartagena, O.F.M. (1563–1618): The Mariology of His Homiliae Catholicae and Its Baroque Scripturism* (St. Bonaventure, NY: Franciscan Institute, St. Bonaventure University, 1978). Also, William J. Malley's review of Sabino Vengco in *Philippine Studies* 27 (1979): 439–42. Vengco reports that Cartagena was a fervent opponent of Molinism who left the Jesuits after the society had officially espoused the defense of Molinism (32–35).

15. See Romanus Cessario, OP, "Premotion, Holiness, and Pope Benedict XIII, 1724–30: Some Historical Retrospects on *Veritatis splendor*," in *Theology and Sanctity*, ed. Cajetan Cuddy, OP (Ave Maria, FL: Sapientia, 2014), 236–56.

Jansenism, in fact, ends with a whimper not a bang. Theological disputes morphed into political ones. De Montfort eschewed the Jansenists. He did not purvey what Leszek Kolalowski has called "Pascal's sad religion."[16] (Recall that Voltaire thought of Pascal as a "sublime misanthrope" who "writes against human nature more or less as he wrote against the Jesuits."[17]) Nothing of the sad, however, invades de Montfort's collected works. His writings are too full of confident rejoicing in the supernatural gifts that God has provided in Jesus and Mary to an admittedly fallen race. *Loin de moi le jansénisme*, the saint cried out.[18] No wonder the aforementioned Pope Clement XI conferred on de Montfort the title of "Missionary Apostolic" during the course of the saintly priest's visit to Rome in June 1706.[19]

What is important for us, de Montfort makes sharing this joy as easy as the praying of a single "Hail Mary." One *Ave Maria*! His teachings on predestination dispel a common misconception about the classical Dominican presentation of the *Prima Pars* of the *Summa Theologiae*, question 23, *de praedestinatione*.[20] The Dominican position on predestination when rightly understood stands immune from the criticism that it inculpates God in the reprobation of the sinner. The grace of predestination rather emerges as a blessed event. No warrant exists for worrying about how to protect the divine innocence—a project in any event that seems otiose to undertake, because the God who needs nothing certainly does not require human efforts to exculpate him.[21]

16. Leszek Kolakowski, *God Owes Us Nothing: A Brief Remark on Pascal's Religion and on the Spirit of Jansenism* (Chicago: University of Chicago Press, 1995), 113.

17. Ibid., 132, citing *Lettres philosophiques ou lettres anglaises: Avec le texte complet des remarques sur les pensées de Pascal* (Paris: Garnier, 1956), 293.

18. Cantique *139*, 55, p. 1578.

19. See S. De Fiores, "Montfort, Louis Marie de," in *Jesus Living in Mary*, 768–72. Pope Clement XI also settled the Chinese rites controversy in favor of the Dominicans.

20. See note 1 above.

21. The contemporary preoccupation with the "divine innocence" has its origin in numerous sources. See Matthew Levering, *Predestination: Biblical and Theological Paths* (Oxford: Oxford University Press, 2011), 135–76. See also F. Michael McLain and W. Mark Richardson, *Human and Divine Agency: Anglican, Catholic, and Lutheran Perspectives* (Lanham, MD: University Press of America, 1999), 2–3. The modern Thomistic attempt to engage this concern is found in Jacques Maritain, *God and the Permission of Evil*, trans. Joseph W. Evans (Milwaukee, WI: Bruce, 1966) and in the writings of Francisco Marín-Sola, OP. For further information on the latter, see Michael D. Torre, *God's Permission of Sin: Negative or Conditioned Decree? A Defense of the Doctrine of Francisco Marín-Sola, O.P., Based on the Principles of Thomas Aquinas* (Fribourg: Academic Press, 2009), and *Do Not Resist the*

De Montfort worked as a pastor and preacher during a period in French history that, to borrow an expression from Ronald Knox, produced a "Battle of the Olympians."[22] The second half of the seventeenth century witnessed exchanges between highly trained clerics such as Bishop Jacques-Bénigne Bossuet (1627–1704) and Bishop François Fenelon (1651–1715) over the orthodoxy of the somewhat less educated but devout laywoman Jeanne Marie Bouvier de la Motte Guyon (1648–1717). Today, the celebrated ultra-supernaturalist controversy about prayer and contemplation and the requirements of Christian virtue interests only the scholarly world or the arcane researcher. At the same time, the view that God always favorably works in the background of a believer's life no matter the moral quality of his conduct finds expression among many contemporary Catholic theologians. De Montfort's life and mission surmount the Jansenist and Quietist controversies that flourished during the seventeenth century. He displays neither dour pessimism nor unctuous presumption. One may begin to explain this accomplishment by the fact that he sought neither salon nor classroom as a venue for his religious explorations. In other words, de Montfort eschewed the swells, the Olympians. Even today, his teaching on predestination better suits those folks on the periphery than it does those university theologians who use Aquinas's texts as a playing field for logical exercises or an excavation site for historical research.

Of course, no sound theologian ought to pit piety against learning. As de Montfort's attentiveness to sound theological authorities indicates, he was not a partisan of Thomas à Kempis (1380–1471), who thought it better to possess contrition than to define it correctly.[23] At the same time, de

---

Spirit's Call: Francisco Marín-Sola on Sufficient Grace (Washington, DC: Catholic University of America Press, 2013). For a Thomistic response to Maritain's engagement, see Steven A. Long, "Providence, Freedom, and Natural Law," *Nova et Vetera* 4 (2006): 557–606. The most recent—and most provocative—examination of the divine innocence at the expense of the Thomist tradition comes from the pen of David Bentley Hart, "Providence and Causality: On Divine Innocence," in *The Providence of God: Deus Habet Consilium*, ed. Francesca Aran Murphy and Philip G. Ziegler (London: T&T Clark, 2009), 34–56.

22. Ronald A. Knox, *Enthusiasm* (Westminster, MD: Christian Classics, 1983), chap. XIV, 319*ff.*

23. Thomas à Kempis, *The Imitation of Christ*, trans. W. Benham (London: J. C. Nimmo & Bain, 1882), no. 3: "What doth it profit thee to enter into deep discussion concerning the Holy Trinity, if thou lack humility, and be thus displeasing to the Trinity? For verily it is not deep words that make a man holy and upright; it is a good life which maketh a man dear to God. I had rather feel contrition than be skillful in the definition thereof. If thou knewest

Montfort, in my view, shows us clearly that in order to grasp the complicated questions that arise around predestination, the student of theology first must discover the truth about living by faith.

Specific Instructions

Figures of Divine Premotion

The book of Sirach, or Ecclesiasticus as it appears in the Latin Vulgate, contains a verse that speaks about Wisdom's dwelling place: "Et dixit mihi: In Jacob inhabita, et in Israël hæreditare, et in electis meis mitte radices." The New American Bible translation runs: "In Jacob make your dwelling, in Israel your inheritance" (Sir 24:8).[24] When he ponders this Vulgate text, Louis de Montfort takes up the allegorical interpretation that identifies Mary with Wisdom. The theme does not originate in de Montfort. His creativeness rather appears in the way that he copiously develops the Marian allegory around the theme of predestination. In his *Secret of Mary*, for instance, de Montfort locates inhabiting, inheriting, and putting down roots within a Trinitarian context where each of the Divine Persons—Father, Son, and Holy Spirit, respectively—instructs Our Lady about her own predestination (Jacob), her inheritance (Israel), and her relationship with all the predestined (roots).[25] What de Montfort explains, especially in *True Devotion*, about Mary and predestination makes of Sirach 24:8 a lodestar. Its allegorical interpretation remains a foundational element of his overall teaching.[26]

Another text that sets the stage for de Montfort's teaching on predestination comes from the Vulgate of Psalms 86:5: "Numquid Sion dicet: Homo et homo natus est in ea, et ipse fundavit eam Altissimus?" In the New American Bible translation, "But of Zion it must be said: 'They all

---

the whole Bible, and the sayings of all the philosophers, what should all this profit thee without the love and grace of God? Vanity of vanities, all is vanity, save to love God, and Him only to serve. That is the highest wisdom, to cast the world behind us, and to reach forward to the heavenly kingdom."

24. The Latin Vulgate *et in electis meis mitte radices* seems to have been lost in the modern editions. It does appear in the twentieth-century translation of the Bible by Ronald Knox, however: "and his command to me was that I should find my home in Jacob, throw in my lot with Israel, take root among his chosen race" (Sir 24:13).

25. *Le Secret de Marie*, 447, no. 15.

26. See, e.g., *Traité de la Vraie Dévotion*, 502–4, nos. 29 and 31.

were born here.' The Most High confirms this" (Ps 87:5). On the basis of this verse, de Montfort allegorizes that each of the elect (*homo et homo*) comes to birth in the Blessed Virgin Mary. Why? She gives birth both to the Head and the members of Christ's Body. De Montfort reasons that were the members to have been born of another mother than the one who gives birth to the Head, such would become monsters in the order of grace.[27] Because they are her spiritual children, Our Lady protects the predestined from the malice of the devil. Jacob along with Abel figuratively represent the elect.[28] The Genesis account of the maneuvering between Jacob and Rebecca supplies de Montfort with a narrative that he will use to explain his teaching on Mary and predestination. *True Devotion*, in numbers 184 and 185, presents a long allegorical account of the mystery of predestination as it appears in the story of Isaac and Jacob (see Gn 27). De Montfort appeals to recognized theological opinions in order to justify his choice to make Jacob a sign of the elect and Esau, who cared little for his birthright, a sign of the reprobate (see Gn 25:34).[29]

Characteristics and Virtues of the Predestined

De Montfort considers that a complete knowledge about predestination arises only among the predestined. No esotericist he, however. First Corinthians supplies the warrant: "We do speak a wisdom to those who are mature" (1 Cor 2:6). In the Vulgate, *Sapientiam loquimur inter perfectos*.[30] Pastoral practice still proceeds along this line. Persons mucked down in adolescent lust, for example, usually require a cooling-off period before they can expect to cherish devoutly the "Hail Mary." Christian maturity requires fortitude. De Montfort often observes that the travails of this life afflict both the predestined and the reprobate. But one can observe the difference in the reactions of each. The saints suffer with joy, the dammed with chagrin. Thus de Montfort likes to affirm that wisdom belongs to the Cross, and the Cross supplies wisdom.[31] In his *Letter to the Friends of the Cross*, de Montfort again makes this claim about

27. Ibid., 504, no. 32.
28. Ibid., 519, no. 54.
29. For a list of authors that de Montfort cites as well as early sources about the saint, see *Ouevres*, xxv–xxxi.
30. See *L'Amour de la Sagesse Éternelle*, 100, 101, no. 14.
31. Ibid., 189, 190, no. 180.

suffering. The predestined accept suffering gladly as a way to participate in Christ, whereas the reprobate remain disgruntled. Choose one of the three crosses on Calvary, counsels de Montfort, that of the saint or of the penitent, though not that of the Bad Thief.[32] Patient endurance reveals the predestined.

De Montfort speaks about the "secret" of the predestined, the "secret" of Mary. His teaching, however, does not advance Gnosticism. Rather, by "secret" he means an actual grace given to those whom God favors with a knowledge of the hidden mysteries of salvation. Broadly speaking, this secret may be compared to what Aquinas teaches about the nature of the gifts of the Holy Spirit: an interior quality of soul that renders a person docile to the movements of the Holy Spirit. This explains why, in a famous introduction to his work *The Secret of Mary*, he does not hesitate to address his reader as "O Predestined Soul."[33] One may recall the Thomist teaching that the gifts of the Holy Spirit flourish in all the mature baptized. *Sapientiam loquimur inter perfectos.* To these perfect souls, de Montfort issues three injunctions: (1) first, that the secret he confides to them should be shared only with those who show signs of religious seriousness of purpose and devotion; (2) second, that the predestined soul actively practice the secret, which may be understood as living the virtues of the Christian life; and (3) third, that the recipient never cease to express gratitude to God for having received so precious an instruction about the Christian life.[34] The secret of Mary advances plain and commonsensical advice. De Montfort considers this secret something that God has revealed to him in a way that is unique for his time. In other words, he possessed a sense of mission. Conversely, what kind of priest would think that God teaches him nothing about salvation?

True Devotion amplifies the characteristics and the virtues that one observes in the predestined. For example, they with Mary crush Satan's head.[35] The predestined exhibit Mary's humility, which, in de Montfort's view, always triumphs over the devil's pride. Still, one may expect that the reprobate will nonetheless persecute the predestined.[36] The predes-

---

32. *Lettre Circulaire aux Amis de la Croix*, 241, 242, no. 33.
33. *Le Secret de Marie*, 442, no. 1.
34. Ibid., 442, 443, no. 1.
35. See *Traité de la Vraie Dévotion*, 518, 519, no. 54.
36. Ibid., 612, 613, no. 190.

tined seek to avoid confrontation with those whose ways point toward perdition. He imagines that Jacob, the youngest son, practiced a kind of sweet admirableness that suited his staying close to home and to his mother, Rebecca.[37] The allegory of Jacob and Rebecca reveals qualities that distinguish the justified from the reprobate. God blesses the predestined in ways that resemble the blessings Isaac bestowed on Jacob (see Gn 27:27–29): (1) the predestined receive a double benediction, the seed of eternal life, which is the gift of grace, *la semance de la gloire*, and a sufficiency of temporal goods; (2) the predestined will rule nations—if not in this life, then in the next; and (3) God also blesses those whom the predestined bless and curses those whom they curse.[38]

As I have mentioned, Louis de Montfort eschewed the highbrow theological exchanges of his period that, significantly, he describes as *sèche, stérile, et indifférente*.[39] His purpose remained missionary, apostolic, and practical; that is, he sought the salvation of souls. He nonetheless was quite adept at devising gimmicks to develop a savoir-faire in his listeners. For example, he composed over two hundred "Canticles," or short ditties, to help the people remember his instruction about Mary and predestination. Among these numerous compositions, which were rhymed and set to popular tunes, were reminders about the qualities that one expects to find in those who live according to the "secret" that de Montfort taught them. One Canticle recalls that obedience imitates Mary's disposition, whereas a false independence becomes the dammed.[40] Another, that the predestined show charity toward the neighbor.[41] That they practice almsgiving.[42] Another Canticle confirms something that I have mentioned already about the teaching of Louis de Montfort, namely, that the predestined exhibit a joyful mien, one that radiates luminously from their foreheads and the eyes.[43] In a small work, *Prayer for Missionaries*, de Montfort calls the Company of Mary, his foundation of missionary priests, a *triette* of predestination. *Triette* means a select little group.[44] So the predestined witness both individually and corporately or communally.

37. Ibid., 613, no. 191.

38. Ibid., 624, 625, no. 207.

39. Ibid., 526, no. 64.

40. Cantique *10*, 10, p. 924.

41. Cantique *14*, 9, p. 970.

42. Cantique *17*, 28, p. 1008.

43. Cantique *25*, 18, p. 1080.

44. *Prière Embrasée*, 18, p. 682. (The standard English rendition is Prayer for Missionar-

Mary and the Predestined

In one of his important works, *The Love of Eternal Wisdom*, de Montfort affirms that it belongs to Mary through the working of the Holy Spirit to "incarnate," so to speak, Christ in the predestined.[45] Again, de Montfort returns to Sirach 24:13 when he assures us that Mary dwells in Jacob, takes Israel for her heritage, and puts down her roots among the elect. Because of this grace given to Mary by God, she can hold in her womb and give birth to those who are the members of Christ.[46] All the elect, in fact, are found in the womb of the Blessed Virgin Mary, who provides for them spiritual nourishment and energy. This theme need not raise questions about the exclusive nature of de Montfort's teaching. How better to explain to the common people the closeness that they enjoy with the Mother of God, whom de Montfort describes as the mold of God?[47] In a familiar passage from *The Secret of Mary*, he counsels the ardent soul to prefer being formed in the womb of Mary, as if she were a mold, rather than being chiseled into the image of God by sculptors (whom de Montfort understands as representing the efforts of individual Christians to make themselves pleasing to God).[48]

De Montfort frequently associates the work of Our Lady with the work of the Holy Spirit. The claim that Mary cooperates with the Holy

---

ies.) See the following note, composed by Simone DeRyeff, on the meaning of the word *triette*, for which no easy English equivalent exists: "Pour triette, voici le résultat de la consultation des plus importants dictionnaires de langue du XVIIe siècle—triette n'est pas attesté comme tel; on peut cependant y voir un diminutif de trie, s. f., dont Cotgrave (dictionnaire français-anglais, 1611) donne la définition suivante: 'A choice, culling, or picking out.'—le substantif trie n'est plus attesté dans les grands dictionnaires de la fin du siècle, qui donnent cependant le verbe trier, dans un sens un peu différent de celui que nous avons actuellement. Voici la définition du *Dictionnaire de l'Académie française*, 1694: 'TRIER. v.a. Choisir entre plusieurs choses, entre plusieurs personnes. Trier du bled. trier des raisins. trier des pois, des lentilles. les Libraires ont trié les meilleurs livres de cette Bibliotheque. il a trié les Medailles les plus curieuses, les plus rares. trier sur le volet. V. VOLET. Ces trois hommes ont esté triez entre les plus habiles de leur compagnie. on a trié ces soldats parmy les meilleures troupes. TRIÉ, ÉE. part. TRIAGE. s.m. Choix. Il signifie et l'action par la quelle on choisit, et la chose choisie. Faire le triage. voila un beau triage. Triage, en terme d'Eaux et forests, se dit de certains contours, de certains quartiers de bois, eu égard aux coupes qu'on en fait. Dans cette forest on coupe cette année un tel triage.' En un mot, il s'agit de la sélection des élus."

45. *L'Amour de la Sagesse Éternelle*, 204, 205, no. 203.
46. Ibid., 209, no. 213.
47. See *Le Secret de Marie*, 447, 448, nos. 14 and 15.
48. Ibid., 449, nos. 17 and 18.

Spirit prompts in de Montfort a startling thought. He points out that within standard Trinitarian theology the Holy Spirit remains "sterile." He proceeds from the Father and the Son, but no person proceeds from him. Nonetheless, this "sterility" finds a remedy in the children that come forth from the womb of the Blessed Virgin Mary, whom one may revere as the spouse of the Holy Spirit. The predestined form the off-spring, so to speak, of the Holy Spirit.[49] That Mary gives birth to the elect provides a central theme of *True Devotion*. The theme emerges as a long commentary on Galatians 4:19: "My children, for whom I am again in labor until Christ be formed in you!"[50] Warrant for this allegorical exegesis dates back at least to the Cistercian Fathers, for instance, Guerric of Igny (d. 1157), who was a friend of St. Bernard.[51]

De Montfort presents his consecration as something that commits the Christian to a practice of interiority, *la pratique interieure*.[52] The venerable saint, who even in his own time was greatly misunderstood, especially by the ecclesiastical apparatchiks, considered himself as a special messenger of this practice, which he calls devotion to Mary. The arcane remained foreign to de Montfort. He rather thought of himself as a messenger of Our Lady's tenderness.[53] In turn, he urged Christians to show her tenderness, which he sees foretold in the tenderness of Jacob. The association derives again from the Vulgate of Genesis, "Nosti quod Esau frater meus homo pilosus sit, et ego lenis" (Gn 27:11). In Latin, *lenis* can mean both smooth-skinned and gentle. So de Montfort simply insists that Christian believers practice the tenderness of Jacob toward a most tender spiritual Mother. When they do, Christians avoid lukewarmness, which results from trying to live the Christian life without tenderness for the Mother of God.[54] In other words, a homey familiarity with the Blessed Virgin Mary, which de Montfort sees foretold in Jacob's demeanor toward his own mother, Rebecca, portends predestination. Given the natural bond between mother and child, the suggestion does not seem

---

49. See *Traité de la Vraie Dévotion*, 497, no. 20.

50. Ibid., 502–5, 507, nos. 29–33 and 37.

51. The text appears on pages 1644–46 in the *Liturgy of the Hours* for the Memorial of the Blessed Virgin on Saturday: "I do indeed praise the ministry of preaching in Paul, but far more do I admire and venerate the mystery of generation in Mary" (1645).

52. *Traité de la Vraie Dévotion*, 520, no. 55.

53. Ibid., 542, no. 85: *elle est tendre*.

54. Ibid., 611, 612, no. 188.

far-fetched. Practice filial tenderness toward Mary. Most folks can grasp de Montfort's advice more easily than they will Madame Guyon's injunctions to abide in the simple state of rest.[55]

Instructions for those who follow the Marian consecration include the following recommendations: (1) Guard interiority with Mary, which de Montfort presents as a preference for retreat from the world. (2) Love tenderly the Mother of God, which de Montfort presents as a way to let Mary teach the predestined souls how to practice complete submission to God, how to avoid sinning, and how to achieve union with God.[56] (3) Obey the Mother of God, which de Montfort explains again with reference to Rebecca's words to Jacob, "Now, son, listen carefully to what I tell you" (Gn 27:8). (4) Preserve great confidence in the goodness and power of the Blessed Mother, whom de Montfort compares to the North Star that ensures safe arrival to heaven. (5) Last, de Montfort counsels his readers, "Be happy!" The reason for this happiness lies in their devotion toward Mary and in their following her "ways" after Proverbs 8:32: "happy those who keep my ways." De Montfort concludes with a warning that those who abuse the devotion are those who claim to practice it but do not keep the commandments.[57] Given the joyful ease that characterizes True Devotion to Mary, one cannot take umbrage at this useful reminder about how to persevere in the grace of predestination.

---

55. See her "A Short and Very Easy Method of Prayer," in *Spiritual Progress: Or Instructions in the Divine Life of the Soul*, from the French of Fénélon and Madame Guyon, ed. James W. Metcalf (New York: M. W. Dodd, Brick Church Chapel, City Hall Square, 1853), chap. 13.

56. These steps compare with the movements to purify, to enlighten, and to perfect that which Aquinas mentions in his discussion of the angels. See *ST* I, q. 108, a. 2, arg and reply 3.

57. See *Traité de la Vraie Dévotion*, 614–19, nos. 196–200.

11

BALTHASAR AND OTHER THOMISTS ON BARTH'S UNDERSTANDING OF PREDESTINATION

Michael Maria Waldstein

John 17:24

For a reflection on Balthasar's understanding of predestination, one can hardly do better than to start with a Johannine text on predestination, namely, John 17:24.[1]

Father, what you have given me,
I will (θέλω) that where I am those too may be with me,
that they may see my glory,
which you have given me because you loved me
before the foundation of the world.

The central affirmation is Jesus's sovereign decree, "I will," a decree not formed apart from the Father's will, received (as everything) from the Father, focused on those the Father has given him. Jesus wills them to be with him where he is.

---

1. For the importance attributed to this text by Balthasar, see Hans Urs von Balthasar, *Herrlichkeit: Eine theologische Ästhetik: Neuer Bund* (Einsiedeln: Johannes Verlag, 1969), III/2/2, 241.

They are to see the glory that is the Father's gift to the Son in the simple now of eternity, a gift given out of eternal love, from our perspective
already before the foundation of the world, and yet never past, but ever
now in the single present eternity that never becomes past. It is often expressed in a Christological reading of Psalm 2. "You are my Son. Today
have I begotten you" (Ps 2:7).

Christ's words "I will" extend the Father's love to those the Father has
given him. Quite logically, Jesus concludes his prayer with this extension
of love. At the same time, he reverses who comes to be in whom. The
destination is that the Father's love for the Son and the Son himself in
person become present in those the Father gave him.

> Just Father, indeed the world has not known you, but I have known you,
> And these have come to know that you sent me.
> And I have made your name known to them and will make it known,
> so that the love with which you loved me may be in them,
> and I in them. (Jn 17:25–26)

The place of the decree "I will" in John 17 is important. Jesus's prayer
as a whole has an expansive movement, like waves going out from a stone
thrown into still water. He prays first for himself (Jn 17:1–8), then for his
disciples (Jn 17:9–19), and finally, in the largest circle, for all who will receive him through their word (Jn 17:20–26). It is toward the end of this
expansive movement that he says, "I will that...where I am those too
may be with me." He sets the destination of the lives of those whom the
Father has given to him. He does so by his own sovereign will, identical
in essence with that of the Father but possessed in a distinct personal
mode.

Many who hear the word "predestination" in a culture deeply formed
by Calvin hear primarily the note of limitation. From the mass of those
predestined to damnation, some are snatched out to be predestined to
live. "I will (θέλω) that where I am those too may be with me." Yet the
primary thrust of the prayer is not to highlight the limits of predestination. Granted, Jesus does not state the universality of predestination as a
fact. What stands in the center of attention is the expansive movement of
the prayer as a whole.

What is the place, the destination, about which he asks, "where I am"?
Earlier in John, he mentions "my Father's house" (Jn 14:2) in which "the
Son remains for ever" (Jn 8:35). Other texts show that this house is the

Father himself. The Son is "in the Father" (Jn 10:38, 14:10, 14:11, 14:20). They cannot reach the Father as their destination without him. "No one comes to the Father except through me" (Jn 14:6). Yet "except through me" implies that "*through me* they *can*" reach this destination. Reaching this destination is the goal of all their longing. "Lord, show us the Father, and that is enough for us" (Jn 14:8), Philip says impetuously to Jesus during the Last Supper discourses. St. Thomas comments, "Seeing the Father is the end of all our desires and actions, so that nothing further will be asked for (or needed)."[2]

In this light one can see why predestination is the very paradise of teleology. It is the one and only way of reaching the end of all human longing, the end that infinitely exceeds all possible human longing: "What eye has not seen nor ear heard, what has not risen up into the human heart, God has prepared for those who love him" (1 Cor 2:9). Becoming "sharers in the divine nature" θείας κοινωνοὶ φύσεως (2 Pt 1:4) infinitely exceeds in goodness all merely created reality.

Origen powerfully expresses the sense of excess of the destination, which is fundamental for understanding predestination. At the beginning of his commentary on John, he writes,

One must dare to say that the Gospels are the first fruits of all Scriptures, but that the first fruits the Gospels is that according to John, whose mind no one can grasp who is not leaning on Jesus' breast and is not receiving Mary from Jesus to be his own mother too.

To be another John, one must also become such as John, shown to be Jesus, so to speak. For if Mary had no son except Jesus, in accordance with those who hold a sound opinion of her, and Jesus says to his mother, "This is your son," and not, "Look, this man also is your son," he has said equally, "Look, this is Jesus whom you bore." Indeed, everyone who has been perfected "no longer lives, but Christ lives in him," and since "Christ lives" in him, it is said of him to Mary, "Look, your son," the Christ.

In order to express that the destination lies beyond any created nature and its power, Origen does not use the later vocabulary "natural" and "supernatural." He uses the radical figures of speech ("so to speak") characteristic of biblical language, "No longer I, but Christ lives in me" and "Woman, this is your son." There is no doubt that such words lift

---

2. "Visio patris est finis omnium desideriorum et actionum nostrarum, ita ut nil amplius requiratur." St. Thomas, *Lectura super Ioannem*, 14:3.

John, and anyone who becomes such as John, far beyond what a creature can reach, namely, to the gift God makes of himself.

Longing for God

Predestination is good news. For the criminal condemned with Jesus to crucifixion, it is certainly good news that Jesus says, "Amen, I say to you, today you will be with me in paradise" (Lk 23:43).

Titian's great painting of this scene, which was chosen as the emblem for this conference on predestination, does not depict the moment in which the criminal hears the promise "You will be with me in paradise." It focuses on an event a little later. Jesus has already died. The criminal accordingly no longer looks at Jesus. He looks up, above Jesus's head, as if toward paradise, toward the fulfillment of the promise. His entire body, particularly his face, expresses the deep longing that the Greeks called *eros*. It is a longing present in every human being as a central point of human nature, an immediate consequence of rationality. Socrates, Plato, Aristotle, Plotinus, and countless other thinkers, poets, musicians, and painters have experienced and unfolded this *eros*. It is the longing for happiness, a longing with an unlimited openness and thus a certain infinity.

In Plato's *Symposium*, the priestess Diotima, who instructs Socrates in the mysteries of eros, explains to him,

"In this place of life, if anywhere, my dear Socrates," said the woman from Mantinea, "[life] is livable for a human being (βιωτὸν ἀνθρώπῳ), for one who contemplates (θεωμένῳ) the beautiful itself…What then," she said, "shall we think if someone sees (ἰδεῖν) the beautiful itself, pure, immaculate, and unmixed…and is able to see clearly (κατιδεῖν) the divine beautiful itself, one in form? Do you think it is a bad life in this place, when one looks (βλέποντος), and contemplates (θεωμένου) it as one ought and has intercourse with it (συνόντος αὐτῷ)?

Or are you not convinced," she said, "that in this place alone the one who sees the beautiful by its own visibility will give birth (τίκτειν), not to images of virtue, because he does not cling to an image, but to true [virtues], because he clings to the True; and that if he gives birth to true virtue and nourishes it he will become beloved by God (θεοφιλεῖ) and, if ever any human, immortal?"

Noteworthy in this text is the strong spousal image and especially the reversal or answering of human ascending love by divine descending love: beloved by God (θεοφιλεῖ).

Augustine seems to know this text or a close paraphrase. He echoes it, including its strong spousal symbolism, in a central passage of the *City of God* in which he explains what the Christian religion shares with the best of pagan religious philosophy and where it differs.

To *see* him as he can be *seen*, and to cling (*cohaerendum*) to him, we cleanse ourselves from every stain of sins and bad desires and consecrate ourselves in his name.

For he himself is the source of our happiness (*fons nostrae beatitudinis*), he himself is the goal of all our striving for an end (*omnis appetitionis finis*)... We tend to him by love (*dilectione*), so that by arriving we might rest, blessed because perfected by this end.

For our good, the final good about which philosophers dispute, is nothing else but to cling (*cohaerere*) to him whose spiritual embrace fills the intellectual soul, if one may so express it, and makes it give birth to true virtues.

Plotinus expresses a similar point, but asks whether such happiness is possible.

One must go up again to the Good, which every soul desires... until, passing in the ascent all that is alien to God, one sees with oneself alone the alone one itself, simple, single, and pure, from which all depends and to which all look and are and live and think: for it is the cause of life and mind and being. If anyone saw it, what loves would he feel, what thirsts, wishing to be mingled together with it, how struck outside himself with joy!...

Here the greatest, the last struggle is set before souls, all toil being for the sake of this, not to be left without a share in the best vision, which, if one attains it, one is blessed in seeing that blessed sight, and, if one fails to attain it, one fails [absolutely]. One does not fail if one fails to win beauty of colors or bodies, or power or office or kingship even, but if one fails to win this and only this, for which one should give up reaching kingship and rule over all earth and sea and sky, if only by leaving and overlooking them one may turn to that and see.[3]

The intensity of human *eros* in this text is overwhelming. Its end is nothing short of the infinite goodness of the divine mystery. Plotinus raises the question of the way that can lead us to this end, but does not answer it. The hypothesis that the divine mystery would come forth to reveal itself seems implausible to him, at least in a form that would profane it. The mystery remains within its own sacred sphere, hidden from

---

3. Plotinus, *On Beauty, Ennead* I.6.7–8.

the profane. He ends his argument with the call to enter, addressed to "the one who can." Who is the one who can? How does he gain the capacity? This decisive question remains open.

But what is the way? What is the means? How can one see the "unmanageable beauty" (Plato, *Symposium* 218e, *Republic* 509a: ἀμήχανον κάλλος) which stays within holy temples and does not go forth to the outside for everyone, even for the profane, to see? Let him go and follow along into the inside—the one who can.[4]

The criminal crucified with Jesus, as Titian portrays him, is near the end of his life. All his traveling along the ways of life toward happiness, all his means and capacities, have come to an end, an agonizing death. Yet his *eros* has been renewed in the midst of intense misery by Jesus's sovereign decree about his destination. "Today you will be with me in paradise." It is not clear how much the criminal understood when he expressed his longing, "Jesus, remember me when you come into your kingship" (Lk 23:42). Yet it is precisely the open-ended thrust of these words, open-ended as the longing expressed by Plotinus, that shows the full dignity and greatness of human nature, of human reason. Reason is an openness to every being, and to being itself.

Natural and Supernatural in St. Thomas's Account of Predestination

It is therefore a deeply biblical, patristic, and classical philosophical starting point when St. Thomas approaches the topic of predestination from the distinction between human nature and the supernatural order.

Finis...	The end
ad quem res creatae ordinantur a Deo,	to which created things are ordered by God
est duplex.	is twofold.
Unus, qui excedit proportionem	One that goes beyond the proportion
naturae creatae, et facultatem;	of a created nature and its power;
et hic finis est vita aeterna,	and this end is eternal life,
quae in divina visione consistit,	which consists in the divine vision,

---

4. Plotinus, *On Beauty, Ennead* I.6.8.

quae est supra naturam cujuslibet creaturae.	which is above the nature of any creature.
Alius autem finis	The other end
est naturae creatae proportionatus,	is proportioned to the created nature,
quem scilicet res creata potest attingere	namely, which a created being can reach
secundum virtutem suae naturae.	according to the power of its own nature.
Ad illud autem,	To that, on the other hand,
ad quod non potest aliquid	which a being cannot reach
virtute suae naturae pervenire,	by the power of its nature,
oportet, quod ab alio transmittatur;	it needs to be shot (or sent) across by another,
sicut sagitta a sagittante mittitur ad signum.	just as an arrow is shot at the target by an archer.
Unde ratio...transmissionis	Hence the account...of the sending over
creaturae rationalis in finem vitae aeternae praedestinatio nominatur.	of the rational creature into the end of eternal life is called setting the destination beforehand (that is, predestination).[5]

The point of departure in predestination is created human nature as a nature defined by a limited end, an end it can reach by its own power, namely, knowing through sensation and entering into love on this basis. "By its own power" does not mean that nature is a realm cut off from God. The first cause is more interior to every natural effect, more immediately, comprehensively, and specifically the origin of that effect than any secondary cause could ever be, as St. Thomas argues at the beginning of his commentary on the *Liber de causis*.

The realm of nature, understood in this way, is an expression of God's wisdom and goodness. Nature is theonomic. It is shaped by the divine wisdom in such a way that by understanding creation precisely as nature, we can understand the natural law as a reflection of God's goodness and wisdom, not as a set of externally imposed decrees of an arbitrary divine will. The natural law becomes clear to us from within our own understanding, so that we can freely govern our acts by it.

5. *Summa Theologiae* (*ST*) I, q. 1, a. 23 co.

The point of arrival in predestination is not merely a created gift, the *gratia gratum faciens*, the grace that makes us pleasing to God. The whole order of grace, St. Thomas argues, is ordered to receiving an uncreated gift, the gift in which God gives himself to us in his infinite goodness (see below).

The infinite distance between the natural and the supernatural is the reason why predestination is needed in the first place. What St. Thomas hears in the word "predestination" is above all that God sends or shoots us over and across a great distance, *oportet quod ab alio transmittatur*, as an archer shoots an arrow at a target far away.

Barth on Double Predestination

No such act of "shooting across" or "sending over" is needed, according to Barth. Double predestination, he holds, is God's first act, the act from which everything else, including creation, takes its origin. God's first act is to predestine Jesus Christ both to eternal life and to damnation. This act is so deeply rooted in God's eternity that it is not merely a plan for a future event. It is the first act to be accomplished *ad extra*. It is the primal flashing-up of light together with its separation from darkness (Gn 1:4). The lamb is "slaughtered from the foundation of the world" (Rev 13:8).

Nature, if it comes into view at all, does so only as an implication of grace. It can only be understood in light of grace. Barth writes,

There is no created nature that does not have its existence, its essence, and its consistency from grace and that can be known in its existence, its essence, and its consistency in any other way than again by grace.[6]

The salvation of all is built with systematic rigor into this sequence of events as the inevitable outcome, despite all the qualifications by which Barth attempts to avoid its automatic necessity. Balthasar concludes about the understanding of double predestination sketched here in its barest outline,

This is the hinge, as it were, or axis of Barth's whole theology. Barth's whole doctrine of God and world, of creation and redemption, of man and provi-

6. Hans Urs von Balthasar, *Karl Barth: Darstellung und Deutung seiner Theologie* (Olten: Hegner Bücherei, 1951; reprint, Einsiedeln: Johannes Verlag, 1976), 187.

dence stands or falls with this axis. Accordingly, the reflection we have set out to achieve must orient itself by this axis.[7]

Balthasar's Response in Defense of Nature

Along this axis, Balthasar's response to the Barthian understanding of double predestination is to affirm exactly what Barth denies, namely, "the consistency within itself (*Eigenständigkeit*) of the natural order and of philosophy, which corresponds to it."[8] Without such consistency of nature and a natural order, Balthasar argues, the gift of grace, of the divine persons themselves, is impossible. The recipient of the gift must be a being with a definite nature.

One of the characteristics of Barth's thinking is the exclusive or at least primary interest in acts and events. He tends to ignore or deny the permanent, identifiable beings with definite natures that perform these acts and participate in these events. He has a particular distaste for the abstraction of natures, because it allegedly negates the only thing that truly counts, namely, dynamic acts and events precisely in their dynamic character.

In this light one can understand the function within the overall argument of the main paragraph in which Balthasar most formally answers the question, what is nature? He begins by affirming, directly against Barth, the essences of creatures as known in abstraction. He goes on to show that, far from denying acts and events, our understanding of essences in the abstract is based on them. He continues by adding in concentric circles around this nature the sorts of things in which Barth is particularly interested. The text begins with a long quote from Scheeben and gives references to St. Thomas, probably to assure Barth that this is indeed the traditional Catholic understanding of nature and not a gilded artifact produced by Balthasar to look attractive to Barth. Headings have been added to this text in order to clarify the steps taken in the argument.

7. Ibid., 201.
8. Ibid., 255.

What Is to Be Defined: The Aristotelian
Concept of Nature

The *philosophical concept of nature*, set forth in a fundamental way by Aristotle and further worked out in detail by the Stoics and Scholastics,

What the word "nature" is first applied to

understands by nature "first of all the origin of a being by begetting and birth,

Nature as the essence of a being in the abstract

then that which is communicated in begetting/birth, namely, the specific essence,

The essence as a principle of movement and activity

first formally inasmuch as it is the principle *of a specific action or passion* (*principium motus*) especially of a specific immanent activity, that is, of a certain condition that corresponds to the constitution of the essence with a view to certain activities of life" (Scheeben, *Dogmatik*, 2:240, cf. Thomas, *Summa* 1.29.1 ad 4).

Defense of this understanding of nature against Barth's actualism

Accordingly, the concept of nature is both static (as essence) and dynamic/teleological, inasmuch as it explains the nature from its *meaning* and activity, that is, from its finality,

Explicit inclusion of items Barth is especially interested in

and inasmuch as one includes—like gradated ever more distant circles around it—all that seems indispensable and ordained to that nature's well-being, namely, its surroundings and the communities of which it is a part (see *Summa* 1–2.6.5 ad 4).

Example: a bird

Take the example of a bird. What belongs to the nature of a bird is not only the abstract ability to fly but also flight itself (and thus its condition, the air), not only the desire for food and the ability to eat it, but also finding it and actually digesting it, and thus the existence of such food, not only the ability to have offspring, but actually having offspring.

The concreteness of the concentric circles around the essence

Of course, this does not mean that each particular potency and endowment must be realized in each individual of the species (see *Summa*, 1–2.84.1 ad 3). It does mean, however that the teleological and dynamic plan of its being—precisely its "nature"—can only be conceived in a world context that is conceived or presupposed as real....

Conclusion: Barth's fear of a merely abstract nature is unfounded

For this reason it is logically impossible to think of a moment in time in which a nature is constituted only "statically" and not at the same time also dynamically [i.e., in terms of these concentric circles of a concrete natural order]. To conclude, it is a philosophically correct formulation of Aristotle's concept of nature if one counts as belonging to a nature (near to a nature) all that belongs to it as its constitution [the essence], its consequences [a concrete fabric of acting and being acted on], and its needs [such as real flying in real air and real eating of real food].

This detailed and multifaceted understanding of nature is what Balthasar upholds in his reading of Barth. It is instructive to bring this passage together with one of Balthasar's texts on William of Ockham that sketches an important part of the overall concern with which he reads Luther, Calvin, and Barth. The text on Ockham underlines the central importance of the text on Aristotle.

This formidable Franciscan [William of Ockham] creates space even more radically [than Scotus] for the sole sovereignty of God when, sweeping away the entire Platonic and Aristotelian tradition, he directly opposes to the yawning abyss of absolute freedom a world which is fragmented into irrational points of reality. With this rupture within the tradition of a mediating or natural (philosophical) theology, every contemplative dimension of the *fides quaerens intellectum* is in principle removed. Theology, which now closes itself in upon itself, must become fideistic and can ultimately be only practical.

And the Franciscan image of God—love beyond the limits of knowledge—must therefore degenerate into an image of horror…since this God of pure freedom might always posit and demand the opposite.[9]

In this text, one can grasp Balthasar's fundamental concern in dialogue with Protestant theology: the defense of nature as reflecting the divine goodness and wisdom is needed for preserving the contemplative dimension of faith, which is unfolded in theology. If any contemporary theologian stands out in emphasizing the need for philosophy in this contemplative dimension, that theologian is Balthasar.

---

9. Hans Urs von Balthasar, *The Realm of Metaphysics in the Modern Age*, vol. 5, *The Glory of the Lord: A Theological Aesthetics*, trans. Oliver Davies (San Francisco: Ignatius Press, 1991), 20.

Steven Long's Vacuole

The Vacuole

In his book *Natura Pura*, Steven Long reads Balthasar as arguing the opposite point, namely, that nature has little, if any, intelligibility in itself, that it is a mere vacuole for grace.

It is here [i.e., in Balthasar's chapter on the concept of nature in Catholic theology] that the transformation of St. Thomas teaching that nature is preface to grace is worked, at the end of which nature is no longer preface, but only postscript to grace, Indeed, "postscript" is perhaps saying too much, for even a postscript has definitive and distinctly cognizable content, even when it refers to the body of the letter. Whereas, for Balthasar nature becomes the equivalent of a theological vacuole or empty Newtonian space, a placeholder for grace.[10]

Long sets aside Balthasar's own explicit statement about the direction of his argument. He does not analyze Balthasar's main paragraph on nature. Balthasar, he argues, holds precisely what he criticizes Barth for.

Worse yet. Although "vacuole for grace" expresses the most radical reading of Barth with some justice, Balthasar leaves considerable room for Barth's ever more serious attention to a robust concept of nature. He does not pin Barth to the vacuole, but praises him for an increasingly rich understanding of nature. Nature, he applauds, entered more and more on its own terms and in its own intelligibility in the course of the years in which Barth carefully developed his thought in detail, whatever the first volume of his *Church Dogmatics* may have said to forestall precisely such developments. Balthasar criticized by Long is more Barthian than Barth criticized by Balthasar.

This paradox calls for an explanation. Why is Long so certain about the reduction of nature to vacuole in Balthasar? A systematic principle rather than detailed exegetical observations about the meaning of particular texts seems to guide his argument. According to Long, if one accepts de Lubac's thesis about the natural desire for the supernatural vision of God, the reduction of nature to a vacuole is the inevitable fruit. Balthasar accepts de Lubac's view. He must therefore think nature is a mere vacuole,

---

10. Steven A. Long, *Natura Pura: On the Recovery of Nature in the Doctrine of Grace* (New York: Fordham University Press, 2010), 54–55.

even if he happens to say the opposite. "In this chapter [on Balthasar], the very error that the last chapter [on de Lubac] was spent correcting will be seen as fructifying in the theology of a great Catholic savant."[11]

A Grammatical Error

A minor argument that does not play an important role in Long's overall argument is useful to begin some critical reflections. Even if it is an unfortunate oversight, it shows a strong push in Long's argument. Long quotes Balthasar as claiming that the concept of nature never entered the field of vision of Vatican I. The sentence on which he bases this interpretation reads as follows in the published English translation: "But there are still other questions about the concept of nature that had never even entered the field of vision of Vatican I." The relative pronoun "that" can with some legitimacy be read either as referring to "the concept of nature" or to "other questions." If it referred to the former, English usage would require a comma before it. In addition, one would tend to use "which" rather than "that." The original German settles the question definitively. The relative pronoun refers to "other questions." A section heading soon after this passage in Balthasar's book is "The Concept of Nature at Vatican I." Balthasar most emphatically sees Vatican I as concerned with the concept of nature in precision from grace. Why a writer of Long's keen intelligence did not consider these passages needs to be explained.

Empty or Full?

Long objects that Balthasar defines the most formal concept of "nature" as "whatever is created." He takes this definition to mean that the natural "has nothing ontologically positive of its own, no proportionate order of defining ends."[12]

One can read Balthasar's statement more simply as affirming that whatever is the result of God creative rather than elevating action can be called natural. "Created by God" in this reading refers to all that falls materially under it, such as the power of locomotion. It is a formal term, but to be taken in its full material extent.

The formal concept "Tibetans" is defined by nothing but Tibetan ori-

11. Ibid., 52.
12. Ibid., 77.

gin or Tibetan citizenship. Yet the term can be used to refer materially to all Tibetans. It does not need to imply that Tibetans have no other attributes, that they lack legs, eyes, ears, and the like. In the same way, to say that whatever in human beings is the result of divine creation is natural can be taken to refer materially to all specific content to which "created" applies. Balthasar's long text on nature quoted above shows that he sees much content in what can generally be described as created. His main example is birds.

Abstraction

The long passage on nature quoted above shows that it is important to distinguish the analogical senses of "nature" in the text. At times, Balthasar speaks about the concentric circles around the essence, for example, bird flight and mating. At other times, he focuses with precision on the essence of particular beings or acts in the abstract. Long's often repeated objection that Balthasar is opposed to abstraction, that he has a wrongly concrete understanding of nature and so on, seems to arise from the tendency to read Balthasar mainly as speaking about nature in the sense of essence.[13]

Although Balthasar's keen aesthetic sense implies a particular love for the concrete, which he shares with Barth, he does not share Barth's distaste for abstraction. He clearly affirms the legitimacy of abstraction and shows that the reasons for Barth's distaste for it are not cogent. The affirmation of an abstract nature is not only compatible with recognition of the full individuality and concrete operation of a being. Abstractive knowledge of the essence is also needed to account for the individual being and its concrete acts. Conversely, these concrete acts tell us "what" a particular being is in the abstract. Long is by inclination particularly focused on the abstract nature. It is not surprising that he transfers this predilection to his reading of Balthasar.

Absolutely Final

Perhaps the most disastrous mistake in Long's reading of Balthasar is his failure to distinguish the many analogical senses of "final" or "ultimate" in Balthasar's text. He quotes Balthasar as writing,

13. Ibid., esp. the section "The Fallacy of Concrete Nature," 83–91.

Thomas never entertains, *even hypothetically*, a final goal that could be unmoored from the supernatural vision of God. According to his medieval presuppositions, it would have been impossible for him even to make the conceptual distinction implied by this problem.[14]

Long writes in response,

These last lines are conspicuous: Thomas not only *does not* entertain the hypothesis that God could have created man without ordering him to the beatific vision, but he could not so much as "make the conceptual distinction implied in the problem." *Of course*, given that God has called man to the beatific vision, it is impossible to place the *finis ultimus* in a purely natural end. But the hypothesis of pure nature is precisely the hypothesis that God *could have*, without any contradiction to His wisdom or Goodness, created man from the beginning without sanctifying grace, without the call to supernatural beatitude. It is *this* which—if it means anything reasonable about Thomas's text—Balthasar must be saying.[15]

Indeed, he *can* mean something quite reasonable about Thomas's text, if one distinguishes between the use of "final goal" *Endziel* in the most formal and unqualified sense, and qualified senses of "end." It is in the latter sense that one says, "The act of seeing is the final end of eyes." Sensory sight in a rational animal is clearly subordinate to other ends, most immediately the end of intellectual knowing.

An end is final in the unqualified sense *if, and only if*, it is through itself all-sufficient, needing and permitting no addition that would subordinate it to some other end. "Lord, show us the Father, and that is enough for us." Seeing the Father is the end of all ends beyond which there cannot be another.

Long uses this formal and unqualified sense of the final end when he argues "it is impossible to place the *finis ultimus* in a purely natural end" on the supposition that God orders us to the beatific vision.[16] "Obviously there cannot be at once two ultimate finalities."[17]

Even if God had not decided to order us to the supernatural end of his own happiness, our natural end could not be final in the unqualified and absolute sense. It could be final only in a qualified sense, still capable of subordination to some other greater end. Inasmuch as we are rational, we can be raised to a higher end, beyond the power of our nature.

14. Ibid., 56.
16. Ibid., 57.
15. Ibid., 56–57.
17. Ibid., 225n5.

In the passage quoted and criticized by Long, Balthasar points out Thomas's habitual practice of adding qualifying phrases to signal that our natural end is final in a qualified and limited sense. It cannot be final in the most unqualified and absolute sense.

When a Theologian Examines the
Natural Desire for Happiness

Balthasar insists again and again in his book on Barth that we must be clear when we speak as theologians and when we speak as philosophers. As a test case, one can take a text from Aristotle's *Nicomachean Ethics*.

Since ends seem to be many, and we choose some of these (e.g. wealth, flutes, and in general instruments) for the sake of something else, it is clear that not all are final. Evidently, the best is something final. Therefore, if there is only some one thing that is final, this will be what is sought, and if there are more, the most final of these.

We call that which is according to itself worthy of pursuit more final than what is so on account of something else; and that which is never desirable through something else [more final] than the things that are desirable both according to themselves and on account of that something else, *and simply final that which is always desirable according to itself and never on account of something else.*

Now of this sort happiness above all seems to be; for this we choose always on account of itself and never on account of something else, but honor, pleasure, mind, and every virtue we choose indeed on account of themselves (for if nothing resulted from them we should still choose each of them), but we choose them also for the sake of happiness, judging that through them we shall be happy. Happiness, on the other hand, no one chooses for the sake of these, nor, in general, on account of anything other than itself.

It seems also from the point of view of self-sufficiency that the same result follows; for the final good is thought to be self-sufficient.[18]

Is Aristotle speaking about a purely natural end in this text, or about the desire for a supernatural end?

It makes a decisive difference whether we attempt to answer this question as theologians, who look at the natural desire for happiness in light of the revelation of God's gift of himself in the beatific vision. The desire for happiness, we may agree with Aristotle, is natural. Yet we desire an end, the finality of which is unqualified and absolute. The desire for

---

18. Aristotle, *Nicomachean Ethics*, 1.7. Emphasis added.

happiness carries us in some way beyond what we can reach by our own natural power. To explain the sense of this "beyond," one can appeal to the *potentia obedientiae* for becoming "sharers in the divine nature," not simply to the common *potentia obedientiae* that is common to all creatures, but one that arises specifically from our rational nature. It is an openness to the vision of God, an openness reflected both in the restlessness of *eros* and in our incapacity to anticipate the gift of God himself.

Many pre-Christian and non-Christian thinkers and artists have documented the unstillable longing of natural *eros* for an absolutely final happiness. In a retrospective view, theologians can see that only the beatific vision can fulfill this longing. In the same retrospective view, they can also see that this natural longing differs in kind from the infused love that prepares us for God's gift of himself.

The Ghost of Michael Baius

Long invokes the heresy of Michael Baius, according to which God owed grace to human beings at creation. By following de Lubac's thesis about the natural desire for God, Long argues, Balthasar is forced into the position of Baius, despite his wish to preserve the gratuitousness of grace.

Here it must be noted that there is a confusion involved in thinking that, *because grace is a personal gift of God, therefore one has addressed adequately the question whether the idea of supernatural beatitude as the only possible natural end does not imply a certain necessity of justice to revelation.* For if one accepts that revelation is a free gift of God and supposes that this makes it possible to say that supernatural beatitude is the only possible end without thereby implying that revelation is necessary, the position of Baius appears to be retained: human nature is consequently so utterly lacking in any proportionate good that, minus the gift of grace, the nature would be penalized or tormented... In the absence of the affirmation of the existence and intelligibility of a proportionate natural end distinct from supernatural beatitude, it appears that a necessity of justice comes to pertain to the need of man for grace, even if this derivative implied consequence is not desired.[19]

One can respond on a preliminary and basic level that Balthasar does not deny natural specifying ends. Nor does he deny the global natural end of happiness. What he insists on is that these ends are imperfect and

19. Long, *Natura Pura*, 62. Emphasis original.

therefore capable of subordination to higher ends. What he denies is that any natural end can be ultimate and absolute in a manner that fully corresponds to the natural desire for happiness.

On a second level, one can respond that Baius's error does not lie only in the conclusion that grace is owed, a conclusion rejected by the Church. Scheeben brilliantly analyzes a complex web of legalistic premises that lead to the conclusion. Baius has little understanding of intrinsic gratuitousness. Scheeben also shows how these premises practically expressed themselves in the complex legal wrangling carried on for years between Baius and the Pope.[20] Yet the true response to Baius must go one level deeper.

Predestination and Gratuitousness

Nature and grace are alike because both are ways in which God communicates his own goodness. Both are deeply theonomic. They are unlike, infinitely more unlike than they are alike, because in creating the natural order, God pours out his goodness in a finite way; in the order of grace, he pours it out infinitely. He gives us not simply a natural created good, not even simply the gift of created grace as a finite reality, but himself.

Per donum gratiae gratum facientis	By the gift of the grace that makes pleasing,
perficitur creatura rationalis ad hoc,	the rational creature is perfected for this,
quod libere non solum ipso dono creato utatur,	not only to use freely the created gift as such
sed ut ipsa divina persona fruatur.	but to enjoy the divine person himself.
Et ideo missio invisibilis	And therefore, the invisible mission
fit secundum donum gratiae gratum facientis;	takes place according to the gift of the grace that makes pleasing
et tamen ipsa persona divina datur.	and yet the divine person himself is given.[21]

---

20. Matthias Josef Scheeben, "Zur Geschichte des Baianismus," *Der Katholik* 2 (1868): 281–308.

21. *ST* I, q. 43, a. 3, ad 1.

The distance between the natural order and the infinite gift of the divine persons comes out particularly sharply in the distinction St. Thomas makes between two kinds of merit in relation to eternal life. When one considers a graced human act as coming from the human will, the merit of that act is not proportioned to the worth or value of the end in the sense that its just reward, in the full sense of justice, is eternal life.

si autem loquamur de opere meritorio,	but if we speak about a meritorious work,
secundum quod procedit ex gratia Spiritus Sancti,	as it comes forth from the grace of the Holy Spirit,
sic est meritorium vitae aeternae	in this way it merits eternal life
ex condigno:	from the same level of dignity,
sic enim valor meriti	for in this way the value of merit
attenditur secundum virtutem Spiritus Sancti moventis nos in vitam aeternam.	is seen according to the power of the Holy Spirit moving us into eternal life.

If is true in the order of grace that acts inspired by supernatural grace cannot, as acts proceeding from our will, be meritorious in the fullest sense and thus lay claim in justice to eternal life, then a fortiori a natural desire for seeing God, which proceeds from our nature as such, cannot establish a claim in justice that the divine persons must give themselves. Nothing can establish such a claim because the gift of the divine persons exceeds all measures. To have overlooked this reason for gratuitousness is one of Baius's main errors. Those who see the denial of the natural desire for the vision of God as necessary for preserving the gratuitousness of grace against Baius grant too much to Baius. They grant the very root of his error.

Conclusion

The denial of the natural longing to see God is as dangerous for the understanding of human nature, if not more so than the error of Baius. By its very nature, reason is open to all that is, even if the sacred fullness of being (*ipsum esse*) lies beyond our reach as an unmanageable beauty (Plato, Plotinus). By this openness, to which a limit can be set only by unnatural violence, we stretch with longing. We stretch beyond what we can know by the power of our own nature. We long for more than we know.

The end we can reach by our own power remains the defining end from which our specific nature derives: we are rational animals, not angels. Knowledge comes to us through the senses. And yet that *defining* end cannot be our *ultimate* end, because we know it is finite and therefore not truly final. To be absolutely and unqualified happy ("that is enough for us")—in union with an end that is not truly final—is contrary to our specific nature. It is contrary to reason.

In a text often quoted by Balthasar, St. Thomas pinpoints what is most noble in our nature. More noble than anything else, more to be treasured and cultivated than anything else, is our openness to a perfect good, even if we cannot reach that good by our own power.

Greater nobility belongs to a nature that can reach the perfect good,
     even if it needs outside help to reach it,
than to a nature that can only reach an imperfect good
     even if it does not need outside help,
          as the Philosopher says in *De coelo*, Book 2...
And therefore the rational creature,
     which can reach the perfect good of happiness,
     but needs divine help for it,
is more perfect than the irrational creature,
     which is not capable of this good,
     but reaches some imperfect good by the power of its own nature.[22]

One can grasp the import of this text more clearly if one listens to someone who is blind to such nobility. In the legalistic and mercantile spirit of Baius, Joannes Baptista Gormaz, SJ, writes against the text just quoted,

I find much is that is altogether displeasing in this answer...
No inclination toward a good in the manner of need (*appetitus indigentiae ad bonum*)
          is given without a debt being incurred [by God]
          to provide the means proportionate to this nature
          for desiring this end, means proportionate, that is, to attaining this
               good.
But [in St. Thomas's text], the means owed to pure nature,
     that is, the means of gaining supernatural happiness,
are impossible for that nature.
Therefore pure nature has no inclination in the manner of need
     for supernatural happiness.

22. *ST* I-II, q. 5, a. 5, ad 2.

This is so true that in order to be perfect, [human nature]
> can only have the inclination in the manner of need for natural
> > happiness...

[If it had an inclination in the manner of need toward supernatural beatitude]
> it would be much more miserable than the other creatures,
> the irrational ones, who can reach their own end on their own
> > level.[23]

This text, which takes a position directly opposed to St. Thomas, is not only redolent with the odor of Baius's legalism but also exemplifies a superficial form of Aristotelianism, one that operates with a univocal understanding of nature. What is naturally desired must be naturally attainable, because nature does nothing in vain.

It is fitting to let Aristotle refute Gormaz.

Nothing that belongs to happiness is incomplete.
> But such a life would be higher than according to man.
> For it is not insofar as he is man that he will live so,
> but insofar as something divine is present in him;
> and by so much as this [the divine] is superior to the composite [a
rational animal]
> is its activity superior to that which is the exercise of the other kind
of virtue.
If intellect is divine compared to man,
> the life according to it is divine compared to human life.
But one should not follow those who advise
> to think human things since one is human,
> and mortal things since one is mortal,
but one must, so far as one can, immortalize,
and do everything to live according to what is highest in oneself,
for even if it be small in bulk,
much more does it in power and value surpass everything.[24]

Aristotle is dimly aware in this text of the need to be "shot across" or "sent across" a great distance, a distance we cannot overcome by our natural power. Had he been told of predestination, it would have been good news for him, as it was to the criminal on the Cross.

---

23. Joannes Baptist Gormaz, *Cursus theologicus* (Augsburg: Georg Schlüter, 1707), 1:256.
24. Aristotle, *Nicomachean Ethics* 10, 1177b27–1178a8.

THE THOMISM OF

ST. IGNATIUS AND THE

SPIRITUAL EXERCISES

*Predestination, Physical Premotion,
and the Sovereignty of Grace*

Christopher M. Cullen, SJ

Introduction

St. Ignatius Loyola (c. 1491–1556) lived in the context of the Renaissance and Reformation. As a result, Ignatius is often seen in light of humanism and Protestantism. Yet Ignatius also lived in the midst of the second major revival of Thomism.[1] He spent years of his life studying both Scholastic philosophy and theology. What is more, when composing the *Constitutions of the Society of Jesus*, Ignatius makes a momentous decision: he prescribes four to six years of theological study for all Jesuit priests and that students of the society be taught "the scholastic doctrine of St. Thomas."[2] Although we find little, or only passing reference, to the

1. See Romanus Cessario, *A Short History of Thomism* (Washington, DC: Catholic University of America Press, 2003), 63–81.
2. George Ganss, SJ, ed., *The Constitutions of the Society of Jesus* (St. Louis: Institute of Jesuit Sources, 1970), nos. 418, 464, 474, 476.

actual theses and doctrinal issues with which Ignatius came into contact in the course of his philosophical and theological studies—a tendency that begins admittedly with Ignatius's autobiography—the case can be, and has been, made that Ignatius is influenced by Aquinas and the Thomistic tradition. Yet the congruity of Ignatius's spirituality with the teachings of Aquinas is greater than has often been considered. Ignatius's *Spiritual Exercises* can be understood to be in harmony with classical Thomism. By examining the congruence between classical Thomism and the *Spiritual Exercises*, "Ignatius the Thomist" can come into focus. By bringing the Thomism of Ignatius to light, we can also come to see how the educational program that Ignatius and the early Jesuits eventually developed flows from a transcendent humanism formed to no small extent under the influence of Aquinas.

Any attempt to examine the theology of Ignatius has to face the fact that Ignatius was not a professional theologian. We must rely on an indirect method to bring to clarity his theological beliefs by inferring them from his writings and, above all, his spiritual writings. There have been recent examinations of Ignatius as a theologian. The most important of these is arguably Hugo Rahner's *Ignatius the Theologian*, first published in 1964.[3] Another such study is an article from 1992 by Avery Dulles, SJ.[4] Dulles summarizes what he regards as the four main themes of "Ignatian theology": Christocentrism, anthropocentrism, ecclesiocentrism, and theocentrism. Dulles begins by defending the idea of considering Ignatius as a theologian. As he points out, the early Jesuits certainly did regard him as such; Jerome Nadal referred to him as "our Father, the theologian."[5] Karl Rahner, SJ, would say that "the theology hidden in the simple words of the *Exercises* belongs to the most important fundamentals of contemporary Western Christianity."[6]

In order to get an accurate understanding of Ignatius's theology, two preliminary points must be considered. First, we need to take care not to

---

3. Hugo Rahner, SJ, *Ignatius the Theologian*, trans. Michael Barry (New York: Herder and Herder, 1968; originally published 1964).

4. Avery Dulles, SJ, "Saint Ignatius and the Jesuit Theological Tradition," *Studies in the Spirituality of Jesuits* 14 (March 1982): 1–21.

5. Ibid., 2. "He aqui a nuestro Padre teólogo." Jerome Nadal, in Rahner, *Ignatius the Theologian,*, 1. Nadal makes this reference in an instruction in Spanish concerning the plan of theological studies proposed by St. Ignatius.

6. Dulles, "Saint Ignatius and the Jesuit Theological Tradition," 2.

associate Ignatius with later theories that became closely identified with Jesuits, such as that of Molinism, which only developed in the generation after Ignatius by Luis de Molina, SJ (1535–1600), or that of probabilism, which also only developed in subsequent generations but became associated with Jesuits. For example, Robert Maryks presents extensive evidence in *Saint Cicero and the Jesuits* that Ignatius and the early Jesuits were not probabilists—they were tutiorists in the tradition of medieval theologians like Bonaventure and Aquinas.[7]

A second important point is to see the unity of humanism itself as a tradition. Humanism is not something radically new that only comes to the intellectual landscape with the Renaissance. The case has been made that there is a humanism not only of the Renaissance but also of the Scholastics. Indeed, there is considerable continuity between medieval and Renaissance humanism, as R. W. Southern's famous work on this topic, *Scholastic Humanism and the Unification of Europe*, brings out:

> Humanism is a word that it is sometimes necessary to use, and there is nothing wrong with it except that it stands for many different things. Any study of the seven liberal arts, which were the foundation of all education from the Carolingian age, implies a certain degree of humanism. That is to say, in studying the Arts you are studying both the human mind and the external world: the human mind in its forms of expression in grammar, rhetoric, and logic; and the external world in the arts of arithmetic, geometry, music, and astronomy. The subjects may be extremely circumscribed, but they depended on the exercise of human powers and not on knowledge drawn from Revelation. They are therefore genuine humanistic studies, and every cathedral school of the period from the tenth to the twelfth centuries was in its general tendency humanistic.[8]

The question is not whether Ignatius was a humanist or a Scholastic; in being the latter, he is also the former. By bringing to light the congruity of Thomism and Ignatian theology, the nature of the humanism of Ignatius comes into greater focus. The difference between Scholastic and Renaissance humanism is to no small extent an argument over which subjects ought to enjoy primacy within the education of the complete human being: the Renaissance humanists favored grammar, poetry, his-

---

7. Robert A. Maryks, *Saint Cicero and the Jesuits: The Influence of the Liberal Arts on the Adoption of Moral Probabilism* (Aldershot, UK: Ashgate, 2008).

8. R. W. Southern, *Scholastic Humanism and the Unification of Europe*, vol. 1, *Foundations* (Cambridge, MA: Blackwell, 1997), 78.

tory, moral philosophy, and rhetoric; the Scholastics regarded theology as the culminating discipline with philosophy, especially metaphysics, as its handmaiden. Ignatius takes a different path from that of certain Renaissance humanists, such as Erasmus, who reject Scholasticism. Ignatius sought to hold together both the humanism of the Renaissance, which culminates in the art of eloquence, and the humanism of the Scholastics, which culminates in the wisdom of revelation.[9] Ignatius and the early Jesuits overcome this dispute by synthesizing the favored subjects of the both the medieval and Renaissance humanists in a carefully ordered plan of studies that culminates in the study of divine wisdom. It is a synthesis made possible to a large degree by the spirituality of the *Spiritual Exercises.*

The Life of Ignatius

Before examining the Thomism of Ignatius, it is helpful to review his life. Ignatius needs to be seen in the context of late medieval chivalric culture. Inigo Lopez, as Ignatius was baptized, came from a land-owning Basque family with connections to the Castilian nobility. At the age of 15, he began his career in the household of the treasurer of King Ferdinand of Castile as a page. When his patron died a few years later, he entered the service of the Duke of Najera and Viceroy of Navarre (Antonio Manrique). In 1521 at the age of 20, he was serving in the military defense of Pamplona. During this battle, he was wounded in both legs by a cannon ball. This wounding was the beginning of a long convalescence and ultimately a whole conversion of life, brought about especially through his reading of the lives of saints. He eventually resolved to serve the divine Lord rather than a merely human one, but realized that he needed some education to do so. To be of "help to souls," as he later expressed his intentions, he would need to receive a formal education.

---

9. John W. O'Malley, *The First Jesuits* (Cambridge, MA: Harvard University Press, 1993), 28. It is important not to see Ignatius in the context of Renaissance humanism alone, as if Ignatius were in fact an Erasmian, as the early Jesuits were sometimes accused of being.

The Education of Ignatius

After two initial years of studies in Latin in Barcelona (under Jeronim Ardèvol), he was to spend a year of study at the University of Alcala.[10] There Ignatius tells us that he studied the logic of Domingo de Soto, OP, the physics of Albert, and Peter Lombard's *Sentences*.[11] But he made these studies hurriedly, "with little foundation," and with considerable distraction owing to his apostolic zeal. So in July 1527 he went to study at Salamanca, but things did not go well there either, especially when he ran afoul of the Inquisition. After twenty-two days of imprisonment, a final judgment was issued that there was nothing reprehensible in his life or doctrine.

Ignatius moved to Paris in February 1528 and restarted his studies. He pursued a course in Latin grammar at the College of Montaigu, on the hill of Sainte-Geneviève.[12] In October 1529, Ignatius moved to the College of Sainte-Barbe, where he began his study of philosophy.[13] There he studied as a student of arts (i.e., philosophy) for three years. He roomed with Francisco de Javier, Pierre Favre, and their tutor, Juan Peña. Peña seems to have been a disciple of one of the famous teachers of the day at Paris, Juan Celaya. Celaya was a follower of the fourteenth-century terminist John Buridan (1295–1363), and had also taught Francisco de Vitoria (1492–1546).[14] Ignatius studied the *Summulae* of Peter of Spain and the logic of Aristotle through commentators. In 1532, Ignatius obtained his bachelor of arts. In order to receive a licentiate, he then studied Aristotle's *Physics*, *Metaphysics*, and *Ethics* as well as the *Parva naturalia*.[15]

---

10. Cándido de Dalmases, SJ, *Ignatius of Loyola, Founder of the Jesuits*, trans. Jerome Aixalá (St. Louis: Institute of Jesuit Sources, 1985), 86.

11. Ibid., 93. "Albert" is presumably Albert the Great. Domingo de Soto's work on logic, the *Summulae*, was not published until 1529, so it probably circulated in manuscript copies beforehand. "Domingo de Soto who, with his fellow-Dominican, Francisco de Vitoria, rejuvenated scholasticism in both Spain and France, was three or four years younger than St. Ignatius." James Brodrick, SJ, *Saint Ignatius Loyola: The Pilgrim Years 1491–1538* (New York: Farrar, Straus and Cudahy, 1956), 167n2.

12. Ignatius first lived in a boarding house with other Spanish students. Because of his lack of funds, he moved to the hospice of Saint-Jacques, which was intended for pilgrims to Compostela (rue Saint-Denis, 133). Dalmases, *Ignatius of Loyola*, 108.

13. Ibid., 112.

14. Brodrick, *Saint Ignatius Loyola*, 242.

15. Dalmases, *Ignatius of Loyola*, 116; Brodrick, *Saint Ignatius Loyola*, 271. Some mathematics and cosmography were also required.

According to the statutes of Paris, no student could proceed to the licentiate examination without having heard lectures on all of these Aristotelian works.[16] On March 13, 1533, Ignatius received his licentiate.[17] Because of the expenses involved in the formal reception of the master of arts, he deferred this for a year but received it on March 14, 1534.[18] On August 15, 1534, he took vows in Paris at a chapel at Montmartre.

Ignatius studied theology for the next year and a half by following the lectures of the Dominicans of the rue Saint-Jacques and the Franciscans. Among his Dominican teachers were the Dominican Jean Benoit and the Franciscan Pierre de Cornes. When Ignatius came to Paris, a revival of Thomism, which had begun earlier in Spain, had already come to the university. The Dominican Peter Crockaert (d. ca. 1514) had been an important leader. For example, he made the momentous decision to replace Peter the Lombard's *Sentences* with Aquinas's *Summa Theologiae* as a basic textbook for theology—a practice that his student, Vitoria, would bring to Salamanca twenty years later. Later Jesuit teachers would follow in this practice.[19] Given this Thomistic revival, it is not surprising that one of the eminent biographers and editors of Ignatius in the twentieth century, Cándido de Dalmases, SJ, summarizes his education by saying, "Ignatius' formation was essentially Thomistic."[20] Ignatius was ordained a priest in 1537 in Venice. The year 1540 marks the official beginning of the order with papal approval of the society. Ignatius served as the first general of the society from its founding in 1540 until his death in 1556.

16. Brodrick, *Saint Ignatius Loyola*, 271.   17. Ibid., 273–74.

18. Dalmases, *Ignatius of Loyola*, 117.

19. Gerald McCool, SJ, *The Neo-Thomisits* (Milwaukee: Marquette University Press, 1994), 17; Cessario, *Short History of Thomism*, 64. As early as 1571 in Dillingen, Jesuits started commenting on Aquinas's *Summa Theologiae* as the textbook in theology. Ulrich G. Leinsle, *Introduction to Scholastic Theology*, trans. Michael J. Miller (Washington, DC: Catholic University of America Press, 2010), 294. "In the renewal of Thomism Jesuits worked side by side with Dominicans. Ignatius himself greatly admired the order and method of St. Thomas, having completed his theological studies at the Dominican convent on the rue Saint-Jacques in Paris." Avery Dulles, SJ, "Jesuits and Theology: Yesterday and Today," *Theological Studies* 52 (1991): 524–38.

20. Dalmases, *Ignatius of Loyola*, 122.

The Writings of Ignatius

Ignatius's writings include two works that are of special importance for our purposes: the *Constitutions of the Society of Jesus*, a labor of love and many years—from 1544 to 1551—as well as of collaboration with other members of the early society, and *Spiritual Exercises*, born to no small degree from his own prayer and mystical experiences. Ignatius also wrote an enormous range of letters, especially during his time as general. Some of these are also relevant.

In the *Constitutions of the Society of Jesus*, Ignatius makes Thomas Aquinas the principal doctor in theology and prescribes that students of the society be taught the Scholastic doctrine of Aquinas: "In theology there should be lectures on the Old and New Testaments and on the scholastic doctrine of St. Thomas; and in positive theology those authors should be selected who are more suitable for our end."[21] While in positive theology Ignatius leaves the selection of authors somewhat open, that is not the case in Scholastic theology. This election of Aquinas is often taken for granted. Yet it should be noteworthy, if not surprising, to anyone familiar both with the prevalence of nominalism at the University of Paris in the sixteenth century and the diversity of schools within the Scholastic tradition by the time of the Renaissance.[22] Ignatius almost certainly encountered this school of thought, especially given his relationship with Peña at Sainte-Barbe. Ignatius did not chose a nominalist as the principal scholastic theologian, nor did he remain silent, leaving it to individuals to choose.[23]

Ignatian Thomism: Reasons for Choosing Aquinas

In his book *The Early Jesuits*, John O'Malley, SJ, refocused attention on Ignatius's Thomism. O'Malley thinks that there are multiple reasons for how this election of Thomas came about. The first reason, he says, is an extrinsic one, that Aquinas was immensely influential in

21. Ganss, *Constitutions*, no. 464.

22. Brodrick, *Saint Ignatius Loyola*, 236–37, 241–46.

23. We know that Ignatius, as early as 1548, recommended Cajetan's *Summula* to Jerome Nadal for his lectures on moral cases that had been requested by the city of Messina. O'Malley, *First Jesuits*, 146.

sixteenth-century Rome, especially as a result of the Dominicans, who were "masters of the Sacred Palace" and so held the chief theological position in the *Studium* of the papal curia.[24] A second reason is that the early Jesuits found elements of Aquinas's teaching compatible with their religious vision, especially his unquestioned orthodoxy. Third would be the clear organization and comprehensiveness of the *Summa Theologiae*, which made this text easy to follow and to teach. A fourth reason is found in Aquinas's adoption of Aristotle's teaching that virtue takes the middle path between two extremes. O'Malley suggests that this was the grounding for Ignatius's moderation on ascetical practices. In general, he thinks the early Jesuits were attracted to the *Secunda Pars* of the *Summa Theologiae*. "Ignatius specifically recommended to Jesuits the study of the second part of Aquinas's *Summa theologiae*, the part dealing with virtues and vices."[25] O'Malley explains that "there may have been other features they found attractive, but the surviving documentation does not provide any apodictic evidence explaining why they rejected the eclectic program the companions followed at Paris and settled on Aquinas."[26]

O'Malley speculates, however, on the possibility of two further reasons, namely, that Thomism defends a basic compatibility between reason and revelation and between nature and grace. The Thomistic synthesis "coincided with the Jesuits' conviction that in their pastoral activities they should not only rely upon God's grace but also use all the 'human means' at their disposal.... Thomistic reason would also help rationalize this conviction."[27] O'Malley explains that the Thomistic view that grace perfects nature provides a better account of the relation between human activity and the influence of grace. The will is wounded and enfeebled by original sin, but not vitiated or destroyed. Grace allows the will to cooperate with it, so that in some mysterious way human responsibility played its part in the process of salvation. O'Malley writes: "This theology is much more easily reconciled with the language of the *Exercises* and the *Constitutions* than a more Augustinian viewpoint."[28]

O'Malley further speculates that Aquinas's teaching on human nature and free will was only the specification of a larger appreciation for all of

24. Ibid., 248.   25. Ibid., 146.
26. Ibid., 249.   27. Ibid.
28. Ibid., 249–50.

created reality. God is ubiquitously present and operative in the Thomistic synthesis. "God could thus be found in all things, as the *Constitutions* stated, succinctly summarizing the essence of the 'Contemplation to Obtain Divine Love' that closes the *Exercises*."[29]

But for all these reasons for adopting Aquinas as the official doctor, O'Malley thinks that the early Jesuits departed from Aquinas on certain other points. For example, he thinks they reject Aquinas's view that theology is principally a speculative doctrine. O'Malley points out that the early Jesuits, such as Nadal and Xavier, inveigh against reducing theology to speculation alone. Erasmus grapples with a similar problem: how to blend mystical and speculative theology. Erasmus's solution, as O'Malley sees it, is to jettison Scholasticism and replace it with the more rhetorical theology of the Fathers.[30] It is clear that Ignatius took a different path. Rather than jettison the Scholastic tradition, he placed it at the center of Jesuit education, as evident in his choice of Aquinas as the theologian of the Society.

The *Spiritual Exercises*

The *Spiritual Exercises* is a manual for a retreat director. It is not designed to be read through. It consists of meditations and contemplations to be done as a retreat director sees fit. Each exercise has a composition of place, a preparatory prayer, a various points, and a closing prayer, often consisting of a colloquy with Mary, Christ, or the Father. As a series of meditations, the *Exercises* is divided into four parts, with a preparatory consideration of what Ignatius calls the "Principle and Foundation." Following this preliminary meditation, Ignatius divides the retreatants prayers into four "weeks" (though the actual number of days on each such part is up to the retreat director). The first week, or series of meditations, is focused on the Fall and human sinfulness; week two is focused on the Incarnation and the life of our Lord; week three is focused on the Passion and Death; week four on the Resurrection and a particularly important closing exercise called the "Contemplation to Attain Divine Love." The retreatant is also given a method for daily examens of conscience and rules for thinking with the Church.

29. Ibid., p. 250; Ganss, *Constitutions*, no. 288.
30. O'Malley, *First Jesuits*, 252.

There are many elements of the *Exercises* that reflect a Thomistic view. They are too numerous to explore all of them in this essay. One, for example, is the quite obvious primacy that Ignatius gives to contemplative activities. While there is no extended argument in Ignatius for the superiority of the contemplative life to the active, as in Aquinas,[31] the *Spiritual Exercises* is first and foremost a series of carefully structured meditations meant to encourage a habit of contemplation in the one making them. The contemplation of the *Exercises* concerns both abstract truths, as in the case of preliminary "Principle and Foundation," and concrete moments in salvation history, which require the active use of the imagination in order to contemplate the biblical scene and the conversations. Much has been written about each of the individual meditations, but what is important for our purposes is the degree to which the retreatant is immersed in acts of contemplation, sometimes recalling fundamental truths of the faith, and at other moments, scenes from salvation history. The *Exercises* grounds the spiritual life in contemplation and meditation. Another Thomistic doctrine is found in the contemplation on the Incarnation, where the motive for the Incarnation is clearly human salvation: "Since They [the Three Divine Persons] see that all are going down to hell, they decree in their eternity that the Second Person should become man to save the human race (*para saluar el género humano*)."[32] But this essay turns to three doctrines of classical Thomism and explores their "fit" with the *Exercises*: predestination, physical premotion, and the intrinsic efficacy of grace.

Predestination

We do well first to call to mind Aquinas's definition of predestination from the *Summa Theologiae*: "Whence it is clear that predestination is a kind of type of the ordering of some persons towards eternal salvation, existing in the divine mind. The execution, however, of this order is in a passive way in the predestined, but actively in God."[33] In this text, Aquinas defines predestination as a kind of ordering in the divine mind.

---

31. Thomas Aquinas, *Summa Theologiae* (*ST*) II-II, q. 182.

32. Ignatius Loyola, *The Spiritual Exercises of St. Ignatius: Based on Studies in the Language of the Autograph*, trans. Louis Pohl, SJ (Chicago: Loyola University Press, 1951), no. 102. *Exercitia Spiritualia*, vol. 1, *Monumenta Ignatiana* (Rome: IHSJ, 1969).

33. Thomas Aquinas, *Summa Theologiae*, I, q. 23, a. 2 resp.

In this way it is a part of providence for whole of creation, as Aquinas makes clear: "We have said above that predestination is a part of providence. Now providence is not anything in the things provided for; but is a type in the mind of the provider, as was proved above."[34] Furthermore, Aquinas distinguishes how "predestination" is present in God and in those ordered: this ordering is executed actively by God and passively in the predestined. We also see this distinction in the following text: "But the execution of providence which is called government, is in a passive way in the thing governed, and in an active way in the governor.... The execution of predestination is the calling and magnification; according to the Apostle (Romans 8:30): "Whom He predestined, them He also called and whom He called, them He also justified" [Vulg]. For Aquinas, predestination is an ordering located in God's own goodness, not in man's goodness or merits, and thus is an act of unfathomable mercy, or "justified."[35]

Ignatius addresses predestination directly in the *Exercises*, specifically in Rules 14 and 15 for "Thinking with the Church." According to Rule 14, "It is granted that there is much truth in the statement that no one can be saved without being predestined and without having faith and grace. Nevertheless great caution is necessary in our manner of speaking and teaching about all these matters."[36]

This leads to Rule 15: "We ought not to fall into a habit of speaking much about predestination. But if somehow the topic is brought up on occasions, it should be treated in such a way that the ordinary people do not fall into an error, as sometimes happen when they say: 'Whether I am to be saved or damned is already determined, and this cannot now be changed by my doing good or evil.' Through this they grow listless and neglect the works which lead to good and to the spiritual advancement of their souls."[37] Note here that Ignatius is simply concerned about whether thinking that a soul is predestined will lead to ceasing to do good works. He is concerned with the effect of the doctrine; he is not commenting one way or another on the question. The fear of a quietism is clearly what is driving these rules on predestination, as we can see in

34. *ST* I, q. 22, a. 1.
35. *ST* I, q. 23, ad 2
36. Ignatius, *Spiritual Exercises*, 160, no. 366.
37. Ibid., 160, no. 367.

Rule 17 for thinking with the Church: Be careful not to generate a poison harmful to freedom of the will. "Hence one may speak about faith and grace as much as possible, with God's help, for the greater praise of the Divine Majesty; but not in such ways or manners, especially in times as dangerous as our own, that works and free will are impaired or thought worthless" (369).[38]

The *Spiritual Exercises* begins with a consideration of man's end in what Ignatius calls the "Principle and Foundation, summarized in its first sentence." "Man is created to praise, reverence and serve God our Lord, and by this means to save his soul."[39] After this propaedeutic consideration, much of the first week of the *Exercises* is a consideration of man's two possible ends in light of revelation and grace: heaven with the elect or hell with the reprobate.[40]

In terms of predestination, two points seem abundantly clear in these texts: (1) predestination is the fact that Ignatius intends the retreatant to consider, and (2) the retreatant is ignorant of his election or nonelection. But this is an ignorance on the side of the retreatant. Nowhere in the meditation on hell does Ignatius suggest that whether we go to hell is entirely up to us. He says near the end: "I will thank Christ because he has not, by the ending of my life, let me fall into any of these classes [of souls in hell]."[41] It is important to note that Ignatius's language seems to imply the moderation of Thomistic nonelection rather than a theory of positive reprobation ("double predestination"). In the meditation on one's own sins, Ignatius asks the retreatant to consider the earth and "how it is that it has not opened up and swallowed me, creating new hells for me to suffer forever."[42] Ignatius clearly intends the retreatant to realize the razor's

---

38. Lainez made strenuous objection at Trent in 1546 to the doctrine of double justification proposed by Girolamo Seripando and others. O'Malley says that Lainez was closer to a nominalist understanding of the relationship of grace to God than to the position of Aquinas (*First Jesuits*, 247). Cf. Diego Lainez, "Disputata de iustitia imputata," in *Disputationes Tridentinae*, 2 vols., ed. Hartmann Grisar (Innsbruck: F. Rauch, 1886), 2:182–83.

39. Ignatius, *Spiritual Exercises*, no. 23.

40. Using the imagination, the second point for the retreatant is "to hear the wailing, the howling, cries and blasphemies against Christ our Lord and against his saints." The third point is "with the sense of smell to perceive the smoke, the Sulphur, the filth, and corruption." The fourth: "to taste the bitterness of tears, sadness and remorse of conscience." The fifth: with the sense of touch to feel the flames which envelop and burn the souls." Ignatius, *Spiritual Exercises*, nos. 66–70.

41. Ibid., no. 71.

42. Ibid., no. 60.

edge on which his life is lived, or to use St. Paul's command, to work out one's salvation in fear and trembling.

These meditations of the first week lead to those of the second. The second week begins with the "Call of the King" and the contemplation on the Incarnation and then continues with moments from the life of Christ. In the contemplation on the Incarnation, Ignatius leads the retreatant to contemplate the great ordering in which he is involved. And it is an ordering not of one life or time, but of all eternity, and it is quite clearly God's ordering.[43] Ignatius asks the retreatant to contrast what the Trinity is doing and what human beings are doing. They are going down to hell.

This second week culminates in meditations on what Ignatius calls the election, which concerns one's state of life. This election is often thought of and spoken of as if Ignatius were referring to the election of the retreatant. But it is clear from the context of the meditations of the first week—namely, on man's end, on the fall of man, and on heaven and hell—that the election is really God's election. The retreatant seeks to know not what he chooses but what God has chosen for him with regard to his life. This election is not about what we want but what God has chosen for us.

Ignatius writes in the introduction on making a choice of way of life: "In every good choice, as far as depends on us, our intention must be simple. I must consider only the end for which I am created, that is, for the praise of God our Lord and the salvation of my soul."[44] Desiring anything apart from this end involves the soul in an inordinate attachment. Ignatius says that every vocation that comes from God is uninfluenced by any inordinate attachment. In the points for this meditation, Ignatius leads the retreatant to consider the great ordering and drama in which they find themselves. Ignatius also places the emphasis on what God is doing. It is God who has ordered the plan. It is not as if there is no predestination to glory for the elect, and God is waiting for the results. It is rather that we, in our limited consciousness, do not know the ending. But the author of this drama has written an ending, for the whole and for each. And the task of the retreatant is to do a series of spiritual exercis-

43. Ibid.
44. Ibid., no. 169.

es—meditations and contemplations, examens of conscience—in order to be found on the side of justice in the end.[45]

Physical Premotion and the Movement of Spirits

Aquinas considers the relation of primary and secondary causality to be vitally important both in the order of nature and of grace. He avoids an occasionalist position that would eliminate secondary causes as well as an autonomous view that eliminates the role of the primary cause. Hence one of the central principles is that God works in every agent by moving it from potency to act. This doctrine follows from the view, rooted in Aristotle, of God as Pure Act who moves the whole natural order. The principle invoked is that "God operates in all creaturely agents" (*Deus operator in omni operante*).

That the primary cause applies the secondary cause to act seems clear in a number of texts in Aquinas. In *Summa contra Gentiles*, Book III, for example, he writes, "Now, the movement of the mover precedes the movement of the movable thing in reason and causally. Therefore, divine help is not given to us by virtue of the fact that we initially move ourselves toward it by good works; instead, we make such progress by good works because we are preceded by divine help." God moves creatures from potency to act in their natural powers.[46] This applies especially to the initiation of the action insofar as the secondary agent passes from the power of acting to actual action. God's motion applies the agent to act, and causes within it and with it both the action and its mode, whether necessary or free. That is to say, this motion is concerned with the exercise of the act.[47] Premotion is a type of divine concurrence; it is divine help (*auxilium*) without rendering the secondary cause a mere instrument. The secondary cause is still a real cause. But Aquinas thinks that "God is the cause of every action, in so far as it is an action," as he says in

---

45. Ibid., nos. 101–9.

46. "Physical promotion was advanced by Báñez as an account of what *Deus operator in omni operante* (*ST* I, q. 105, a. 5) means: God operates in all creatures agents—including free creaturely agents—by moving them to act."

47. R. P. Phillips, *Modern Thomistic Philosophy*, vol. 2, *Metaphysics* (Westminster, MD: Newman Bookshop, 1934), 343–44. The name for this view of creaturely operation and the numerous details that it entails are often taken from Domingo Báñez, OP (d. 1604). *New Catholic Encyclopedia*, comp. T. C. O'Brien (Detroit, MI: Thomson/Gale, 2003), "premotion, physical."

his discussion of sinful acts. Physical promotion is a type of help in the natural order. It is distinct from the supernatural help (*auxilium*) that is grace, yet it is still understood to be a type of help.

Aquinas writes: "So, the soul cannot prepare itself to receive the influence of divine help except in so far as it acts from divine power. Therefore, it is preceded by divine help toward good action, rather than preceding the divine help and meriting it, as it were, or preparing itself for it."[48] This point is especially important in the movement of the will from potency to act. The will is not a self-mover in some absolute sense. Were it so, then it would be an island of autonomy in a sea of secondary causes that need divine concurrence in order for them to function as secondary causes.

The Renaissance Thomist Domingo Báñez (1528–1604) worked to specify Aquinas's teaching on divine concurrence. Báñez studied under Francisco de Vitoria and after teaching in various sites taught for twenty years at Salamanca. Recent work on Báñez by Robert Matava expresses clearly Báñez's doctrine of physical promotion, which clearly specifies divine concurrence:

According to Báñez's theory of physical promotion, God determinately and indefectibly moves the creatures free will from a state of potency to a state of act by a created motion that is distinct from and naturally antecedent to the creature's own free act. It is this *motio*, or changing, which is called a physical promotion.... The motion is call physical because it is an influx of God's efficient causality as opposed to an instance of his final or formal causality. In short, the physical promotion is a causal impulse from God, an inflow if divine efficient causality that is passively received into the human will, stimulating the will to actively elicit its own free operation.[49]

An understanding of God's help as a physical premotion within human nature is especially valuable when it comes to Ignatius's *Spiritual Exercises*, because the soul can then be seen as a mirror in which God's movements can be discerned. This view of the relation between divine and human action is obviously important for Ignatius's *Spiritual Exercises*. These exercises require as a precondition that God is moving us from within. Of course, this is true in the order of grace. God moves us with

---

48. Thomas Aquinas, *Summa contra Gentiles* III, ch. 149, no. 2.

49. Robert Matava, *Divine Causality and Human Free Choice: Domingo Bañez, Physical Premotion, and the Controversy de Auxiliis Revisited* (Boston: Brill, 2016).

the help that is his grace. Ignatius writes "that we cannot by ourselves bring on or retain great devotion, intense love, tears, or any other spiritual consolation, but that all these are a gift and grace from God our Lord."[50]

But this also seems true in the order of nature, at least with regard to the movements of the soul as operations of natural powers moving from potency to act. The *Exercises* requires extensive use of the retreatant's natural powers of intellect, will, memory, imagination, and the senses in the actual doing of the *Exercises*.

The Thomist position is deeply congruent with Ignatius's conception of the spiritual life and the exercises he recommends for its growth and development. The Thomist conception leaves ample room for grace as an influence that moves the human soul, but an understanding of physical premotion also renders the movements of the soul in the exercise of its natural operations as also of potential import. This is not to say that such a view means that every movement of the intellect, the will, and the appetites is specified in its object as revelatory of the divine will, nor as leading to God. But this view does say that God is at work in the intimacy of the human soul, in the most profound sort of way, insofar as the powers of the soul move from potency to act in their operations. Ignatius understands consolation to be any movement that increases the faith, hope, or charity of the believer; desolation is any movement to decrease these theological virtues. The spiritual life and all its movements are of potential value as consolations drawing the soul nearer to God through growth in the theological virtues, and they are of potential import as to the divine will made manifest in the movements of the heart.

Ignatius calls the retreatant to a "discernment" of spirits. But this discernment aims not to find our will for ourselves but God's will for us. The *Exercises* is often concerned with making what Ignatius calls an election about one's life. In order to arrive at the election, a discernment of spirits becomes crucial. We see this in the consideration of poverty, for example: Ignatius makes clear that he thinks that God leads souls by attracting them to spiritual or actual poverty, to reproaches and contempt.[51] But a discernment of spirits conceived as a mere sorting through

50. Ignatius, *Spiritual Exercises*, no. 322. Or, as Ignatius prays on many occasions, "I should beg God our Lord to deign to move my will." Ibid., no. 180.

51. Ibid., no. 146. What is more, God can give the soul consolation without any preceding cause. Ignatius explains what he means by this: "I mean without any previous perception or

of what we want and what God wants is misleading. If our souls are understood to be autonomous domains of psychological operations without divine concurrence or influence, then there is no need for a discernment of spirits as Ignatius conceives it. In his view, the movements of our souls are revelatory of how God is moving us from within. Ignatius seems to take a middle ground between two extremes on interior prayer: one would be to see the interior movements of the soul to be radically autonomous, requiring no divine agency of any sort, including divine concurrence; the other extreme would be to see movements of the soul as entirely the work of divine agency, not only with regard to the exercise of the act from potency to act, but also with regard to the specification of the act. The former would render the spiritual exercises purely a mental exercise without revelatory import with regard to God; the latter seems to exclude secondary agency, which also seems far from how Ignatius conceives his *Exercises*. If we understand our souls to be autonomous domains, then it seems that the foundation of the *Exercises* is lost. But if our souls are moved from potency to act by God as Pure Act, the spiritual life is a realm of transcendence.

We cannot know with certitude whether we are among the elect or reprobate, but we can discern the spirits that move within us, of whether we are moved by consolation or desolation, and whether our consolations are false, or not from God, insofar as the specifying object of the intellect or will is not in conformity with the divine order and the divine will for the individual. We find Ignatius focusing on interior movements over and over again.

We find the issue of divine concurrence in creation to be the central point of contemplation at the very summit of the *Spiritual Exercises*, in the "Contemplation to Attain Divine Love" at the end of week four: "I will consider how God labors and works for me in all the creatures on the face of the earth." "I will consider how God dwells in creatures; in the elements, giving them existence; in the plants, giving them life; in the animals, giving them sensation."[52] By this point in the *Exercises* it is clear that God is working within the interior of the soul and in the whole of creation.

---

understanding of some object by means of which the consolation just mentioned might have been stimulated" (no. 330).

52. Ibid., no. 235.

Grace

Classical Thomism's teachings on grace are an attempt to account for the great mystery of grace at work in the human soul. It has generally made various distinctions in order to affirm both the profound power of God's help and the freedom of the human agent. Aquinas affirms what we could call the sovereignty of grace: grace is necessary for salvation and the efficacy of efficacious grace is not derived from the human will. This latter point leads to a distinction between sufficient and efficacious grace. The former confers the power to perform a particular action; the latter actualizes this power to act. The grace that brings about the salutary act is understood to be intrinsically efficacious and not dependent on the consent of the human will for its efficacy.

While this distinction is not explicitly affirmed in Ignatius's writings, it does seem to be reconcilable with the *Exercises*. For example, Ignatius insists that God can give the soul consolation without any preceding cause. Ignatius explains what he means by this: "I mean without previous perception or understanding of some object by means of which the consolation just mentioned might have been stimulated."[53] What is more, Ignatius seems to view grace as irresistible at times. He writes in a letter on the discernment of spirits to Teresa Rejadell in 1536: "It often happens that our Lord moves and forces us interiorly to one action or another by opening up our mind and heart, i.e., speaking inside us without any noise of voices, raising us entirely to His divine love, without our being able to resist His purpose, even if we wanted."[54]

The Spiritual Exercises reflects a man who has thought extensively about grace and the effect of its movement in souls. Ignatius's notion of grace is deeply influenced by the great Thomistic synthesis on nature and grace, and his theology is one of balance founded in that of Thomas Aquinas. *The Spiritual Exercises* reflects a clear attempt to maintain the importance of nature, freedom, and grace. It reflects a strong emphasis on the role of secondary causality, human freedom, and the meritorious character of charitable deeds performed under the influence of grace. Ignatius presupposes the fundamental integrity of the will in its operations

53. Ibid., no. 330.
54. St. Ignatius Loyola, "Letter 4 to Teresa Rejadell," in *Personal Writings*, Penguin Classics (New York: Penguin, 1996), 133–34.

throughout the *Exercises*. In many passages, Ignatius affirms the power of the will to choose the right and good. And thus it makes possible meritorious acts. Aquinas ties the possibility of merit to God's ordering; hence predestination and the possibility of meritorious acts are joined.[55] Ignatius makes frequent reference to the meritorious character of good works, and so, given his notion of predestination and freedom, it should not be surprising the vigor with which he emphasizes meritorious acts at various points.[56]

In this regard, the *Exercises* chooses a different view than that of the Protestant Reformers' rejection of the meritorious nature of good works in the mystery of salvation. Yet Ignatius clearly emphasizes the necessity of grace for human salvation, whether one is considering the end of human life, the predestination of the saints, the way that the Cross serves as the standard for all human decisions, or the ontological foundation for the discernment of spirits.

Jesuit Education

Ignatius worked with the early Jesuits to create a system of schools; these schools became one of the largest purveyors of Aristotelianism and Thomism in the history of Western education. O'Malley makes the point that the early Jesuits did not know what they were getting into when they took up schools, as if they were just one more ministry on the list. "They

---

55. *ST* I-II, q. 114, a.1, resp. "Now it is clear that between God and man there is the greatest inequality: for they are infinitely apart, and all man's good is from God. Hence there can be no justice of absolute equality between man and God, but only of a certain proportion, inasmuch as both operate after their own manner. Now the manner and measure of human virtue is in man from God. Hence man's merit with God only exists on the presupposition of the Divine ordination, so that man obtains from God, as a reward of his operation, what God gave him the power of operation for, even as natural things by their proper movements and operations obtain that to which they were ordained by God; differently, indeed, since the rational creature moves itself to act by its free-will, hence its action has the character of merit, which is not so in other creatures."

56. *ST* I-II, q. 114, a. 3, resp. "I answer that, Man's meritorious work may be considered in two ways: first, as it proceeds from free-will; secondly, as it proceeds from the grace of the Holy Ghost. If it is considered as regards the substance of the work, and inasmuch as it springs from the free-will, there can be no condignity because of the very great inequality. But there is congruity, on account of an equality of proportion: for it would seem congruous that, if a man does what he can, God should reward him according to the excellence of his power."

did not grasp that this ministry had an intrinsic dynamism that would change the organization undertaking it."[57]

There is admittedly a tension borne of trying to find the compatibility between an education in humane letters, which is the first stage in the early Jesuit schools, and an Aristotelian philosophy and Thomistic theology on the other, for the second and third stages.[58] Yet the election for Aquinas in theology fits quite well with Ignatius's decision to make "Aristotelian philosophy the main constituent of the entire program of arts in the universities he was to found,"[59] as George Ganss, SJ, points out, especially given the degree to which Aquinas works to synthesize Aristotelian doctrines with Christian revelation. Aristotle received much prominence in the philosophy curriculum of the early Jesuit schools. The eminent scholar of the Aristotelian commentatorial tradition, Charles Lohr, SJ, speaks of a "Jesuit Aristotelianism."[60] He points out that it was also Nadal, who completed a brief tract, *De studiis Societatis*, while rector of the first Jesuit college at Messina in the 1540s, that was to serve as the draft of the *Ratio studiorum*. This tract includes an extensive list of texts from Aristotle that were to be used. This list would be familiar to any student enrolled at an arts faculty in a medieval university. Furthermore, the medieval practice of commenting on Peter Lombard's *Sentences* in theology was abandoned quite early among the Jesuits in favor of the *Summa Theologiae*.[61] Dulles summarizes the work of the Jesuits in what

57. O'Malley, *First Jesuits*, 242.

58. O'Malley thinks it is "a compatibility vaguely adumbrated in the 'Rules for Thinking with the Church.'" *First Jesuits*, 226. Cf. Ignatius, *Spiritual Exercises*, nos. 363 and 242.

59. George Ganss, SJ, *Saint Ignatius' Idea of a Jesuit University: A Study in the History of Catholic Education* (Milwaukee: Marquette University Press, 1956), 15.

60. Charles Lohr, SJ, "Jesuit Aristotelianism and Sixteenth-Century Metaphysics," in *Paradosis: Studies in Memory of Edwin A. Quain* (New York: Fordham University Press, 1976), 203–20. Jerome Nadal, SJ, completed a brief tract, *De studiis Societatis*, while rector of the college at Messina, indicating the texts from Aristotle to be used: logic, Porphyry's *Introduction* and Aristotle's logical works; natural philosophy, Aristotle, *Physics*, *De caelo et mundo*, *De generatione et corruptione*, *Meteora*, *De anima*, *Metaphysics*; moral philosophy, *Nicomachean Ethics*. This list gets repeated many times, as Lohr points out: Constitutions of the University of Gandia 1549/50; Nadal tract of 1552, *De studii generalis dispositione et ordine* (MPL 143); Martin Olave, SJ, instruction of 1553; Diego Ledesma, *De atrium liberalium studiis* (1570/71).

61. As early as 1571 in Dillingen, Jesuits started commenting on Aquinas's *Summa Theologiae* as the textbook in theology. Ulrich G. Leinsle, *Introduction to Scholastic Theology*, trans. Michael J. Miller (Washington, DC: Catholic University of America Press, 2010), 294.

he calls "the age of Trent" (from about 1550 to the late eighteenth century): "In the sixteenth century theology was in disarray because medieval scholasticism had been devastated by the mockery of the humanists and hostility of the Protestant reformers. The Jesuits together with the Dominicans, were the primary architects of a new, updated scholasticism in which discipline and order were restored."[62] This investigation of the congruity between Ignatius spirituality and Thomism sheds light on the educational system developed by Ignatius.

Conclusion: Finding God in All Things

This essay has considered Ignatius as a theologian in the context of the Thomistic tradition. It first examined evidence for understanding Ignatius as a Thomist. Then it turned to three doctrines central to classical Thomism in order to test the congruence between Ignatius's *Exercises* and Thomism. Finally, this essay has tried to indicate ways in which the Thomism of Ignatius provides the intellectual foundation for the humanism of Jesuit education—a humanism that endeavors to synthesize the humanism of the Renaissance and that of Scholasticism.

Ignatius strikes a balance between the antinomies of the spiritual life: between contemplation and action, nature and grace, freedom and predestination. Ignatius also strikes a balance between the objective and subjective dimensions of the spiritual life: both what God has done for us in creation and salvation history and what he is doing for us in the movements of the soul. God is working within and without, in the order of nature and the order of grace. It is but for the human being to recognize this "principle and foundation" of reality and of the spiritual life and so to "find God in all things." "And there are diversities of operations, but the same God, who worketh all in all" (1 Cor 12:6).

62. Dulles, "Jesuits and Theology," 537.

THOMAS AQUINAS'S

DE PRAEDESTINATIONE

AS CONFESSIO

Barry David

To hope for all souls is imperative; and it is quite tenable that their salvation is inevitable. It is tenable, but it is not specially favorable to activity or progress.

G. K. Chesterton

Introduction

This essay analyzes Thomas Aquinas's teaching on divine predestination in the *Summa Theologiae* (*ST*) I, q. 21, a. 8,[1] ostensibly his "final deci-

Epigraph. G. K. Chesterton, *Orthodoxy* (New York: Doubleday, 1908/1936/1990), 135.

1. For analysis of Thomas's teaching in *ST* I, q. 23, aa. 1–8, see M. M. Adams, "The Problem of Hell: A Problem of Evil for Christians," in *A Reasoned Faith*, ed. E. Stump (Ithaca, NY: Cornell University Press, 1993), 301–27, 304–5; S. Bulgakov, *The Bride of the Lamb*, trans. B. Jakim (Grand Rapids, MI: W.B. Eerdmans, 2002), 216–17; J. Dool, "Predestination, Freedom, and the Logic of Love," *Logos* 11, no. 3 (2008): 105–25; R. Garrigou-Lagrange, *Predestination*, trans. Dom B. Rose (Charlotte, NC: Tan Books, 1939, 1998), 70–89, 183–220; N. Healy, "Creation, Predestination, and Divine Providence," in *The Providence of God*, ed. F. A. Murphy and P. G. Zeigler (London: T&T Clark, 2009), 208–28, 222–26; M. Levering, *Predestination: Biblical and Theological Paths* (New York: Oxford University Press, 2011), 79–81; and M. Paluch, *La Profondeur de l'Amour Divin: Évolution de la Doctrine de la Pre-*

sion on the question,"[2] by relating it to rival teachings on predestination
upholding contrary accounts of predestination's ultimate outcome while

---

destination dans l'Oeuvre de Saint Thomas d'Aquin (Paris: J. Vrin, 2004), 189–235, 246–47.
While Garrigou-Lagrange finds Thomas's predestinarian teaching compelling insofar as it
upholds the absolute primacy of divine predilection/love (Predestination, 75, 78), whereby
the related threats of Pelagianism and semi-Pelagianism can be vanquished (Predestination,
187–91), the other commentators cited above concur concerning the primacy of divine predilection in predestinarian teaching. But they maintain that Thomas applies this principle
only narrowly (e.g., Dool, "Predestination, Freedom, and Love," 121–24; Levering, Predestination, 83). Their common view is that Thomas's doctrine of predestination in ST I, q. 23, aa.
1–8, effectively denies God a universal salvific will; i.e., it denies that everyman has the
opportunity to attain bliss. This essay agrees that Thomas's teaching on predestination is
vitiated by a truncated notion of God's love but considers it in terms of a significant tension
within Thomas's theological method of confessio. Therefore, in light of defining confessio
as man's/imago dei's right relationship with God and neighbor, consisting in his coordi-
nate acknowledgment of ontological dependence on divine goodness/love and response of
gratitude to God, I claim that Thomas's teaching on predestination in ST I, q. 23, aa. 1–8, is
informed by unduly restricted doctrines of divine goodness and human love.

2. Garrigou-Lagrange, Predestination, 70. According to J. P. Torrell, Saint Thomas Aquinas, vol. 1, The Person and His Work, trans. R. Royal (Washington, DC: Catholic University
of America Press, 1996), 328, 333, Thomas writes ST I, q. 23, aa. 1–8, during the years 1265–67.

As this volume evinces, Thomas discusses predestination in many other parts of his corpus. This includes: (1) On Truth 6, 1–6 (~1256–59; Torrell, Saint Thomas Aquinas, 328)—for
commentary, see Paluch, La Profondeur de l'Amour Divin, 112–53; (2) ST III, q. 24, aa. 1–4,
concerning Christ's predestination (~1272–73; Torrell, Saint Thomas Aquinas, 329)—for recent analysis, see R. Nutt, "From Eternal Sonship to Adoptive Filiation: St. Thomas on the
Predestination of Christ," chap. 3, this volume; (3) Commentary on the Letter of Saint Paul to
the Romans, 8.6–9 (~1263–68; Torrell, Saint Thomas Aquinas, 328, 340)—for recent study, see
M. Levering, "Aquinas on Romans 8: Predestination in Context," in Reading Romans with
St. Thomas Aquinas (Washington, DC: Catholic University of America Press, 2012), 196–215;
(4) Commentary on St. Paul's Letter to the Ephesians, 1,1 (~1263–68; Torrell, Saint Thomas
Aquinas, 328, 340)—for discussion, see M. Dauphinais's "Predestination as the Communication of Divine Goodness in Aquinas's Commentary on Ephesians," chap. 5, this volume;
and (5) Literal Exposition on Job (~1263–65; Torrell, Saint Thomas Aquinas, 328)—for recent
commentary, see M. Levering, "Aquinas on the Book of Job: Providence and Presumption,"
in Reading Romans with St. Thomas Aquinas, 7–33. See also M. Levering, "Predestination in
John 13–17? Aquinas's Commentary on John and Contemporary Exegesis," The Thomist 75,
no. 3 (2011): 393–414.

General studies of Thomas's teaching on predestination include: Bulgakov, Bride of the
Lamb, 215–17; M. J. Farrelly, Predestination, Grace, and Free Will (Westminster, MD: New-
man Press, 1964), 114–21; Garrigou-Lagrange, Predestination; H. Goris, "Divine Foreknowl-
edge, Providence, Predestination, and Human Freedom," in The Theology of Thomas Aqui-
nas, ed. R. Van Nieuwenhove and J. Wawrykow (Notre Dame, IN: University of Notre Dame
Press, 2005), 99–122; D. B. Hart, "Providence and Causality: On Divine Innocence," in The
Providence of God, ed. F. A. Murphy and P. G. Zeigler (London: T&T Clark, 2009), 34–56;
Healy, "Creation, Predestination, and Divine Providence," Hick, Evil and the God of Love
(New York: Palgrave Macmillan, 1966/2007/2010), 93–114, 169–98; Levering, Predestination,
9–11, 75–83, 96–97, 188–92, 194–201; M. McCarthy, Recent Developments in the Theology of
Predestination (Rome: Pontifical Lateran University, 1995), 31–63; M. G. Most, Grace, Pre-

sharing a similar methodology. On this basis, three claims are distinguished: (1) that the entire human race attains eternal bliss;[3] (2) that a

---

destination, and the Salvific Will of God: New Answers to Old Questions* (Front Royal, VA: Christendom Press, 1997), 305–38; Paluch, *La Profondeur de l'Amour Divin*; and H. U. Von Balthasar, *Dare We Hope "That All Men Be Saved"? With a Short Discourse on Hell*, 2nd ed., trans. D. Kipp and L. Krauth (San Francisco: Ignatius Press, 1988/2014), 54–63, 160–62, 204.

   3. Some contemporary Christian theologians and philosophers of religion claim that Christianity (variously understood) mandates that all humans attain eternal bliss. Among the theologians are Bulgakov, *Bride of the Lamb*, 482–526; D. B. Hart, *Atheist Delusions: The Christian Revolution and Its Fashionable Enemies* (New Haven, CT: Yale University Press, 2009), 154; idem, "Providence and Causality: On Divine Innocence," 34–56, 46–50; and J. Moltmann, *The Coming of God: Christian Eschatology*, trans. M. Kohl (Minneapolis, MN: Fortress, 1996), 235–55.

   Recent philosophers claiming an eschatological outcome of universal salvation include especially Hick, *Evil and the God of Love*, 337–64; and Adams, "Problem of Hell," 301–27. These thinkers assert, to varying degrees, that God's Irenaean-like person-making project entails both that God is directly responsible for moral and natural evil and that his project terminates in universal salvation. Another group of philosophers upholds universal salvation as a corollary to the doctrine that God is self-sufficient, goodness/love, omnipotence, omniscience, and wisdom. This perspective is shared by: T. Talbot, "The Doctrine of Everlasting Punishment," *Faith and Philosophy* 7 (1990): 19–42; idem, "Freedom, Damnation, and the Power to Sin with Impunity," *Religious Studies* 37 (2001): 417–34; idem, "Towards a Better Understanding of Universalism," "Christ Victorious," "A Pauline Interpretation of Divine Judgement," and "Reply to My Critics," in *Universal Salvation? The Current Debate*, ed. R. A. Parry and C. H. Partridge (Grand Rapids, MI: W. B. Eerdman, 2003), 3–14, 15–31, 32–52, 247–73; idem, "Universalism," in *The Oxford Handbook of Eschatology*, ed. Jerry Walls (New York: Oxford University Press, 2007), 446–61; E. Reitan, "Universalism and Autonomy: Towards a Comparative Defense of Universalism," *Faith and Philosophy* 18 (2001): 222–40; idem, "Eternal Damnation and Blessed Ignorance: Is the Damnation of Some Incompatible with the Salvation of Any?" *Religious Studies* 38, no. 4 (2002): 429–50; idem, "Human Freedom and the Impossibility of Eternal Damnation," in *Universal Salvation?*, 125–42; and J. Kronen and E. Reitan, *God's Final Victory: A Comparative Philosophical Case for Universalism* (New York: Bloomsbury, 2013).

   I do not include in group A earlier thinkers like Origen (185–254 AD); Gregory of Nyssa (332–98 AD); Gregory of Nazianzus, Bishop of Constantinople (329/30–90 AD); Maximus the Confessor (~580–662 AD); and Eriugena (~815–77 AD) or recent thinkers like K. Barth (1886–1968) and Von Balthasar (1905–88), with whom the doctrine of universal salvation is commonly associated. This is because recent scholarship debates whether any of those thinkers uphold universal salvation as a certitude. It is evident, however, that they imply or consider the possibility of such an outcome. For diverse opinions on the meaning of "universalist" claims in the aforementioned thinkers, see, e.g., M. Ludlow, "Universalism in the History of Christianity," in *Universal Salvation?*, 191–218; D. Hilborn and D. Horrocks, "Universalistic Trends in the Evangelical Tradition: An Historical Perspective," in *Universal Salvation?*, 219–44; Levering, *Predestination*, 1–4, 29–35, 38–44, 65–67, 135–54, 162–76, 192–97; and Von Balthasar, *Dare We Hope*, 18–53, 64–88, 129–35, 181–204. For insightful commentary on the relationship between Von Balthasar's and Thomas's view on "hoping for the salvation of all," see J. G. Trabbic, "Can Aquinas Hope 'That All Men Be Saved?,'" *Heythrop Journal* 57 (2016): 337–58.

majority of the race, and possibly the entirety, attains bliss;[4] and (3) that,

4. I comprise group B from (see note 4 above) Origen, Gregory of Nyssa, Bishop Gregory of Nazianzus Eriugena, Barth, and Von Balthasar—and to this I add Chesterton (1874–1936; see note 1 above), Pope John Paul II (1978–2005), Pope Benedict XVI (2005–13), and Levering, *Predestination*.

Within *Crossing the Threshold of Hope*, trans. J. and M. McPhee, ed. V. Messori (Toronto: Alfred A. Knopf, 1994), John Paul II (aka Karol Wojtyla, 1920–2005) shares Chesterton's emphasis on man's right practical response to God by concluding his discussion of hell by citing, on the one hand, the biblical teaching on "the *purifying fire*" and, on the other, the Church's requirement to preserve "its eschatological awareness" to lead "man to eternal life" (186–87). In the former regard, however, John Paul II writes that "the 'living flame of love'... is above all a purifying fire.... God makes man pass through such an interior purgatory of his sensual and spiritual nature in order to bring him into union with Himself. Here we do not find ourselves before a mere tribunal. We present ourselves before the power of Love itself. Before all else it is Love that judges. God, who is Love, judges through love. It is Love that demands purification, before man can be made ready for that union with God which is his ultimate vocation and destiny" (186–87). See also Healy, "Creation, Predestination, and Divine Providence," 224–25.

For his part, Pope Benedict XVI (aka Joseph Ratzinger, b. 1927) echoes John Paul II's account of the purifying fire in his encyclical letter *Spe Salvi* (November 2007). Sounding much like his predecessor, he writes: "Some recent theologians are of the opinion that the fire which both burns and saves is Christ Himself, the Judge and Savior. The encounter with him is the decisive act of judgement. Before his gaze all falsehood melts away. This encounter with him, as it burns us, transforms and frees us, allowing us to become truly ourselves. All that we build during our lives can prove to be mere straw, pure bluster, and it collapses. Yet in the pain of this encounter, when the impurity and sickness of our lives become evident to us, there lies salvation. His gaze, the touch of his heart heals us through an undeniably painful transformation 'as through fire.' But it is a blessed pain, in which the holy power of his love sears through us like a flame, enabling us to become totally ourselves and thus totally of God" (http://w2.vatican.va/content/benedict-xvi/en/encyclicals/documents/hf_ben-xvi_enc_20071130_spe-salvi.html, section 47, p. 25). See also Healy, "Creation, Predestination, and Divine Providence," 226.

Group B also includes Levering's *Predestination* because his doctrine implies the possibility of an eschatological outcome anywhere from minority to universal salvation. *Predestination*'s principal point is that the biblical, especially New Testament, teaching on predestination includes (1) that God offers the entire human race, i.e., each human individual, the *opportunity* for salvation and (2) that some will ultimately refuse his offer and thereby suffer unending torment. In other words, although only some humans will attain salvation, God somehow offers to every person, rather than (contra Augustine and Aquinas) to only some, the opportunity to attain salvation. Levering argues, therefore, that a properly biblical approach to predestination upholds two conflicting truths (cf. Most, *Grace, Predestination, and the Salvific Will of God*, 3–4, 305–7) that are irreconcilable until "the eschaton," and have been enunciated as such in Catherine of Siena's and Francis de Sales's Thomistic-centered teachings on predestination. These two truths, properly upheld as doxological affirmations (197)—cf. Garrigou-Lagrange, *Predestination*, 221–22 (noted by Levering, *Predestination*, 198n50)—are: (1) "that God superabundantly loves each and every rational creature" and (2) that "this provident God, from whose infinite love all created goodness arises, permits the permanent free rebellion of some rational creatures" (199). Hence the key to articulating a biblical doctrine of predestination in our era rests in "retrieving Catherine's and Francis's

as Aquinas insists, only a minority of the race attains bliss. According to Garrigou-Lagrange, it is "the common opinion of the Fathers and early theologians that the majority of human beings are not saved." [5]

---

perspective, rooted in Aquinas's theocentric theology" (200). Cf. Most, *Grace, Predestination, and the Salvific Will of God*, 629. Until the *eschaton*, then, Bible-centered theologians should promulgate the aforementioned form of particular salvation.

Levering's argument implies, however, that after the *eschaton*, one of two outcomes will prevail. Either humans will then see how principles (1) and (2) are compatible (and be completely reconciled thereto) or, as the primacy of principle (1) suggests, (2) will be canceled out by (1) owing to universal salvation. *Predestination*'s principal object, then, consists in identifying and justifying the biblical message of predestination that God wants promulgated until the *eschaton*. Hence, although Levering claims that the Bible teaches particular salvation (199–200)—which means that either a minority or majority portion of the race attains salvation—his key principles imply that God might ultimately guide the race to universal salvation. I include Levering in group B rather than C on account of the fluidity of his position and its key implications. Cf. H. G. Frankfurt, "On God's Creation," in *Reasoned Faith*, 128–41. Although Frankfurt expresses significantly different views of God and humanity than Levering's, his argument can ultimately be classified in the same manner, as maintaining that God's creation of humanity is only completed when mankind willingly accepts God's law (141).

5. *Predestination*, 219. In category C, I couple Aquinas with Augustine of Hippo, e.g., *City of God* 21.12, because Aquinas's teaching on predestination is commonly classified as "Augustinian." See, e.g., Bulgakov, *Bride of the Lamb*, 212–17; Dool, "Predestination, Freedom, and the Logic of Love," 105, 111, 114; Garrigou-Lagrange, *Predestination*, 5–54, 70–84; Healy, "Creation, Predestination, and Divine Providence," 223–24; Hick, *Evil and the God of Love*, 93–114; McCarthy, *Recent Developments in the Theology of Predestination*, 1–30; Paluch, *La Profondeur de l'Amour Divin*, 190–93, 202–3, 246; and Von Balthasar, *Dare We Hope*, 54–58, 130. This essay agrees that Thomas's teaching is essentially Augustinian in terms of its (1) interpretation of Romans 8–9, (2) related accounts of the primacy of divine predilection and minority salvation, and (3) pervasive rhetorical element. But unlike other commentators, it also considers that Thomas's teaching is Augustinian because its *confessio* (or *imago dei*) methodology upholds human recognition of both the primacy of divine goodness and the practical importance of responding to God with gratitude. In that respect, I imply not only that most every doctrine of predestination is Augustinian but also that some teachings on predestination, including Augustine's, are more successful instantiations of *confessio* than others.

For extensive discussion of Augustine's doctrine of predestination, see inter alii G. Bonner, *Freedom and Necessity: St. Augustine's Teaching on Divine Power and Human Freedom* (Washington, DC: Catholic University of America Press, 2007), 17–33, 97–132; Bulgakov, *Bride of the Lamb*, 213–15; P. Cary, "Augustinian Compatibilism and the Doctrine of Election," in *Augustine and Philosophy*, ed. P. Cary, J. Doody, and K. Paffenroth (Lanham, MD: Rowman and Littlefield, 2010), 79–102; Garrigou-Lagrange, *Predestination*, 39–54; Hick, *Evil and the God of Love*, 59–69, 82–89, 169–98; Levering, *Predestination*, 44–54; idem, *The Theology of Augustine* (Grand Rapids, MI: Baker Academic, 2013), 71–87; D. J. McQueen, "Augustine on Free Will and Predestination: A Critique of J. M. Rist," *Museum: West Africa Journal of Theology* (1974): 17–28; P. Rigby, *The Theology of Augustine's Confessions* (Cambridge: Cambridge University Press, 2015), 65–199; J. M. Rist, *Augustine: Ancient Thought Baptized* (Cambridge: Cambridge University Press, 1994), 133–35, 266–89, 307–9; idem, "Au-

Why are these perspectives alike? A charity-centered approach to biblical interpretation (rooted in St. Augustine's *Confessiones* [*Conf*] 12.18.27–31.42 and its closely related *imago dei* theological anthropology [*Conf* 13.22.32]) assumes that each perspective judges that man's right relationship with God and neighbor depends on embracing a correlate (1) cognitive insight into God and human nature and (2) practical response thereto. On the one hand, *confessio* means *recognizing* both the irreducible primacy of divine goodness—that is, a self-sufficient and triune, yet Creator and Incarnate, God makes and governs humanity entirely for the latter's benefit—and the implication that human thought and action *should* therefore manifest gratitude toward God, that is, an imperative for gratitude. On the other hand, *confessio* entails the concrete practical response that man *actually* structures his thought and action to manifest divine gratitude. Therefore, although the aforementioned perspectives on predestination are regulated by *confessio*'s correlate of decisive knowledge of divine goodness *and* the practice of divine gratitude, they differ concerning its content. The first party believes that gratitude is cultivated by distinguishing an ultimately unlimited application of divine goodness; the second party maintains that gratitude is encouraged by upholding a significant, unto potentially unlimited, sharing of divine goodness; and the third party, represented in *de praedestinatione*, holds that gratitude is stimulated by a strictly limited application of divine goodness. Relying on these distinctions, I argue that although each of the aforementioned views has value, Aquinas's view is less perfect in one respect because its decisively limited account of divine goodness restricts the scope of human gratitude.

---

gustine on Free Will and Predestination," *Journal of Theological Studies* 20 (1969): 420–47; G. W. Schlabach, "Augustine's Hermeneutic of Humility: An Alternative to Moral Imperialism and Moral Relativism," *Journal of Religious Ethics* 22, no. 2 (1994): 299–330; Von Balthasar, *Dare We Hope*, 32–53; J. Wetzel, "Snares of Truth: Augustine on Free Will and Predestination," in *Augustine and His Critics*, ed. R. Dodaro and G. Lawless (London: Routledge, 2000), 124–41 (134–38); and idem, "Predestination, Pelagianism, and Foreknowledge," in *The Cambridge Companion to Augustine*, ed. E. Stump and N. Kretzmann (Cambridge: Cambridge University Press, 2001), 49–58.

While the vast majority of commentators find that Augustine's doctrine of predestination contradicts divine goodness or human responsibility, some—like McQueen, Rigby, Schlabach, and Wetzel—find salutary its emphasis on the absolute priority of divine love and the human response thereto of humility and confession (e.g., Wetzel, "Snares of Truth," 137–38; and Rigby, *Theology of Augustine's Confessions*, 147–99). No commentator claims that Augustine's concrete teaching on predestination is biblically or philosophically coherent, however; each welcomes modification.

The Metaphysics of Universal Bliss:
Key Components

The principal distinction concerning the scope of predestination will be reconsidered later in this essay.[6] For now, I concentrate on the doctrine that God's providence brings about universal bliss, because our preceding distinction shows it is both the most popular opinion and a prominent view in the contemporary era.[7] This is probably because it upholds a rigorously theocentric metaphysical perspective that is instantiated in the three related elements of human solidarity, divine goodness or love, and human responsibility. First, the claim that the entire race attains bliss upholds a robust doctrine of human solidarity, which is probably one of the foremost points of agreement between the secular and the sacred *weltanschauungs* structuring the modern era's march toward globalization.[8] It is admirable that "no one is left behind" or, put differently,

6. This section's principal argument is capable of relating together apparently rival claims made by secularists and by the Bible. On the one hand, Albert Camus writes, "if all are not saved, what good is the salvation of one only?" *The Rebel: An Essay on Man in Revolt*, trans. A Bower (New York: Vintage Books/Random House, 1956/1984, 1991), 304. On the other hand, St. Paul states, "How deep are the riches and wisdom and knowledge of God! How inscrutable his judgments, how unsearchable his ways! For 'who has known the mind of the Lord? Or who has been his counselor? Who has given him anything as to deserve return?' For from him and through him and for him all things are. To him be glory forever. Amen" (Rom 11:33–36). Although Camus and Paul disagree concerning ultimate realities, they might concur on the reasonableness of the idea of universal human salvation to the extent that the latter is implied by a coherent notion of God.

7. See, e.g., Levering, *Predestination*, 133–37, 175, who attributes the recent focus on universal salvation to a widespread desire to protect "the divine innocence." For helpful discussion of the origin and nature of contemporary teachings on predestination, see McCarthy, *Recent Developments in the Theology of Predestination*, 64–221.

8. I have in mind the apparently seminal comments on and approach to solidarity by H. de Lubac, *Catholicism: Christ and the Common Destiny of Man*, trans. L. C. Sheppard and E. Englund (San Francisco: Ignatius Press, 1947/1950/1988), 13–20, 25–81; the Vatican II document *Gaudium et Spes*, esp. Part I, cc. 1–4; and Pope John Paul II's encyclical letters *Sollicitudo Rei Socialis* (1987), paragraphs 9, 21, 23, 26, 33, 36, 38–40, 45–4, and *Laborem Exercens* (1981), paragraphs 8 and 20. See also Von Balthasar's approval of Péguy's depiction of Joan of Arc. Von Balthasar claims that Péguy "begins with the fact that every individual human being is indispensable to eternal bliss itself. All enjoy solidarity in salvation: hence no individual can be damned; thus Péguy central figure is his (fictional) Joan of Arc, who surrenders herself to damnation and fire for the salvation of all." H. U. Von Balthasar, *Theo-Drama*, vol. 4, *The Action*, trans. G. Harrison (San Francisco: Ignatius Press, 1994), 418, taken from Levering, *Predestination*, 162n121. Cf. Von Balthasar, *Dare We Hope*, 86–87. For the importance of solidarity among secular thinkers, see inter alii Camus, *The Rebel*, 13–22, 302–6; and J. P. Sartre, "Existentialism Is a Humanism," in *Essays in Existentialism* (New York:

that the human race is considered as if "one body."[9] Upholding universal bliss implies that divine election, God's predestining his Church in
time, is only temporally—and consequently only temporarily—about
"one instead of others." Perhaps following *inter alii* Paul's *Letter to the
Ephesians* (1.2–14)[10] and the Gospel of Matthew's "parable of the laborers
in the vineyard" (Mt 20:1–16),[11] there is an implied distinction between
"first fruits" and "only fruits" such that what is prior in time is ultimately
ordered toward what is common to and fully enjoyed by each in the afterlife. Hence the aforementioned first fruits are both the first of many
fruits in the order of time and, other things being equal, the first of all,
of the entire race, becoming "fruit" before the ultimate end.[12] This view

Citadel Press, 1965, 1993), 31–62, at 35–38, 50–53. Although these thinkers disagree about the
nature of an "authentic" human life, each upholds a robust doctrine concerning the biologi-
cal, psychological, and, in principle, sociopolitical unity of the human race.

9. See, e.g., Bulgakov, *Bride of the Lamb*, 266–68, 488, 515–16; Talbot, "Christ Victorious,"
in *Universal Salvation?*, 18–22; and Von Balthasar, *Dare We Hope*, 86–87.

10. Eph 1:3–14: "Praised be the God and Father of our Lord Jesus Christ, who has bestowed on us in Christ every spiritual blessing in the heavens. God chose us in him before
the world began, to be holy and blameless in his sight, to be full of love, he likewise predestined us through Christ Jesus to be his adopted sons—such was his will and pleasure—that
all might praise the glorious favor he has bestowed on us in his beloved. It is in Christ and
through his blood that we have been redeemed and our sins forgiven, so immeasurably generous is God's favor to us. God has given us the wisdom to understand fully the mystery,
the plan he was pleased to decree in Christ, to be carried out in the fullness of time: namely
to bring all things in the heavens and on earth into one under Christ's headship. In him we
were chosen; for in the decree of God, who administers everything according to his will and
counsel, we were predestined to praise his glory by being the first to hope in Christ." All
biblical quotations are from the New American Bible.

11. Mt 20:1–16: "*The Laborers in the Vineyard*. 'The reign of God is like the case of the
owner of an estate who went out at dawn to hire workmen for his vineyard. ... I am free to
do as I please with my money, am I not? Or are you envious because I am generous?' Thus
the last shall be first and the first shall be last."

12. For analysis, see Talbot, "Christ Victorious," in *Universal Salvation?*, 25–27. Commenting on 1 Cor 15:22–24 to support his preceding interpretation of Rom 5 (18–22), Talbot
claims that there is a three-step process wherein all become alive in Christ. He writes, "It
is as if Paul had in mind a procession or a parade, and he quickly listed three segments of
the procession: At the head...is Christ, the first fruits; behind him are those who belong to
Christ at his coming; and behind them are 'the remainder'—that is, those at the end of the
procession—who are there when Christ 'hands over the kingdom to God the Father, after he
has destroyed every ruler and every authority and power' (v. 24)" (26). For a contrary view,
see I. H. Marshall, "The New Testament Does *Not* Teach Universal Salvation," in *Universal
Salvation*, 55–76, at 64–65, 69–70, 72–74. According to Marshall, Talbot's mistaken claim
about universalism entails misinterpretation of the relevant biblical text. Nevertheless, even
if Talbot misjudges Rom 5, universalism requires that some are converted to Christ in the
afterlife or after his return in glory and last judgment. On this point, see Bulgakov, *Bride of
the Lamb*, 466–526; and Moltmann, *Coming of God*, 250–339.

is not only that divine election leads to bliss *and* that these elect shall attain bliss, but also that nonelection, in a way, leads to bliss. Therefore providence employs election and, in some manner, nonelection to bring about the salvation of all. According to this view, election does not mean "one instead of others" or "one for the sake of some others" but "one for the sake of all others."[13] Moreover, because election precedes salvation, it seems that those elected in history—that is, *before the afterlife, somehow, in and through God's goodness*—help in the eventual conversion of those not elected in history.[14] In other words, those in whom salvation is explicitly begun before the afterlife play a decisive role in the explicit beginning of salvation in those having that beginning in the afterlife. Therefore, because the entire race is predestined to bliss, some can know and love that before the afterlife while the rest will know and love it in the afterlife. As such, a distinction is made between *predestination to bliss* and *predestination to election*; while God predestines each to bliss, he only predestines some, apparently a minority, to election.

Second, theists with a decisive metaphysical bent can be well pleased by the prospect of universal bliss because there is manifested a rigorous doctrine of God as goodness or love.[15] If the self-sufficient, omnipotent, and omniscient Creator *is* love, the ultimate destiny of humanity, created in his image and likeness,[16] is to participate in his love as lovers, through his love, of his love.[17] It is obvious that inequities appear in the eschatological process on account of certain particularities pertaining to divine election. For example, why are these persons elected instead of those? Why do some taste God's mercy/goodness before others? But this can be mollified by considering, on the one hand, original sin and personal sinfulness and, on the other, the outcome of universal bliss. The reasons why only some are elected in this life and why some taste more

13. Cf. P. Cary, *Inner Grace: Augustine in the Traditions of Plato and Paul* (New York: Oxford University Press, 2008), 121–26; and R. K. Soulen, *The God of Israel and Christian Theology* (Minneapolis, MN: Fortress Press, 1996), 114–40.

14. For discussion of conversion after this life and after this "world" ends, see Bulgakov, *Bride of the Lamb*, 500–526; Hick, *Evil and the God of Love*, 345–64, 374–76; and Kronen and Reitan, *God's Final Victory*, 3.

15. See, e.g., Bulgakov, *Bride of the Lamb*, 47–49, 127–29; Dool, "Predestination, Freedom, and the Logic of Love," 115–24; and Levering, *Predestination*, 187–92, 195–201.

16. See *inter alii* Gen 1:26–27; Augustine, *Confessions*, 13.22.32; and *ST* I, q. 45, a. 7.

17. See Bulgakov, *Bride of the Lamb*, 507; Dool, "Predestination, Freedom, and the Logic of Love," 123–24; and John Paul II and Benedict XVI, as cited above in note 5.

of God's goodness "before" others can largely be explained by original sin and personal sinfulness obstructing, but not completely blocking, divine goodness.[18] Most importantly, because the entire race attains bliss, the aforementioned particularities pertaining to election are ultimately relative, that is, merely historical rather than absolute or eternal. Because those particularities are consequent upon human sinfulness, the infinite God uses them to bring about his end goal of universal bliss.

Third, belief in universal bliss implies a rational account of human responsibility. Because man owes his being to God's goodness, his proper response to God consists in gratitude and he is helped in this by divine goodness.[19] If man is not grateful, it is, as original sin and personal sinfulness makes clear, his own fault; however, he can become grateful by cooperating with divine goodness in this life and *will become* grateful by cooperating in the afterlife.[20] Hence the relationship between divine goodness and human responsibility ultimately matches up with understanding God as ineffable first cause and man as secondary, participating cause.

An interesting result of the above emphases, moreover, is that divine predestination is squarely identified with God's providential governance of humanity. Unlike claims by Augustine of Hippo (e.g., *City of God* [CG] 21.12) and Thomas Aquinas (e.g., *de praedestinatione*) that predestination (like reprobation) is a species of God's providence for humanity, here predestination, and consequently the eschatological outcome of universal bliss, is the same as God's plan for the human race. My principal point at this juncture, however, is that some find congenial the eschatology of universal bliss because it upholds a satisfying metaphysical account of God and man. In accord with a variety of authoritative theocentric teachings,[21] *belief* in universal bliss embraces God as self-sufficient yet

---

18. Another objective reason is that the nature of the human race, as Augustine notices (see *CG* 12.22–23), is developmental so that it attains its ultimate number and wisdom by way of communal development. So, there would always have been temporal distinctions requiring that some human persons share in God's goodness "before" and "after" others. If, from the beginning, the race was originally slated for linear progress, temporal distinctions would be a necessary part of the divine plan to bring the race to fulfillment.

19. See Dool, "Predestination, Freedom, and the Logic of Love," 107–9.

20. See note 16 above.

21. I have in mind the many creedal definitions of the nature of and relationship between the divine and human natures of Christ (e.g., the Creed of Chalcedon [451 AD]) and the nature and relationship of the divine persons comprising the Godhead (e.g., the Nicene Creed [325 AD]).

sine qua non Creator and first cause (i.e., as irreducible divine goodness/ love) and human responsibility, both for the individual and for the race, as secondary, since created and consequently cooperative cause.

Put differently, the account of universal bliss distinguished above can satisfy a rigorously theocentric study of God and humanity because it embraces the ineffable God-in-himself as the irreducible first principle or paradigm whereby humanity is interpreted.[22] The eschatological relationship between God and man is judged according to the structure of the Godhead—as proceeding from and returning to God, so that the entirety is "from Him, and through Him, and for Him."[23] By contrast, those opposing a teaching of universal bliss interpret the God–man relationship either by a nontheocentric paradigm combining theocentrism and non-

22. On this point, see Hart, "Providence and Causality," 36–37, 46–50; and Thomas's illuminating analysis of Lombard's *Sentences*, Book 4, 49, 1.3, reply to query 1 ("Does everyone desire bliss?"). Thomas writes: "And because all things issue from God in so far as he is good...everything created tends to desire good in the way appropriate to it, according to the imprint it receives from its creator. And so things describe a sort of circle (*quaedam circulatio*), coming out from good and tending towards it (*a bono egredientia, in bonum tendunt*), a circle completed in certain creatures (*Haec...circulatio in quibusdam perficitur creaturis*) but remaining incomplete in others. For creatures not ordered towards contact with the first good from which they have come out, but only to a sort of imitation of him, don't complete the circle (*non perfecte habent hanc circulationem*); but reasoning creatures—the only creatures who can come into a sort of contact with their first beginning itself—do. They attain God through knowledge and love, and in that attainment bliss consists." T. McDermott, trans., *Selected Philosophical Writings* (Oxford: Oxford University Press, 1993), 336–37 (Latin is added). In this context, Thomas's teaching is theocentric because the created order is considered in light of God-in-himself. What is not God is created, and therefore (because every effect is like its cause) objectively from and back to him, and persons are especially so, being directly from and back to him. In this passage, Thomas states what universalism upholds as the objective structure of created reality; Thomas does not claim, however, that this is how the human race's relationship with God always or inevitably works.

In any event, it is evident that Thomistic metaphysics includes a decidedly theocentric approach to being wherein a teaching of universal salvation can be grounded and (looking toward the remainder of this essay) has at hand the principal conceptual resources to furnish a more reasonable account of divine predestination than Thomas offers in *ST* I, q. 23, aa. 1–8. That said, it is also compelling to consider the reasons for which *ST* I, q. 23, rejects these possibilities. This is especially so in light of the fact (which I consider later) that Thomas structures his *Summa Theologiae* by the aforesaid *exitus-reditus* pattern. For commentary on *ST*'s *exitus-reditus* pattern, see inter alii: W. J. Hankey, *God in Himself: Aquinas' Doctrine of God as Expounded in the Summa Theologiae* (New York: Oxford University Press, 1987), 8–17, 29–35, 141–42; and D. J. Merriell, "Trinitarian Anthropology," in *Theology of Thomas Aquinas*, 123–42, 123.

23. Rom 11:36. Cf. Moltmann's comments (*Coming of God,* 263) concerning Thomas's teaching on the *exitus-reditus* structure of divine creating; Moltmann draws the inference that "the time of the world as a whole takes the form of the *circulatio*, the circle."

theocentrism or by a strictly nontheocentric paradigm. These paradigms maintain either that man cannot attain eternal bliss[24] or that one portion of humanity attains bliss on account of God's primary causality while the other portion does not because it, rather than God, exercises primary causality.[25] Each view contradicts a consistently theocentric account of the nature of and relationship between God and humanity.

St. Thomas Aquinas's *De Praedestinatione*

We analyze St. Thomas's teaching in *ST* I, q. 23, aa. 1–8,[26] by commencing with its challenging doctrine of reprobation.[27] In *ST* I, q. 23, a. 3, and onward, Thomas claims that God reprobates some men; he ordains that the race's majority maintains an unrepentant sinful disposition and terminates, for that reason, in eternal hell. Taking as its analogue the immediately previous teaching on divine providence (*ST* I, q. 22, aa. 1–4),[28]

24. I refer to ancient pagan philosophy generally and, minimally, to empiricist currents within modern and contemporary philosophy standing in the tradition of Hume.

25. This is implied by any teaching on predestination that denies universal salvation. Bulgakov, *Bride of the Lamb*, 483, writes that "the final accomplishment therefore includes an ontological failure, precisely in its dualistic character: alongside the eternity of the kingdom of God, one affirms the equal eternity of hell. The world is therefore a failure. God's Wisdom has stopped impotently before an insuperable boundary set by creaturely freedom."

26. All English translations and Latin citations of the *Summa* are taken from the Benzinger Brothers edition, 1947, translated by Fathers of the English Dominican Province.

27. In a decisive way, Thomas's teaching on predestination in *ST* I, q. 23, aa. 1–8, instantiates the view of Christ's last judgment expressed in Mt 25:41–46. "Then he will say to those on his left: 'Out of my sight, you condemned, into that everlasting fire prepared for the devil and his angels!' ... These will go off to eternal punishment and the just to eternal life." While this section considers Thomas's *de praedestinatione* from a metaphysical perspective, subsequent sections will study his argument's biblical orientation.

28. Thomas claimed that providence, consisting in God's *prudential* plan whereby God orders his creation to its end of sharing in his goodness (*ST* I, q. 22, a. 1), is properly ordered to "the good of the whole" *bonum totius* or to God's "plan of universal nature" *de intentione naturae universalis* (*ST* I, q. 22, a. 2, ad 2). Unlike a provider for a particular thing, who will endeavor to keep his object from suffering defect "as far as he can," God permits certain objects to suffer defects beneath his providence because his principal goal is the universal good. So, God "allows some little defect to remain lest the good of the whole should be hindered" (*ST* I, q. 22, a. 2, ad 2).

Thomas's analogy is helpful, but the relationship between his analogues, viz., a creature and God, is decidedly narrow—rather than properly wide as had been made clear in *ST* I, q. 22, a. 2, ad 1–2—especially in *ST* I, q. 2, a. 2, ad 3, and in *ST* I, q. 13, a. 5. Thus far, Thomas presents God as if God is "one being among beings"—and, as *ST* I, q. 23, aa. 1–8, shows, this will lead to the erroneous view that man, who is really *imago dei* (*ST* I, q. 45, a. 7), is likewise "one being among beings."

Nevertheless, on the basis of his original analogy, Thomas adds that because divine creation includes generable and corruptible natures, it follows that God ordains the corruption of some natures to effect the "perfect good of the universe" *bonum universi perfectum*, viz., for the generation and perpetuation of other natures. Implying that God employs something akin to the principle of double effect, Thomas writes: "Since God, then, provides universally for all being, it belongs to His providence to permit certain defects in particular effects, that the perfect good of the universe may not be hindered, for if all evil were prevented, much good would be absent from the universe. A lion would cease to live, if there were no slaying of animals; and there would be no patience of martyrs if there no tyrannical persecution" (*ST* I, q. 22, a. 2, ad 2; cf. *ST* I, q. 47, a. 2, ad 2, and *ST* I, q. 48, a. 2, ad 3).

As the last phrase shows, Thomas extends his claim from natural to moral evil, asserting that moral evil is permitted for the sake of manifesting the virtue of patience. In other words, God permits evil acts to ensure that the universal good includes, in general, the good of virtue and, in particular, the virtue of patience. Consequently, just as God permits certain natural defects for the universal good, he permits certain moral defects for that same end. Preparing for his subsequent discussion of *predestination* in *ST* I, q. 23, aa. 1–8, Thomas adds that God's relationship with the just differs from his relationship with the wicked. Although "everything happening from the exercise of free will must be subject to divine providence" so that "human providence is included under the providence of God as a particular under a universal cause," God exercises his providence over the just in a more excellent way than over the wicked. Whereas in the one case "He prevents anything happening which would impede their final salvation," in the other case he is said to "abandon" the wicked (*dicitur eos dimittere*) because "He does not restrain the wicked from the evil of sin" *quod impios non retrahit a malo culpae* (*ST* I, q. 22, a. 2, ad 4).

Thomas teaches, then, that God's providential governance of humanity is a species within his overall providence so that what pertains to the latter pertains to the former. As some natural and generable things are ordained for the sake of others, so evil acts are ordained to inspire virtuous acts and, more significantly, wicked persons are ordained to inspire the just. Therefore, as the universal good for the subhuman creation ordains individuals for the welfare of species, so the universal good for humanity ordains one part of the race, viz., the wicked, for the welfare of its opposite, viz., the just.

It is evident that Thomas's analogue for interpreting God's governance of humanity is composed of three parts: (1) God-in-himself (insofar as his willing the universal good ordains different portions of humanity, viz., the just and the wicked, to manifest the universal good), (2) fallen nature (insofar as certain individuals or species are for the sake of perpetuating certain species), and (3) fallen humanity (insofar as certain evil actions and wicked persons are meant to inspire virtuous actions and just persons). Taken all together, Thomas's analogue for interpreting God's providence for humanity is nontheocentric because it originates in his vitiated comparison of God's providence to a form of providence ostensibly exercised by a creature (see *ST* I, q. 22, a. 2, ad 2). And he builds his subsequent argument, including his doctrine of God's governance of humanity, on the aforesaid reduction of the divine nature that that analogy implies. This spoils Thomas's teaching on God's governance of humanity both in *ST* I, q. 22, a. 2, ad 2 and 4, and in *ST* I, q. 23, aa. 1–8.

Thomas's teaching on divine providence is studied inter alii by Bulgakov, *Bride of the Lamb*, 204–12; R. Garrigou-Lagrange, *Providence: God's Loving Care for Men and the Need for Confidence in Almighty God* (Rockford, IL: Tan Books, 1937/1998); Goris, "Divine Foreknowledge, Providence, Predestination, and Human Freedom"; Hick, *Evil and the God of Love*, 93–98; Hart, "Providence and Causality: On Divine Innocence"; Healy, "Creation, Predestination, and Divine Providence"; and J. Webster, "On The Theology of Providence," in *Providence of God*, 158–75.

ST I, q. 23, 3, claims that because providence permits defects in some of its subjects, defects are permitted in some of its human subjects. This means that providence predestines "those ordained to eternal salvation" *qui divinitus ordinantur in aeternam salutem* while permitting "some to fall away from that end" *aliquos ab isto fine deficere*. The latter is named reprobation (*reprobatio*), being "a part of providence in regard to those who turn aside from ... [the end of eternal life]" "pars providentiae respectu illorum qui ab hoc fine decidunt."[29] Thomas explains more about reprobation by contrasting it with its opposite. Whereas "predestination includes the will to confer grace and glory, reprobation includes the will to permit a person to fall into sin (*reprobatio includit voluntatem permittendi aliquem cadere in culpam*), and to impose the punishment of damnation on account of that sin (*et inferendi damnationis poenam pro culpa*)."[30] Moreover, while divine predestination causes what the predestined have in the present, namely, grace, and the glory they will have in the future, divine reprobation does not cause what the reprobated presently have, namely, sin, but only "what is assigned in the future—namely eternal punishment (*scilicet poenae aeternae*)."[31] Why so? Because sinning causes the sinner to be abandoned by God and "deserted by grace" *a gratia deseritur*, reprobation does not incite sinning but ordains the sinner to have an "eternal punishment" *poenae aeternae*, ultimately due to sinning,[32] because eternal damnation is the final outcome of the sinner's abuse of free will.[33]

It is evident, therefore, that whereas Thomas's analogue for the predestined is God-in-himself, that is, *theocentric*, his analogue for the reprobated is *nontheocentric* because it results from some combination of upholding fallen nature, fallen man, and God-in-himself as his interpretative paradigm. Looked at in one way, this antithesis is rooted in Thomas's account of providence in *ST* I, q. 22, a. 2, because the latter includes theocentric and nontheocentric analogues.[34] One analogue is theocentric insofar as God's action on his predestined is identical with his concern to

---

29. *ST* I, q. 23, a. 3.

30. *ST* I, q. 23, a. 3. This is a consistent implication from the immediately preceding *ST* I, q. 22, a. 2, ad 4.

31. *ST* I, q. 23, a. 3, ad 2.   32. *ST* I, q. 23, a. 3, ad 2.

33. *ST* I, q. 23, a. 3, ad 2 and 3.

34. See note 30 above for study of Thomas's doctrine of providence in *ST* I, q. 22, a. 2.

bring about the "universal good" in respect of human virtue; the opposing analogue is nontheocentric because God's action on the reprobated is
identical with his decision to elicit the universal good regarding human
vice. Viewed from the perspective of the metaphysical standard stated
before, we see that Thomas's nontheocentric analogue arises by reducing
God to the level of creature and some portion of humanity to subhuman status (see *ST* I, q. 23, a. 7).[35] Put differently, although Thomas's distinction among humanity keeps in view the reality of human sinfulness
(both original and personal) obstructing the race from its proper object,
it overlooks the objective theocentric paradigm structuring God's relationship with the race. While Thomas's focus on sin has immediate existential value, because manifesting that sinning entails self-contradiction,
a strictly theocentric perspective claims that the race's true relationship
to the universal or perfect good means it is ordained toward and ultimately established in virtue. Because sinning, by misappropriating the
divine goodness, delays rather than defeats God's plan for the race,
Thomas's subordination of a theocentric to nontheocentric paradigm has
some merit. But his teaching on eternal reprobation contradicts the natures of divine goodness and human responsibility.

On the basis of Thomas's vitiated principle of interpretation, *ST* I, q.
23, aa. 4, 5, and 7, discuss the reprobated using various nontheocentric
analogues, albeit to make different points. *ST* I, q. 23, a. 4, claims that
God withholds love and election from those he reprobates,[36] and *ST* I, q.
23, a. 5, ad 3, argues that God predestines some and reprobates others to
manifest his goodness. Using fallen nature (from *ST* I, q. 22, a. 2) as his

---

35. As Dool, "Predestination, Freedom, and the Logic of Love," 112, writes: "It...rais-
es the spectre of a God who treats some human persons in a purely instrumental way, as
though they were nothing more than a means to a greater end (or at least allows them to
become such within his providential order). The inherent value of the human person given
by God in creation seems to be at risk within Thomas's vision."

36. *ST* I, q. 23, a. 4. Thomas writes: "Predestination presupposes election (*electionem*)
in the order of reason; and election presupposes love (*dilectionem*)....the predestination of
some to eternal salvation presupposes, in the order of reason, that God wills their salvation;
and to this belong election and love:—love, inasmuch as He wills them this particular good
of eternal salvation; since to love is to wish well to anyone, as stated above...election, inasmuch as He wills this good to some in preference to others (*inquantum hoc bonum aliquibus
prae aliis vult*); since He reprobates some (*cum quosdam reprobet*), as stated above [*ST* I,
q. 22, a. 3]....In God....His will, by which in loving He wishes good to someone, is the cause
of that good possessed by some in preference to others."

analogue, Thomas claims that just as "the completion of the universe"
ad completionem universi requires different grades of being—some higher, others lower—so the human race is divided into the predestined and
the reprobated. Thereby God manifests his mercy as "sparing" *parcendo*
some (the predestined), and his justice by "punishing" *puniendo* others
(the reprobated). In other words, insofar as the universal good contains
higher and lower grades of being, it has higher and lower human responses to virtue. Then, while combining analogues of fallen man *and*
of divine goodness, Thomas completes his argument by asserting that
it is not unjust for God to prepare "unequal lots for not unequal things"
inaequalia non inaequabilus praeparat.[37] In this respect, Thomas's claim
that God's division of the race into the predestined and the reprobated
appears to rely, on the one hand, on the gratuitousness of divine goodness—strictly speaking, predestination, like being *in the first place*, is not
owed by God to any creature (it is not "granted as a debt" but "gratuitously" "si praedestinationis effectus ex debito redderetur, et non daretur ex gratia"[38])—and, on the other hand, to the fact that the race is fall-
en. Finally, *ST* I, q. 23, a. 7, ad 3, appeals to the closely related analogues
of fallen nature and fallen man to argue that a minority is predestined
to salvation. Using the first analogue, Thomas teaches that "the good exceeding the common state of nature is found in the minority." Then, relying on human society as his interpretative standard, Thomas instructs
that those having "a profound knowledge of things intelligible are a very
small minority in respect to the rest" *qui attingunt ad habendam profun-
dam scientiam intelligibilium rerum.*[39] These arguments not only show
how Thomas justifies his doctrine of reprobation by employing nontheocentric analogues, but also suggest, as I consider below, that he wishes
readers to infer that they should be extraordinarily grateful for experi-
encing predestination.

Based on a theocentric metaphysical standard, Thomas's teaching on
reprobation is unsatisfying because it contradicts the natures of divine
goodness and human responsibility. Most importantly, we note that
Thomas's account of reprobation flows from a nontheocentric analogue
taking its cue generally, from his misleading treatment of providence in

---

37. *ST* I, q. 23, a. 5, ad 3.   38. *ST* I, q. 23, a. 5, ad 3.
39. *ST* I, q. 23, a. 5, ad 3.; a. 7, ad 3.

ST I, q. 22, a. 2, and particularly, from fallen nature, fallen man, or some combination of fallen man, fallen nature, and God-in-himself. For these reasons it posits a narrow, rather than wide, analogy between God and creatures[40] and transposes this perspective on its interpretation of God's ultimate relationship with the human race. Therefore, while Thomas rightly emphasizes that human sinning is self-contradictory, his teaching that sinning brings eternal self-contradiction denies a theocentric account of the God–man relationship. This tension in Thomas's doctrine is fruitful insofar as it indicts sinning, but it is ultimately misleading because it subordinates divine goodness.

On the other hand, *de praedestinatione* also contains significant positive elements. First, Thomas's specific teaching on predestination as such is metaphysically apt because, from beginning to end, its principal analogue is theocentric. Throughout *ST* I, q. 23, aa. 1–2 and 4–8, Thomas makes it crystal clear that God is first and final cause of predestination, and human responsibility is his secondary and cooperative cause. Employing God-in-himself as analogue, *ST* I, q. 23, a. 1, argues that predestination is properly attributed to God because he alone, as providential Creator, has ordained man for an end "which exceeds all proportion and faculty of created nature" "qui excedit proportionem naturae creatae et facultatem." Accordingly, Thomas defines predestination as "the type of the...direction of a rational creature towards the end of life eternal" "ratio praedictae transmissionis creaturae rationalis in finem vitae aeternae."[41] Predestination, therefore, is a part of providence having God-in-himself, rather than fallen nature or fallen man, as analogue. *ST* I, q. 23, a. 2, depends on this theocentric perspective by arguing that predestination places the effect of being predestined in its subjects. In other words, while the plan for predestining belongs to divine "activity," the plan's effect is found in the predestined in a passive way.[42] Thomas's crucial point

---

40. See Thomas's consistent teaching in *ST* I, q. 1, a. 9, ad 3, *ST* I, q. 2, a. 2, ad 3, and *ST* I, q. 13, a. 5, that God is more unlike than like his creatures. Hence Hart, "Providence and Causality," 35, writes that "it is precisely because God is not situated within any kind of ontic continuum with the creature that we can recognize him as the ontological cause of the creature, who freely gives being to beings." Strong agreement with his point is voiced by Adams, "Problem of Hell," 308; and Dool, "Predestination, Freedom, and the Logic of Love," 107–9.

41. *ST* I, q. 23, a. 1.

42. *ST* I, q. 23, a. 2. Thomas writes: "Whence it is clear that predestination is a kind of type of the ordering of some persons towards eternal salvation, existing in the divine mind

here, following from *ST* I, q. 23, a. 1, is that God is first cause of predestination and the predestined are his effect; because God is first cause, man's proper role is responsive, cooperative, or receptive. Who can disagree with that?

Thomas continues explicating his theocentric analysis of predestination in *ST* I, q. 23, aa. 4–8. *ST* I, q. 23, a. 4, argues that God chooses or elects his predestined because he wills to them the good of eternal salvation, that is, he chooses them so that they can choose him;[43] *ST* I, q. 23, a. 5, maintains that God's predestining his elect causes the merits he foreknows in them; that is, God's choice causes them to merit because "whatsoever is in man disposing him towards salvation (*quidquid est in homine ordinans ipsum in salute*), is all included under the effect of predestination (*comprehenditur totum sub effectu praedestinationis*); even the preparation for grace."[44] *ST* I, q. 23, a. 6, argues that God's predestining "certainly and infallibly takes effect" *certissime et infalliliter consequitur sum effectum* because it includes rather than destroys the free will found in his elect.[45] *ST* I, q. 23, a. 7, maintains that God knows *certissima ratione* the exact number and identity of those he has predestined,[46] and *ST* I, q. 23, a. 8, argues that predestination can be furthered by the prayers of the saints because God's predestining determines the secondary causes and effects belonging thereto.[47]

In each of these matters, we emphasize agreement with Garrigou-

---

(*in mente divinam existens*). The execution (*executio*), however, of this order is in a passive way in the predestined (*est passive quidem in praedestinatis*), but actively in God (*active autem est in Deo*)."

43. *ST* I, q. 23, a. 4. In Thomas's words, "For by His will, by which in loving He wishes good to someone, is the cause of that good possessed by some in preference to others (*est causa quod illud bonum ab eo prae aliis habeatur*). Thus it is clear that love precedes election in the order of reason, and election precedes predestination. Whence all the predestinate are objects of election and love."

44. *ST* I, q. 23, a. 5.

45. *ST* I, q. 23, a. 6.

46. *ST* I, q. 23, a. 7. Thomas writes: "Therefore we must say that to God the number of the predestined is certain (*sit certus*), not only formally, but also materially."

47. *ST* I, q. 23, a. 8. In Thomas's words: "So, as natural effects are provided by God in such a way that natural causes are directed to bring about those natural effects, without which those effects would not happen; so the salvation of a person is predestined by God in such a way, that whatever helps that person towards salvation falls under the order of predestination (*ut etiam sub ordine praedestinationis cadat quidquid hominem promovet in salutem*); whether it be one's own prayers or those of another; or other good works, and such like, without which one would not attain to salvation."

Lagrange et al. concerning the acuity of Thomas's teaching; its unfailing emphasis on God as first cause and human responsibility as secondary, cooperative cause is eminently capable of warding off the gamut of Pelagian and semi-Pelagian criticisms.[48] Although Thomas's overall teaching on God's providential governance of humanity lacks metaphysical exactness, his doctrine of God's predestining is metaphysically apt, being correct by subalternation for upholding right understanding and encouraging right response. Thomas's doctrine of predestination, like that of reprobation, takes its cue from the preceding treatment of providence in *ST* I, q. 22, a. 2; however, Thomas's specific focus on God's governing his elect employs a properly wide, rather than narrow, analogy. In this instance, Thomas correctly emphasizes that human sinning is self-contradictory, but his teaching on the primacy of divine goodness/mercy upholds the essence of the God–man relationship. Consequently, question 23's doctrine of predestination as such is both accurate and fruitful insofar as it indicts sinning while subordinating it to the divine goodness.

This leads to my next point: the name *de praedestinatione* signifies that Thomas's formal object in *ST* I, q. 23, aa. 1–8, is God's predestining and, through that, the effects thereby caused in its subjects. Thomas's topic is therefore theological before it is anthropological; it concerns the self-sufficient God who, as *ST* I, q. 19, aa. 2–3, shows, creates by suppositional rather than by absolute necessity.[49] So, *ST* I, q. 23, aa. 1–8's specific teachings on reprobation and final eschatology are essentially secondary, functioning as side dishes or *antitheses* highlighting the central doctrine of *ST* I, q. 23, aa. 1–8. This means that Thomas's thoughts on those matters have something of a rhetorical role by allowing him to distinguish the nature of predestination *through contrasting* the privileged status of God's elect with the ignominious status of the reprobated. While the party to and for whom Thomas writes, namely, "beginners in theology"[50]

---

48. See Garrigou-Lagrange, *Predestination*, 183–93; and Paluch, *La Profondeur de l'Amour Divin*, 202–3.

49. *ST* I, q. 19, a. 3. Thomas writes: "Hence, since the goodness of God is perfect, and can exist without other things inasmuch as no perfection can accrue to Him from them, it follow that His willing things apart from Himself is not absolutely necessary (*non sit necessarium absolute*). Yet it can be necessary by supposition (*necessarium est ex suppositione*), for supposing that He wills a thing, then He is unable not to will it, as His will cannot change."

50. See *ST* I, prologue. Thomas writes: "Because the Master of Catholic Truth ought not only to teach the proficient, but also to instruct beginners (*incipientes*) (according to the

(an elite minority in medieval society; see *ST* I, q. 23, a. 7, ad 3),[51] owes its origin and sharing in beatitude to God's merciful predestination (*ST* I, q. 23, aa. 1–8), the nonpredestined owe their unhappy origin and ultimate destiny to rejecting God (*ST* I, q. 23, a. 3). It is obvious that Thomas endeavors to encourage his *reader* in the all-important divine gratitude. In fact, *ST* I, q. 23, a. 7, claims that God ordains the reprobate to encourage his elect;[52] as noted above, *ST* I, q. 23, a. 7, ad 3, strongly implies that God's elect should be extraordinarily grateful for his gratuitous mercy upon them.[53] Thomas here employs contrast and comparison, that is, antitheses, for rhetorical purpose to show that because predestination is entirely gratuitous, it should evoke a response of gratitude in its recipients.

Moreover, a glance both at Thomas's inheritance and at *ST* gives evidence for *de praedestinatione*'s rhetorical element. In the first place, Aristotle makes the general point in *Rhetoric* 3.9–11 that antithesis is a formidable mode of persuasion to virtue.[54] And this approach colors Thomas's fundamental method in *ST*. As fine scholars like W. J. Hankey have shown, the entire *ST*, containing each particular question and article, has an *exitus-reditus* structure imitative of the processions structuring the Godhead.[55] We note that within this overarching pattern up-

---

Apostle...*I Cor.* iii. 1, 2), we purpose in this book to treat of whatever belongs to the Christian Religion, in such a way as may tend to the instruction of beginners (*ad eruditionem incipientium*)." For helpful commentary on Thomas's intention to write for "beginners," see Torrell, *Saint Thomas Aquinas*, 142–46; for consideration of how this affected Thomas's approach to predestination, see Paluch, *La Profondeur de l'Amour Divin*, 197.

51. There is an implied parallel between the nature of Thomas's audience and his claim in *ST* I, q. 23, a. 7, ad 3, that "they who attain to a profound knowledge of things intelligible are a very small minority in respect to the rest." It is likely that Thomas intends this parallel to encourage his audience in divine gratitude because these persons are privileged to be both learned and Christian.

52. *ST* I, q. 23, a. 7. Thomas writes: "It is not exactly the same thing in the case of the number of the reprobate, who would seem to be pre-ordained by God for the good of the elect (*qui videntur esse praeordinati a Deo in bonum electorum*), in whose regard 'all things work together unto good' (Rm 8:28)."

53. *ST* I, q. 23, a. 7, ad 3. In Thomas's words, "The good that exceeds the common state of nature is to be found in the minority, and is wanting in the majority.... Since their eternal happiness, consisting in the vision of God, exceeds the common state of nature...those who are saved are in the minority. In this especially, however, appears the mercy of God (*in hoc etiam maxime misericordia Dei apparet*), that He has chosen some for that salvation, from which very many in accordance with the common course and tendency of nature fall short (*quod aliquos in illam salute erigit, a qua plurimi deficient secundum commune cursum et inclinationem naturae*)."

54. Aristotle, *Rhetoric*, 3.9–11 (1410a–12b).

55. Hankey, *God in Himself*, 8–17, 29–35, 141–42. Cf. Merriell, "Trinitarian Anthropology,"

holding the primacy of God-in-himself, each particular article of each question has a contrast and comparison structure. Each article begins with Thomas's statement of views opposed to his own—namely, the objections—but then proceeds to his positive teaching, initially in his *sed contra* and *respondeo*, and finally in his replies to the objections, namely in his explicit response to the views stated at the outset. Hence Thomas's contrast and comparison structure commonly terminates in a synthesis wherein the initial objections are responded to through the medium of his *respondeo*'s decisive argument. Most importantly, when the structure of each article (and question) is viewed in subordination to the *Summa*'s general *exitus-reditus* pattern, we see Thomas implying that his *antithesis* mode of presentation—that is, the essentially dialectical nature of human discourse (and presumably many of the imperfect dialectical realities it describes, including historical divisions in the human race)—is ultimately grounded in and informed by the Godhead's *exitus-reditus* pattern. Put differently, Thomas's practice of *antithesis*, both in his articles and more largely in the overall structure within which they are found, implies a zeal to inspire virtue in his readers through encouraging them in the *reditus* dimension of their essential *exitus-reditus* relation with God.[56] (I speculate later on what this pattern implies concerning question 23's teachings on predestination, reprobation, and final eschatology.)

With respect to *de praedestinatione*'s rhetorical element, my second claim is that several members of the biblical tradition note how providence contrasts the obedient with the disobedient, and some underscore the latter's rhetorical value. In Sirach 33:10–15, Joshua-Ben-Sira claims that God structures human communities and relationships by the mode of antithesis to inspire obedience;[57] in Ephesians 1:3–12[58] and Romans

---

123–42, at 123; A. N. Williams, "Mystical Theology Redux: The Pattern of Aquinas' *Summa Theologiae*," *Modern Theology* 13 (1997): 53–74; and Torrell, *Saint Thomas Aquinas*, 148–59.

56. See, again (note 24 above), Thomas's illuminating analysis of Lombard's *Sentences*, Book 4, 49.1.3, reply to query 1, viz., "Does everyone desire bliss?"

57. Sir 33:10–15: "So too, all men are of clay, for from earth man was formed; Yet with his great knowledge the Lord makes men unlike; in different paths has them walk. Some he blesses and makes great, some he sanctifies and draws to himself. Others he curses and brings low, and expels them from their place. Like clay in the hands of a potter, to be molded according to his pleasure, So are men in the hands of their Creator, to be assigned by him their function. As evil contrasts with good, and death with life, so are sinners in contrast with the just; See now all the works of the Most High: they come in pairs, the one the opposite of the other."

58. Eph 1:3–12: "Praised be the God and Father of our Lord Jesus Christ, who has be-

11:30–2,[59] St. Paul asserts that God governs humanity by antitheses to bring about "the obedience of all." And beginning in *CG* 11.18,[60] St. Augustine absolutizes[61] the ontological distinction between the predestined and nonpredestined. He claims that providence's goal is eternal antithetical communities, namely, the city of God (ultimately heaven) and city of Man (ultimately hell),[62] while noticing and avidly emphasizing the

stowed on us in Christ every spiritual blessing in the heavens. God chose us in him before the world began, to be holy and blameless in his sight, to be full of love, he likewise predestined us through Christ Jesus to be his adopted sons—such was his will and pleasure—that all might praise the glorious favor he has bestowed on us in his beloved. It is in Christ and through his blood that we have been redeemed and our sins forgiven, so immeasurably generous is God's favor to us. God has given us the wisdom to understand fully the mystery, the plan he was pleased to decree in Christ, to be carried out in the fullness of time: namely to bring all things in the heavens and on earth into one under Christ's headship. In him we were chosen; for in the decree of God, who administers everything according to his will and counsel, we were predestined to praise his glory by being the first to hope in Christ."

59. Rom 11:30–32: "Just as you were once disobedient to God and now have received mercy through their disobedience, so they have become disobedient—since God wished to show you mercy—that they too may receive mercy. God has imprisoned all in disobedience that he might have mercy on all."

60. In Augustine's words, "For God would never have created a man, let alone an angel, in the foreknowledge of his future evil state, if had not known at the same time how he would put such creatures to good use, and thus enrich the course of the world history by the kind of antithesis which gives beauty to a poem. 'Antithesis' [*Antitheta*] provides the most attractive figures in literary composition: the Latin equivalent is 'opposition' [*opposita*], or, more accurately 'contra-position' [*contraposita*]. The Apostle Paul makes elegant use of antithesis in developing a passage in the Second Epistle to the Corinthians,... [2 Cor. 6, 7–10]...The opposition of such contraries [*contraria contrariis opposita*] gives an added beauty to speech; and in the same way there is beauty in the composition of the world's history [*saeculi pulchritude componitur*] arising from the antithesis of contraries [*contrariorum oppositione*]—a kind of eloquence in events instead of in words. This point is made very clearly in the book Ecclesiasticus, 'Good confronts evil, life confronts death: so the sinner confronts the devout. And in this way you should observe all the works of the Most High; two by two; one confronting the other' [Sir 33:14–15]." H. Bettenson, trans., *St. Augustine, City of God* (New York: Penguin Books, 1972/1984), 11.18, 449 (Latin is added).

On Augustine's structuring his entire *CG* according to the manner of antithesis, see the helpful comments of P. L. McKinnon, "Augustine's *City of God*: The Divided Self/The Divided *Civitas*," in *The City of God: A Collection of Critical Essays* (New York: Peter Lang, 1995), 319–52, 322–23, who explicitly underscores H.-I. Marrou's similar insight in *Saint-Augustin et la fin de la culture antique* (Paris: E. De Broccard, 1938), 80. In McKinnon's words (Augustine's *City of God*, 322), "the conceptual and structural order of the work as a whole...may be described as an example of *syncrisis*, or concatenated antitheses, on a grand scale. Implicitly, Augustine's reliance upon this rhetorical strategy is an imitation of the creative signature of God discernible within the logic of human history."

61. Cf. Plotinus, *Enneads* 3.2–3 (*On Providence*).

62. Augustine writes: "Now the reason why eternal punishment appears harsh and unjust to human sensibilities, is that...under their condition of mortality man lacks...the sense which would enable him to feel the gravity of the wickedness in the first act of dis-

rhetorical dimension of this antithesis toward producing human obedience.[63] In this respect, Thomas's approach to predestination in *ST* I, q. 23, stands within the biblical, but specifically Augustinian, tradition because he both absolutizes the ontological distinction between the predestined and the elect and uses it for the rhetorical purpose of encouraging his reader in divine gratitude.[64] It is obvious that Thomas's teaching on the aforementioned antithesis would have been more acceptable if he had followed Paul instead of Augustine.[65] But this aside, why does Thomas absolutize that antithesis?

On *Confessio*

Thomas's methodology in *de praedestinatione* belongs neither to metaphysics nor to ethics but is, as *ST* I , q. 1, aa. 1–10 advertises, theological; that is, it belongs to what is distinguished as "sacred doctrine" *sacra doctrina*.[66] However, insofar as *de praedestinatione* includes (1)

---

obedience. For the more intimate the first man's enjoyment of God, the greater his impiety in abandoning God. By doing so he merited eternal evil....In consequence, the whole of mankind is a 'condemned lump' [*universa generis humani massa damnata*]...The result is that there is no escape for anyone from this justly deserved punishment, except by merciful and undeserved grace [*nisi misericordi et indebita gratia liberetur*]; and mankind is divided between those in whom the power of merciful grace [*misericors gratia*] is demonstrated, and those in whom is shown the might of just retribution [*veritas ultionis*]." St. Augustine, *City of God*, 21.12, 988–89. (Latin is added.)

63. See Moltmann, *Coming of God*, 247, who claims that by introducing into theology the "Aristotelian theorem of juxtaposition," Augustine manifests that the "deeper reason for this terrible doctrine of predestination is not to be found in theology...[but in]...aesthetics." Cf. Hick, *Evil and the God of Love*, 82–85, on the apparent fallacy of subordinating teachings on providence and predestination to an aesthetic perspective.

64. E.g., *ST* I, q. 23, a. 7, ad 3.

65. Thomas seems to think that on this question the Pauline and Augustinian traditions are essentially identical. As Farrelly writes, "It is clear that [Thomas] held that absolute predestination was causally antecedent to God's foreknowledge of man's merits, and eternal reprobation was likewise antecedent to man's personal sins. The reason for this teaching was not philosophical. It was the authority of St. Paul as interpreted by St. Augustine." Farrelly, *Predestination, Grace, and Free Will*, 121. As Most, *Grace, Predestination, and the Salvific Will of God*, 4–5, 307, points out, however, Thomas's identification of St. Paul's meaning in Romans 8–9 with St. Augustine's interpretation thereof is wrong, and to some extent Thomas tries to distance himself from it.

66. For commentary on Thomas's account of *sacra doctrina* in *ST* I, q. 1, aa. 1–10, see inter alii Torrell, *Saint Thomas Aquinas*, 156–59; and J. Weisheipl, "The Meaning of *Sacra Doctrina* in *Summa Theologiae* I, q. 1," *The Thomist* 38 (1974): 49–80. Most commentators assert that Thomas's approach to predestination in *ST* I, q. 23, aa. 1–8, is rooted, from beginning to end, in his unswerving loyalty to biblical revelation. See, e.g., Farrelly, *Grace, Predestination, and*

key elements in metaphysics and ethics,[67] (2) secondary teachings on reprobation and eschatology, and (3) a pronounced rhetorical emphasis, what kind of theological teaching is *this*? To my mind, it instantiates the essentially biblical mind-set of *confessio*.[68]

In general, *confessio* designates the mind-set of the self-consciously imperfect lover of God and neighbor; it consists in praising and worshipping God (hence the *Latin* term *confessio*[69]) so that God and neighbor are loved and by which biblical doctrine is therefore approached and interpreted.[70] Rooted in the biblical tradition (e.g., David's Psalms), but decisively developed by St. Augustine of Hippo (354–431 AD) in his famous *Confessiones*,[71] *confessio* contains several complementary components to which a coherent teaching on divine predestination should conform.

---

the Salvific Will of God, 115; Garrigou-Lagrange, *Predestination*, 90–106; Levering, *Predestination*, 75–83; Most, *Grace, Predestination, and the Salvific Will of God*, 3–5, 305–7; and Paluch, *La Profondeur de l'Amour Divin*, 190, 233–34, 246.

67. My point is that Thomas's doctrine includes teachings about the nature of God and the nature of human happiness and how it is attained, but his doctrine is not about those things as such, because he claims at the outset (*ST* I, q. 23, a. 1) that knowing and attaining beatitude depend decisively on divine aid. Hence Thomas claims that his formal object exceeds what belongs to the disciplines of metaphysics and ethics.

68. In *Confessions* 12, St. Augustine expresses the spirit of *confessio* governed biblical interpretation. He writes, "Let us love the Lord our God with all our heart...soul...mind, and our neighbor as ourselves (Matt. 22.37.9). On the basis of those two commandments of love, Moses meant whatever he meant in those books [*Confessions* 12.25.35]...[and] May all of us who...perceive and affirm that these texts contain various truths, show love to one another, and equally may we love you, our God, fount of truth—if truth is what we are thirsting after and not vanity [*Confessions* 12.30.41]." H. Chadwick, trans., *Saint Augustine, Confessions* (New York: Oxford University Press, 1992, 265 and 270.) Taking its cue from Augustine's doctrine of *confessio*, this section considers Thomas's approach to *confessio* in *ST* I and the implied central content of a *confessio* approach to predestination.

69. On the meaning of *confessio* as "praising God," see: P. Brown, *Augustine of Hippo: A Biography* (Boston: Faber and Faber, 1967), 175–81; J.-L. Marion, *In The Self's Place: The Approach of Saint Augustine*, trans. J. L. Kosky (Stanford, CA: Stanford University Press, 2012), 11–55; J. J. O'Donnell, *Augustine: Confessions*, vols. 1–2, *Introduction* (Oxford: Clarendon Press, 1992), xlii–li, 2:3–5; J. Ortiz, "Creation in the *Confessions*," in *Saint Augustine: The Confessions*, Ignatius Critical Editions, ed. D. V. Meconi (San Francisco: Ignatius Press, 2012), 475–90, 488–89; P. Rigby, *The Theology of Augustine's Confessions* (Cambridge: Cambridge University Press, 2015), 6–33; and G. Wills, *Saint Augustine's Childhood: Confessiones Book One* (New York: Viking/Penguin Group, 2001), 13–15.

70. See Augustine, *Confessions*, 12.30.41–31.42. Cf. Thomas's *Commentary on the Sentences of Peter Lombard*, "Commentary on the Master's Prologue."

71. Augustine writes *Confessions* ~397–401 AD. Recent studies include: R. McMahon, *Augustine's Prayerful Ascent: An Essay on the Literary Form of the Confessions* (Athens: University of Georgia Press, 1989); C. J. Starnes, *Augustine's Conversion: A Guide to the Argument of Confessions I–IX* (Waterloo, ONT: Wilfred Laurier University Press, 1990);

What comprises the developed mode of *confessio*? In the first place, it is a mortal person's explicitly Trinitarian relationship with God. The subject not only understands that man as such, though vitiated by original sin and personal sinfulness, is constituted as *imago dei* according to his intellectual nature,[72] but also that he is properly so by explicit conformity, through God's grace, to God[73] and that perfect unity with

J. J. O'Donnell, *Augustine: Confessions*, vols. 1–3, *Introduction and Text* (Oxford: Clarendon Press, 1992); K. Paffenroth and R. P. Kennedy, eds., *A Reader's Companion to Augustine's Confessions* (Louisville, KY: Westminster John Knox Press, 2003); C. G. Vaught, *The Journey toward God in Augustine's Confessions: Books I–VI* (Albany: State University of New York Press, 2003); idem, *Encounters with God in Augustine's Confessions: Books VII–IX* (Albany: State University of New York Press, 2004); and idem, *Access to God in Augustine's Confessions: Books X–XIII*, (Albany: State University of New York Press, 2005).

72. See *ST* I, q. 1, a. 45, ad 7; q. 93, a. 4. Thomas writes: "Since man is said to be the image of God (*imaginem Dei*) by reason of his intellectual nature (*secundum intellectualem naturam*), he is the most perfectly like God according to that in which he can best imitate God in his intellectual nature. Now the intellectual nature imitates God chiefly in this, that God understands and loves Himself (*quod Deus seipsum intelligit et amat*). Wherefore we see that the image of God is in man in three ways. First, inasmuch as man possesses a natural aptitude for understanding and loving God (*Uno quidem modo, secundum quod homo habet aptitudinem naturalem ad intelligendum et amandum Deum*); and this aptitude consists in the very nature of the mind, which is common to all men (*et haec aptitudo consistit in ipsa natura mentis, quae est communis omnibus hominibus*).... Wherefore on the words, 'The light of Thy countenance, O Lord, is signed upon us' (Ps. 4:7), the gloss distinguishes a threefold image of 'creation,' of 're-creation,' and of 'likeness.' The first is found in all men (*Prima ergo imago invenitur in omnibus hominibus*)."

For commentary on Thomas's account of man as *imago dei*, see: M. Brown, "*Imago Dei* in Thomas Aquinas," *Saint Anselm Journal* 10, no. 1 (Fall 2014): 1–11; R. Cessario, *Christian Faith and the Theological Life* (Washington, DC: Catholic University of America Press, 1996), 38–48; J. A. Di Noia, "*Imago Dei-Imago Christi*: The Theological Foundations of Christian Humanism," presented at Congresso Tomista Internazionale, Instituto Universitario Virtual Santo Tomàs, Rome, September 21–25, 2003; I. Eschmann, "St. Thomas Aquinas, the Summary of Theology I–II: The Ethics of the Image of God," in *The Ethics of St. Thomas Aquinas: Two Courses*, ed. E. A. Synan (Toronto, ONT: Pontifical Institute of Mediaeval Studies, 1997), 159–231; T. Hibbs, "*Imitatio Christi* and the Foundation of Aquinas's Ethics," *Communio* 18 (1991): 556–73; D. J. Merriell, *To the Image of the Trinity: A Study in the Development of Aquinas's Teaching* (Toronto, ONT: Pontifical Institute of Mediaeval Studies, 1990); idem, "Trinitarian Anthropology," in *To the Image of the Trinity*, 123–42; and J. P. O'Callahan, "*Imago Dei*: A Test Case for St. Thomas's Augustinianism," in *Aquinas the Augustinian*, ed. M. Dauphinais, B. David, and M. Levering (Washington, DC: Catholic University of America Press, 2007), 100–144.

73. *ST* I, q. 93, a. 4. Thomas writes: "Now the intellectual nature imitates God chiefly in this, that God understands and loves Himself. Wherefore we see that the image of God is in man in three ways.... Secondly, inasmuch as man actually and habitually knows and loves God, though imperfectly (*Alio modo, secundum quod homo actu vel habitu Deum cognoscit et amat, sed tamen imperfecte*); and this image consists in the conformity of grace (*et haec est imago per conformitatem gratiae*.)....Wherefore on the words, 'The light of Thy countenance, O Lord, is signed upon us' (Ps. 4:7), the gloss distinguishes a threefold image of

God can only be attained, by his grace, in eternity.[74] On the one hand, *explicit imago dei* understands that man is *imago dei* by nature. In an earlier Augustinian form, man as such is constituted as *imago dei* by his co-implicate activities of awareness/memory (*memoria*), understanding (*intelligentia*), and love (*voluntas/amor*), having their respective exemplars in God the Father, Word, and Holy Spirit.[75] In the Thomistic form focused on here, rooted in *ST* I, q. 45, a. 7, and q. 93, aa. 1–9, man is *imago dei* because mind's nature and activity represent the divine processions. Because mind is structured by the powers of intellect (*intellectus*) and of will/love (*voluntas/amor*), it represents the divine processions insofar as its intrinsic conjunction of intellect and will both conceives a word (*verbum conceptum*)—imitating the Father's begetting of his Divine Word, and entails love proceeding (*amor procedens*)—thereby representing the Spirit's proceeding from the Father and from the Son.[76] Because the word

---

'creation,' of 're-creation,' and of 'likeness.'... the second [is found] only in the just (*secunda in iustis tantum*)."

74. *ST* I, q. 93, a. 4. Thomas writes: "Now the intellectual nature imitates God chiefly in this, that God understands and loves Himself. Wherefore we see that the image of God is in man in three ways.... Thirdly, inasmuch as man knows and loves God perfectly (*Tertio modo, secundum quod homo Deum actu cognoscit et amat perfecte*); and this image consists in the likeness of glory (*et sic attenditur imago secundum similitudinem gloriae*). Wherefore on the words, 'The light of Thy countenance, O Lord, is signed upon us' (Ps. 4:7), the gloss distinguishes a threefold image of 'creation,' of 're-creation,' and of 'likeness.'... the third [is found] only in the blessed (*tertia vero solum in beatis*)."

75. Augustine, *De Trinitate*, 10.4.18–9, 14.3.13.

76. My claim is especially based on interpreting Thomas's doctrines in *ST* I, q. 45, a. 7, and q. 93, a. 7. In the former passage, Thomas identifies the rational creature as *imago dei* insofar as, having intellect (*intellectus*) and will (*voluntas*), its thinking and loving imitate the processions of the divine persons whereby a word is produced and love proceeds (*invenitur repraesentatio Trinitas per modum imaginis, inquantum invenitur in eis verbum conceptum et amor procedens*). In *ST* I, q. 93, a. 7, Thomas considers the distinction between the divine persons "by reason of the procession of the word from the speaker (*secundum processionem verbi a dicente*), and the procession of love connecting both (*et amoris connectentis utrumque*)." Taken altogether, I infer that the "principle from which understanding proceeds looks to be the correlate to the Father, while the *verbum* is the correlate of the Son of God, the Divine *Verbum*, and the springing forth of love is the correlate of the Holy Spirit who proceeds from both." O'Callaghan, "*Imago Dei*," 100–144, here 137.

Thomas's account of mind as *imago dei* might also be stated in terms of the first principles structuring intellect and will, viz., the law of noncontradiction and the first principle of practical reason, viz., "good is that which all things seek" (*ST* I-II, q. 94, a. 2). Hence mind's highest "word proceeding/produced" pertains to knowing God as truth and loving him as good. See also *ST* I, q. 2, a. 1, ad 1 (cf. *ST* I-II, q. 2, a. 8, and q. 3, a. 1) concerning Thomas's teaching on the ultimate orientation of man's innate desire for happiness, and Thomas's specific accounts of the trajectories of intellect (*ST* I-II, q. 3, a. 8) and of will/love (*ST* I-II, q. 5, a. 8) in his *Treatise on Happiness*. In every instance, Thomas argues that man has a natural

produced represents what mind is reflecting on or enjoying, Thomas is claiming that mind is *imago dei* owing to its intellectual nature[77] and in each of its acts.[78] Therefore, in both its earlier Augustinian and later Thomistic form, mind is considered *imago dei* because there is existential likeness and spiritual orientation between its specific operations and specific members of the Godhead. According to Augustine, this informs each co-implicate activity;[79] for Thomas, this structures the co-implicate powers of intellect and will in terms of the word and love their interaction innately produces.[80] Because mind is objectively *imago dei*, each and every human thought and action, notion and love, presupposes ontological kinship with the Godhead.[81]

On the other hand, *imago dei* understands that a person is properly such by self-consciously conforming oneself to the Godhead.[82] With the aid of divine grace, *imago dei* both recognizes what is stated above concerning its natural structure and actively corresponds with the Godhead. Hence *explicit imago dei* both knows and behaves in conformity with the insights (1) that being, including its own, depends on God; (2) that God is the truth of being; and (3) that its proper response to God (Father, Word, and Spirit) consists in unconditional gratitude because all that it is, apprehends, and loves (viz., God and being) is from, through, and to him. In the latter regard, *explicit imago dei* responds to Father, Word, and Spirit with love because it is grateful for (1) existing; (2) being formed by the Word and reformed by Christ, the Word made flesh to overcome the privative state in which the race has placed itself owing to original

---

orientation toward the enjoyment of God. "Man's fundamental orientation towards God, his capacity for God, is tied to his creation in the image of God.... Whatever he may say about the fulfillment of this capacity for God in the beatific vision, Aquinas insists that the capacity is rooted in human nature. God has created man with this capacity, and in the *Summa* Aquinas connects this capacity to the image of God in man." Merriell, "Trinitarian Anthropology," 124–25.

Recent studies of Thomas's account of man's natural orientation toward God include: B. Ashley, "What Is the End of the Human Person? The Vision of God and Integral Human Fulfillment," in *Moral Truth and Moral Tradition*, ed. L. Gormally (Dublin: Four Courts Press, 1994), 68–96; L. Feingold, *The Natural Desire to See God* (Washington, DC: Catholic University of America Press, 2004); and J. Haldane, "Philosophy: The Restless Heart and the Meaning of Theism," *Ratio* 19, no. 4 (2006): 421–40.

77. *ST* I, q. 45, a. 7; q. 93, a. 4. 78. *ST* I, q. 93, a. 7.
79. *De Trinitate*, 14.4.15–16. 80. *ST* I, q. 45, a. 7.
81. *ST* I, q. 93, a. 7.
82. For Thomas, see *ST* I, q. 93, a. 4; for Augustine, see *De Trinitate*, 14.4.15 and 14.5.22–5.

and personal sin; and (3) being led heavenward to its *telos* by the Holy Spirit.[83] Likewise, *explicit imago dei* also recognizes that its transition from implicit to explicit to perfect *imago dei*—that is, from natural to supernatural and finally to perfect union with God—depends on corresponding with his grace.[84]

Confessio's third cardinal characteristic, rooted in the Trinitarian mind-set described above, is that the nature and progressive development of *imago dei*, from explicit to perfect, functions as the prism or eyeglass through which *it* understands the reality falling outside of mind's immediate spiritual relationship with God.[85] On this basis, *imago dei* analyzes all things in light of the nature and mandate of the eternal Incarnate *Logos*, that is, that God creates, structures, and governs all things for the purpose of developing *imago dei*. Therefore, because the eternal Incarnate *Logos* consists in Godhead and human nature eternally established together and, by that reality, mandates love of God and neighbor, *imago dei*'s interpretation of those things standing outside of its immediate self-certain relationship with the Godhead—for example, Bible, philosophy, history, and nature—is anchored in recognizing the primacy of divine goodness and practicing divine gratitude. Hence *imago*

---

83. In *ST* I, q. 45, a. 7, Thomas maintains that each creature constitutes a representation of the Trinity (*repraesentatio Trinitatis*) by the mode of trace (*per modum vestigium*) insofar as each (1) exists as a substance (*subsistit in suo esse*)—thereby representing the Father, "the principle from no principle"; (2) has a form and species (*habet formam per quam determinatur ad speciem*)—manifesting "the Word as the form of the thing made by art"; and (3) is ordained to some end (*quod habet ordinem*)—representing "the Holy Ghost, inasmuch as He is love, because the order of the effect to something else is from the will of the Creator." Hence Thomas's teaching on the nature of *explicit imago dei* in *ST* I, q. 93, a. 4, means that it is grateful to God for its existing, essence, and ordination to beatitude.

84. For Augustine, see *De Trinitate*, 14.5.23–24; for Thomas, see again his account of the image "in the conformity of grace" at *ST* I, q. 93, a. 4. Thomas claims that mind is properly *imago dei* (what I name *explicit* or *elect imago dei*) when it focuses on God: "According to Aquinas, not just any inner procession of word and love suffices for the mind to be the image of the Trinity. It has to be the inner word that expresses the mind's knowledge of God, the inner love that impels the mind towards God. God must be the object of the intellect and will; and reflexive acts of knowledge and self-love will suffice only if they in fact lead the mind to God." Merriell, "Trinitarian Anthropology," 133.

85. For Augustine, see *Confessions*, 13.12.13; for Thomas, see *ST* I, a. 93, a. 8. In that article, Thomas does not say exactly what I have asserted above, but it is implied by his distinction therein between the nature of immediate (*directe et immediate*) and mediate (*indirecte et mediate*) knowledge and love of God. If the nature of mind, when properly *imago dei*, consists in knowing and loving God, then that mind-set will think and love all things—whether God or creatures—in light and for the sake of its knowing and loving God.

dei approaches those things in light of recognizing their ultimate *telos*, and study thereof fortifies its spiritual orientation toward God. (By that principle, Augustine interprets the origin and destiny of God's Church,[86] divine providence,[87] and the Godhead,[88] and, closer to home, Thomas Aquinas interprets *inter aliis* Lombard's *Sentences* and constructs his *Summa Theologiae*.[89])

Put differently, as the Godhead, through Christ, is Incarnate and "truth cannot contradict truth," right understanding of reality always encourages knowledge of God and piety. *Confessio* therefore properly entails a hermeneutic of interpretation structured by a cognitive dimension on the one side, namely, that one's being and activity is owed to ineffable divine goodness, and on the other side, by a correlate imperative to practice divine gratitude. Moreover, because *imago dei* has two phases of development in fallen history (i.e., in the *saeculum*), namely, from *implicit* to *explicit imago dei* and from *explicit imago dei* toward *perfect imago dei* (attainable only in the afterlife), it is implied that *explicit imago dei*, following the divine example in Christ, properly tailors its common or official doctrine for the benefit of all.[90] This means (using Ockham's razor) that common doctrine is targeted more at those transitioning from *implicit* to *explicit imago dei* than at those developing from *explicit* to *perfect imago dei*. That is because each party shares, so long as they dwell in this world, the fundamental spiritual state wherein all *imago dei* development occurs, namely, a constant warring against a nontheocentric (or "fleshly") mind-set (see Rom 8:1–13). Put differently, mind wavers between embracing a nontheocentric or theocentric *weltanschauung*.

Moreover, *explicit imago dei*, being "stronger" in doctrine because it is more established in charity, is called by Christ's example (by *imitatio Christi*; see Phil 2:1–11) to humble itself in the service of God and neighbor. This does not mean it ceases pursuing truth but that it distinguishes

---

86. *Confessions*, 13.12–38.
88. *De Trinitate*, 1–15.
87. *CG*, 11–22.
89. Hankey, *God in Himself*, 19–35.
90. Does this imply an "esoteric" doctrine? (See Levering, *Predestination*, 194.) Only in the sense that some insights into the meaning of Scripture can be more developed or astute than others. By the law of charity (*lex divinitatis*), however, which is concerned with the welfare of the entire community, each interpreter is required to submit private insight into common doctrine whenever that is needed. So, encouragement for intellectual and spiritual development occurs within the context of the *lex divinitatis*'s decisive concern for the welfare of the collective to which each interpreter belongs.

between common doctrine and private opinion. That said, *explicit imago dei* propounds common doctrine that upholds divine goodness and
encourages divine gratitude in accordance with the aforementioned
assessment of *imago dei*'s spiritual condition. So, while it welcomes the
advanced to continue their journey in the spirit of charity, it prudently
draws a line in the sand safeguarding the welfare of those moving toward
or newly established in the lifestyle of *confessio*.[91] Perhaps it is for this
reason that Father Thomas originates his account of divine providence
(*ST* I, q. 22, aa. 1–4), and by implication of predestination (*ST* I, q. 23, aa.
1–8), with the claim that God's providence is governed by his prudential
consideration of the human condition. Thomas introduces providence as
a species of prudence: "For it is the chief part of prudence, to which two
other parts are directed—namely, remembrance of the past, and understanding of the present, inasmuch as from the remembrance of what is
past and the understanding of what is present, we gather how to provide
for the future."[92]

My fourth point is that *confessio*'s opposing mind-set is *praesumptio* (i.e., presumption).[93] In general, it means one thinks and lives in a
manner contradicting one's intrinsic *imago dei* structure. At one extreme, the presumptuous mind-set holds that God absolutely owes to
one existing, reforming, and eternal bliss; at the other extreme, *praesumptio* claims that absolute gratitude is owed, not to the Creator but to
the created by ordering oneself to some essentially finite—that is, tribal,
familial, nationalistic, or imperialistic (or merely empirical, mental, or
metaphysical)—structure. Despite their particular differences, each extreme overlooks the utterly gratuitous nature of divine goodness and,
by consequence, human responsibility's proper response of gratitude.
For example, our immediately preceding distinction concerning *explicit
imago dei*'s approach to common and to private doctrine implies specific
forms of presumption pertaining to predestination. On the one side, a
presumptuous mind-set might propound a common teaching that God

---

91. This means that, in principle, explicit *imago dei* can pinch truth in the service of
charity; i.e., it can sacrifice some part of the truth on the altar of love in the service of sharing common doctrine. What a paradox!

92. *ST* I, q. 22, a. 1.

93. For Augustine, see *Confessions*, 7.20.26; for Thomas, see *ST* II-II, q. 21, aa. 1–4. Cf.
Von Balthasar, *Dare We Hope*, 17.

leads all persons to bliss; on the other, it could promulgate a common teaching that God only leads to bliss a minority. It is arguable that each approach denies charity by overlooking *imago dei*'s existential condition. As I explain below, while a doctrine of universal salvation can uphold the primacy of divine goodness at the cost of deemphasizing the importance of human responsibility, a teaching asserting minority salvation can underscore human responsibility by undercutting the primacy of divine goodness.

Wherever present, *praesumptio* denies *confessio*'s hermeneutic key, namely, recognition of divine goodness *coupled with* an imperative to gratitude. A properly developed *confessio* approach, however, upholds divine goodness and human responsibility in their right order. It acknowledges, on the one hand, that all good/being/existence is ultimately received, as gift, from divine goodness and, on the other, that anything vitiated— that is, any human or subhuman reality suffering privation—is, in some manner, produced by human responsibility opposing itself to God. By acknowledging its existential debt to divine goodness, *confessio* asks that it be healed, schooled, and led to its *telos* of blissful union with God.

Keeping in mind the above distinctions, what belongs to a *confessio* doctrine of divine predestination? It has three obvious elements.

1. *Synthesis of God and man.* It upholds the divine goodness, rooted in the uncreated self-sufficient Creator, as first principle and human responsibility as secondary, created principle. Consequently, writer and reader should respond to divine goodness with unqualified gratitude for the gift of existing, essence, and ordination to eternal bliss. In this instance, the word conceived by intellect and by love proceeding signifies God himself. As such, mind is properly *imago dei*.

2. *Synthesis of God and man through Christ, the God-man.* Owing to God-in-Christ's canceling the demerits of original sin and personal sin, *imago dei* responds to divine goodness, manifested in divine mercy, with gratitude because, humanly speaking, what is given by Christ is more than mere goodness. And because human responsibility is, by its own doing, less than it ought to be, *imago dei* does the good it ought not simply by the grace of divine goodness but by the grace of divine mercy. In this instance, too, the word conceived by intellect and by love proceeding signifies, through Christ, God himself. As such, mind is properly *imago dei*.

3. *Synthesis encouraged by explicit imago dei's reflecting, in light of its spiritual union with God, on a providentially established antithesis between different portions of humanity.* Interpreting created being through the prism of *confessio, imago dei*'s gratitude toward divinity is encouraged by contrasting its privileged relationship with God to that of the unprivileged. In this instance, *imago dei*'s synthesis with God motivates positing and studying, in that light, an antithesis between the predestined and the reprobated. It is important to note two things about this. First, the antithesis posited between the *being redeemed* and the *not yet being redeemed is not for its own sake* but is informed by the principal, because absolute synthesis between *imago dei* and divine goodness. Second, while the word produced in the former instance directly represents God—who is absolute and irreducible, or his objective relationship with man, which by his gratuitous choice to create man is also absolute and irreducible—the word produced in the second instance, and which is allied to the first word, signifies what is contingent and reducible. This is because, taken on its own, it manifests neither God-in-himself nor his created union with man. So whereas mind, being united with God by the activities of intellect and love and, consequently, by the nature of the word proceeding, is explicitly *imago dei* in every instance, the formal object considered in this instance does not match up with God-in-himself. I return to this important distinction below.

For now, we note that a doctrine of divine gratitude informs (1), (2), and (3) above. However, whereas (1) and (2) are intrinsically irreducible, it happens that (3)—arising through and for the sake of (1) and (2)—is not. This is because, while the ontology between divine goodness and human responsibility—and, consequently, between goodness and the predestined—is eternal, the ontology between both divine goodness and the reprobated and the elect and the reprobated is contingent.

Assessing *De Praedestinatione* as *Confessio*

De praedestinatione instantiates a biblical mind-set of *confessio*.[94] This is because Thomas's *theological* doctrine therein properly includes what

94. The previous section suggests that a *confessio* approach to divine predestination is properly grounded in Christ's humility—perhaps as the latter is articulated by St. Paul in

structures a Trinitarian knowledge and love of God and neighbor: both decisive knowledge of God and encouraging writer and reader alike in divine gratitude. *ST* I, q. 23, a. 1, defines predestination as "a type in the divine mind whereby God orders the rational creature to eternal life." But that account of God's plan of action, and its human consequences, is neither promulgated nor received in a vacuum. Rather, it is evident both to Thomas and to his audience, those so-called beginners in theology, that the God he describes (and mediates, in a way, to his audience) is self-sufficient (e.g., *ST* I, q. 19, a. 3) and therefore creates by suppositional, that is, conditional, rather than by absolute necessity. Because God creates by free will (*ST* I, q. 19, a. 10), the inference is easily and properly drawn that each (reader) owes not only mere existing to God but also, because of God's merciful response to inherited (viz., original sin) and personal sinfulness, being on the path to eternal bliss. Hence the gratitude owed to God's goodness in the first place is underscored, in a way, by that owed to his mercy, that is, to what is, humanly speaking, a greater manifestation of goodness. This imperative for gratitude is emphasized by the fact that even awareness of gratitude depends on divine goodness. So, while decisive knowledge of God, as described above, is *de praedestinatione*'s principal cognitive dimension, gratitude toward God is the question's *practical imperative*.

These correlates not only function as *ST* I, q. 23's hermeneutic key but also delineate the ontological and, consequently, cognitive and affective boundaries of *confessio*—the one correlate signifying what belongs to intellect (*intellectus*), the other what informs will/love (*voluntas/amor*). Stated in terms of *confessio*'s *imago dei* mind-set (cf. *ST* I, q. 45, a. 7, and q. 93, aa. 1–9), divine gratitude entails that intellect's proper object consists in reflecting on the nature and depth of divine goodness and that will's/love's proper activity lies in practicing divine gratitude. In this regard, we recognize the Trinitarian mind-set of *confessio* in two related ways. First, will, by God's grace, both inspires and responds to intellect's

---

Phil 2:5–7: "Your attitude must be that of Christ: Though he was in the form of God, he did not deem equality with God something to be grasped at. Rather, he emptied himself and took the form of a slave, being born in the likeness of men. He was known to be of human estate, and it was thus that he humbled himself, obediently accepting even death, death on a cross!" This section measures Thomas's *de praedestinatione* by the standard of *confessio* and finds his teaching somewhat deficient.

insight, namely, to the "word conceived" *verbum conceptum*, that gratuitous goodness structures its immediate relationship with God. Second,
intellect properly interprets nondivine or contingent reality through a
prism of the aforementioned cognitive certitude and practical imperative. Because the purpose of God's relationship with his elect is eternal, blissful union—rather than the lesser form of union his elect presently enjoys or the implicit union structuring those presently oriented
away from him (see *ST* I, q. 93, a. 4), namely, the nonelect—it follows
that divine goodness has structured *all things* to manifest itself and encourage a response of gratitude. While the original "word conceived"
verbum conceptum pertains to the objective and absolute, since eternal,
relationship between God and man, the second "word conceived" considers the contingent, since temporal, relationship between the predestined and so-called nonpredestined. Based on its co-implicate cognitive
certitude and practical imperative, *imago dei* judges that the antithetical
relationship's *telos* includes encouraging its own essentially Trinitarian,
synthesis-structured and synthesis-producing, relationship with God.
Hence *ST* I, q. 23, a. 7, asserts that *imago dei*'s comparison of its present
and future plight with that of the apparently nonpredestined manifests
both its present dependence on and need for ever-greater devotion to
God.[95]

In this respect, we also noticed a pronounced rhetorical component in
Thomas's presentation. *De praedestinatione*'s employing an antithesis to
encourage gratitude parallels an approach found within many of Thomas's important predecessors. While Aristotle's *Rhetoric* upholds using
antitheses to inspire virtue (*Rhetoric*, 3.9–11)—which we note that Thomas employs in each question and article throughout his *ST*—biblical authorities like Joshua Ben-Sira (Sir 33:10–15) and St. Paul (Eph 1:3–12 and

95. While speaking in *ST* I, q. 23, a. 7, of God's certain knowledge of the number of God's
elect, Thomas compares this to God's knowledge of the number of the reprobate, remarking
that while God preordains his elect "for the good of the universe," he preordains the reprobate for "the good of the elect." Thomas writes: "Now of all creatures the rational creature is
chiefly ordained for the good of the universe, being as such incorruptible; more especially
those who attain to eternal happiness, since they more immediately reach the ultimate end.
Whence the number of the predestined is certain to God; not only by way of knowledge, but
also by way of a principal pre-ordination. It is not exactly the same thing in the case of the
number of the reprobate, who would seem to be pre-ordained by God for the good of the
elect (*qui videntur esse praeordinati a Deo in bonum electorum*), in whose regard all things
work together unto good (*quibus omnia cooperantur in bonum*) (Rm 8:28)."

Rom 11:30–32), and theological authorities like St. Augustine (*CG* 11.18), notice and employ antitheses between the godly and ungodly to persuade their audience in godliness. Nevertheless, our *confessio*-centered analysis shows that while the contingent "word" representing an antithesis between the predestined and the supposed nonpredestined is commonly first in the order of human discovery—and may even be needed to motivate joining with God in the first place—the absolute "word," representing the principal cognitive teaching, and its correlate imperative for gratitude, is first in the order of being. The contingent word, therefore, is for the sake of, since dependent upon, the absolute word.

I will soon return to this matter because Thomas's granting of absolute status to the contingent word implies that his *confessio* approach to predestination contains a misleading—perhaps even presumptuous—element. It is true that mind moves from *ratio* to *intellect*, that is, from discovery to insight. Broadly viewed, mind is always in a state of discovery, but this is in different degrees because some starting points, as the state of *intellect* shows, are more accurate than others. Insofar as *explicit imago dei* is more developed than *implicit imago dei*, its perspective on being is more insightful. But because we recognize two phases of *imago dei*, it is evident that each party requires each word. To develop *imago dei*, how are these words rightly related and expressed?

For now, I emphasize that viewing *de praedestinatione* as *confessio* has certain interpretative advantages because it both highlights the philosophical strength in Thomas's teaching and gives reasonable explanation for the latter's sometimes bewildering treatment of reprobation. On the one hand, claiming that Thomas's formal object includes a complimentary knowledge of God and imperative for human responsibility allows us to recognize specific metaphysical and ethical excellences in Thomas's teaching. Because *de praedestinatione* upholds the infinite God as *sine qua non* first and final cause, and human responsibility's proper response to God as humble gratitude, it is evident that *ST* I, q. 23, can easily fend off various Pelagian and semi-Pelagian challenges. Owing to being created and suffering the consequences of original sin and personal sinfulness, man—and therefore human knowing and willing—is not only in a state of imperfect act toward his *telos* with God, for which he requires special divine aid (i.e., a relatively greater sharing in divine goodness), but his need is also exacerbated by his privative state. Consequently, man's attaining his *telos* requires what is, humanly speaking, a more intensive participation in divine goodness than if he had not fallen, wherefore Thomas claims throughout *de praedestinatione* that man needs divine mercy.

Even if Thomas's overall teaching is weakened by arguing that God "predestines" only some to bliss, his treatment of the predestined is right by subalternation. Thomas might be mistaken about the status of "all men," but the particular (i.e., the "some men") he analyzes conforms to the universal proposed by those a strictly theocentric paradigm of interpretation to divine providence. Additionally, Thomas's secondary focus on predestination's effect in historical human community has merit insofar as it attempts to explain what remains perplexing even in our own era, namely, that "to some it is given while from others it is withheld." While Thomas might wrongly identify the election of a minority with the salvation of a minority, the nature of election requires explanation. Exactly what does God place in his elect? And why are *these* persons elected instead of *those*? Election is certainly mysterious, but Thomas is surely right that only some are predestined to election in this world and, in this respect, that election's ultimate reason is found in God's will (*ST* I, q. 23, a. 5, ad 3). Thomas's account of predestination has merit because it helps toward comprehending the mystery of divine election.

But how does our *confessio* analysis render intelligible *de praedestinatione*'s problematic aspects? I mean its related teachings on reprobation and eschatology, claiming that the majority of humanity is both destined for and suffers eternal hell. Because Thomas's principal cognitive certitude is theological and its correlate practical imperative consists in cultivating divine gratitude—or, put differently, because Thomas's method is *imago dei*—he is concerned with eschatology and reprobation so far as his notions thereof encourage his predestination-friendly audience in the aforementioned hermeneutic. This, I think, gives some reason why *de praedestinatione* juxtaposes contradictory theocentric and nontheocentric interpretations of God's action upon humanity. It is somewhat strange to say, but, as shown before, *ST* I, q. 23, ultimately employs two distinct paradigms related by contradictory opposition, alternately upholding (concerning predestination) and denying (in the case of reprobation) metaphysically sound doctrines of God and man, because its teaching strives to be biblical; it is *confessio* rather than metaphysics or ethics.

On this score, Thomas's marvelous metaphysical insights into God and human nature, stated elsewhere, along with *de praedestinatione*'s emphasis on ineffable goodness and divine gratitude, give ample reason to believe that his effort in *ST* I, q. 23, is informed by *confessio*'s *sine qua non* virtue of charity.[96] Because charity, as Christ shows (e.g., Phil 2:1–11), properly motivates its subjects to share goodness by practicing humility, it might be claimed that Father Thomas is a well-established, second-phase *imago dei* theologian writing to benefit those in first- or second-stage *imago dei*. One can suppose that he intends to encourage both a mind-set transitioning from a nontheocentric to a theocentric perspective and a growing theocentric mind-set. It is therefore possible that Thomas's accounts of predestination, reprobation, and eschatology side with those who are "weaker" in knowledge and love because, as previously mentioned, these share by subalternation with the "stronger" the common ground of warring against a nontheocentric or imperfect theocentric mind-set. On this basis, the stronger, who know and love more, are encouraged by serving the weaker, who know and love less. And it is also conceivable that Thomas subtly instructs his stronger brethren by structuring his entire *Summa*, as noted before, by a theocentric *exitus-reditus* pattern to make evident an important limitation to his doctrine in the *Summa*'s every question and article—including a limitation in *ST* I, q. 23's treatment of predestination.[97]

96. For Thomas's teaching on charity in his *Summa*, see *ST* II-II, q. 23, aa. 1–8.

97. On this point, see the insightful connection that Di Noia makes between Thomas's doctrine of man as *imago Dei* in *ST* I, a. 93, and the *exitus-reditus* structure of the entire *Summa Theologiae*. "A critical feature of this more comprehensive appraisal of Aquinas's theology of the *imago Dei* has involved recognition that his explicit consideration of the matter as part of the theology of creation in question 93 of the Prima Pars cannot be treated in isolation but must be located within the broader context of the overall argument of the *Summa Theologiae*. It is well known that the structure of this argument is framed in terms of Aquinas's distinctive appropriation of the *exitus-reditus* scheme. This structure has immense significance for his theology of the *imago Dei*: the human being created in the image of God is by the very fact of his human nature and from the very first moment of his existence directed toward God as his ultimate end." "*Imago Dei-Imago Christi*," 9. Di Noia's claim implies that Thomas informs his earlier teaching on predestination by the *exitus-reditus* pattern because, by placing that teaching within his treatise on *God and His Perfections* (*ST* I, qq. 1–26), he makes clear to his privileged, *imago dei*, readers that they are indebted to God both for their origin (*exitus*) and opportunity to attain their proper destiny (*reditus*). But note also Dool's comments ("Predestination, Freedom, and the Logic of Love," 121–24) concerning the limitation Thomas places on his teaching on predestination by considering it in advance of his study of the divine processions (*ST* I, qq. 27–43). According to Dool, Thomas's account of predestination is informed

Nevertheless, as the above considerations are speculative, it is evident that *de praedestinatione* is an imperfect manifestation of *confessio*. For one thing, our distinction between the absolute and relative "word," or between the "synthesis"—man's objective, ontological relationship with God—and the "antithesis"—providence's distinction between the elect and nonelect—shows that Thomas's treatment might have greater intellectual success by (1) focusing on predestination's origin in God and its effects on his human subjects, (2) avoiding definite negative judgments about those outside the domain of divine election, and (3) expanding its account of salvation from a minority to, at least, a majority. This is for four closely related reasons.

First, Thomas's assertion of an eternal antithesis between the predestined and the reprobated contradicts *de praedestinatione*'s principal cognitive certitude concerning divine goodness. Because it makes sense to claim, in light of original sin and personal sinfulness, that the self-sufficient, yet Creator, God freely applies his goodness in a special way to some persons in the context of applying it in the best possible way to all, *confessio* need not assert that God shares his goodness both in a special and in the best possible way only with some. Admittedly, Thomas maintains that God applies his goodness to all, namely, to the predestined and to the so-called reprobated alike ("since He wills good to all, He loves all"; *ST* I, q. 23, a. 4, ad 1). But claiming that God shares the highest dimensions of his goodness with only some human persons contradicts ineffable goodness. It is true that God creates and consequently predestines by suppositional, rather than absolute, necessity, that is, by his free rather than absolute will (*ST* I, q. 19, a. 10).[98] However, the marvelous aspect of God's suppositional necessity is that he has freely bound *humanity* to himself so that, *by his free choice*, humanity's sharing

---

by considering God's love from the perspective of a relatively truncated "creative dimension" (121) rather than from the perspective of its all-encompassing "personal, unitive" (122) dimension. Thomas, therefore, could furnish a better account of predestination by considering "the intricacy of how God's unitive love empowers the human person... through the logic of love that, by its very nature, creates freedom for either communion or rejection" (124).

All told, these commentators imply that the location of Thomas's teaching on predestination can benefit his specific *imago dei* audience, but it causes that teaching to fail as common doctrine. This is akin to my principal judgment concerning *de praedestinatione*.

98. This contradicts Thomas's claim (*ST* I, q. 23, a. 4, ad 3) that God predestines by his consequent or simple will rather than by his antecedent will because the proper inference (from *ST* I, q. 19, aa. 3 and 10) is that God's consequent will reiterates his antecedent will.

in his goodness is allied with his willing his own goodness. Because God has pledged himself to willing the best for humanity, it is misleading to say that he *ultimately* withholds the depth of his goodness from some while sharing it with others. Thomas's restrictive account of God's sharing his goodness contradicts *confessio*'s proper analogue—namely, the Godhead, as Father, Word, and Spirit stand opposed to each other—implying that Father alone is God, Word is not consubstantial with Father and Spirit, and Spirit is not consubstantial with Father and Word. By that same principle, Thomas's teaching on reprobation denies the unity of the human race because, among other things, human responsibility, a secondary (since created) principle, is made more important than the first cause of created being! A doctrine of eternal reprobation means that finite responsibility conquers infinite goodness.

Second, because Thomas absolutizes a self-evidently contingent antithesis, he weakens his emphasis on divine gratitude. To begin with, Thomas's imperative for gratitude is grounded, proximately considered, in *understanding* that everything "good" one is and has depends on divine goodness. Anything "good," then, is essentially a divine gift, completely unmerited since entirely gratuitous. I believe this is well expressed in St. Paul's statement, "What do you have that you did not receive?" (1 Cor 4:7). So, one is grateful for divine goodness. But the belief that God ultimately withholds his goodness from some persons contradicts the nature of goodness. If I am grateful that God gives to me what he ultimately withholds from others, I am thankful for his special favor. But I cannot identify God as goodness itself. That is not the case, however, if I recognize that the highest good he gives to me he *can and probably will* give to all (cf. Rom 11:30–32, Eph 1:2–14, and the parable of the laborers in the vineyard in Mt 20:1–16). Under that circumstance, I can identify God as goodness and become grateful without reserve. This being so, the nature of *de praedestionatione*'s imperative for gratitude implies that God's best gift is given to more than a minority of humanity.

My third point might be the most decisive. Thomas's claim that providence's antithesis has absolute status understates man's nature as *imago dei*. I have already mentioned that a *confessio* teaching on predestination requires *explicit* (i.e., elect) *imago dei* to cultivate the ontological synthesis between itself and God through considering the eternal divine goodness, the eternal divine mercy in Christ and, *through these*, an antithesis structuring human history between the elect, composed of *explicit imago dei*, and the nonelect, composed of *implicit imago dei*. Therefore, while *imago dei*'s (i.e., man's) synthesis with God (whether *implicit* or *explicit*) is absolute, not all the objects *explicit imago dei* considers to cultivate it are absolute. Divine goodness and Christ are absolute because each is God himself, but the aforementioned antithesis composed of historical communities is not absolute because it includes the nonelect, who are apart from God as not yet enjoying explicit union with him. Hence the antithesis that *elect imago dei* considers is contingent because, although each of its composing theses includes God, the formal object of reflection is *principally* rightly and wrongly oriented persons. It is between what, on the one hand, is ultimately absolute (viz., *explicit imago dei*) because human being is properly subordinate to divine being, and, on the other, what is ultimately contingent (viz., *implicit imago dei*) because, in that instance, divine being is actively subordinated to human being. So, *elect imago dei* rightly contemplates the antithesis to which it belongs while recognizing that antithesis as contingent.

How, then, should *confessio* view that antithesis? If it is likely that each person—or, at minimum, the majority—is predestined, the principal difference between the opposing theses concerns some destined to bliss in the next life through election in this life and others destined for bliss in the next life apart from election here. In the spirit of Ephesians 1, this antithesis encourages divine gratitude, as I am thankful for receiving in advance some part of what will be received by very many. And I can now work toward achieving that end both in myself and for others. It is true that being elected makes me subject to God's special favor, but my awareness of the circumstances brought into play by the presence of original and personal sin, *together with* knowing that God is ineffable goodness, allows me to understand that each person can *eventually* receive whatever good I now receive—and much more. My gratitude is cultivated by observing an antithesis between one party presently enjoying God's special favor and another that does not. I am not required to hold that the relationship between the elect and the nonelect is absolute.

This implies that *de praedestinatione*'s claim that providence's antithesis is between the predestined and the reprobated—and, at that, ultimately between a minority predestination and majority reprobation—veers toward presumption. *Confessio* mandates viewing providence's antithesis to encourage both decisive knowledge of God and divine gratitude. Because that antithesis is contingent, however, granting it absolute status means that in this one respect an absolute word is conflated with a relative word, or, put differently, what is adventitious to mind is wrongly identified with mind's irreducible spiritual orientation toward God. This contradicts *de praedestinatione*'s correlate cognitive dimension and imperative to gratitude.[99]

My fourth point, closely related to the previous three, is arrived at by analyzing *ST* I, q. 23, by the standard of a biblical teaching on predestination.[100] On this basis, I claim that Thomas's teaching stands at an extreme—albeit at the better extreme in one respect—owing to its doctrine of minority salvation. My assertion is supported in two manners, depending on one's account of the biblical standard. In the first place, the Bible's teaching on predestination can be judged ambiguous. Is its doctrine particular election and minority salvation,[101] or particular election and universal salvation?[102] Or is it some middle claim of particular election and of majority unto universal salvation' achieved by applying

---

99. Put differently, Thomas subordinates (1) infinite divine goodness to finite human responsibility, (2) mind to will, and (3) both the Son to the Father *and* the Spirit to both the Father and the Son.

100. I believe that the Bible is ambiguous on this point. The Bible seems to be clear concerning particular election, but the end result thereof is either (1) minority salvation, (2) majority salvation, or (3) universal salvation. On this matter, I share Adams's opinion that there are "a variety of different biblical, indeed New Testament views, each of which deserves separate and careful consideration." "Problem of Hell," 318n35. To my mind, each of those views can belong to the domain of *confessio* insofar as each encourages human recognition of ineffable divine goodness and the practice of divine gratitude.

101. Mt 7:13–14: "Enter through the narrow gate. The gate that leads to damnation is wide, the road is clear, and many choose to travel it. But how narrow is the gate that leads to life, how rough the road, and how few there are who find it!"

In his subsequent Parable of the Last Judgment (Mt 25:31–46), Matthew speaks of how Christ will distinguish "the sheep," i.e., the godly, from "the goats," i.e., the ungodly, sending the former to heaven and the latter to hell. In his words, "Then he will say to those on his left: 'Out of my sight, you condemned, into that everlasting fire prepared for the devil and his angels!'...These will go off to eternal punishment and the just to eternal life." Taken in conjunction with the earlier statement in Mt 7:13–14, this passage can be judged to explain some of the mechanism of minority salvation.

102. In Rm 5:18–19, Paul writes: "To sum up, then: just as a single offense brought condemnation to all men, a single righteous act brought all men acquittal and life. Just as through one man's disobedience all became sinners, so through one man's obedience all shall become just." In 1 Tm 2:4, Paul writes: "for he [i.e., God] wants all men to be saved and come to know the truth."

Ockham's razor to the aforesaid views?[103] I defend my assertion by considering the relationship between the above distinctions and the three views of predestination defined above. These were: first, group A, claiming particular election coupled with the certitude of universal salvation; second, group B, embracing particular election while advocating something between majority and universal salvation; and third, group C (the Augustinian-Thomistic outlook), proclaiming particular election and minority salvation.

These opposed doctrines can be related to a biblical standard in two ways. If the biblical view, as first reported, is unclear and therefore determined by the standard of *confessio*, then (1) group A stands at one extreme, positing universal salvation as a certitude; (2) group C, the Augustinian-Thomistic perspective, stands at the other extreme, upholding minority salvation; and (3) group B stands toward the middle or mean, claiming something within the range of majority unto universal salvation. By the framework of Aristotle's famous teaching on "the mean,"[104] I measure the above views according to what has been hitherto identified as biblical doctrine's *confessio* or *imago dei* hermeneutic key. On that basis, group A's account of universal salvation is open to the charge of presumption because such an outcome can easily negate the imperative to gratitude.[105] The Augustinian-Thomistic perspective (group C) is also misleading, because asserting minority salvation easily weakens recognizing ineffable divine goodness. By contrast, group B stands closest to the mean, because claiming an ultimate eschatology ranging from a majority unto universal salvation has the advantage of upholding divine goodness *in conjunction with* divine gratitude.

---

103. Some commentators imply that the term "all" in the above texts is rightly interpreted to mean "many" rather than "everyone." Marshall, "New Testament Does *Not* Teach Universal Salvation," 55–66.

104. Aristotle, *Nicomachean Ethics*, 2.6–9.

105. For discussion of the practical advantages of proclaiming universal salvation, see Adams, "Problem of Hell," 325, and Kronen and Reitan, *God's Final Victory*, 181–84. All told, these commentators assert that teaching universal salvation encourages the response of (1) recognizing the utterly gratuitous divine goodness, (2) gratitude toward God, (3) love of neighbor, and (4) zeal to evangelize. By contrast, as previously noted, Aquinas (*ST* I, q. 23, a. 1, ad 4) claims it would not be fitting for each to know whether he is predestined, as "those who were not predestined would despair; and security would beget negligence in the predestined." Either way, many would behave badly. It is interesting to note, however, that Aquinas is open to the possibility that some, "by special divine privilege," could know they are predestined.

Still, Thomas's teaching is, in one respect, located at the better extreme as it protects the imperative of gratitude that group A weakens. On
this score, Thomas wisely claims (*ST* I, q. 23, a, 1, ad 4) that "even if by a
special privilege their predestination were revealed to some, it is not fitting that it should be revealed to everyone; because, if so, those who were
not predestined would despair; and security would beget negligence in
the predestined." Therefore, although group A's doctrine of universal salvation can better signify the primacy of divine goodness than group C's
teaching of minority salvation, it easily militates against inspiring divine
gratitude. Hence group B's approach is "towards the mean" because its t
doctrine concerning the extent of human salvation upholds the primacy
of divine goodness while encouraging divine gratitude. By the measure
of *confessio*, group B manifests a reasonable biblical standard.

What happens when the three responses are assessed by a biblical
standard consisting in particular election *and* majority unto universal
salvation? Obviously, the outcome is essentially the same as above. While
group A stresses divine goodness to the detriment of inspiring gratitude, group C emphasizes gratitude to the disadvantage of manifesting
divine goodness. Once again, group B's view is closest to the mean, as it
is capable of manifesting divine goodness together with inspiring divine
gratitude. And, in the same respect as before, Thomas's doctrine is at the
better extreme in one respect because, all things considered, it can inspire gratitude in its adherents more readily than group A's teaching can
encourage its followers in gratitude.

In any event, it is obvious that Thomas's assertion of minority salvation removes his teaching from the mean because his zeal to encourage
gratitude militates against his zeal to uphold the absolute primacy of
God's goodness. Put differently, whether one establishes a biblical teaching on predestination by the measure of *confessio* or measures *confessio*
by the standard of a biblical teaching on predestination, it is evident that
Thomas's doctrine of predestination should be developed to include a
doctrine of majority unto universal salvation.[106]

106. As stated before, Levering, *Predestination*, 197–201, argues that this can be accomplished by developing Thomas's teaching on predestination through the aid of de Sales's and
Siena's teachings on predestination. Levering likes that Thomas's (essentially theocentric)
philosophical theology contains the resources needed to uphold (at full strength) the two
doxological principles required to ground a coherent biblical teaching on predestination,
viz., that (1) God's goodness/love is ineffable or infinite and (2) some human persons ulti-

mately reject God's ineffable goodness and suffer eternal damnation (178). Therefore, while Thomas holds both principles but decisively subordinates the first principle to the second (194–95), de Sales and Siena, from within a Thomistic perspective, embrace both principles *at full strength*, i.e., apart from subordinating any one to the other. For this reason, these divines develop Thomas's doctrine so that it matches up with a properly biblical account of predestination.

My study implies three related responses to Levering's claim. First, even if de Sales and Siena hold that a majority is saved, their claim that some certainly suffer eternal damnation ultimately subordinates principle 1 to principle 2 because it places a restriction on the scope of divine goodness. So, each principle is upheld at full strength, but this is relative rather than absolute because each principle is already limited by its relationship with the other. Second, if Levering finds that Thomas's teaching is underdeveloped on account of emphasizing the second doxological principle to the detriment of the first, then our study shows that there are other ways of developing Thomas's teaching for the better—and to an even greater extent than de Sales and Siena allow. For example, Popes John Paul II and Benedict XVI (see note 5 above) in one way both include and deny the de Sales and Siena position. They deny the *certitude* that some—i.e., a minority—suffer eternal damnation by substituting in its place a *belief* that some—i.e., a minority—are lost. But these popes are also open to the possibility of universal bliss. In other words, relative to Levering's position, they imply that doxological principle (2) could ultimately be negated by doxological principle (1). Does this mean that their approach is not biblical?

My third point attempts to answer these questions by focusing on the difference between Levering's and my account of a "proper" biblical hermeneutic informing a biblical doctrine of predestination. I have argued that this hermeneutic is not exactly what Levering has stated, though the latter is both very close and helpful. Instead of locating the hermeneutic key in the two humble doxological principles that Levering cites, I claim it is found in *confessio*—in the way of humbly upholding unlimited emphasis on divine goodness with unlimited recognition and practice of divine gratitude. Therefore, while Levering implies that biblical teaching in advance of the *eschaton* properly proclaims an outcome of majority salvation and excludes universal salvation, *confessio* implies that biblical teaching can proclaim an outcome of majority salvation in conjunction with allowing for the possibility of universal salvation. Additionally, whereas Levering's account of what should prevail before the *eschaton* subordinates his principle (1) to his principle (2) on the basis of claiming that some are certainly damned, the principles underlying *confessio* can be upheld at full strength (according to the manner that Levering, following G. K. Chesterton [vii], claims is ideal) because they are not already mutually limited or, put differently, because of their openness, when combined, to the possibility of universal human bliss.

Confessio is therefore capable—albeit as private rather than as common doctrine—of granting more to divine goodness and to human responsibility than Levering's account allows. It seems that these doctrines generally agree concerning the limits of common doctrine, i.e., about what befits Church proclamations on the topic of predestination before the *eschaton*. But a *confessio* mind-set maintains that relatively more can be understood or considered about divine predestination in advance of the *eschaton*. While Levering's hermeneutic key claims one authentic mind-set and, consequently, no proper distinction between a common doctrine and an ostensibly more developed private opinion (though his hermeneutic key, like *confessio*, is obviously open to opinions less developed than the norm), *confessio* claims two normative mind-sets by distinguishing between common doctrine and a relatively more developed private opinion or between *imago dei* generally and *explicit imago dei* in particular. Therefore, while the one hermeneutic implies that the aforementioned popes' opinions about ultimate eschatology are not biblical, the other holds differently, maintain-

Conclusion

All told, a *confessio doctrine of predestination* can welcome a more extensive manifestation of divine goodness and response of divine gratitude than Thomas's *de praedestinatione* allows.[107]

In particular, group B implies a more perfect manifestation of *confessio* owing to its openness toward a *majority unto universal bliss*. Why is that? Although in one way group A's teaching on universal bliss manifests the divine goodness to a greater extent than group B's eschatological doctrine, the latter is more capable of inspiring divine gratitude. Because group B holds to a teaching of majority unto universal bliss rather than to the certitude of universal bliss (which group A holds), it places relatively greater emphasis on the need to practice gratitude. Moreover, although Thomas's—group C's—doctrine of predestination upholds the importance of practicing gratitude, its teaching of a minority salvation militates against recognizing the primacy of divine goodness. Therefore group B's teaching is superior, as it upholds the primacy of divine goodness *and* the importance of practicing gratitude. While none of these teachings harmonizes perfectly the divine goodness with the practice of gratitude, we see that group B's doctrine is more palatable because it is more capable of effecting that harmonization.

On this basis, then, group B is better able to subordinate (1) the contingent to the absolute word, (2) temporal to eternal being, and (3) finite responsibility to infinite divine goodness. Moreover, concerning *confessio*'s *imago dei* structure, understanding providence's antithesis to be contingent rather than absolute upholds what belongs both to our decisive analogue—the divine processions between Father, Word, and

---

ing that these popes are not speaking *ex cathedra*, or for the sake of formulating common doctrine, but as private *confessio*-centered interpreters.

107. The Gospel of Luke implies that a *confessio* teaching on divine predestination must be loyal to Christ's humility; otherwise, the interpreter is presumptuous and made subject to divine punishment at the *eschaton*. Hence (Lk 9.23–26): "Jesus said to all: 'Whoever wishes to be my follower must deny his very self, take up his cross each day, and follow in my footsteps. Whoever would save his life will lose it, and whoever loses his life for my sake will save it. What profit does he show who gains the whole world and destroys himself in the process? If a man is ashamed of me and my doctrine, the Son of man will be ashamed of him when he comes in his glory and that of his Father and his holy angels.'" My conclusion holds that a *confessio* approach to divine predestination has more scope than Thomas's *confessio* interpretation in *ST* I, q. 23, aa. 1–8.

Spirit constituting the Godhead—and to its image—the word conceived and love proceeding—produced by the intrinsic conjunction between intellect and will constituting not only mind as such but also, especially, when mind is properly focused on God. Divine predestination is therefore fittingly considered to bring about particular election for the sake of *majority to universal bliss* instead of for *minority bliss.*

St. Thomas's *de praedestinatione* is a meritorious exercise in *confessio* because its focus on harmonizing divine goodness *and* divine gratitude shows that its theological and anthropological center holds. But the exercise in *confessio* implied by those advocating the possibility of an eschatological outcome between a *majority and universal bliss* can have more merit, as it is capable of adding emphasis to the cognitive and affective boundaries comprising *de praedestinatione*'s biblical hermeneutic key. Because *predestination is made for man, not man for predestination*, that approach can do a relatively better job with the correlate knowledge and practical imperative informing the intellect and will of those predestined, it seems, to study the mystery of predestination.

CONTRIBUTORS

SERGE-THOMAS BONINO, OP, is a Dominican priest who teaches theology and philosophy and is presently the dean of the Faculty of Philosophy at the Pontifical University of St. Thomas Aquinas-Rome (Angelicum). Former director of *Revue Thomiste*, the Very Reverend Fr. Bonino serves as the general secretary of the International Theological Commission. Fr. Bonino is the president of the Pontifical Academy of St. Thomas Aquinas and has received the honor of Master of Theology from the Order of Preachers, a title the Order bestows upon its most distinguished theologians.

ROMANUS CESSARIO, OP, is a fellow of the Pontifical Academy of Saint Thomas Aquinas and a professor of theology at St. John's Seminary in Brighton, Massachusetts. The author of numerous books and articles on Catholic theology and spirituality, Father Cessario received the Master of Sacred Theology degree from the Order of Preachers in 2013.

CHRISTOPHER M. CULLEN, SJ, is an associate professor of philosophy at Fordham University. His research has focused on medieval Scholasticism, with special attention to Bonaventure and the Augustinian tradition. He wrote a systematic study of the Seraphic Doctor's philosophy and theology, titled *Bonaventure* (Oxford University Press, 2006). He has also written on Bonaventure's principal mentor, Alexander of Hales, and on his important disciple, John Peckham, as well as on contemporary neo-Thomism.

MICHAEL DAUPHINAIS is an associate professor of theology at Ave Maria University. He holds the degrees of BSE from Duke University, MTS from Duke Divinity School, and PhD from the University of Notre Dame. He has published in the areas of Thomistic theology, theological exegesis, and Catholic higher education.

BARRY DAVID holds a PhD from the University of Toronto. He is an associate professor in the Department of Philosophy at Ave Maria University and chairperson emeritus. He is the author of a variety of articles in medieval philosophy, ethics, and metaphysics, and coeditor of *Aquinas the Augustinian* (Catholic University of America Press, 2007).

LAWRENCE FEINGOLD is an associate professor of theology and philosophy at Kenrick-Glennon Seminary in St. Louis, Missouri. He is a convert to the Catholic faith, entering the Church in 1989. He is the author of *Faith Comes From What Is Heard: An Introduction to Fundamental Theology*; *The Natural Desire to See God According to St. Thomas Aquinas and His Interpreters*, and a three-volume series titled *The Mystery of Israel and the Church*.

MATTHEW LAMB, Cardinal Maida Professor of Theology at Ave Maria University, received a licentiate in sacred theology from the Pontifical Gregorian University and a doctor of theology from the University of Münster in Germany. An ordained Catholic priest, he has published four books, edited or coedited six books, and authored over 150 articles in refereed journals and books.

STEVEN A. LONG is a professor of theology at Ave Maria University and author of *Teleological Grammar of the Moral Act* (now in its second edition); *Natura Pura: On the Recovery of Nature in the Doctrine of Grace*; and *Analogia Entis: On the Analogy of Being, Metaphysics, and the Act of Faith*. He is codirector of the Aquinas Center for Theological Renewal at Ave Maria University, and a corresponding member of the Pontifical Academy of St. Thomas Aquinas.

ROGER W. NUTT is an associate professor of theology, codirector of the Aquinas Center for Theological Renewal, and editor-in-chief of Sapientia Press at Ave Maria University. His books include a translation of Thomas Aquinas's disputed question *De unione verbi incarnati* and *Elements of Sacramental Theology: A Catholic Introduction*.

THOMAS M. OSBORNE JR. is a professor in the Department of Philosophy and the Center for Thomistic Studies at the University of St. Thomas in Houston, Texas. He has published many articles on medieval and late scholastic philosophy and theology, as well as the monographs *Love of Self and Love of God in Thirteenth-Century Ethics* and *Human Action in Thomas Aquinas, John Duns Scotus, and William of Ockham*, for which he received the Charles Cardinal Journet Prize.

JOSEPH G. TRABBIC is an associate professor of philosophy in the Department of Philosophy at Ave Maria University. He earned his PhD in philosophy from Fordham University in 2008. His research interests include Aquinas, Heidegger, medieval philosophy, continental philosophy, philosophy of religion, and metaphysics. He has published his work in these areas in various scholarly journals.

MICHAEL MARIA WALDSTEIN is the Max Seckler Professor of Theology at Ave Maria University. He is author of a new translation of John Paul's *Man and Woman He Created Them: A Theology of the Body*, as well as numerous journal articles.

THOMAS JOSEPH WHITE, OP, is the director of the Thomistic Institute at the Dominican House of Studies. He is the author of several books, including *The Incarnate Lord: A Thomistic Study in Christology*, and coeditor of the theological journal *Nova et Vetera*. He is an ordinary member of the Pontifical Academy of St. Thomas Aquinas.

INDEX

Thomism and Predestination: Principles and Disputations was designed and typeset in Minon by Kachergis Book Design of Pittsboro, North Carolina. It was printed on 50-pound Tradebook and bound by Thomson Reuters of Eagan, Minnesota.